W9-ADL-033

WHEN
RACE
TRUMPS
MERIT

WHEN RACE TRUMPS MERIT

HOW THE PURSUIT OF EQUITY SACRIFICES EXCELLENCE, DESTROYS BEAUTY, AND THREATENS LIVES

HEATHER MAC DONALD

ISBN: 978-1-956007-16-9

First Edition
Published by DW Books
DW Books™, a division of The Daily Wire®

Daily Wire
1831 12th Avenue South
Suite 460
Nashville, TN 37203

www.dailywire.com

PRINTED IN THE USA

CONTENTS

PART III: LAW AND ORDER

Introduction

A CULTURAL REVOLUTION

The year 2020 may go down as a pivotal moment in American history. Major institutions—from corporations and the media to higher education and professional sports—endorsed the view that the United States is defined by systemic racism. The death of George Floyd under the knee of a Minneapolis, Minnesota, police officer in May 2020 epitomized such bias, according to elite opinion leaders. The riots following Floyd's death were portrayed as a wake-up call: address America's pervasive discrimination or face even greater disruption.

Those fiery months spawned a cultural revolution that could prove as transformative as its 1960s antecedent. That earlier youth-led upheaval challenged the adult establishment's allegedly oppressive norms of propriety in the name of liberation. This time the targets are the very fundamentals of a fair society: meritocracy, fealty to the rule of law, and respect for our civilizational inheritance. All are now tarred as impediments to racial justice.

The driving concept behind this revolution is disparate impact. Under this ideology, any standard or behavioral norm which negatively and disproportionately affects blacks is presumed to be a tool of white supremacy. If academic admissions standards for colleges and high schools result in a student body in which the percentage of black students is less than that of the national population (13 percent), then those standards must be lowered for the sake of racial equity. If the enforcement of criminal law results in a prison population that is more than 13 percent black, then that enforcement must be unwound. If hiring and promotion criteria mean that a workplace is not proportionally "diverse," then those criteria must be abandoned.

Disparate impact analysis first arose in the law as a way to expand the reach of civil-rights-era discrimination statutes. Those early statutes banned deliberate discrimination: an employer could only be found guilty of a civil rights violation if he intentionally discriminated against a minority applicant. A 1971 Supreme Court case, Griggs v. Duke Power Co., changed that rule.[1] Even if an employer had no intent to discriminate and had used color-blind standards for hiring or promotion, the court held that he could still be liable under the 1964 Civil Rights Act if those job requirements—such as a certain level of literacy or a high school diploma—disproportionately affected underrepresented minorities and were not required by business necessity.

Disparate impact analysis has been used to invalidate school discipline policies,[2] bank lending standards,[3] and written tests for first responders.[4] Now the disparate impact approach has jumped from judicial opinions and the Code of Federal Regulations into the world at large. Disparate impact analysis is no longer primarily a legal tool but a cultural one. Even if it were extirpated from the law, it would continue to alter our world by discrediting high standards and color-blind policies.

The key to disparate impact thinking is the presumption of racial proportionality. Absent some form of unfairness, it is assumed that the racial demographics of every institution would match that of the population at large. If blacks are underrepresented in science research labs or overrepresented among arrested felons, the only allowable explanation is racism. The possibility that such racial disparities reflect the actual distribution of skills or differences in behavior is taboo.

The real estate website Redfin, for example, declared in 2021 that it would not provide potential home buyers with information about neighborhood crime rates. According to Redfin's chief growth officer, there were "troubling signs" that crime data were biased. The victims of crime were "more likely to describe their offender as young, male, and Black than would be expected given the representation of those groups in the population."[5] It was not conceivable that young black males may, in fact, commit crime at a higher rate than their population percentage.

In June 2022, bioethicist Ezekiel Emanuel and epidemiologist Cary Gross called on Congress to require that the National Institutes of Health (NIH) fund science researchers who "look like the country."[6] Currently, blacks receive less than 2 percent of NIH support for the most cutting-edge science—a mark of funding inequity according to the NIH itself.[7]

Until recently, San Francisco's acclaimed Lowell High School admitted a majority of its students based on middle school GPA and a standardized admissions test. Lowell's student body was 82 percent non-white,[8] but because blacks were underrepresented compared to their share of San Francisco's population, the school board in 2021 accused Lowell of "perpetuat[ing] segregation and exclusion."[9] Henceforth, Lowell would use a lottery for admissions. (The receipt of Ds and Fs shot up 300 percent in the first lottery-enrolled class.)[10]

Gifted and talented programs are being dismantled because blacks are not proportionally represented in them.[11] The University of California now refuses to consider SAT and ACT scores in its undergraduate admissions decisions because those tests have a disparate impact on blacks and Hispanics.[12]

The SAT was a "racist test," said the Board of Regents' then–Vice Chair Cecilia Estolano.[13] The American Bar Association will likely declare the Law School Admission Test optional for entrance to law schools based on the same disparate impact reasoning.

But racial disparities in outcomes are overwhelmingly the result of measurable differences in achievement and behavior, not the result of racism. All objective measures of academic knowledge document an average skills gap that makes the expectation of proportional representation across all meritocratic institutions unrealistic. If black researchers are not proportionally represented among recipients of the NIH's most prestigious science grants, it is not because the NIH is discriminating against competitively qualified scientists. The victims of violent street crimes—themselves disproportionately minority—provide the data showing that blacks commit crime at much higher rates than other groups.

To be sure, America's treatment of blacks was heartbreakingly cruel and gratuitously sadistic for centuries. That mistreatment extended well past the Civil War and the formal elimination of de jure segregation, and it was found in the North as well as the South. White Americans' long-standing reflex to put blacks in their place undercuts every paean to the country's foundational commitment to freedom. Frederick Douglass's bitter comment on the antebellum Fourth of July celebrations—"your shouts of liberty and equality" are, to a slave, a "hollow mockery"—needs to be ever juxtaposed to the narrative of American exceptionalism.[14]

Yet, hard as it would have been to imagine even in the middle of the twentieth century, the country has radically changed course. Far from discriminating against blacks and other underrepresented minorities, virtually every mainstream institution today is trying to admit, hire, and promote as many non-Asian minorities as possible. (Asians are not affected by disparate impact; on average, they exceed standards rather than fall below them.) Philanthropists and corporations spend millions each year on social-uplift programs to close the racial achievement gap. Taxpayer dollars are as liberally distributed from government coffers toward the same end. We so take these efforts for granted that we don't even see them; they have no effect on the dominant narrative about white indifference and exploitation.

And now, even the greatest achievements of the West are being subjected to disparate impact analysis. The most devastating charge that can be levelled against a tradition today is that its practitioners have historically been white. Classical music, European art, and science are on the defensive for their demographic past as well as for inadequate "diversity" in the present. Objectivity, individualism, a respect for the written word, perfectionism, and promptness have been tarred as markers of whiteness because insisting on those values has a disparate impact on blacks.[15]

There is little precedent for this civilizational self-cancellation. During the Chinese Revolution, the masses turned on the elites. Now, in the US, the elites turn on everyone else, denouncing their fellow citizens as racists and the American past as monolithically shameful. The French Revolution left intact French reverence for Rabelais, Pascal, Racine, Moliere, and Voltaire. Today's cultural guardians—museum directors, orchestra leaders, humanities professors—have declared their highest mission to be anti-racism, which means accusing the works under their care of white supremacy.

What happens when a culture condemns itself so decisively? We don't yet know. But we are robbing children of an essential source of identity through a one-sided take on the past and a groundless indictment of the present. The highest function of schooling is to pass on an inheritance, as the philosopher Michael Oakeshott explained.[16] That function is now all but obliterated. Serious humanistic learning has been decimated. The greatest sin of the diversity crusaders is to teach students to revile some of the most sublime creations of the human spirit.

The concept of disparate impact is destroying America's core institutions in the name of fighting invented racism. It is putting future scientific advances at risk by substituting racial quotas for meritocracy. It is unwinding decades of progress in fighting urban crime by declaring color-blind law enforcement racist. The nonstop denunciation of the West's civilizational inheritance may well be contributing to America's drug-addicted malaise and to rising mental distress among the young. This cultural self-cancellation impoverishes the imagination, stunts the capacity for wonder and joy, and strips the future of everything that gives human life meaning: beauty, sublimity, and wit.

We are in uncharted territory.*

---

*A note on methodology: this book invokes group averages. Those averages say nothing about the capacities of any member of a particular group, who must be assessed on his own merits. Thousands of individuals from groups with lower average skills vastly outperform individuals from groups with higher average skills. But since the disparate impact crusade deals in bulk numbers—using racial percentages in institutions to identify alleged racism—that crusade must be rebutted with bulk numbers as well.

THE BIAS FALLACY

The United States is being torn apart by an idea: that racism defines America. George Floyd's death catapulted this claim into national prominence.

On May 25, 2020, a clerk at a Minneapolis grocery store called 911 to report that a customer (George Floyd) had just used a counterfeit bill. The customer was "awfully drunk" and "not in control of himself," the employee said.[1] The clerk and his fellow workers had tried to persuade Floyd, now parked in a Mercedes SUV outside the store, to return the cigarettes he had just bought with the counterfeit twenty-dollar bill. Floyd had refused, so the clerks called the police.

Two Minneapolis police officers responded. Floyd, patently high, resisted the officers' efforts to put him in their patrol car, admitted that he had been using drugs, and told them that he couldn't breathe. After several violent struggles, the officers eventually laid a cuffed Floyd facedown on the ground. By then, two other Minneapolis officers had arrived at the scene. The senior officer, Derek Chauvin, put his knee on Floyd's neck and back and kept it there for the next nine minutes, while Floyd repeatedly said that he could not breathe. Floyd's breathing grew shallow, and he stopped speaking or moving. Floyd went into cardiac arrest and was pronounced dead at the Hennepin County Medical Center.

The county's autopsy concluded that the pressure exerted on Floyd's neck and back was the proximate cause of Floyd's fatal heart attack. Floyd had recently ingested enough fentanyl to fell a non-habitual user; that fentanyl consumption, supplemented by methamphet-amines, may have increased Floyd's risk of death, the coroner found. Floyd's severe coronary artery disease and enlarged heart were also contributing causes.[2]

Floyd's last moments were caught on cell phone video and streamed around the world. Chauvin's nonchalance as Floyd's life ebbed away was horrifying to behold. In April 2021, a Minneapolis jury convicted Chauvin of murder and manslaughter, for which he received a state prison sentence of twenty-two-and-a-half years. (As of February 2023, all federal and state charges against two of Chauvin's fellow officers had been resolved through pleas or guilty verdicts, leaving only one fellow officer facing a bench trial on a manslaughter charge.)

But however callously Chauvin had behaved, there was no evidence, other than his and Floyd's skin color, that Chauvin had been motivated by race. Nevertheless, the political and cultural establishments imme-diately turned Chauvin into the very embodiment of systemic racism and Floyd into its martyr. Floyd was lionized as a civil rights hero, de-spite a violent criminal history that would have shamed the nation's early civil rights leaders. In the days after his death, riots broke out across the US; institution after institution pledged to fight the struc-tural racism that Floyd's killing supposedly represented.

Soon, activists and their media allies were marshaling a more sweeping set of facts to prove the dominance of white supremacy: the absence of a proportional representation of blacks in a range of organi-zations. The activists claimed that insufficient diversity is the result of racial bias. The press served up exposés of this industry's or that com-pany's too-white workforce to illustrate the allegedly damning lack of racial proportionality in elite America. The concept of disparate impact had been weaponized and turbocharged.

In one short stretch during the summer of 2020, the *Wall Street Journal* ran stories headlined "Wall Street Knows It's Too White"[3] and "A Decade-Long Stall for Black Enrollment in M.B.A. Programs."[4] The *Los Angeles Times* asked: "Why are Black and Latino people still kept out of the tech industry?"[5] In another article, the *Los Angeles Times* documented its own "painful reckoning over race."[6] The *New York Times* pumped out news features and op-eds alleging racism in food journalism, Hollywood, publishing, and sports management. The *Chronicle of Higher Education* painstakingly covered alleged racial bias in the STEM (science, technology, engineering, and math) fields. All the articles invoked employment ratios as proof of racism.

This journalistic theme has deep roots. For decades, reporters could all but guarantee themselves front-page placement by tallying shortfalls in the "diversity" of a firm or profession. Depending on the moment, sex counts might dominate the discrimination genre, as during the height of the #MeToo movement. More recently, however, the press has gone back to race tallies. Indeed, female leadership buys an institution no credit from the media if that leadership is white.

These current diversity exposés are distinguished from their predecessors not just by their frequency. Virtually all mainstream institutions now agree that a nonracially proportionate workforce—including their own—proves racism. Organizations preemptively accuse themselves of discrimination without waiting for the inevitable indictment. The publisher of the *Science* family of journals denounced his own publications for "the discrimination, subjugation, and silencing of minority colleagues and voices."[7] The American Mathematical Society pledged to "address systemic inequities that exist in [the] mathematics community."[8] The dean of the Harvard Business School announced: "We have not fought racism as effectively as we could have and have not served our Black community members better."[9] (The capitalization of "black" has become de rigueur in progressive publications. As the *Columbia Journalism Review* explains: "*Black* reflects a shared sense of identity and community," whereas capitalizing "white" would risk "following the lead of white supremacists."[10])

After the George Floyd riots, the following ratios tumbled out of news pages to buttress the racism charge: 3.7 percent of Google's employees and contractors are black, compared with about 13 percent black representation in the country at large; at Salesforce, 2.9 percent of employees are black; at Facebook (now Meta), 3.8 percent of employees are black; and at Microsoft, 4.5 percent of employees are black. Black investors make up less than 1 percent of venture capitalists and less than 1 percent of the start-up founders whom those venture capitalists underwrite. Some venture-capital firms—among them, Kleiner Perkins, Sequoia, Benchmark, and Greylock—have no black partners at all.[11]

Eight percent of MBA students are black, according to the main business school accreditor. In 2020, 5 percent of Harvard Business School students were black. In 2019, about 4.1 percent of chief executives were black, according to the Bureau of Labor Statistics.[12] Three percent of venture capital funding went to black-founded companies in 2020.[13] In 2020, the newsroom at the *Los Angeles Times* was 61 percent white, though the population in Los Angeles County is 26 percent white. Black journalists at the *Los Angeles Times* make up 5.2 percent of the staff, though the county is 8 percent black.[14]

At WNYC, the nation's largest public radio station, fifteen of the 157 staff members responsible for content were black in 2020; only five of these fifteen had direct reports, and only one had a staff. WNYC's newsroom leadership was "almost uniformly white," according to the *New York Times*, and most reporters were white.[15]

The press and activists slice and dice the numbers to get the black proportions as low as possible. At Google, though 3.7 percent of employees and contractors were black in 2020, only 2.6 percent of leadership and 2.4 percent of technical workers were black. Blacks made up 3.8 percent of Meta's employees in 2020, but only 3.1 percent of those were in leadership roles, and 1.5 percent of those were in technical roles.[16]

Racism journalism backs up such demographic data with personal anecdotes alleging employment discrimination. A mental-health advocate provided the rule for evaluating these testimonials: "If a Black person tells you that they're feeling something is racist, just believe them."[17] This "just believe" mandate is the credo of the #MeToo movement as well. To test a claim of discrimination or sexual assault against the evidence makes official victims "unsafe" and violates their sanctity.

Thus, the routine complaints of employees in nearly every workplace are converted into unfalsifiable proof of discrimination when articulated by a particular group of employees. If a white job applicant is not hired, it is acceptable to assume that he was less qualified than other applicants. If a black job applicant is not hired, it is because of discrimination. If a white employee is not promoted, it is possible that another employee was more deserving. If a black employee is not promoted, it's because his employer is resistant to blacks, as a 2020 legal complaint against Facebook alleges.[18] Facebook (now Meta) is desperately trying to boost black and Hispanic representation in its workforce. Yet, if we are to believe that 2020 complaint, filed by a black Facebook manager and two failed applicants to the company, Facebook's "white managers" make it harder for blacks to get hired and promoted, thus undermining Facebook's own costly diversity efforts.[19]

A black virtual-effects specialist in Los Angeles told the *Los Angeles Times* that peers and supervisors constantly undermined her. "I can't really think of any space I've been in where it wasn't assumed that someone was smarter than me," she said. "People, speaking generally of non-Black people, always make the assumption that I don't know how to code, that I don't have any tech skills, that I got a job because of affirmative action; it's just ridiculous."[20] White employees at a virtual-reality start-up were promoted, she claimed, while she got pushed out.

A black food writer recounted in the *New York Times* that the editor of *Saveur* magazine barely lifted his head while interviewing her for an entry-level position and didn't read her résumé.[21] Such peremptory behavior exemplifies the racial microaggressions that have kept the writer back, she claimed.

A "social-impact manager" at Pinterest, a social media site, received a minor rebuke during a performance review.[22] She had successfully urged the company to adopt a racial-justice initiative. However, according to her supervisor, she should have presented Pinterest's decision-makers with other options as well. The supervisor's critique reflected the company's bias against minority employees, she said.

A reporter at the *Los Angeles Times* felt targeted by higher-ups. "Some days, I would cry and ask the editors: 'Why am I being treated this way?'" she told the paper. Then she realized that she was experiencing not just personal but "institutional" racism.[23]

An assistant professor of counselor education at the University of Virginia was denied tenure. The University of Virginia, like Big Tech, is desperate to hire and promote as many minorities as possible. Its education school is an outpost of woke correctness. Nevertheless, the tenure denial was the result of racism, especially since the tenure committee had no "people of color" on it. "Black people, including Black academics, have to be twice as good," the professor's wife told the *Chronicle of Higher Education.*[24]

Feeling undermined by peers, being passed over for inferior candidates, and feeling unappreciated in job interviews was once considered the ordinary lot of office workers. These petty indignities become proof of racism, however, when suffered by blacks. It is taboo to suggest that noncompetitive qualifications ever play a role in any lack of black advancement.

Woe to a CEO who hires a high-placed white professional in the current climate. The *Wall Street Journal* began an October 2020 story on the lack of diversity in finance with a profile of Wells Fargo's new CEO, Charles Scharf. When Scharf began at Wells Fargo in 2019, he brought trusted colleagues with him from J.P. Morgan and the Bank of New York Mellon to fill crucial positions. The *Journal* plunged in the knife: all were "white men."[25]

Scharf had asked for this blow, however. In June 2020, he had told Wells Fargo employees that he would tie executives' bonuses to the diversity of their units and that he would double the number of black senior leaders by 2025. Such promises were part of the flood of anti-racism pledges that were pouring out of C-suites in response to the Floyd riots. The day after Scharf's June 16 diversity email, he announced Wells Fargo's new head of wealth management, another lateral hire from JPMorgan. The *Journal*'s punch line was visible from a mile away: the hire was another white man. It was not necessary to ask if comparably qualified black bankers were available for the job; the *Journal* simply assumed that they were. Indeed, it is unlikely that before Scharf announced Wells Fargo's latest diversity mandates, he had evaluated the composition of the relevant hiring pool. Nor did he likely reconcile those new hiring mandates with the thousands of planned layoffs designed to offset the bank's falling revenues.

Supervisors grovel before the charge that they have discriminated against black applicants and employees. In June of 2020, the co-managing editor of the *Los Angeles Times* said she was "personally" doing a "lot of self-assessment."[26] "It's hard when you realize that you have failed in some ways. I'm sorry for that, and I am pledging to do better." The *Times*'s deputy managing editor would also "do better." And the executive editor, Norman Pearlstine, would do best of all. "I have been taking a hard look in the mirror," Pearlstine told the staff that month. "I haven't liked everything I have seen." But in October 2020, Pearlstine announced that he was leaving the paper, unable to withstand the racial quota brigade.

In 2017, the director of a food heritage group, the Southern Foodways Alliance, received accolades from the *New York Times* for organizing the Southern food revival.[27] By June 2020, director John Edge was apologizing for being white. "I want to embrace the critique," Edge told the *Times*.[28] "I'm still at it and I appreciate it." Admittedly, Edge's remedial options were limited, given his skin color. "Time has run out" for him, said his critics. The University of Mississippi announced in September 2020 that it would audit the Southern Foodways Alliance for "institutional racism and patriarchy."[29]

Given management's prostration before every charge of bias, it is no surprise that diversity demands are increasing in stridency and scale. Following the Floyd riots, the *Los Angeles Times* was pressured to hire eighteen black journalists, regardless of need or revenues, and to issue a public apology for racism.[30] Public radio station WNYC had to hire two black reporters and two black producers in 100 days to make amends for hiring a white woman as editor-in-chief.[31] None of WNYC's white diversity advocates, including its influential talk-show host Brian Lehrer, volunteered to resign in order to rectify the station's racial imbalance. In October 2022, New York Public Radio, the parent organization of WNYC, hired its first black CEO, perhaps purely a coincidence.[32]

Companies' self-initiated diversity goals are no less sweeping. Half of Meta's workforce will come from "underrepresented communities" (i.e., black and Hispanic) by 2023, announced then–Chief Operating Officer Sheryl Sandberg in 2020—a remarkably ambitious pledge in light of the firm's then–3.9 percent black workforce.[33] At Google, the number of blacks and other "underrepresented" minorities in its leadership ranks will grow 30 percent by 2025, according to Chief Executive Officer Sundar Pichai.[34]

A long series of similar pledges preceded these ones; none were fulfilled. Apparently, systemic racism overrode whatever good-faith intentions the promisers had at the time. What is never asked is the proportion of competitively qualified blacks in the hiring or promotion pool. It is assumed that such competitively qualified candidates are available in the same measure as in the population at large.

They are not. The underrepresentation of blacks in many professions is the result of the unequal distribution of skills, not of bias. Sixty-six percent of black twelfth graders nationally were "below basic" in twelfth-grade math skills in 2019, as measured by the National Assessment of Educational Progress (NAEP) exam.[35]

A "basic" score means that a student has mere "partial" mastery of grade-related concepts. Basic twelfth-grade math knowledge includes the ability to perform routine arithmetic calculations with or without a calculator and the ability to recognize linear functions in graphs.[36] Sixty-six percent of black twelfth graders were not even partially competent in such skills. Only 7 percent of black twelfth graders were proficient in twelfth-grade math. NAEP defines "proficient" as giving a "solid academic performance" and demonstrating "competency."[37] Math-proficient twelfth graders can calculate using ratios and exponents. The number of black twelfth graders rated "advanced" in math was too small to show up statistically.

By comparison, 29 percent of white twelfth graders were below basic in twelfth-grade math in 2019, 28 percent were proficient, and 4 percent were advanced. Twenty percent of Asian twelfth graders were below basic in twelfth-grade math in 2019, 37 percent were proficient, and 15 percent were advanced.

The picture was not much better in reading. Fifty percent of black twelfth graders were below basic in twelfth-grade reading in 2019, 16 percent were proficient readers, and 1 percent were advanced readers.[38] By comparison, 21 percent of white twelfth graders were below basic in twelfth-grade reading, 38 percent were proficient readers, and 9 percent were advanced readers. Twenty-one percent of Asian twelfth graders were below basic in twelfth-grade reading, 37 percent were proficient readers, and 14 percent were advanced readers.

Black students never catch up to their white and Asian peers. There aren't many professions where someone possessing less than even partial mastery of reading and math will qualify for employment.

The ACT and the SAT measure a more selective group of students than the NAEP, but even within that smaller pool of college-intending high school students, the gaps remain wide. The American College Testing organization, which administers the ACT, rated 10 percent of black high school seniors college-ready in math in 2021, compared to 44 percent of whites. Six percent of black twelfth graders were fully college-ready when ACT scores in English, science, and reading were taken into account along with math. Whites were five times as likely to be ready for college-level work in all four ACT subject areas.[39]

The College Board, which administers the SAT, used to report SAT scores in fifty-point increments (on an 800-point scale). Such information shows how racial groups cluster at the highest and lowest tails of the SAT curve, a distribution that predicts eligibility for the most cognitively demanding professions. (In the late 2010s, the College Board stopped reporting SAT scores in fifty-point increments, presumably on the usual equity grounds.) In 2015, only 2 percent of all test takers with a math SAT between 750 and 800 were black, according to the Brookings Institution. Sixty percent of math scorers in the 750 to 800 tranche were Asian, and 33 percent were white. By contrast, blacks made up 35 percent of all test takers with rock-bottom scores between 300 and 350. Whites made up 21 percent of such low scorers, and Asians made up 6 percent.[40]

Physicists, mathematicians, and the most cutting-edge medical researchers and engineers are ordinarily drawn from an applicant pool that received the uppermost range of math scores. In a meritocratic hiring system, the most challenging jobs in law and finance will also be filled from that upper range.

As for average SAT scores, the average total SAT score in 2021 (on a 1600-point scale) was 934 for blacks. For whites, the average score was 1112, and for Asians, it was 1239.[41] Most white and Asian students who presented a combined SAT score of 934 would have little chance of admission to a selective college.

The SAT gap is replicated in graduate-level standardized tests. Between July 2020 and June 2021, the average score on the quantitative section of the Graduate Record Exams (GRE) for US citizens was 150.7 out of 170. The Asian average was 154.9; the white average, 151.1; and the black average, 144.6.[42] The Massachusetts Institute of Technology's 2019-2020 engineering program had an average GRE quantitative score of 166;[43] students in the University of California's engineering programs averaged 166, as did graduate students in University of Southern California's program, and students at Berkeley's mechanical engineering program averaged 165.[44] The proportion of blacks whose quantitative GRE scores would qualify them for these programs, absent racial preferences, is negligible compared to whites and Asians.

The organizers of the post-Floyd STEM protests, such as #Shut-DownSTEM, #ShutDownAcademia, and #BlackInTheIvory, argue that bias drives the lack of black representation in quantitative STEM fields. Brian Nord, a visiting astronomer at the University of Chicago and organizer of Strike for Black Lives, complained in June 2020 of being "one of the few Black physicists of [his] generation," a disproportion which shows, he said, "how white supremacy pervades [his] professional spaces."[45]

But there are simply not enough black STEM PhDs to go around. In 2021, blacks made up 1 percent of all doctorates awarded in physics to US citizens and permanent residents, according to the annual Survey of Earned Doctorates from the National Center for Science and Engineering Statistics. Blacks earned 3.2 percent of all mathematics and statistics doctorates, 3.4 percent of all doctorates in computer science, 3.5 percent of all doctorates in chemistry, and 4.2 percent of all doctorates awarded in engineering disciplines.[46] There were no black PhD graduates in medical physics, atmospheric physics, chemical and physical oceanography, plasma/high-temperature physics, logic, number theory, robotics, or structural engineering.[47] How academic STEM departments and Silicon Valley tech firms are going to fulfill their diversity pledges in light of that dearth of supply is a mystery. Yet in July 2020, MIT's president blamed his own institution for not effectively making headway on "racial equity and inclusion," despite years of effort to meet diversity quotas.[48] Virtually every other college leader has issued the same self-indictment.

The Law School Admission Test (LSAT) is similarly skewed. The gap between white and black scores on the LSAT is large: a study of the 2013-2014 LSAT found that the white average score was over 10 points higher than the average black score.[49] In 2004, only twenty-nine blacks, representing 0.3 percent of all black LSAT takers, scored 170 (out of 180) or above on the LSAT, which is the average entrance score for the nation's highest-ranked law schools, such as Yale, Harvard, and Stanford. There were 1,900 whites who scored at least a 170, representing 3.1 percent of all white test takers. The average LSAT for the top ten law schools in 2004 was 165. Only 1 percent of black test takers—or 108 blacks nationwide—scored at least 165 that year. By contrast, over 10 percent of white test takers—or 6,689 whites nationwide—scored at least 165.[50] That gap has only grown, and it affects law school outcomes. Of black law school graduates, 22 percent never pass the bar exam after five tries, compared with 3 percent of white test takers, according to a study by the Law School Admissions Council.[51] The skills measured by the LSAT and the bar exam—verbal reasoning, command of English, and logical thinking—are required for a range of professions, such as corporate management and consulting, banking, and journalism.

As for the law itself, if corporate law firms do not have a proportional number of black partners, it is not for lack of trying. Black law students are hired as summer law interns and first-year associates at rates far above their representation among law school graduates, according to research by UCLA law professor Richard Sander.[52] Partners and associates in those elite firms are subjected to relentless unconscious-bias and cultural-competence training, and the firms often offer exclusive mentoring programs to "diverse" lawyers. But the academic skills gap eventually becomes too consequential to ignore, especially regarding the drafting of legal documents. By the time partner decisions roll around, few blacks remain in the pipeline to promote. Nevertheless, in 2019, nearly 200 corporate general counsels signed an open letter threatening to pull their business from law firms where the partners were not "diverse," putting even greater pressure on firms to hire and promote based on race.[53]

Average results on the business school admissions test, the Graduate Management Admissions Test (GMAT), explain the lack of proportional representation in the corporate arena. The GMAT measures critical-reasoning skills and problem-solving abilities. The mean score for the GMAT for black test takers in 2020 was 463, on an 800-point scale. The average for whites was 573, for Asians 601, and the overall average was 561.[54] Only 19 percent of blacks scored 600 or higher in 2020, compared with 49 percent of "non-underrepresented populations" (diversity-speak for whites and Asians). Sixty-two percent of black test takers scored less than 500.[55]

In 2019, students entering the top ten business schools, as ranked by *The Economist*, had average GMATs ranging from 704 to 733.[56] The *Journal of Blacks in Education* estimated in 2006 that only 1 to 2 percent of black GMAT takers scored above 700, a proportion that has likely not changed.[57] A former Harvard Business School professor told the *Wall Street Journal* in June 2020 that he had quit to protest the school's systemic "anti-black practices."[58] An expectation of high-level quantitative skills was likely among those anti-black practices. Far from discriminating against blacks, the Harvard Business School admits at least twice as many black applicants as their average GMAT scores would predict.[59] Nevertheless, Dean Nitin Nohria claims that the school's efforts at racial justice have been "painfully insufficient."[60]

California lawmakers agree with Nohria's approach to business qualifications, which makes proportional representation the measure of fairness and race an aspect of competence. Oblivious to the pipeline problem, California mandates minority representation on the boards of corporations headquartered in the state, regardless of whether the quota hires possess business expertise; other states will follow suit.

Behavioral differences also undercut the expectation of proportional representation. One-third of all black males have a felony conviction.[61] Such convictions do not happen by chance; they signal involvement with the street culture of guns, drugs, and impulsivity, none of which are selling points to employers. The prevalence of out-of-wedlock births in the black community (over 70 percent of all black births) means that a high percentage of black females are burdened with solo child-rearing responsibilities.[62] Such responsibilities make advancement more difficult, no matter the amount of employer-paid leave.

As long as data on the skills and behavior gaps remain available, it is possible to challenge the myth of bias, at least in theory. So those facts must themselves be canceled, as well as anyone who publicizes them. That is the ultimate motivation for the movement to end the use of standardized tests in admissions. All minimally selective institutions of higher education practice race-norming in the evaluation of test results already, meaning that they judge the scores of blacks and Hispanics on a different scale than those of whites and Asians. The cutoff score, below which the school will not consider an applicant, is much higher for whites and Asians than for blacks and Hispanics. Standardized tests do not impede racial preferences; colleges simply ignore the results for the sake of diversity.

The reason to eliminate standardized assessments is rather to put the College Board and the Educational Testing Service out of business entirely—and with them, any possibility of an objective measure of intellectual skills. The College Board was dealt a body blow in May 2021 when the University of California barred the consideration of the SAT and the ACT in admissions. The SAT and ACT are "racist metrics," according to a lawyer who challenged the University of California's use of objective admissions tests.[63] Nearly 2,000 colleges have banned the submission of college entrance test scores or made submission optional, but none have the financial clout of the University of California, the largest consumer of College Board products.

Graduate programs have been dropping the GREs because of their disparate impact. In a sample of eight STEM disciplines at 50 top-ranked universities, the percentage of programs requiring the GRE General Test dropped from 84 percent in 2018 to 3 percent in 2022. Thirty-six percent of the programs surveyed by *Science* magazine banned GRE submission entirely in 2022. The GRE "unfairly privileges" white men, a Boston University professor told *Science.*[64]

The rejection of objective standards of accomplishment is nihilistic. One could argue that the academic skills gap itself reflects structural racism in the distribution of school funding and private capital. (Such a claim ignores the billions of public and private dollars that the US, with the best of intentions, has allocated to close the gap.) But to maintain that color-blind tests are meaningless in demonstrating cognitive mastery is to deny the very possibility of assessing accomplishment. Knowledge and skill exist, and they are measurable—if not always perfectly. Standardized tests are under attack only because blacks and Hispanics, on average, score poorly on them. The SAT was developed in the mid-twentieth century to overcome college admissions biases that favored traditional White Anglo-Saxon Protestant (WASP) elites. It allowed students from non-elite backgrounds and social classes to demonstrate superior academic capacity. Now, because of disparate impact, the diversity movement deems color-blind measures of competence to be unjust instruments of racial exclusion. If there were no group differences in outcome, however, no one would think about eliminating the very measures that were introduced to overcome group favoritism.

The next step in the unwinding of objective standards is to reject the notion of accomplishment itself. It has become career-ending to hold that some individuals or cultures achieve more than others. The ever-more sweeping deprecation of Western civilization refuses to acknowledge the West's unparalleled contributions to human progress. And now the behavioral norms that lead to individual success are being relativized as well. The National Museum of African American History & Culture in Washington, DC, declared in the summer of 2020 that rationality, the two-parent family, punctuality, self-control, and being polite were "white" traits.[65] The museum, part of the Smithsonian Institution, thus strengthened the underclass stigma against "acting white," defined as trying hard in school and obeying one's teacher. How the Smithsonian's leaders thought that they were helping black children by teaching them to scorn "hard work" and "delayed gratification" goes unexplained.

The museum eventually removed its chart on "white culture" from the internet after an outcry from conservative media.[66] Yet this typology of whiteness has been a dreary feature of corporate diversity trainings and freshman orientations since the 1990s—and the removal of the chart was only a minor setback in the ongoing attack on bourgeois virtues. The KIPP charter school network long distinguished itself with its high expectations for inner-city children and its insistence on self-discipline and conformity to basic norms of respect. No longer. In the summer of 2020, it retracted its motto "Work Hard. Be Nice." as part of its push to "dismantle systemic racism."[67]

America's elites have apparently decided that if, after five decades of massive financial outlays on inner-city education, income transfers, and social services, the academic skills gap has still not closed, it is time to break up the objective yardsticks that measure it. The same will happen regarding crime data. At present, data that show the vastly disproportionate rate at which blacks commit criminal offenses are still available from a handful of local police departments. Expect to find such facts even harder to pry from government agencies until they are disappeared entirely.

Thousands of blacks outperform whites and Asians thanks to study and self-discipline. But the ubiquity of racial preferences casts doubt on their achievements and leaves them open to the suspicion that they advanced because of the color of their skin. The question, *Do you owe your college seat or your job to affirmative action?* is not racist. The question is almost unavoidable under the current regime.

PART I

SCIENCE AND MEDICINE

Chapter One

MEDICINE'S RACIAL RECKONING

The post–George Floyd racial reckoning hit the field of medicine like an earthquake. Medical education, medical research, and standards of competence have been upended by two related hypotheses: that racial disparities in the demographics of the medical profession and racial disparities in health outcomes are the products of systemic racism. Questioning those hypotheses is professionally suicidal. Vast sums of public and private research funding are being redirected from basic science to political projects aimed at dismantling white supremacy. The result will be a declining quality of medical care and a curtailment of scientific progress.

Virtually every major medical organization—from the American Medical Association (AMA) and the American Association of Medical Colleges (AAMC) to the American Association of Pediatrics (AAP)—has embraced the idea that medicine is an inequity-producing enterprise. The AMA's 2021–2023 Organizational Strategic Plan to Embed Racial Justice and Advance Health Equity is virtually indistinguishable from a black studies department mission statement. The plan's anonymous authors seem aware of how radically its rhetoric differs from medicine's traditional concerns. The preamble notes that "just as the general parlance of a business document varies from that of a physics document, so too is the case for an equity document." (Such shaky command of usage and grammar characterizes the entire eighty-six-page tome, making the preamble's boast that "the field of equity has developed a parlance which conveys both [*sic*] authenticity, precision, and meaning" particularly ironic.) The "parlance of equity is manifest," according to the preamble, in the equity plan's "invocation-like recognition of 'land and labor acknowledgement,'" as well as in the "recognition of the specific harms of the past including those of the more recent past (termed 'truth and reconciliation')."[1]

Having been thus forewarned, the reader plunges into a thicket of social-justice maxims: physicians must "confront inequities and dismantle white supremacy, racism, and other forms of exclusion and structured oppression, as well as embed racial justice and advance equity within and across all aspects of health systems." The country needs to pivot "from euphemisms to explicit conversations about power, racism, gender and class oppression, forms of discrimination and exclusion." (The reader may puzzle over how much more "explicit" current "conversations" about racism can be.) We need to discard "America's stronghold of false notions of hierarchy of value based on gender, skin color, religion, ability and country of origin, as well as other forms of privilege."

A key solution to this alleged oppression, according to the AMA, is identity-based preferences throughout the medical profession. The AMA strategic plan calls for the "just representation of Black, Indigenous and Latinx people in medical school admissions as well as . . . leadership ranks." The lack of "just representation," according to the AMA, is due to deliberate "exclusion," which will end only when we have "prioritize[d] and integrate[d] the voices and ideas of people and communities experiencing great injustice and [those who are] historically excluded, exploited, and deprived of needed resources such as people of color, women, people with disabilities, LGBTQ+, and those in rural and urban communities alike."

According to medical and STEM leaders, to be white is to be racist per se; apologies and reparations for that offending trait are now expected. In June 2020, the journal *Nature* identified itself as one of the culpably "white institutions that is responsible for bias in research and scholarship."[2] In January 2021, the editor-in-chief of *Health Affairs* lamented that "our own staff and leadership are overwhelmingly white."[3] The AMA's strategic plan blames "white male lawmakers" for America's systemic racism.

And so medical schools and medical societies are discarding traditional standards of merit in order to alter the demographic characteristics of their profession. As with all disparate impact analyses, that demolition of standards rests on an a priori truth: that there is no academic skills gap between whites and Asians, on the one hand, and blacks and Hispanics, on the other. Therefore, any test or evaluation on which blacks and Hispanics, score worse than whites and Asians is biased and should be eliminated.

The United States Medical Licensing Exam (USMLE) is a prime offender. At the end of their second year of medical school, students take Step One of the USMLE, which measures knowledge of the body's anatomical parts, their functioning, and their malfunctioning; topics include biochemistry, physiology, cell biology, pharmacology, and the cardiovascular system. High scores on Step One predict success in a residency; highly sought-after residency programs, such as surgery and radiology, use Step One scores to help select applicants.

Black students are not admitted into competitive residencies at the same rate as whites because their average Step One test scores are a standard deviation below those of whites,[4] representing, in statistical terms, a massive gap. (Standard deviation measures how dispersed data are from a mean.) Step One has already been modified to try to shrink that gap; it now includes nonscience components such as "communication and interpersonal skills." But the standard deviation in scores has persisted. In the world of anti-racism, that persistence means only one thing: the test is to blame. It is Step One that, in the language of anti-racism, "disadvantages" underrepresented minorities, not a lesser degree of medical knowledge.

The Step One exam has a further mark against it. The pressure to score well inhibits minority students from what has become a core component of medical education: anti-racism advocacy. A fourth-year Yale medical student describes how the specter of Step One affected his priorities. In his first two years of medical school, the student had "immersed" himself, as he describes it, in a "student-led committee focused on diversity, inclusion, and social justice." The committee lobbied the administration for changes in the curriculum, the admissions process, and research funding. The student ran a podcast about health disparities. All that political work was made possible by Yale's pass-fail grading system, which meant that he didn't feel compelled to put studying ahead of diversity concerns. Then, as he tells it, Step One "reared its ugly head." Getting an actual grade on an exam might prove to "whoever might have thought it before that [he] didn't deserve a seat at Yale as a Black medical student," the student worried.[5]

The solution to such academic pressure was obvious: abolish Step One grades. Since January 2022, Step One has been graded on a pass-fail basis. The fourth-year Yale student can now go back to his diversity activism without worrying about what a graded exam might reveal. Whether his future patients will appreciate his focus is unclear.

Medical school bureaucrats cheer on this reorientation to advocacy. A career advisory dean at the George Washington University School of Medicine & Health Sciences describes a conversation she had with a student who had done so poorly on her Step One test that she would have a hard time "matching" (med-school argot for landing) her preferred residency in obstetrics and gynecology. The advisor insisted that the student's test scores were less important than her "passion for social justice." (How that passion might help a doctor treat a uterine rupture during delivery is also unclear.) In the career advisor's view, the student's "feelings of incompetence" were arbitrary and unjustified. Yet they were "impacting" the student's clinical performance. Arguably, it was the student's struggles with core science concepts that were impacting her clinical performance. No matter. Making Step One pass/fail will help students more "effectively tell their stories to residency programs," since it is apparently a student's "story" that hospitals should use in selecting interns.[6]

Every other measure of academic mastery has a disparate impact on blacks and thus is in jeopardy.

Membership in the medical school honor society, Alpha Omega Alpha (AOA), influences resident selection and faculty hiring. White students are nearly six times as likely as black students to be inducted into Alpha Omega Alpha, according to the *Journal of the American Medical Association*.[7] Time to change the membership criteria. In 2020, the then–president of AOA suggested consideration of a potential inductee's "relationship skills" and of any "unequal barriers" he may have faced.[8] Success! The University of Pennsylvania's Perelman School of Medicine, among others, happily converted to a "holistic" selection system in 2021, adding community activities (think: anti-racism advocacy) to class standing. The percentage of minority selectees rose from 10 to 26 percent, reports Stanley Goldfarb, an emeritus professor and former associate dean of curriculum at the Penn medical school.[9]

In the third year of medical school, professors grade students on their clinical knowledge in what is known as a Medical Student Performance Evaluation (MSPE). The MSPE uses qualitative categories like Outstanding, Excellent, Very Good, and Good. From 2010 to 2015, white students at the University of Washington School of Medicine received higher MSPE ratings than underrepresented minority students, according to a 2019 analysis.[10] The disparity in MSPEs tracked the disparity in Step One scores.

The parallel between MSPE and Step One evaluations might suggest that what is being measured in both cases is real. But the a priori truth holds that no academic skills gap exists. Accordingly, the researchers proposed a national study of medical school grades to identify the *actual* causes of that racial disparity. The conclusion is foregone: faculty bias. As a Harvard medical student put it in *Stat News*: "biases are baked into the evaluations of students from marginalized backgrounds."[11]

A 2022 study of clinical performance scores also proposed that foregone conclusion. Professors from Emory University, Massachusetts General Hospital, and the University of California, San Francisco, among other institutions, analyzed faculty evaluations of internal medicine residents in such areas as medical knowledge and professionalism.[12] On every assessment, black and Hispanic residents were rated lower than white and Asian residents. The researchers hypothesized three possible explanations: bias in faculty assessment, effects of a non-inclusive learning environment, or structural inequities in assessment. Stanley Goldfarb tweeted out a fourth possibility: "Could it be [the minority students] were just less good at being residents?"[13]

Goldfarb had violated the a priori truth. Punishment was immediate. Predictable tweets called him, inter alia, a "garbage human being."[14] Michael S. Parmacek, chair of the University of Pennsylvania's Department of Medicine, sent a school-wide email addressing Goldfarb's "racist statements." Those statements had evoked "deep pain and anger," Parmacek wrote. Accordingly, he said, the school would be making its "entire leadership team" available to "support" its students and faculty. Parmacek took the occasion to reaffirm that doctors must acknowledge "structural racism."[15]

That same day, the executive vice president (EVP) of the University of Pennsylvania Health System and the senior vice dean (SVD) for medical education at the University of Pennsylvania medical school reminded faculty, staff, and students via email that Goldfarb was currently an emeritus professor, a status which presumably posed less of a danger to school safety than an active professorship would. The EVP and the SVD affirmed Penn's efforts to "foster an anti-racist curriculum" and to promote "inclusive excellence."

Despite the allegations of faculty racism, disparities in academic performance are the predictable outcome of racial admissions preferences. In 2021, the average score for white applicants on the Medical College Admission Test (MCAT) was in the seventy-first percentile, meaning that it was equal to or better than 71 percent of all average scores.[16] The average score for black applicants was in the thirty-seventh percentile[17]—a full standard deviation below the average white score. The MCATs have already been redesigned to try to reduce this gap; a quarter of the questions now focus on social issues and psychology.[18]

Yet the gap persists. So medical schools use wildly different standards for admitting black and white applicants. From 2013 to 2016, only 8 percent of white college seniors with below-average undergraduate GPAs and below-average MCAT scores were offered a seat in medical school; less than 6 percent of Asian college seniors with those qualifications were offered a seat, according to an analysis by economist Mark Perry.[19] Medical schools regarded those below-average scores as all but disqualifying—except when presented by blacks and Hispanics. Over 56 percent of black college seniors with below-average undergraduate GPAs and below-average MCATs were admitted, as were 31 percent of Hispanic students with those scores, making a black student in that range more than seven times as likely as a similarly situated white college senior to be admitted into medical school, and more than nine times as likely as a similarly situated Asian senior.[20] Race plays such a large role in medical school admissions that a free online calculator of acceptance likelihood uses only four variables: GPA, MCAT score, state of residence, and ethnicity.[21]

Such disparate rates of admission hold in every combination and range of GPA and MCAT scores. Contrary to the AMA's Organizational Strategic Plan to Embed Racial Justice and Advance Health Equity, blacks are not being "excluded" from medical training; they are being catapulted ahead of their less valued white and Asian peers. The "hierarchy of value based on . . . skin color" is the reverse of the one denounced by the AMA.

Though mediocre MCAT scores keep out few black students, some activists seek to eliminate the MCATs entirely. Admitting less-qualified students to PhD programs in the life sciences will lower the caliber of future researchers and slow scientific advances. But the stakes are higher in medical training, where insufficient knowledge can endanger a life in the here and now. Nevertheless, some medical schools offer early admissions to college sophomores and juniors with no MCAT requirement, hoping to enroll students with, as the Icahn School of Medicine at Mount Sinai puts it, a "strong appreciation of human rights and social justice."[22] The University of Pennsylvania medical school guarantees admission to black undergraduates who score a modest 1300 (on a 1600-point scale) on the SAT, maintain an even more modest 3.6 GPA in college, and complete two summers of internship at the school.[23] The school waives its MCAT requirement for these black students; University of Pennsylvania's non-preferred medical students score in the top 1 percent of all MCAT takers.

Disparate impact dogma holds that differences in MCAT scores must result from test bias. Yet the MCATs, like all beleaguered standardized tests, are constantly scoured for questions that may presume forms of knowledge particular to a class or race. This "cultural bias" chestnut has been an irrelevancy for decades, yet it retains its salience within the anti-testing movement. MCAT questions with the largest racial variance in correct answers are removed. External bias examiners, suitably diverse, double-check the work of the internal MCAT reviewers. If, despite this gauntlet of review, bias still lurked in the MCATs, the tests would underpredict the medical school performance of minority students. In fact, they overpredict it—black medical students do worse than their MCATs would predict, as measured by Step One scores and graduation rates.[24] (Such overprediction characterizes the SATs, too.) Nevertheless, expect more medical schools to forgo the MCATs, in the hope of shutting down the test entirely and thus eliminating a lingering source of objective data on the allegedly phantom academic skills gap. (Indeed, in 2015, the American Association of Medical Colleges stopped publishing the distribution of MCAT scores, as opposed to the average, by race. The AAMC cites as the reason the "sensitivity of the data and small sample sizes for some race/ethnicity categories."[25])

Opposition to the preference regime requires a certain reckless courage. In 2020, the director of the electrophysiology fellowship program at the University of Pittsburgh Medical Center called for the color-blind evaluation of future doctors based on their "personal merits" rather than on their racial identities.[26] Director Norman Wang argued that years of research showed that students admitted under a racial quota disproportionately end their studies because of poor grades and have a harder time passing the medical licensing exam. Because of their weaker academic records, black medical students are less likely to be admitted into a residency program than whites and Asians, even though graduate medical school education also doles out large racial preferences.

A cardiologist in Virginia responded that Wang's paper was emblematic of "systemic racism."[27] The article sends the message to minority trainees that they owe their position to affirmative action and that their presence in a medical specialty reflects a decline in standards, the cardiologist complained. Actually, the data on medical school admissions show that the large majority of blacks attend the schools they do thanks to racial preferences, which continue throughout a trainee's medical career. If preferences were not so key in engineering "diversity," academic gatekeepers would not so fiercely defend them as the only mechanism capable of producing diversity.

The director of diversity and inclusion at the Mayo Clinic tweeted that the paper should inspire rage and activism.[28] The president-elect of the American Heart Association, who chairs the Department of Preventive Medicine at Northwestern University, wondered how the paper could have been published, given its "unbalanced, unscientific, and untrue statements."[29] The president-elect offered no examples of such untrue statements. The AAMC claimed that the paper lacked factual accuracy, also without providing any examples.[30] One of Wang's colleagues at the University of Pittsburgh medical school tweeted that she and other faculty denounce this individual's racist beliefs and paper.[31] She was apparently unwilling to sully herself by naming the reprobate.

Both the paper and Wang himself were soon retracted. The editor of the *Journal of the American Heart Association* condemned "discrimination and racism in all forms,"[32] apologized for publishing the article, and retracted it.[33] The *Journal* would be "improving" its peer-review system, the editor said, to ensure that it avoids such "missteps" (i.e., publishing the facts) in the future. The AAMC expressed its hope that other journals would revise their peer-review process as well, with the undoubted goal of ensuring that a challenge to racial preferences does not occur again.

Wang lost his position as a director at the University of Pittsburgh Heart and Vascular Institute. His supervisors banned him from any contact with medical students and residents. Wang's lawsuit against the University of Pittsburgh and its employees for First Amendment and contractual violations is ongoing.[34]

Meanwhile, even medical professors who have not challenged diversity orthodoxy need to be reeducated to ensure that their grading and hiring practices do not provide further evidence of the skills gap. Faculty are routinely subjected to workshops in combating their own presumed racism. On May 3, 2022, the Senior Advisor to the National Institutes of Health Chief Officer for Scientific Workforce Diversity, Charlene Le Fauve, gave a seminar at the University of Pennsylvania medical school titled, "Me, Biased? Recognizing and Blocking Bias."[35] Le Fauve's mandate at NIH is to "promote diversity, inclusiveness, and equity in the biomedical research enterprise through evidence-based approaches."[36] Yet her presentation rested heavily on a measure of bias that evidence has discredited: the Implicit Association Test (IAT). Le Fauve insisted that the IAT has "identified" over 100 types of bias. She asserted that psychologist Daniel Kahneman's theory of fast and slow thinking was simply another version of the implicit bias conceit. In fact, Kahneman's work has nothing to do with the IAT. Moreover, the IAT's creators have acknowledged that it lacks validity and reliability as a psychometric tool.[37]

Increasing amounts of faculty time are spent on such anti-racism activities. On May 16, 2022, the anti-racism program manager at the David Geffen School of Medicine at the University of California, Los Angeles, hosted a presentation from the director of strategy and equity education programs at the Icahn School of Medicine at Mount Sinai titled "Anti-Racist Transformation in Medical Education."[38] Mount Sinai's dean for medical education and a medical student joined the presentation, since spreading the diversity message apparently takes precedence over academic obligations in New York.

Grand rounds is a century-long tradition for passing on the latest medical breakthroughs. Originally, a doctor would present a particularly challenging case, complete with patient, to his fellow practitioners; Thomas Eakins's great 1889 painting, *The Agnew Clinic*, portrays one such early grand rounds at the University of Pennsylvania. Now, rounds are often a conduit for anti-racism reeducation. On May 12, 2022, the vice chair for diversity and inclusion at the University of Pittsburgh's Department of Medicine gave a grand rounds at the Cleveland Clinic on the topic: "In the Absence of Equity: A Look into the Future." Afterward, attendees would be expected to describe "exclusion from a historical context" and the effects of "hierarchy on health outcomes"; attendance would confer academic credit toward doctors' continuing-education obligations.[39] On November 18, 2022, the Department of Pediatrics in the Stanford School of Medicine offered a grand rounds titled "Creating Native American Pathways to Diversify the Healthcare Workforce to Address Health Inequities."[40]

The medical school curriculum itself needs to be changed, say diversity advocates, to lessen the gap between the academic performance of whites and Asians, on the one hand, and blacks and Hispanics, on the other. Doing so entails replacing pure science courses with credit-bearing advocacy training. More than half of the top fifty medical schools surveyed by the Legal Insurrection Foundation in 2022 already required courses in systemic racism.[41] That number will increase after the AAMC's new guidelines for what medical students and faculty should know transform the curriculum further.

According to the AAMC, newly minted doctors must display "knowledge of the intersectionality of a patient's multiple identities and how each identity may present varied and multiple forms of oppression or privilege related to clinical decisions and practice." They must be able to articulate how their own "identities, power, and privileges" influence interactions with patients and the health care team. Faculty are responsible for teaching how to engage with "systems of power, privilege, and oppression" in order to "disrupt oppressive practices."[42] Failure to comply with these requirements could put a medical school's accreditation status at risk and lead to a school's closure.

Mandatory instruction in such politicized concepts will help diversify the faculty and administration—for who better to teach about oppression than a person of color? (Part of the appeal of diversity trainings and bureaucracy, whether in academia or the corporate world, lies in the creation of new employment slots dedicated to diversity activities, which can be diversely filled without as great a sacrifice of meritocratic standards.) But being indoctrinated in "intersectionality," as the AAMC demands, does nothing to improve a student's clinical knowledge. Every moment spent regurgitating social-justice jargon is time not spent learning how to keep someone alive whose body has, for example, just been shattered in a car crash. Advocates of anti-racism training never explain how fluency in "intersectional" critique improves the interpretation of an MRI or the proper prescribing of drugs.

The UCLA medical school has gotten a jump start on the AAMC's new diversity competencies. It has replaced the third-year curriculum—traditionally devoted to rotations through various clinical practices—with eight elective concentrations. Only one of those electives—Basic, Clinical, and Translational Research—appears to be related to actual scientific knowledge. A more typical option is Health Justice and Advocacy, which will instruct students on how to be "advocates for justice" by learning about "human rights" and the "social determinants of health."[43] It is easy to guess the likely demographics of the Health Justice and Advocacy track, which will provide another route for shrinking the GPA and honor society gaps. (UCLA's law school used a similar strategy: introducing a critical race theory concentration in order to admit more minority students without overtly violating California's ban on racial admissions preferences.)

Teaching students how to engage in political work is not a medical school's comparative advantage; teaching cell pathology is. Doctors already complain that third- and fourth-year interns know less science than before, thanks, in part, to the non-scientific components inserted into the curriculum. Every substitution of political advocacy for science will further shrink future doctors' knowledge.

The academic skills gap, confirmed in every measure of knowledge before and during medical school, does not close over the course of medical training, despite remedial instruction. Yet the lower representation of blacks throughout the medical profession is solely attributed to racism on the part of the profession's gatekeepers. *Nature* accused itself of denying a "space and a platform" to black researchers, without naming any such researchers against whom it had discriminated or any editor who had done the discriminating.[44] In April 2022, the Institute for Scientific Information decried the fact that the proportion of black authors in medical research did not match US census data on the population at large.[45] Black representation had not improved between 2010 and 2020, lamented the Institute. If white supremacy lay behind that lack of progress, it was a mystery as to why the proportion of published Asian researchers over the same decade had outstripped Asian population changes.

Despite the persistent academic skills gap, a minority-hiring surge is underway. Many medical schools require that faculty search committees contain a quota of minority members, that the committees be overseen by a diversity bureaucrat, and that they interview a specified number of minority candidates. One would have to be particularly dense not to grasp the expected result. In recent years, the Wake Forest School of Medicine, the Memorial Sloan Kettering Cancer Center, the Cleveland Clinic Taussig Cancer Center, Virginia Commonwealth University's School of Pharmacy, the Uniformed Services University of the Health Sciences, the University of Chicago Comprehensive Cancer Center, the University of Pittsburgh Division of Medical Hermatology/Oncology, the Massey Cancer Center at Virginia Commonwealth University, the University of Miami Miller School of Medicine, and the

Department of Medicine at UCLA's medical school have hired black leaders. These candidates may all have been the most qualified, but the explicit calls for diversity in medical administration inevitably cast a pall on such selections. In at least one case, the runner-up possessed a research and leadership record that far surpassed that of the winning candidate. But he lacked the right demographic characteristics.

It matters who heads research ventures and medical faculties. Top scientists can identify the most promising directions of study and organize the most productive research teams. But the diversity push is discouraging some scientists from competing at all. When the chairmanship of UCLA's Department of Medicine opened up, some qualified faculty members did not put their names forward because they did not think they would even be considered, according to an observer. "It's the end of the road for me as a Jewish male doctor," a cancer researcher told me.[46]

College seniors, deciding whether to apply to medical school, can also read the writing on the wall. A physician-scientist reports that his best lab technician in thirty years was a Yale graduate with a BS in molecular biology and biochemistry. The former student was intellectually involved and expert in cloning. His college GPA and MCAT scores were high. The physician-scientist recommended the student to the dean of Northwestern's medical school (where the scientist worked at the time), but the student did not get so much as an interview. In fact, this "white, clean-cut Catholic," in the words of his former employer, was admitted to only one medical school.

Such stories are rife. A UCLA doctor says that the smartest undergraduates in the school's science labs are saying: "Now that I see what is happening in medicine, I will do something else."[47]

Funding that once went to scientific research is now being redirected to diversity cultivation. The NIH and the National Science Foundation are devoting millions in taxpayer dollars to "[support] the diverse and inclusive workforce needed for tomorrow's life-saving medical interventions"[48] and to "broaden the implementation of evidence-based systemic change strategies that promote equity."[49] Private research support is following the same trajectory. The Howard Hughes Medical Institute (HHMI) is one of the world's largest philanthropic funders of basic science, and arguably the most prestigious. Airline entrepreneur Howard Hughes created the Institute in 1953 to probe into the "genesis of life itself." Now diversity in medical research is at the top of HHMI's concerns. In May 2022, it announced a $1.5 billion effort to cultivate scientists committed to running a "happy and diverse lab where minoritized scientists will thrive and persist," in the words of the Institute's vice president.[50] "Experts" in diversity and inclusion will assess early-career academic scientists based on their plans for running "happy and diverse" labs. Those applicants with the most persuasive happy lab plans could receive one of the new Freeman Hrabowski scholarships.[51] The scholarships would cover the recipient's university salary for ten years and would bring the equivalent of two or three NIH grants a year into his academic department.[52] If an applicant's happy lab plan fails to ignite enthusiasm in the diversity reviewers, his application will be shelved, no matter how promising his actual scientific research.

The HHMI program and others like it amplify the message that doing basic science, if you are white or Asian, is not particularly valued by the STEM establishment. The number of scientific breakthroughs that will be forgone in response to this messaging is incalculable.

The leaders of today's medical schools, professional organizations, and scientific journals would reject the foregoing critique. Teaching racial-justice concepts and advocacy is not a swerve from medicine's core competencies and obligations, they would argue; it is the highest fulfillment of those obligations. Racial disparities in health, they would say, are the biggest medical challenge of our time, and they are a social, not a scientific, problem. If blacks have higher rates of mortality and disease, it is because systematic racism confronts them at every turn. Changing the demographics of the medical profession is essential to eliminating the sometimes lethal racism that black patients encounter in health care. Changing the profession's awareness of its own biases is also key to achieving medical equity. And changing the orientation of medical research—away from basic science and toward race theory—simply moves medicine to where it can be most effective.

Here we encounter the second a priori truth: health disparities are the product of systemic racism; any other explanation is taboo and will be as ruthlessly punished as the questioning of admissions preferences.

On February 24, 2021, Edward Livingston, deputy editor for clinical reviews and education at the *Journal of the American Medical Association* (*JAMA*), recorded a podcast with Mitchell Katz, president of New York City Health and Hospitals, called "Structural Racism for Doctors—What Is It?" Livingston, a UCLA surgeon, asked Katz to define structural racism. Katz gave as examples the routing of diesel trucks through poor neighborhoods and disparities in access to top-level medical care. Livingston responded that Katz had described a "very real" problem: impoverished neighborhoods with poor quality of life and little opportunity, where most residents are black and Hispanic. Livingston agreed with the urgency of making sure that all people "have equal opportunities to become successful." His only quibble was with the current emphasis on "racism." Such an emphasis "might be hurting" the cause of racial equality, by alienating potential supporters who do not think of themselves as biased and who are "turned off by the whole structural racism phenomenon." Livingston himself had been taught to revile discrimination and yet was being told that he was racist. The focus, as Livingston saw it, should be on socioeconomic disparities, not alleged racial animus.

After the podcast became an instant totem of white supremacy, *JAMA* disappeared it from the web. Livingston himself was disappeared from *JAMA* shortly thereafter. (Back at his home base at the UCLA medical school, he faced a show trial from fellow faculty members.) *JAMA*'s Editor-in-Chief Howard Bauchner, a professor of pediatrics and public health at Boston University, apparently sensed that he might be next on the chopping block and started issuing serial apologies. The disappeared podcast, Bauchner declared, was "inaccurate, offensive, hurtful, and inconsistent with the standards of *JAMA*." *JAMA* would be "instituting changes that will address and prevent such failures from happening again"—a "failure" being defined as deviation from racial justice orthodoxy. Bauchner genuflected further in an official statement: "I once again apologize for the harms caused by this podcast and the tweet about the podcast."[53] (*JAMA* had promoted the podcast with a tweet, asking: "No physician is racist, so how can there be structural racism in health care?"[54]) For good measure, Bauchner also commented in a moderated conversation with Harvard T.H. Chan School of Public Health affiliates, apologizing for the "harm" caused by the tweet and podcast and expressing his "commitment" for *JAMA* to "further discuss issues of structural racism."[55]

JAMA was once a leading forum where physicians and other scientists could present research to their peers. Now *JAMA*'s overseers regard a fundamental component of the scientific method—debate—as out of bounds, at least regarding the diversity agenda. Livingston's disagreement with Katz and the "structural racism" conceit was over language, not substance. Yet because Livingston suggested taking the "racism" out of the "structural racism" phrase and focusing instead on equal opportunity, he had, in Bauchner's widely shared view, harmed blacks and violated professional standards of journalism. No disagreement is tolerated.

Meanwhile, Bauchner's efforts to distance himself from the "offensive" dialogue were not bearing fruit. Ominously, an AMA committee put him on administrative leave pending an "independent investigation"—as if there were a complex backstory to what were clearly Livingston's personal opinions. By June 2021, Bauchner, too, was out, even though, as he ruefully observed, he "did not write or even see the tweet, or create the podcast."[56] The diversity bureaucracy, always resourceful in exploiting perceived race crises, leveraged the episode to expand its reach. In May 2021, in penance for the Livingston debacle, the AMA rolled out another sinecure-stuffed plan to dismantle its own structural racism and the racism inherent in medicine.

The chance that the AMA would not appoint an intersectional editor-in-chief to replace the hapless Bauchner was zero. But just to be safe, the AMA named a black epidemiologist specializing in racial disparities to lead the search and staffed the search committee with suitably diverse members. A cardiologist who has analyzed the lack of racial diversity among *JAMA* editors acknowledged the inevitability of the outcome. "I expected them to choose a woman of color, to shield themselves against more criticism," cardiologist Ray Givens told *Stat News*.[57] Limiting the editor search to females "of color" drastically shrinks the applicant pool and thus the likelihood of finding the best possible candidate. Such meritocratic considerations are passé, however. The new editor, Kirsten Bibbins-Domingo, is a "health-equity researcher"—also an overdetermined fact, given the career course of many black MDs.

Bibbins-Domingo has already announced her determination to bring in "new voices" (who will inevitably be chosen on the basis of race), to ensure that the *JAMA* family of journals regularly "name" structural racism as the cause of health inequities.[58] Will those new voices be conducting the most cutting-edge clinical science? It doesn't matter: basic science is, at best, irrelevant to structural racism and, at worst, complicit in it.

Livingston's challenge to the idea that health disparities are caused by racism was sui generis among medical journalists. The hold of that idea within medical publishing is otherwise absolute. The *New England Journal of Medicine*, another formerly august institution now in thrall to racial politics, presents a nonstop stream of articles on such topics as the "Pathology of Racism,"[59] "Toward Antiracist Allyship in Medicine,"[60] and "How Structural Racism Works — Racist Policies as a Root Cause of US Racial Health Inequities."[61] More specialized reviews publish works like "Reductions in Racial Disparities in Colorectal Cancer."[62]

Entire issues of scientific journals have been devoted to racism. *Scientific American* published a "special collector's edition" on *The Science of Overcoming Racism* in the summer of 2021.[63] The edition was dominated by paeans to the Implicit Association Test, denunciations of the police, and scorn for any suggestion of patient self-efficacy. (Prescribing weight loss to black women, for example, is a "racist" way to fight obesity, wrote a sociology professor and a nutritionist.[64]) A special issue of *Science* in October 2021 addressed "Criminal Injustice" and "Mass Incarceration."[65] The issue opened with an editorial by a social-work professor claiming that the US crime rate is "comparable to those in many Western industrial nations."[66] This is a fanciful proposition, in light of the fact that the American firearm homicide rate is twenty-two times higher than the average of European Union countries.[67]

Like the AMA's Organizational Strategic Plan to Embed Racial Justice and Advance Health Equity, many of these anti-racism articles consist of the formulaic rhetoric of academic victim studies, supplemented by the personal narratives that characterized early critical race theory in law schools. Others, though, try to quantify the racism that allegedly produces higher levels of illness and mortality in blacks. Those efforts, done through regression analysis, do not capture the personal behaviors that affect the course of disease, such as compliance with a doctor's orders, adherence to a medication regime, and keeping follow-up appointments. (Regression analysis analyzes large tranches of data to determine the relationship, if any, among different variables—say between the number of ads a company runs and its revenues or between obesity and health outcomes.) In some cases, the statistical search for racism did not account for the differences in the illnesses suffered by black patients and white patients at the start of the study.

Nevertheless, the second a priori truth—that health disparities are necessarily the product of systemic racism—has devalued basic science and encumbered medical research with red tape. The fight against cancer has been particularly affected.

Cancer grant applications must now specify who, among a lab's staff, will enforce diversity mandates and how the lab plans to recruit underrepresented researchers and promote their careers. White and Asian oncologists are assumed to be part of the problem of black cancer mortality, not its solution, absent corrective measures. According to the NIH, leadership of cancer labs should match national or local demographics, whichever has a higher percentage of minorities. In Baltimore, which is over 60 percent black, only 10 percent of black eighth graders can read proficiently.[68] Should Johns Hopkins's comprehensive cancer center nevertheless have 60 percent black physician-administrators?

Grant applicants seek the services of the burgeoning diversity-consulting profession to make sure that their proposals sound the right diversity notes. As with the Howard Hughes Medical Institute's Freeman Hrabowski scholarships, an insufficiently robust diversity plan means that a cancer research proposal will be rejected, regardless of its scientific merit. Discussions about how to beef up the diversity section of a grant proposal have become more important than discussions about tumor biology, reports a physician-scientist. "It is not easy summarizing how your work on cell signaling in nematodes applies to minorities currently living in your lab's vicinity," the researcher says. Mental energy spent solving that conundrum is mental energy not spent on science, he laments, since "thinking is always a zero-sum game."[69]

A lab's diversity gauntlet has just begun, however. The NIH insists that participants in drug trials must also match national or local demographics. If a cancer center is in an area with few minorities, the lab must nevertheless present a plan for recruiting them into its study, regardless of their local unavailability. Genentech, the creator of life-saving cancer drugs, held a national conference call with oncologists in April 2022 to discuss products in the research pipeline. Half of the call was spent on the problem of achieving diverse clinical trial enrollments, a participant reported. Genentech admitted to having run out of ideas.

There is no evidence that racist researchers are excluding minorities from drug trials on nonmedical grounds, nor has anyone presented a theory as to why they would. The barriers to such drug trial diversity include a higher incidence among blacks of disqualifying comorbidities, more challenging personal lives, and a suspicion of the medical profession (which that same profession constantly amplifies with its drumbeat about racism). Those barriers to drug-trial diversity are not recognized by grant evaluators, however.

In May 2022, a physician-scientist lost her NIH funding for a drug trial because the trial population did not contain enough blacks.[70] The drug under review was for a type of cancer that blacks rarely get. So there were almost no black patients with that disease to enroll in the trial in the first place. It's better, however, to foreclose development of a therapy that might help predominantly white cancer patients than to conduct a drug trial without black participants.

The diversity-driven requirement of racial proportionality in drug trials is perplexing, since diversity advocates insist that race is a social construct, without biological reality. Suggesting that genetic differences exist between racial groups will brand you a racist. The AMA's Organizational Strategic Plan to Embed Racial Justice and Advance Health Equity sneers that "much of medicine still looks for cultural, behavioral or even genetic explanations" to explain racial gaps in life expectancy. Such a focus rests on "discredited and racist ideas about biological differences between racial groups," according to the AMA. In May 2022, the American Association of Pediatrics announced that it was eliminating "race-based" medicine, defined as including a patient's race in assessments of some health risks. If race does not exist, as received wisdom now has it, then the racial makeup of clinical trials should not matter.

The idea that race is merely a social construct is anti-scientific, however. DNA analyses show that there are at least five distinguishable races. The refusal to acknowledge race is also anti-health. Blacks with sub-Saharan roots have a high rate of kidney disease, for example, thanks in part to a more frequent genetic mutation. Drug companies have sought a treatment for that mutation. The reaction to that research has been unhinged. A lecturer in ethics at Columbia University and author of the book *Medical Apartheid* told the *New York Times* in May 2022 that knowledge about the genetic variant might drive the medical establishment toward "a blame-the-victim approach signaling an inherent flaw in African Americans."[71] This is fictional. No one thinks that possessing a genetic mutation means that the possessor is "inherently flawed." The activists are terrified, however, that work in basic science will supplant the political crusade against white supremacy. They would rather stop medical progress than improve blacks' quality of life, if doing the latter acknowledges biological reality.

Biological reality comes into play in another kidney-related area. A common blood test for kidney health understates healthy kidney function in black patients. Nephrologists therefore adjusted the test results for black patients to estimate their kidney function with greater accuracy. Then the activists showed up, arguing that this correction must be abolished. The American Society of Nephrology and the National Kidney Foundation announced that they no longer supported the separate reporting of the kidney function measure for black patients.[72] The University of Pennsylvania health system, among others, proudly presented its changed reporting protocol as part of the fight against medical racism.[73] A more complicated diagnostic formula was widely adopted. But no patient was damaged by the original, more straightforward formula, nor was that original formula based on racism.

The proponents of the systemic racism hypothesis are making a large bet with potentially lethal consequences. In accordance with the idea that racism causes racial health disparities, they are changing the direction of medical research, the composition of medical faculty, the curriculum of medical schools, the criteria for hiring researchers and for publishing research, and the standards for assessing professional excellence. They are substituting training in political advocacy for training in basic science. They are taking doctors out of the classroom, clinic, and lab and parking them in front of anti-racism lecturers. Their preferential policies discourage individuals from pariah groups from going into medicine, regardless of their scientific potential. They have shifted funding from the investigation of pathophysiology to the production of tracts on microaggressions.

The advocates of this change insist that these measures are essential to improving minority health. But what if they are wrong? If it turns out that individual behavior, pathogens that disproportionately infect certain groups, and other genetic dispositions have a more proximate influence on health than supposed structural racism, then this reorientation of the medical project will have impeded progress that helps all racial groups. Obstetricians working in inner-city hospitals report that black mothers have higher rates of complications during pregnancy and in delivery because of higher rates of morbid obesity, hypertension, and inattention to prenatal care and prenatal-care appointments. Packing those doctors off to diversity reeducation will not improve black childbirth outcomes. It will, though, divert attention from solutions that could improve those outcomes—such as help with keeping appointments and complying with a medication regime or encouragement of exercise and weight loss. And yet we are told that efforts directed at behavioral change are racist and that convincing patients that they have power over their health is victim-blaming.

Higher rates of COVID-19 fatalities among blacks is the latest favored proof of medical racism, amplified by a 2022 Oprah Winfrey and Smithsonian Channel documentary *The Color of Care*.[74] State and federal health authorities gave priority to minorities in vaccination and immunotherapy campaigns, however, and penalized the highest-risk group—the elderly—simply because that group is disproportionately white. Those are not the actions of white supremacists. The likelier reasons for disparities in COVID-19 outcomes are vaccine hesitancy and obesity rates. When the constant refrain about medical racism intensifies vaccine resistance among blacks, the widened mortality gaps will be used to confirm the racism hypothesis, in a vicious circle.

Medical science has been one of the greatest engines of human progress, liberating millions from crippling disease and premature mortality. It has also seen its share of dead ends and misconceptions, from the miasma theory of contagion to the use of thalidomide to treat morning sickness. Science goes astray when politics become paramount, as in the denial of plant genetics and natural selection under Stalin. (Stalin-era agronomist Trofim Lysenko insisted that acquired characteristics could be passed on to subsequent generations, a logically necessary capacity if humans were to be molded into a revolutionary vanguard. Applied to agriculture, Lysenkoism resulted in grain harvest failures and famine.)

The scientific method and the spirit of open debate that lie behind that method are natural corrections to such fatal errors. Now, when it comes to the contention that racism is the defining trait of the medical profession and the source of health disparities, holding opposing views is grounds for being purged. The separation of politics and science is no longer seen as a source of empirical strength; it is instead a racist dodge that risks "reinforcing existing power structures," according to the editor of *Health Affairs*.[75]

The guardians of science have turned on science itself.

Chapter Two

HOW 'DIVERSITY' SUBVERTS SCIENCE

The National Institutes of Health supports a multidisciplinary neuroscience initiative to expand understanding of the brain. Research applications include treatments for Alzheimer's, Parkinson's, autism, and depression. On June 10, 2021, then–NIH Director Francis Collins announced a new requirement for participating in the brain initiative: neurologists, molecular biologists, and nanophysicists seeking NIH funding must now submit a plan showing how they will enhance "diverse perspectives" throughout their research. Scores on the plan for enhancing diverse perspectives will inform funding decisions.

This new requirement was part of Collins's effort to atone for what he called biomedical science's "stain" of "structural" racism. The NIH already supports more than sixty diversity and inclusion initiatives, but those have apparently failed to eradicate the NIH's own racism.

Each "plan for enhancing diverse perspectives" must show how the principal investigator will "empower" individuals from groups traditionally "underrepresented" in biomedical research, such as blacks, the disabled, women, and the poor. Institutions are also covered by the diversity mandate. Researchers working on an NIH neuroscience grant should be drawn from institutions that are traditionally underrepresented in biomedical research, including "community-based" organizations.

Collins provided no evidence for "structural racism" other than demographic data on NIH's grant applicants and recipients. Under disparate impact theory, that is evidence enough. Black applicants are "present in far fewer numbers compared with their representation in the U.S. population, 13.4%," according to Collins's announcement.[1] In 2020, 2.3 percent of the 30,061 funding applications the NIH received came from black scientists. As noted previously, less than 2 percent of NIH grants go to black principal investigators.[2]

But grant attainment, particularly in STEM fields, reflects the skills gap discussed earlier. In 2019, twenty blacks nationwide received a doctorate in a neuroscience field—1.9 percent of all such degrees awarded in the neurosciences. There were three newly minted black PhDs in biophysics (1.7 percent of the total) and twenty-one in biochemistry (2.6 percent of the total). Genetics and genomics departments graduated eight black PhDs (2.3 percent of the total), and molecular-biology departments fourteen (2.5 percent of the total). In electrical engineering, a feeder into nanotechnology, there were eighteen black PhDs (1 percent of the total).[3]

The NIH is determining research priorities to maximize the number of black grant recipients. Black researchers submit comparatively few pure science proposals to the NIH, instead favoring public-health projects.[4] Accordingly, Collins also announced an additional $30 million in grants for addressing the "impact of structural racism and discrimination on minority health" and another $60 million for projects "aimed at reducing health disparities."[5] Such a reallocation of resources is expected to boost the NIH's diversity numbers, whatever its scientific necessity.

Notwithstanding the NIH's determination to "provide full opportunity and participation to individuals and groups underrepresented in neuroscience,"[6] the mission of federal science agencies is not compensatory hiring. Underrepresented groups are underrepresented for reasons unrelated to discrimination by the academy. Any scientific agenda that imposes extraneous criteria on the selection of researchers will reduce the quality of the talent pool and divert attention away from the generation of new knowledge.

The diversity agenda subverts science in a more fundamental way. The standard argument for what is called "inclusive excellence" is that being black or female affects how one analyzes scientific problems. But science is a universal language—one that unites its participants in a discourse of reason, transcending the particularities of today's grievance-inspired identity categories. That universality is science's beauty and strength. The NIH's diversity obsession, now pervasive throughout the federal science bureaucracies and in academic STEM departments, is a betrayal of the Enlightenment ideals that have alleviated so much human suffering.

Collins's new initiative was part of a pattern. In 2020, the NIH announced a new round of "Research Supplements to Promote Diversity in Health-Related Research."[7] Academic science labs could get additional federal money if they hired "diverse" researchers; no mention was made of relevant scientific qualifications. This grant solicitation expanded the agency's social-justice agenda into novel territory. Besides the usual preferences for blacks, Hispanics, and women, the NIH would fund student researchers who were or had been homeless, who were or had been in foster care, who had been eligible for free school lunches, or who had received WIC payments (a food program for low-income mothers) as a child or mother. None of these conditions has anything to do with scientific capacity.

The federal science agencies—not just the NIH, but also the National Science Foundation and the Centers for Disease Control and Prevention—have absorbed the vocabulary of academic victimology, from "heteronormativity" and "stereotype threat" to "intersectionality." (The theory of stereotype threat holds that black students on average perform poorly on tests because they are worried about confirming the stereotype that they perform poorly on tests.) Science labs angling for the latest NIH diversity supplements will increase their chances of federal funding by hiring an intersectional woman (i.e., one who is also an underrepresented minority, disabled, or from a "disadvantaged background").

In 2022, the National Science Foundation dedicated $29 million, consistent with previous years, to its "ADVANCE" program, which uses "intersectional approaches in the design of systemic change strategies" to combat bias in the STEM fields. Successful applications recognize that "gender, race and ethnicity do not exist in isolation from each other and from other categories of social identity." The NSF funders are particularly concerned about policies that "do not mitigate implicit bias in hiring, tenure, and promotion" and that lead to "women and racial and ethnic minorities being evaluated less favorably."

The NSF also bankrolls the tortuously named "Inclusion across the Nation of Communities of Learners of Underrepresented Discoveries in Engineering and Science" program, known by the acronym INCLUDES.[8] INCLUDES has dedicated millions to develop a "bias awareness intervention tool" and to remediate "microaggressions and implicit biases" in engineering classrooms. It spent $300,000 incorporating "indigenous knowledge systems" into Navajo Nation Math Circles in the hope of developing Native American mathematicians. INCLUDES's August 2022 grant solicitation offers $2 million a year to diversity "alliances" that disseminate the so-called "science" of broadening STEM participation.[9] When Congress created the NSF in 1950 to "promote the progress of science,"[10] it likely did not have such "science" in mind.

In 2019, then–NIH Director Collins urged his biomedicine colleagues to boycott any "high-level" scientific conference that did not have women and underrepresented minorities in marquee speaking spots. Critics refer to these male-dominated abominations as "manels." A manel is the product of "subtle (and sometimes not so subtle) bias" that prevents a fair evaluation of merit, according to Collins.[11] But research on hiring in scientific fields contradicts the notion that unequal representation is the result of discrimination. Italian physicist Alessandro Strumia, for example, found that in a sample of 70,000 physicists since 1970, women were hired with fewer citations on average than their male peers.[12]

COVID-19 worries did nothing to lessen the identity-politics obsession. On April 20, 2020, five weeks after the World Health Organization had declared COVID-19 a global-health pandemic, the NIH and

CDC announced the availability of grants to increase the "diversity" of biomedical research labs.[13] Academic virologists working on respiratory failure, say, could receive hundreds of thousands more in taxpayer dollars if they could find a "diverse" student to add to the project. No scientific justification for the new diversity hire was needed; indeed, high school students were eligible, despite the virtual certainty that they would contribute nothing of value. In fact, such new hires would be a drag on any medical advance, since the scientists had to pledge to mentor the students, taking time and attention away from their scientific research. Those mentees would be chosen not because of their science skills—they would not need to present any—but because of their group's underrepresentation in STEM.

The NSF also increased spending on the intersectional ADVANCE program during the pandemic, while the New York City health department required its contact tracers to recognize "institutional and structural racism" and show a "demonstrated commitment" to victims of such racism (i.e. people of color, LGBTQ+ people, immigrants, and justice involved persons [translation: criminals]).[14]

If the federal science agencies did not treat COVID-19 as a reason to make biomedical research meritocratic, then the legislative branch and the White House do not view China as a sufficient threat to override the diversity crusade either. China has already surpassed America in several subspecialties of quantum information science, which entails massive computations and nearly instantaneous communications. China leads in critical areas of artificial intelligence, all of which have military applications.[15] The next global conflict could well involve the deployment of Beijing's growing technological prowess. But cultivating America's best STEM talent to compete with China is subordinate to the pursuit of alleged racial justice.

In August 2022, President Joe Biden signed a bill intended to counter China's growing dominance in semiconductor manufacturing and to spur the development of other technologies critical to national security. The $280-billion CHIPS and Science Act is shot through with the usual diversity mandates and giveaways. An entire title is devoted to "broadening participation in science"—an aim tangential to geopolitical competition. In order to broaden participation in science, federal research agencies are directed to "mitigate bias in the merit review process." Such bias is evidenced by unequal outcomes in grant awards, according to disparate impact theory. Lack of bias is evidenced by proportional representation in grant-making, regardless of the sacrifice of meritocratic standards that such proportional representation requires. The CHIPS and Science Act directs federal research agencies to eradicate "institutional barriers limiting the recruitment and retention of historically underrepresented minorities." Here, too, those barriers are manifest simply by the lack of proportional representation in agency employment.

The law creates a new Chief Diversity Officer (and office) in the National Science Foundation. It is hard to conceive how much more diversity-obsessed the NSF can become, but that difficulty reflects merely a failure of imagination. This superfluous diversity bureaucracy will support research on "diversity, equity, and inclusion in the technology sector"—something that NSF has already been doing to the tune of millions of taxpayer dollars a year, but will now do at an even more frenzied rate. Bureaucrats working in the new office of the Chief Diversity Officer will develop and monitor training for university administrators and faculty on "unbiased recruitment and evaluation of underrepresented minority candidates"—more code for racial preferences. More STEM funding will be funneled into "minority-serving institutions," regardless of whether those institutions are producing cutting-edge research on a par with Chinese science.[16]

The flip side of boosting black and Hispanic participation in STEM is to depress white and Asian participation, which is the aim of much K-12 policy. Gifted and talented programs in elementary and high school math are being shut down or watered down across the US because of their disparate impact.[17] California's education bureaucracy is proposing to dismantle accelerated math classes because blacks are not proportionally represented in them. Without such equity reforms, math instruction merely perpetuates "white supremacy," according to a manifesto cited in early drafts of the new California math guidelines.[18] Under the proposed curriculum, mathematically gifted students would not accelerate into advanced classes until the eleventh grade, in order to create more inclusive (i.e., racially proportional) math classrooms in middle school and early high school. Algebra I would be deferred until the ninth grade, in the hope that more black and Hispanic students would be able to master it. (Deferring introductory algebra means compressing subsequent courses like pre-calculus and Algebra II into a shorter period of time, which ironically would increase the difficulty for less gifted students.) A watered-down course called "data science" would be offered as an alternative to pre-calculus and calculus. (Data science courses are spreading across the country as a substitute for traditional math.)

China takes the opposite tack to this levelling mania. It identifies its top math talent early on and gives mathematically gifted students accelerated instruction. Its rigorous university entrance exams reward effort and achievement, not identity. Undergraduate math competitions provide a pipeline to the best graduate programs in STEM. These efforts are working. As of 2018, China ranked number one in the international tests of K-12 math, science, and reading known as PISA; the US ranked twenty-fifth.[19] Chinese teams dominate Stanford's challenge for machine-reading comprehension and the International Olympiad in Informatics, reports the Kennedy School's Belfer Center.[20] Highly trained STEM PhDs are pouring out of China's graduate schools. China will likely overtake the US in research dominance in the coming years, predicts the editor of the 2022 World University Rankings. While the absolute number of US universities among the top 100 research institutions— thirty-four—remained much higher than China's seven, the trend was not auspicious. The number of US universities in the top 100 dropped by nearly 21 percent between 2018 and 2022, while the number of Chinese universities in the top 100 rose 250 percent. China has already displaced the US in the production of high-impact research studies, according to a 2022 paper in the journal *Scientometrics*.[21]

Diverting ever more US STEM resources from the pursuit of scientific knowledge to the pursuit of alleged racial equity all but guarantees that a hard-charging, merit-driven China will win the war for scientific and technological dominance, giving it a massive military advantage. Yet when President Biden had the opportunity to choose a new director for the Department of Energy's Office of Science, a major engine of militarily crucial basic science, he chose identity politics over meritocracy. DOE's Office of Science is the largest funder of the physical sciences in the US, overseeing x-ray synchrotrons, the development of nuclear weapons, and ongoing research on nuclear fusion. Its directors, usually physicists themselves, typically have exercised managerial authority in the nation's major physics labs before taking over the office. Such qualifications and experience helped science office directors choose whether the agency should, say, try to expand understanding of fundamental particle physics or of the physics of the universe, or decide how much attention should be given to solid-state lighting, to semiconductors, or to artificial intelligence.

Biden, however, nominated a soil geologist from the University of California, Merced. Asmeret Asefaw Berhe had no background in physics, the science of energy, or the energy sector. She had never held a position as a scientific administrator. Berhe's only managerial experience consisted of having served since 2020 as an interim associate dean of UC Merced's graduate division.[22]

She would, however, be the first black woman to head the $7 billion office, and that, along with her invitation to be a speaker at the TED conference in 2019 and her advocacy for inclusion, anti-harassment, and anti-bullying, was reason enough to appoint her.[23]

Each day, the Office of Science turns out dozens of "one-pager" descriptions of projects and proposals. It is unlikely that a soil geologist (even one with an MS in political ecology) would have the knowledge to evaluate proposals for advanced scientific computing research and nuclear physics, or to make the policy judgments that those "one-pagers" require. Berhe would, however, be able to bring racial-justice concerns to the heart of the Energy Department's science work. Her soil biogeochemistry lab at UC Merced strove, according to its website, to "create a dynamic, diverse, and equitable STEM community that represents the public." It developed and tested "sexual harassment bystander intervention training programs . . . that incorporate experiences of diverse women." Her lab recommends readings on racism and offers tips on writing the "diversity, equity, and inclusion" statements that are increasingly required of academic science hires.[24]

It was fitting that Berhe taught at the University of California, Merced. UC Merced was created as a diversity campus, in the hope of minting more Hispanic graduates with a UC degree. Berhe herself benefited from UC's obsessive diversity push, having received a President's Postdoctoral Fellowship, a program that "seeks applicants with the potential to bring to their academic and research careers the perspective that comes from their non-traditional educational background or understanding of the experiences of members of groups historically underrepresented in higher education."[25]

An academic physicist who has worked on five multibillion-dollar DOE projects wonders if Berhe "can know merit when she sees it."[26] Preference beneficiaries such as Berhe, this physicist observes, tend to "think that merit is a myth and that hierarchies of achievement are arbitrary." Berhe has argued that the lack of race and sex diversity in STEM is due to exclusion. Her co-authored articles include: "Leaky Pipeline vs. Vicious Obstacle Course: Metaphors for the Persistent Exclusion of Minoritized Scholars from STEM," "A Critical Feminist Approach to Transforming Workplace Climate in the Geosciences through Community Engagement and Partnerships with Societies," and "Hostile Climates Are Barriers to Diversifying the Geosciences."

An electrical engineer at a prestigious California university compared Berhe's nomination to "putting a newspaper delivery boy in charge of Google."[27]

Berhe was confirmed for the Office of Science directorship in May 2022 over Republican opposition. Four months later, the Office of Science announced that starting October 1, 2022, all future applications for funding must include a detailed statement of how the applicant's research—say, into nuclear and high-energy physics—would "promote equity and inclusion as an intrinsic element to advancing scientific excellence."[28]

As with the medical industry's cancellation of Ed Livingston and Norman Wang, a juggernaut now crushes anyone who even unintentionally challenges diversity hiring in STEM. On November 1, 2021, astronomer John Kormendy withdrew an article from *Proceedings of the National Academy of Sciences* (PNAS), after a preprint version that he had just posted on the web drew sharp criticism for threatening the conduct of "inclusive" science.[29] Three days later, the preprint version was scrubbed as well (though a PDF can still be found online).[30] The paper had passed the journal's three-person peer-review system and was awaiting publication.

Kormendy, an expert on supermassive black holes and professor emeritus at the University of Texas at Austin, had proposed a method for reducing the role of individual subjectivity in scientific hiring and tenure decisions. He created a model that predicted a scientist's long-term research impact from the citation history of his early publications. He tested the results of his model against a panel of twenty-two prestigious astronomers, many of whom had advised the federal government on scientific research priorities and had served as jurors on high-profile astronomy prizes. That panel rated the research impact of the 512 astronomers whom Kormendy had run through his model; the panel's conclusions closely matched the model's results. Kormendy's paper stressed that hiring decisions should be made "holistically." Scientific influence was only one factor to consider; achieving gender and racial balance in a department was also a legitimate concern, he wrote. Such genuflection to diversity ideology earned Kormendy no protection from the diversity avengers.

Formulas for quantifying scientific influence on the basis of a citation record are hardly new. PNAS itself published the proposal for one such famous measure, known as the "h-index."[31] But that was in 2005. In 2021, a different standard for evaluating ideas applies: do they help or hinder females and underrepresented minorities in STEM? Kormendy's model, tweeted an astrophysicist at the City University of New York, "JUST TOOK ANY TINY STEPS WE ARE MAKING TOWARDS EQUITY AND THREW THEM OUT OF THE WINDOW" (capitalization in the original).[32] An astronomer in Budapest objected that Kormendy had failed to consult with "relevant humanities experts" about cumulative bias against females and minorities.[33] Equally damningly, Kormendy had suggested that the profession should hire female and minority scientists, who, in the words of the Budapest astronomer, "match the success rate of the majority (i.e., men)."[34]

After Kormendy withdrew the paper, a University of Texas colleague tweeted about her hopes that the work of doing "science inclusively" could now continue.[35] Other astronomers directed potshots at the panel of twenty-two raters for being a "bunch of old people" from Western universities who were not representative of the "astronomy community."[36] But scientific expertise is not democratic. These were scientists at the top of their field, whose accomplishments would, in earlier times, have been a source of authority.

Naturally, the fact that nineteen of Kormendy's panelists were men was a red flag. Kormendy had tried to get more female raters, but they had turned down his offer to join the project in higher proportion than the males he solicited.[37] (The three females who did agree to serve as panelists rated female astronomers higher than the male panelists did. Kormendy's attribution of this discrepancy to bias on the part of the *males* won him no credit.)

None of the paper's critics spelled out how publication metrics (known as "bibliometrics") conflict with equity. Several rebuffed or ignored attempts to seek clarification. Presumably, the critics sense (correctly) that quantitative measures of scientific influence will show that white males have had the greatest impact on science to date. That finding would not be inequitable on its face, however, unless we define equity as equality of outcome.

Some of Kormendy's rating panelists issued apologies as well. Brian Schmidt, vice-chancellor of the Australian National University and a Nobel Prize winner, wrote on Twitter: "As an unintended consequence [o]f this article, I hope our field can be more [r]eflective of our hiring practices, and the inequitable gatekeeping that occurs into astronomy to this day. I am sorry for my involvement."[38]

Kormendy acknowledges no errors in his research. "I didn't do anything [methodologically] wrong," he told me. "I trust my techniques; I trust the results. I checked for bias in great detail."[39] Nevertheless, he issued an apology: "I now see that my work has hurt people. I apologize to you all for the stress and the pain that I have caused. Nothing could be further from my hopes. I fully support all efforts to promote fairness, inclusivity, and a nurturing environment for all."[40]

The Kormendy retraction is at least the fifth instance in recent years of cancelling a scientific paper based on its perceived negative impact on equity in STEM. (Kormendy's peer-reviewed book on his hiring algorithm was also rescinded by the publisher—the Astronomical Society of the Pacific Conference Series—in June 2022[41] and all printed copies presumably destroyed.) Previous journalistic cancellations include a mathematical model to explain why evolution would select for greater variability in inherited traits among males of a species, and an empirical study comparing the benefits of male and female mentorship in STEM (male mentorship proved more advantageous). The authors of the latter retracted article expressed "deep regret" for having "caused pain."

Professional honors must also be reversed if they conflict with a diversity quota. In October 2021, a few days before the Kormendy retraction, a committee that awards fellowships for the American Geophysical Union cancelled the slate of finalists that peer scientists had forwarded to it because the three finalists were all white men. Better not to award a fellowship at all than to give it to a white male. The leader in the cancellation effort admitted that the finalists, who specialized in the study of snow and ice, were "truly, amazingly deserving." But the cancellation would result in a "fairer process," she told *E&E News.*[42]

The cancelling committee presented no evidence of unfairness in the nomination process, apart from the unacceptable result. Indeed, the entire American Geophysical Union fellowship process was decidedly pro-female: female finalists overall had nearly a 50 percent greater chance of being selected for a fellowship than male finalists. That disparity was not regarded as unfair, just as the higher ratings given to female scientists by female raters in the Kormendy study were not regarded as biased.

No STEM job or honor awarded to a female or an underrepresented minority can now be free from the suspicion that the selection was the result of "equity" concerns. "Diverse" conference panels are equally suspect, in light of former NIH Director Collins's call to boycott "manels."

The "only thing on anyone's mind now is redressing inequities," Kormendy told me, adding that he supports that "honorable" aim. But it is "risky" to "mute our emphasis on excellence," Kormendy later added in a group email, especially when astronomers in Europe and China still place a "ferocious" focus on scientific accomplishment.[43] "Equity" is extraneous to science. Science *does* have a liberatory effect, freeing humans from crippling submission to natural forces. But it achieves that liberation through the hard-won attainment of knowledge. Step by step, we are shutting down the open inquiry and the cultivation of excellence that makes scientific knowledge possible.

PART II

CULTURE AND ARTS

Chapter Three

THE CRUSADE AGAINST CLASSICAL MUSIC

Disparate impact analysis is sweeping across the arts as well as the sciences. Any European art form is now presumptively racist due to the lack of racial diversity in its past. Likewise, any lack of racial proportionality among present members of an arts organization is exclusively attributed to racism.

The campaign against classical music has been particularly heartbreaking. Orchestras and opera companies are said to discriminate against black musicians and composers. The canonical repertoire—the product of a centuries-long tradition of musical expression—is allegedly a function of white supremacy.

Not one leader in the field has defended Western art music against these charges. Their silence is emblematic. Other supposed guardians of Western civilization, whether museum directors, humanities professors, or scientists, have gone AWOL in the face of similar claims, lest they themselves be denounced as racist.

The attack against classical music is worth examining in some detail, for it reveals the logic that has been turned against nearly every aspect of Western culture over the last few years. That logic displays a hatred of beauty, a brittle intolerance of the past, and a self-righteous certainty that the orthodoxies of the present are uniquely just.

The crusade began within days of George Floyd's death. The classical music profession deemed itself implicated in that death. On June 1, 2020, the League of American Orchestras issued a statement confessing that, for decades, it had "tolerated and perpetuated systemic discrimination against Black people, discrimination mirrored in the practices of orchestras and throughout our country." The League was "committed to dismantling" its "role in perpetuating the systems of inequity that continue to oppress Black people" and expected its member orchestras to respond in kind.[1]

That response was immediate. The Hartford Symphony Orchestra apologized for its "history of inaction to effectively confront the racist systems and structures that have long oppressed and marginalized Black musicians, composers, and communities."[2] The Seattle Opera announced that it would "continue to prioritize" anti-racism and "make amends" for causing harm.[3] Opera Omaha sent a message to its "black community": "We know that you are exhausted and recognize we will never fully understand the depth of your suffering. We know that part of your exhaustion comes from the heartbreak of our silence, inaction, and half-measures." Every communication that the opera sends out now concludes with the tagline: "We will listen more than we speak, but will not be silent in the face of injustice."[4]

Black musicians produced manifestos complaining of their mistreatment at the hands of white administrators and conductors. Weston Sprott, a trombonist with the Metropolitan Opera Orchestra, along with three musicians from three other ensembles, declared in the *New York Times* that the reason there are not "more Black artists in orchestras" is "racism."[5] Six black opera singers made a YouTube video about opera racism at the invitation of the Los Angeles Opera. LA Opera's President, Christopher Koelsch, introduced the discussion. "I come to you today as the white male leader of this institution," he said, staring dazedly at the camera. LA Opera was committing "anew to self-examination and . . . to do[ing] our part to heal wounds that are hundreds of years old." Most of the discussion centered on Floyd's death, but tenor Russell Thomas also told of being rebuked for routinely showing up late and for talking on his cell phone during rehearsals for an unnamed opera. "They were putting me in my place," Thomas said, though his behavior was the result of his uncle dying in a car accident, he maintained. Only a black singer would be denied a "basic amount of consideration," he claimed.[6]

Professional disappointments were likewise chalked up to racism. Soprano Lauren Michelle claimed that the reason she has not had a more prominent career in the United States was that she was black. "The truth is I am an award-winning international opera singer who has only been hired once at an 'A' house in the United States," she wrote on her blog.[7] Michelle did not address why her black contemporaries, such as Eric Owens and Lawrence Brownlee, have sung in "A-houses."

Music conservatories admitted their supposed racial backwardness. The Juilliard School's president, Damian Woetzel, and Juilliard's director of Equity, Diversity, Inclusion, and Belonging Initiatives together pledged that the school would become a "community that not only rejects racism, but that is actively anti-racist, working to tear down systemic racism and injustice." As part of that "work," the school created a blacks-only Zoom "space for healing."[8] Juilliard's head of music theory wrote to his colleagues that "it's high time the whiteness of music theory is examined, critiqued and remedied."[9]

The classical music press, presiding over an art form whose salience shrinks by the year, produced a torrent of commentary explaining to readers why they should view classical music as culpably white. In September 2020, *New Yorker* critic Alex Ross apologized for being a "white American," writing about a world that is "blindingly white, both in its history and its present."[10] The love of classical music on the part of nineteenth-century American patrons and performers was a smoke screen for white supremacy, Ross suggested. For good measure, he invoked a standard from the student-gripe portfolio to buttress his argument for classical music's racism: the portrayal of the Moor Monostatos in Mozart's fairy-tale opera, *The Magic Flute*. (Monostatos is a slave in the temple of the priest Sarastro; he is portrayed comically as scheming, lustful, and bumbling.)

The lead reviewer for the *New York Times*, Anthony Tommasini, urged that orchestra auditions no longer take place behind a screen in order to address the "appalling racial imbalance" in orchestral ranks.[11] Currently, musicians' identities are concealed by a screen through most, if not all, stages of an orchestral audition to prevent favoritism or bias (a process known as a "blind audition"). But color blindness is now regarded as discriminatory, since it favors merit over race.

Fellow *Times* critic Joshua Barone called for reforming "opera's culture" by placing "anti-racism front and center."[12] A *Washington Post* critic alleged that systemic racism "runs like rot through the structures of the classical music world."[13] *Vox* explained that Beethoven's Fifth Symphony was a symbol of white male "superiority and importance."[14] *BBC Magazine* columnist Tom Service also purported to deconstruct the alleged greatness of the canonical repertoire: "The link between patriarchal power in the West and the fact that the classical canon is made of lookalike faces of Great Men is more than coincidental."[15] *Slate* complained that referring to well-known composers only by their last names exacerbates classical music's exclusionary practices. The Louisville Orchestra, for example, had advertised the performance of a Beethoven symphony and the debut of a composition memorializing Breonna Taylor by "Davóne Tines" and "Igee Dieudonné." To assume that Davóne Tines and Igee Dieudonné need to be "fullnamed," whereas Beethoven does not, replicates classical music's "centuries of systematic prejudice, exclusion, sexism, and racism," according to *Slate*.[16] (Note to readers: if you are not yet aware of Tines and Dieudonné, you are not alone.)

Classical music radio announcers and executives instructed their audience to hear inequity in the cascade of human feeling coming from their radio speakers. Garrett McQueen, a former announcer for American Public Media, told a Composers Forum roundtable in June 2020: "You are complicit in racism every time you listen to Handel's 'Messiah.'"[17] (Handel briefly held stock in a slave-trading company—stock which he had received as payment for a commission.)

Academia, the source of today's race obsession, weighed in with gusto. The Music Library Association decried its place in a "social structure that allows the marginalization and extrajudicial killing of people of color, particularly Black and indigenous individuals."[18] A music theory professor from Hunter College, Philip Ewell, received widespread acclaim for his denunciations of classical music's racism.

Ewell has whiteness on the brain. During the Floyd riots, Ewell compiled a glossary of music-related euphemisms for whiteness: "authentic, canonic, civilized, classic(s), conventional, core ('core' requirement), European, function ('functional' tonality), fundamental, genius, German ('German' language requirement), great ('great' works), maestro, opus (magnum 'opus'), piano ('piano' proficiency, skills), seminal, sophisticated, titan(ic), towering, traditional, and western." Since everything is about race, according to Ewell, any time you seem not to be talking about race—referring to someone's piano skills, say—you are actually talking about race by dint of ignoring the topic. (Connoisseurs of deconstruction will recognize the rhetorical technique here of turning an "absence" into a supposed "presence.")

Ewell also engaged in the mandatory Beethoven takedown. The only reason we deem the Ninth Symphony a masterpiece is Beethoven's whiteness and maleness, he wrote on his blog. Beethoven's Ninth Symphony is "no more a masterwork than Esperanza Spalding's 12 Little Spells," Ewell insisted.[19] Spalding is a jazz singer; *Twelve Little Spells* is an album of experimental jazz numbers about sixteen body parts and functions. The texts ("Our eyeballs are hollow but presently hold shape/ Around a gooey filling") are not, to say the least, the equivalent of Friedrich Schiller's "Ode to Joy" (with which the Ninth Symphony concludes). To place Spalding's slight compositions at the same level of complexity, emotional force, and historical significance as the Ninth Symphony is objectively ludicrous.

Ewell backed up his aesthetic relativism with attempted logic: "To state that Beethoven was any more than, say, above average as a composer is to state that you know all music written on planet Earth 200 years ago when Beethoven was active as a composer, which no one does."[20] Judgments of greatness imply no such encyclopedic knowledge, however. We may deem a meal great, for example, without implying that we have eaten every other meal available on the planet at that moment.

Ewell's whiteness obsession is standard in music departments now. What catapulted him to iconic status was his denunciation of the early twentieth-century music theorist Heinrich Schenker. Schenker developed an influential system of analysis that identifies the most important elements of a musical phrase in order to explain the phrase's emotional impact and its role within a work's thematic development. In a keynote address at a November 2019 music theory conference, Ewell argued that Schenker's ranking of notes and harmonies within a composition is merely a stand-in for a white-supremacist ranking of the races. The "white racial frame" of Schenkerian analysis has kept blacks from becoming music theorists, Ewell maintained.[21]

Ewell's speech was ecstatically received. Alex Ross's September 2020 article on racism and classical music amplified Ewell's "white racial frame" thesis further. And when a few music theorists dissented from that thesis, Ewell became Exhibit A for how the classical music field allegedly oppresses minorities.

With such near unanimity regarding classical music's racial sins, it is no wonder that the demands issued to compensate for those sins have been breathtaking in ambition. Those coming from the Sphinx Organization were typical. Sphinx has been advocating for race consciousness in classical music since 1997. It holds separate competitions for young black and Hispanic musicians, supports minority-only ensembles, and provides color-coded training and financial assistance. Since the Floyd riots, it has been churning out a series of diversity demands more extensive than any demands it had previously proposed.

Its first set of demands opened with a call for orchestras, opera companies, and conservatories to "examine the supremacist logic embedded in traditional Western art and music/repertoire." After impugning the Western music tradition, Sphinx then laid down racial quotas for that allegedly white supremacist activity: at least 20 percent of soloists each concert season should be "Black and Latinx"; 40 percent of candidates for auditions and administrative jobs should be "Black and Latinx"; and 20 percent of the repertoire performed each season should be "reflective [*sic*] of Black and Latinx composers."[22] At least 10 percent of every musical budget should be spent compensating for past racial inequities in programming (what such compensation might mean was not explained).

Sphinx's next set of demands was published in the *New York Times* in September 2020.[23] The numbers had changed, suggesting a certain arbitrariness in how they were computed. Sphinx President Afa Dworkin, writing with Anthony McGill, principal clarinet of the New York Philharmonic, now insisted that 15 percent of a music organization's budget (up from the previous 10 percent) should go toward "addressing systemic racism" (what that meant was, again, left unspecified). This 15 percent reallocation should continue for the next decade. The diversity component in every audition was down to 25 percent from 40 percent, but if an orchestra or conservatory did not rustle up the requisite diversity quotient for its audition, it could not select a winning candidate, no matter how qualified the finalist.

In January 2021, Sphinx issued more audition guidelines.[24] Traditionally, if a musician is of a known high caliber, having played with another prestigious orchestra, say, he may skip the early stages of an audition and go right to the semifinals or finals (which may still be blind). Sphinx now proposed that those automatic advancements include a whopping 25 percent or more of "Black and Brown" musicians. This is mathematically impossible, and Sphinx should know it, since it has been decrying the low numbers of minorities in orchestras for two decades. Blacks make up 1.8 percent of all orchestral musicians, which includes noncompetitive community ensembles. Filling at least 25 percent of all automatic advancement slots with minorities from top-ranked orchestras is not doable, even assuming that there were enough automatic advancements in each audition to be able to set aside 25 percent of them for any type of quota.

Sphinx's January audition guidelines suggested selecting musicians on nonmusical grounds, as the *New York Times*'s Anthony Tommasini had recommended. Orchestras should hire diversity consultants to develop "extra-musical evaluation" criteria for orchestral positions, such as serving as an institutional spokesman.

Board members also found themselves in the crosshairs for being too white, with the added infraction of being too rich. Simon Woods, head of the League of American Orchestras, apologized for his whiteness during a discussion at the Peabody Institute in February 2021 and then lamented that nondiverse board members were given power to help define the "vision" of orchestras.[25] Anyone in the classical music business today should be down on his knees in gratitude for the existence of wealthy donors who want to contribute to the "vision" of orchestras. The American philanthropy tradition is still without parallel in other countries, but donors are abandoning high culture for more popular causes. Supporting social and racial justice organizations confers a thousand times more prestige than supporting opera, as the stampede of New York's wealthiest to the galas of the anti-poverty Robin Hood Foundation demonstrates. Pressuring those remaining fine-arts boards to find "diverse" board members, no matter their connection to music or their willingness to finance struggling ensembles, is a destructive self-indulgence.

Even in the best of financial circumstances, the demands of classical music's new race activists would have been startling in their scope. But at a time when every classical music budget had been blown apart by the coronavirus lockdowns, such ambition required considerable confidence in one's bargaining power. The bet paid off. Orchestras and opera companies rushed to adopt racial hiring benchmarks and to take on costly new diversity bureaucracy.

Long before 2020, the Metropolitan Opera had been running in the red. The coronavirus blackout put it on the ropes, eliminating $150 million in earned revenues. In December 2020, Metropolitan General Manager Peter Gelb told his employees that financial cutbacks were a life-and-death matter: "What we're trying to do is keep the Met alive, and the only way to achieve that is to reduce our costs." In a letter to the stagehands' union, Gelb wrote: "The health crisis has compounded the Met's previous financial fragility, threatening our very existence."[26]

In February 2021, Met musicians had gone nearly a year without pay, and the stagehands' union was locked out of the house. Yet that month, the Met's first chief diversity officer started work. The new position was necessary in order to ensure that the Met is an "organization that is adamantly opposed to racism," as a Met spokesman put it in an email.[27] Otherwise, there would apparently be some suspicion that the Met, populated by immaculately progressive staff in the most liberal big city in the country, might favor racism.

The Met's new Chief Diversity Officer, Marcia Sells, had been the dean of students at the nation's highest-paying law school—Harvard. Her six-figure Harvard salary doubtlessly was increased to cover the move to New York. Sells would likely also have been promised her own staff. She has no background in music, much less opera. Yet she is now entrusted with creating "artistic pathways" at the Met for "people of color," according to a press release.[28]

Presumably, the Met would have compiled a firm empirical basis for this new financial commitment, given the sacrifices that it is asking its existing employees to make. Has the Met in recent years failed to hire the most qualified musician because of his skin color or otherwise denied opportunities to minorities? I asked the spokesman. The Met had "nothing further to add at this time," came the response.[29]

In March 2020, the musicians of the Philadelphia Orchestra agreed to a 20 percent pay cut in the hope of reducing an estimated $15 million deficit by year-end. That projection was arrived at before anyone imagined that Philadelphia's Kimmel Center would remain dark for the next twelve months. Yet in October 2020, the orchestra created a new vice presidency position for Inclusion, Diversity, Equity, and Access. "We have been working on a rigorous analysis of the organization at all levels, taking critical steps to implement real and sustainable change to become an ever more inclusive, diverse, equitable, and accessible organization," explained Philadelphia Orchestra President and CEO Matías Tarnopolsky in announcing the new title.[30] Philadelphia's Vice President of Inclusion, Diversity, Equity, and Access, Doris Parent, also has no musical background. Her two bachelor's degrees are in psychology and family studies; her master's degree in business administration is from the University of Phoenix. She will nevertheless be "shaping" the orchestra's future, according to Tarnopolsky.

The Cincinnati Symphony Orchestra hired its first chief diversity and inclusion officer in March 2021—someone, as usual, without a classical music background. Ideally, the orchestra would be "reflective of Cincinnati"—i.e., 40 percent black—Executive Director Jonathan Martin had said.[31] Short of that ideal for now, the organization sent its musicians, board, and staff to diversity training and put a black composer on every live-streamed performance during its 2021-2022 season.

In Spring 2021, the Juilliard School announced a pandemic-related tuition increase, prompting student protest. Perhaps the school should have refrained from bulking up its diversity bureaucracy instead. It had recently added an Equity, Diversity, Inclusion, and Belonging (EDIB) program manager to work alongside the school's director for EDIB Initiatives and other diversity staff. Juilliard's new bias response deputies are steeped in "trauma-informed practices" so that they can understand how Juilliard's systemic bias "manifests" and how to mitigate it. Faculty are being trained to recognize their racial biases. All aspects of the school will now be examined "through the lens of inclusion," Juilliard's provost announced in September 2020.

In light of such changes, the evidence for current discrimination in the classical music field must be overwhelming. In fact, it does not exist.

The primary fact adduced to prove systemic bias is the underrepresentation of black orchestral musicians. As of 2014, only 1.8 percent of the players in top ensembles were black.[32] Meantime, the proportion of Asians rose, from 3.4 percent to over 9 percent (and many more in some top orchestras), though Asians, too, are non-white in an allegedly white supremacist field.[33] When Asians began their conquest of Western classical music in the second half of the twentieth century, there were fewer Asian instrumentalists and composers to serve as ethnic role models than there were black instrumentalists and composers to serve as role models for blacks.

The official explanation for that steady underrepresentation of blacks in orchestral ranks is racism. Suggesting that there aren't enough competitively qualified blacks in the audition pipeline is taboo. Anthony Tommasini briefly considered that supply-side explanation before calling for the de-blinding of auditions. But he gave the last word to Sphinx President Afa Dworkin, who insisted, in Tommasini's words, that the "pipeline is not the problem, and that talented musicians of color are out there and ready."[34]

Conductors and members of audition committees disagree. Leonard Slatkin has served as music director in Detroit, St. Louis, Washington, DC, New Orleans, London, and Lyon, and has served as principal guest conductor in Pittsburgh, Los Angeles, Minneapolis, and Cleveland. Filling Sphinx's quotas for auditions would be "impossible" at the present time, he wrote by email. "There are not enough black and other minority musicians studying at music schools or conservatories, let alone in the audition pool."[35] At Juilliard, blacks make up 6.3 percent of the total student body in music, drama, and dance.[36] The drama division, roughly half black,[37] accounts for a large part of that total black share. The school would not provide the breakdown for the music division alone.

At the National Symphony Orchestra in Washington, black audition entrants are rare, though there is no minimum experience requirement, says someone who oversees the process.[38] Even if the screen was removed, there are very few black musicians to hire. Proponents of the racism narrative never explain why conductors, perfectionists by nature, would turn down the most qualified musician in favor of someone more likely to maul an exposed solo, just because that inferior musician was white.

In fact, conductors want "the best possible player for the best possible concert because [they] will be blamed otherwise," says a former music festival leader. "I've never observed someone not getting the job because he was black."[39]

Zubin Mehta conducted the Los Angeles Philharmonic from 1962 to 1978 and then went on to direct the New York Philharmonic for another thirteen years. There was "never" any racial component to auditions, Mehta said in a phone interview. Nor have boards discouraged the hiring of black musicians, as is alleged. "No one ever told me you can't engage someone because he's black," Mehta says.[40] Dorothy Chandler, Los Angeles's premier arts philanthropist for decades, welcomed Mehta's hiring of Henry Lewis as assistant conductor in 1961.

Asked if he had seen racism in the field, pianist Emanuel Ax replied, "Of course not!" Though he added that he would have "no idea about auditions."[41] No black pianist has asked Ax to teach him (which is how Ax gets students), though he would welcome such a request.

Violinist Joseph Striplin played with the Detroit Symphony Orchestra, the St. Louis Symphony Orchestra, and the Metropolitan Opera's touring orchestra. When the Grosse Pointe Symphony Orchestra's conductor fell ill, Striplin was asked to fill in. He now leads that orchestra. There was discrimination in the past, but it's not the 1940s anymore, Striplin says. "Orchestras would be more than happy to have more blacks."[42]

Both of John McLaughlin Williams's parents were pianists who passed on to him their love of classical music. His father's hopes for a musical career were dashed by mid-century racial attitudes. But the classical music industry is "not racist now, by any means," says Williams, a conductor, violinist, and pianist.[43] Williams has never witnessed someone not getting a job because of the color of his skin. But after hundreds of years of discrimination, blacks assume—and understandably so, Williams says—that if they are not picked for something, it is because of their race.

In July 2020, bassoonist Monica Ellis accused the orchestral profession of protecting a "white framework built to benefit white people."[44]

To the contrary, the field has been obsessed with diversity for decades. Since the early 1970s, fellowship programs for black and Hispanic musicians have poured forth, including from the New York Philharmonic, the Houston Symphony Orchestra, the Chicago Symphony Orchestra, and the Pittsburgh Symphony Orchestra.[45] Grantees in these programs typically get to play with the orchestra, receive training for auditions, and are given priority in tryouts. At present, more than a dozen of the country's top orchestras provide fellowships for minority players, according to the *Pittsburgh Post-Gazette*,[46] while many others give stipends to minority musicians as audition support. Orchestras have also sent their musicians into public schools in the hope of creating more minority players.

Music schools have encouraged black enrollment, though now they lambaste themselves as exclusionary. In 1986, Juilliard established the Aaron Diamond Foundation Fellowships for minority students, endowed with millions of dollars. Rather than requiring minority students to come to New York to audition for entrance into the school, Juilliard set up regional auditions across the country. Minority applications rose fivefold, but minority admissions stayed low, since most applicants were not qualified. The school needed to start earlier in the process, then–Juilliard president Joseph Polisi told funder Irene Diamond. So the conservatory brought local black and Hispanic elementary school students to the New York campus for individual tutoring and group lessons. The school provided each student with an instrument to play at home and one to play at school. It reached out to parents in the hope of involving them in their child's music education. Today, the Music Advancement Program serves about 100 students a year.

So prized have been black students and musicians that they are treated with kid gloves. Violinist Earl Carlyss was a member of the Juilliard String Quartet for twenty years and a teacher for even longer. In the 1960s, Carlyss helped determine whether students at the Peabody Institute in Baltimore would continue into their next year of study. One violinist played so poorly that Carlyss mentioned him to the dean. "We know," came the answer, "but no one has had the nerve to boink him." At Michigan State University, Carlyss tried to correct a student's sloppy playing. Two weeks later, nothing had changed. "Have you practiced?" Carlyss asked. "I don't have to," the student responded. "I'll always have a job."[47]

Prejudice tragically limited black musical opportunity in the first half of the twentieth century. But even in that cruel period, some black musicians were recognized and elevated, complicating the monolithic story of oppression that the classical music profession is now telling about itself. These musicians included bassist Charles Burrell, cellist Donald White, and double bassist Henry Lewis. Lewis became music director of the New Jersey Symphony Orchestra in 1968 and eventually conducted nearly every other major American orchestra, sometimes accompanying his then-wife, mezzo-soprano Marilyn Horne. James DePreist was mentored on the podium by Leonard Bernstein, the most well-known and influential American conductor of all time (as well as one of America's greatest musical theater composers). The late Michael Morgan, conductor of the Oakland Symphony, received a Tanglewood fellowship at nineteen, the youngest such recipient. Morgan became Leonard Slatkin's assistant at the St. Louis Symphony at twenty-three. Starting in 1986, he worked for seven years as assistant conductor at the Chicago Symphony Orchestra under Sir Georg Solti and Daniel Barenboim.

Since at least the 1970s, performing ensembles have sought new works from black composers. George Walker's numerous commissions came from the New York Philharmonic, the Cleveland Orchestra, the John F. Kennedy Center for the Performing Arts, and the New Jersey Symphony Orchestra, among other groups. Walker's *Lilacs for Voice and Orchestra*, commissioned by the Boston Symphony Orchestra in honor of a black tenor, won the Pulitzer Prize for Music in 1996. Walker received fellowships from the Fulbright, Whitney, Guggenheim, Rockefeller, Koussevitzky, and MacDowell foundations.

And yet we are to believe that music ensembles, having commissioned pieces from black composers, then turned around and suppressed those same composers out of racial bias. If few contemporary, black-composed works entered the regular repertoire, the reason is the same as that affecting new works by white composers: audiences continue to reject post-tonal idioms, no matter how many honors the academy confers on their practitioners.

Today, black musicians are welcomed with open arms. One musician with a major orchestra marvels at the oppositional stance taken by some of his fellows, such as clarinetist Anthony McGill and his brother, flutist Demarre McGill: "The business has handed these guys opportunity after opportunity. To turn around and say: 'It's a racist industry!' I want to shake them. They should be ambassadors!"[48] Another leading player notes that the McGills "aren't the exception; they are the rule. People fall over black students to give them every opportunity to have a shot. I did it, too. Since 1990, at least, black privilege has been in effect in classical music."[49] Opera singers—such as Pretty Yende, Angel Blue, and Julia Bullock, all enormously talented in their own right—have enjoyed an extra boost to their careers from being black, according to a former opera executive.[50]

If, before 2020, being black was an asset in a field already agonizing about diversity, going forward it will provide jet propulsion. In July 2022, the Baltimore Symphony Orchestra announced its choice to replace outgoing conductor Marin Alsop. At twenty-nine, Jonathan Heyward would be the second youngest conductor in history to lead one of America's top ten orchestras. Zubin Mehta was twenty-six when appointed to lead the Los Angeles Philharmonic in 1962. Unlike Heyward, Mehta had already guest conducted some of the world's most prestigious ensembles, such as the Vienna, Berlin, and Israel Philharmonic orchestras. In 2022, Heyward was starting his second year as chief conductor of the Nordwestdeutsche Philharmonie, ranked twentieth among Germany's orchestras—respectable, but not world-class.

The Baltimore search process began with extensive diversity and inclusion trainings for orchestra staff; the ensemble's book club featured

Ibram X. Kendi's writings. The orchestra's board and management were unambiguous that a "diverse" conductor would best accord with Baltimore's majority-black population. The press release for Heyward's appointment lauded the selection's significance for "budding musicians who will see themselves better reflected in such a position of artistic prominence."[51]

Heyward may well be the most promising leader that the orchestra could have found. But the circumstances of his hiring suggest that his race (he is biracial) was the deciding qualification.

Commissions are pouring in to black composers, and many orchestras are putting a black-authored work on every program. Expect a rash of new Black Lives Matter–themed works, such as Carlos Simon's "An Elegy: A Cry from the Grave,"[52] dedicated to Trayvon Martin, Eric Garner, Michael Brown, and others "murdered wrongfully by an oppressive power," and Jonathan Woody's "Nigra Sum Sed Formosa: I Am Black but Beautiful." The latter work is a "fantasia on microaggressions" and the "stereotypes around blackness and black musicians."[53]

Black musicians are highly sought after for consultancy jobs and newly created fellowships. Small performing ensembles seeking philanthropic support are now grilled on their racial makeup. If their musicians, staff, or board are too white, they can forget about a grant. Many groups are going under.

Even early-music ensembles, a rarefied subspecialty of performance focused on pre-nineteenth-century compositions and instruments, are feeling the post-Floyd heat. The Continuo Foundation, a British philanthropy that supports early-music groups, now conditions its grants based on an ensemble's programming of works by "women and people of color" and on the "diversity" of their performers and administrators. But there were virtually no black composers in medieval and Renaissance Europe, since the continent was overwhelmingly Caucasian. Female composers were rare (thus the eternal fuss over Hildegard von Bingen). As for performers, blacks have only recently started going into the early-music field.

There are not enough of them now to seed every early-music group that desperately needs financial support (i.e., every early-music group).

Conservatories are creating separate programs for blacks. The Manhattan School of Music announced in October 2020 a new Artist Scholars program, peopled exclusively by black "performers, educators, activists, directors, choreographers, and administrators."[54] In November, one of its Artist Scholars gave a Zoom lecture on the American minstrel tradition; the talk was incoherent. The Artist Scholar congratulated himself repeatedly on his "very Brechtian theatrical technique." Twentieth-century German playwright Bertolt Brecht sought to prevent audiences from falling victim to theatrical illusion in order to lead viewers to a properly Marxist interpretation of his plays. Brecht's characters periodically addressed spectators directly with reflections on the play's class politics, thus breaching the imaginary "fourth wall" separating actors from audience. In the opinion of the Artist Scholar, a brief segment in his lecture superimposing the original lyrics of "Ol' Man River" onto Paul Robeson's cinematic performance of the song was a major theatrical coup of "Brechtian-Weillian irony and dissonance." It was not. The school's provost thanked the Artist Scholar afterward for his "spectacular presentation."[55]

If institutional support and encouragement of black musicians have been unequivocal for decades, why has their percentage in orchestras barely budged? Because over the last sixty years, two of the three main sources for exposing a child to classical music—a music-promoting culture and music education—have dried up. Violinist Joseph Striplin had a "classic inner-city mother," he says, but he had the good fortune to come of age in the 1940s and 1950s, when "music was vibrant in the country and at school." Classical music themes were ubiquitous on television shows and in the movies. Every junior high and high school in Detroit had its own orchestra; students were taken to the Detroit Symphony Orchestra Young People's Family Concerts at the Masonic Temple and the Ford Auditorium. "We heard and we saw; the orchestra was massive to my young eyes," he says. Striplin attended the prestigious Cass Technical High School and played in its orchestra with students who had had lessons since they were young. "I loved this music and knew I needed to find out how to play like that," he says.[56]

Since then, music education has been decimated, and classical music has disappeared from the public sphere. From 1962 to 1989, the percentage of high schools with orchestras fell from 67 percent to 17 percent, according to *Billboard*.[57] Seventy-seven percent of schools that were polled in a University of Illinois study claimed they dropped piano instruction; 40 percent dropped string instruction. If a child's home is not exposing him to classical music, he is likely not being exposed at all.

Today, blacks are not being pushed out of classical music; they are not being pushed in by their families at a rate necessary to compete. "Unless you start the violin at age seven, you won't be auditioning for the New York Philharmonic when you're 25," says Emanuel Ax.[58] And it is overwhelmingly Asian families who insist on such early discipline, placing the same emphasis on mastering an instrument (or two) as was once found in Jewish homes. Parents sacrifice for private lessons; the household stays quiet when a child is practicing.

Without encouragement at home, the best hope for creating more black classical musicians is to restore widespread music education. The anti-racism advocates have said little about that imperative, however. It's easier to extract racial quotas from compliant organizations than it is to engineer a change as profound as exposing students to a vanishing musical aesthetic. Packing off every opera and orchestra administrator to implicit bias training will not produce a single competitively qualified black musician. Nor will potential students be inclined to pick up the violin after learning that its repertoire belongs to a white supremacist tradition. But more power is to be gained by pushing the racism line than by pursuing the unlikely rebirth of public-school music training. So the search has been on to find racial scapegoats.

Chapter Four

SCAPEGOATS AND
THE RISE OF MEDIOCRITY

Until August 2020, Dona Vaughn had been the longtime artistic director of opera at the Manhattan School of Music. Her experience included singing, acting, and directing on and off Broadway and on opera stages. The Manhattan School of Music's 2019 production of Saverio Mercadante's little-known opera buffa *I Due Figaro* showed her influence in stunningly charismatic and witty student performances.[1]

Vaughn was committed to championing minority musicians—so much so that she endowed a scholarship for them at her alma mater, Brevard College in North Carolina. "In all my years of teaching," she said at the time, "I often have wished that more minority members were encouraged to pursue a music profession."[2] Besides the classics, she produced socially conscious contemporary works, giving the first professional staging, for example, at the Fort Worth Opera Festival of a feminist opera about a seventeenth-century nun.

The mob cares nothing for facts, though. On June 17, 2020, Vaughn was teaching a class via Zoom on musical theater. An unidentified participant, whose name and image were blacked out, asked her, out of the blue, how she could justify having produced Franz Lehár's allegedly racist operetta *Das Land des Lächelns* (The Land of Smiles) several years earlier. (The racial sin, in this case, was allegedly against Asians.) Vaughn cut the questioner off for raising an issue irrelevant to the current discussion.

The fuse was lit. A Manhattan School of Music student petition was immediately forthcoming. Vaughn must be fired because she is a "danger to the arts community," it thundered. The petition resurrected a meme from the time of the Lehár production: that Vaughn had cast a black singer as a butler, thus proving her racism. A rule banning blacks from playing servant characters would put off-limits some of the most essential roles in the repertoire, including Leporello in *Don Giovanni* and Figaro and Susanna in *The Marriage of Figaro* (the latter role Kathleen Battle owned for years at the Met). For good measure, the petition threw in unspecified "reports" of "homophobic aggression and body shaming." The petition quickly garnered 1,800 signatures. Phony Instagram accounts under Vaughn's name suddenly appeared on the Web, containing fake inflammatory material.

Vaughn's colleagues, cowering from the mob, let her twist in the wind. Almost none came to her defense. Vaughn was fired, and replaced by a black male.

The Manhattan School of Music administration apparently made no effort to speak with Vaughn's former students, who would have rebutted the false charges against her. Howard Watkins is a black assistant conductor at the Metropolitan Opera and a faculty member at Juilliard; he has accompanied world-famous singers and conducted at some of the most prestigious venues in the industry. In a heartfelt character reference after she had been fired, he chronicled his history with Vaughn. In 1988, he was enrolled in the Lindemann Young Artist Development Program at the Metropolitan Opera. Vaughn was the program's stage director and acting coach. Watkins wrote that Vaughn was responsible for many of his greatest experiences there. "Her classes provided all of us with specific tools towards improving our artistic growth and understanding. . . . It is tremendously sad that the students of Manhattan School have been deprived of the opportunity of learning from someone with vast knowledge, the passionate desire to see them succeed, and the integrity to say what must be said for them to grow." As for the homophobia charge, Watkins's "interracial relationship" with his male domestic partner "has clearly never been the slightest concern to her whatsoever," nor would it even occur to her to "cast according to race or sexual orientation."[3]

Bass-baritone LaMarcus Miller—also black—worked in Vaughn's Opera Workshop and Opera Lab at the Manhattan School of Music in the early 2010s. She was a "pillar of integrity" and the "epitome of a mentor," he says. "I've only seen her be tremendously inclusive, while holding students accountable for their actions."[4]

Days after the firing, the anonymous petition instigator posted a follow-up: "Victory! Dona D. Vaughn has been removed from her position at MSM. Thank you to everyone who supported this petition. The work is never over and I hope you all feel strengthened by this victory."[5] The "hope" is well-founded; on to the next takedown.

As for Vaughn, she's "still in total shock," she says. "I do not have words to describe it. It's guilt by allegation."[6]

Another academic is fighting back against a similarly false allegation of racism. Timothy Jackson is a music theory professor at the University of North Texas, the former director of the Center for Schenkerian Studies, and the former editor of the *Journal of Schenkerian Studies*. After Hunter College musicologist Philip Ewell launched his race-based attack on Schenkerian music theory in November 2019, Jackson put out a call to members of the Society for Music Theory (including to Ewell) to submit a response. The majority of essays, published in the July 2020 *Journal of Schenkerian Studies*, were critical—some timidly, others more forthrightly; five were supportive. Few stated the obvious: that to equate tonal hierarchies with racial hierarchies is lunatic.

Like most practitioners of academic high theory, Ewell is blinded by the similarity of words while ignoring their contextual meaning. A hierarchy of keys and of harmonies within those keys is constitutive of Western tonal music and of some non-Western music as well. It has nothing to do with alleged racial hierarchy. Ewell's position means that tonal music is itself racist. Every composer writing in a tonal idiom, including composers of color, would be engaged in a racist enterprise. So would be anyone in any field of activity that recognizes dominant and subdominant elements—

whether art analysis, evolutionary biology, chemistry, or engineering. Distinctions between gravitational, nuclear, and electromagnetic forces would render our very universe a site of cosmic racism. Of course, the rhetorical slippery slope holds no terrors for Ewell. Sweeping other fields into the "white racial frame" would not cause him to rethink his argument; there can never be too many examples of white supremacy.

Jackson's response focused on Ewell's denunciations of Schenker as a proto-Nazi. Ewell had failed to mention Schenker's outsider status as an Austrian Jew or his widow's death in a concentration camp. Ewell's silence on these matters, Jackson wrote, may be related to black anti-Semitism, which was once again in evidence in a spate of attacks on elderly Jews in New York. Ewell has called for more rap repertoire in music curricula. Before acceding to that demand, Jackson advised, music departments should grapple with rap's anti-Semitism and misogyny. The underrepresentation of blacks in music theory is due to the fact that few blacks "grow up in homes where classical music is profoundly valued," Jackson concluded, before issuing a call to demolish "institutionalized racist barriers."[7]

This attempted self-inoculation failed, as it always does. The Executive Board of the Society for Music Theory and music theory students and professors nationally denounced him for "replicating a culture of whiteness," in the words of the Society for Music Theory Executive Board.[8] Jackson's colleagues at the University of North Texas blasted him for publishing a symposium "replete with racial stereotyping and tropes." Ewell's own racial stereotyping was taken as simple truth.

Jackson must be fired for his history of "particularly racist and unacceptable" actions, according to the graduate students. Jackson was also accused of breaching scholarly norms in publishing the symposium; those charges were tendentious.

If Jackson made a mistake, it was to refute Ewell's thesis on irrelevant biographical grounds and to deploy Ewell's own ad hominem method against Ewell himself. Instead, he should have refused to get involved in the parsing of Schenker's German nationalism and focused on the absurdity of the harmony-race analogy itself.

In December 2020, Jackson was removed from his editorship of the *Journal of Schenkerian Studies*. The chair of Jackson's department informed him that the university was ceasing its financial and institutional support for the journal and for the Center for Schenkerian Studies, essentially cancelling both institutions. Jackson is suing the university and the university's regents for violating his First Amendment rights.[9] Whatever the legal outcome, he will remain a pariah among colleagues and students.

The biggest victim in the racial attack on classical music is the music itself. Once the poison of identity politics is injected into a field, it can never recover its prelapsarian innocence. Every time an industry insider or critic disparages our greatest composers for being too white and too male, he gives neophytes, especially young people, another reason to close their ears to this legacy. At the 2021 Peabody Institute conference mentioned earlier, where the League of American Orchestras' Simon Woods apologized for his own whiteness, Woods voiced dread at also seeing the "whiteness" on the stage and in the audience once concerts resumed. This is professional malpractice: the irrelevant introduction of race will drive desperately needed new audiences out of, not into, the concert hall.

Seeking to make classical music politically acceptable, orchestras and conservatories are resurrecting lesser-known black composers from the past. (Other black composers, such as Samuel Coleridge-Taylor and William Grant Still, have been played, at least on radio stations, for decades now, and rightly so.) This enterprise would ordinarily call for celebration. The canon is performed to death. The more previously unfamiliar music we know, the greater our understanding of what it has meant to be human, since music traces the movement and yearnings of its composer's soul. Rediscovering black contributions to classical music is particularly meaningful. But the stated rationale for this resuscitation destroys its value. Every past composer now being presented on radio stations and in concert halls is said to have disappeared from public attention because of racism. That claim is, in most instances, fanciful.

Perhaps 98 percent of all composers in the classical tradition are not listened to or even recognized today. Those forgotten artists were almost all white males. It is the sad fate of most composers to recede into obscurity, if they were even lucky enough to have had their music performed during their lifetimes. To charge history with racism for having allowed black composers to have also fallen into obscurity requires proof of overwhelming merit strong enough to overcome the usual oblivion meted out to everyone else. That high burden of proof is rarely met.

The composers enjoying the greatest prominence at the moment are Joseph Bologne, Chevalier de Saint-Georges (1745–1799), and Florence Price (1887–1953). The hyperbole surrounding their works is astonishing.

Bologne was the son of a Guadeloupe plantation owner and a slave; he spent most of his life in Parisian court society. Throughout his twenties, Bologne enjoyed an annuity from his father's estate, but he has not been canceled for having profited from slave labor.

Bologne is commonly referred today as the "black Mozart." That comparison is laughable enough in its own right. Bologne is fluent in the classical style, with a pleasing capacity for forward momentum. His works are recognizable on the radio for their simple construction. They possess none of the melodic gift and emotional depths that have led the world's greatest composers to bow down before Mozart in dazed gratitude.

But the "black Mozart" label is insufficiently hagiographic. It is Mozart who should be called the "White Chevalier," says Bill Barclay, a playwright-composer.[10] This is preposterous. If Bologne were white, his oeuvre would remain marginal. Other contemporaries of Mozart, such as Antonio Rosetti, Joseph Martin Kraus, and Josef Mysliveček, deserve revival before Bologne. It was not Bologne's mixed-race status that consigned him to the same fate as nearly all his white colleagues, but his banality.

Florence Price has a major advantage over Bologne: she is of mixed ancestry and female, and thus intersectional. Price is most frequently compared with Antonín Dvořák. This, too, is overblown, though her American-vernacular style drew inspiration from the Czech composer,

especially in its use of black spirituals. The Symphony No. 3 in C minor
(from 1940), considered her masterwork, starts promisingly, with eerie,
shifting chords emanating from the brass. There are moments of bois-
terous exaltation—above all, in one of her signature African "juba"
dances in the third movement—that incorporate early jazz harmonies.
But the work is thematically inert and repetitive; its melodies, truncated.
Frequent climaxes are generated artificially through cymbal clashes.
Indeed, Price's cymbal scoring makes Tchaikovsky's fondness for the
instrument look ascetic.

An influential pedagogue calls Price's harmony, rhythm, and materials "fourth-rate."[11] Long before the current Price boom, a prominent
conductor searched for a piece of hers that he could, in good conscience,
program. He couldn't find one, though he has happily conducted the
works of other black composers, such as William Grant Still, Ulysses
Kay, and Alvin Singleton.[12]

Sometimes the challenge proves too much even for the most willing
boosters. The *Financial Times*, reviewing a Boston Symphony Orchestra
concert from November 2020, admitted that Price's String Quartet in G
was "slight." Not to worry, said the paper, it is "none the worse for that."[13]

The Chicago Symphony Orchestra premiered Price's First Symphony
in 1933; it was favorably reviewed in the *Chicago Daily News* as "worthy
of a place in the regular symphonic repertory."[14] The WPA Orchestra of
Detroit and several women's orchestras played her compositions. If her
works failed to find that lasting place in the repertory, it was not because of a racial lockout. Ironically, the critics who champion Price now
are ordinarily fierce advocates of the avant-garde. In Price, however,
they elevate an aesthetically conservative style that would hold little
interest for them if practiced by a white male.

The hype being ladled onto recently revived black composers is not
innocuous. The inflation is in the service of accusation and resentment.
By blurring real distinctions in musical value, the racial boosters make it

harder for new listeners to learn what makes this tradition monumental. Someone ignorant of classical music should not be told that there is no difference between Beethoven and Esperanza Spalding, between Dvořák and Florence Price. A newcomer should start with the peaks, not the shallows. The wild applause that breaks out after a Price performance is due to its current political significance, not to its musical merits. Her works and those of other lesser-known composers deserve a grateful hearing. But the rapturous praise is condescending. In the meantime, works of more likely interest, such as operas by William Grant Still, remain a tantalizing mystery.

As the lies about classical music accumulate, not one conductor, soloist, or concertmaster has rebutted them. These influential performers know that Beethoven's late piano sonatas and quartets are not about race but about pushing beyond ordinary human experience into an unexplored universe of unsettling silences and space. They know that Schubert's song cycles are not about race but about yearning, disappointment, and fleeting joy. They know that the Saint Matthew Passion is not about race but about crushing sorrow that cries out in pain before finally finding consolation. To reduce everything in human experience to the ever more tedious theme of alleged racial oppression is narcissism. This music is not about you or me. It is about something grander than our narrow, petty selves. But narcissism, the signal characteristic of our time, is shrinking our cultural inheritance to a nullity.

These conductors and soloists are silent, though their knowledge has led them deep into that greatest of all human dramas: the evolution of expressive style. They can trace how the erotic languor of Chopin's nocturnes and concerti became even more dangerously seductive in Brahms's and Rachmaninoff's piano works. They know that even one composer, not even in the first tier of name recognition, in this kaleidoscopic tradition—whether Smetana, Sibelius, or Granados—contains more expressive depth than any individual can possibly fathom in a lifetime. These successful musicians have felt the terrifying anticipation—a moment without parallel in the repertoire—as a pianist sits quietly in front of the orchestral beast at the start of one of the great romantic piano concerti as waves of sound pour over him, or as he issues his own challenge first, whether a thunderclap or a whisper, and is answered in turn. The leaders have experienced this, and yet they say nothing.

Their silence breeds such inanities as Alex Ross's chastising the alleged racism of *The Magic Flute*'s comic Moor Monostatos.[15] The complaint is stunningly trivial when measured against the majesty of Mozart's output. More importantly, it overlooks the conventional nature of dramatic expression. Monostatos is no more a serious portrait of a North African than Papageno (another character in *The Magic Flute*) is a serious portrait of a bird catcher. Both exist within the realm of comic tropes. If we are looking to take racial offense at libretti that Mozart did not even write, we could also complain about bumbling, manipulated, or hysterical whites, whether Count Almaviva, Donna Elvira, Masetto, Leporello, or Elettra. But every iteration of such a childish accusation serves as another excuse for the uninitiated to keep their ears and minds shut.

Classical music's insider critics throw in a class bias count for good measure; these pseudo-Marxist accusations are as specious as the racism charge. To be sure, many seventeenth- and eighteenth-century composers had court patrons—and we should thank those nobles for underwriting such musical treasures, however capricious their will and taste. Pre-revolutionary opera seria legitimated absolute rule while also trying to nudge its royal attendees closer to Enlightenment ideals of tolerance and justice. The eighteenth-century Classical style is infused with nobility and grandeur; the French Baroque with the formality of Versailles. So what? With the arguable exception of opera seria, music written for wealthy patrons—whether Telemann's *Tafelmusik* or Haydn's symphonies—is not about class but about the abstract logic of musical expression. Western classical music has at times emerged from or elicited political passions. But those passions were usually associated with nationalist movements against monarchical regimes, exemplified by the frenzy that broke out in Pest in response to Berlioz's orchestration of the anti-Habsburg "Rákóczi

March." Most canonical composers were at odds, quietly or vociferously, with their respective governments.

The present-day scourges impugn concert protocols as a classist means of excluding a "diverse" audience. But it was the bearers of inherited privilege during the ancien régime who treated music as a backdrop to be gambled and flirted through. It was the nonaristocratic classes who started attending to music with silent devotion, as it became more complex and demanding in the nineteenth century. Timothy Jackson's maternal and paternal grandparents, impoverished refugees from Central and Eastern Europe, bought his mother and his father a cheap violin and a dilapidated piano, respectively, during the Great Depression and scraped together enough money to pay for lessons. His working-class parents had done hard menial labor all their lives, but they heard classical music as a "call from another world, divine, mysteriously exalted, pointing to a higher plane of existence," he wrote in his article for the Schenker symposium.[16]

Today's warriors against "classism" would presumably accuse José Antonio Abreu, a Venezuelan socialist economist, of being an unwitting tool of white "patriarchal power," in the words of the *BBC Magazine*.[17] Abreu founded El Sistema, a program of free classical music training for barrio children in Caracas, in the belief that playing Bach, Schubert, and Brahms would help deliver them from poverty and crime into a better world. El Sistema, Abreu said in 2008, was meant to "reveal to our children the beauty of music [so that] music shall reveal to our children the beauty of life."[18] Philip Ewell can sneer at Beethoven as, at best, "above average." The *BBC Magazine* can snark that the formula for musical "greatness" appears to be "wild hair + cantankerousness + 32 sonatas" but is, in fact, a "manufactured quality" designed to "sell scores of 'greatness' to as many people as possible." The graduates of El Sistema know better. Gustavo Dudamel, conductor of the Los Angeles Philharmonic and El Sistema's most famous product, said during a live HD concert broadcast in 2011: Beethoven is "not just the reference point of classical music; he is the master of us all." The Seventh Symphony is "happiness. It's the only word that I find perfect for this music."

Though the keepers of our tradition surely know that classical music is a priceless inheritance, having devoted their lives to it, fear paralyzes them as that legacy goes down. Among the leaders I contacted were conductors Daniel Barenboim, Dudamel himself, Riccardo Muti, Franz Welser-Möst, Valery Gergiev, Gianandrea Noseda, Charles Dutoit, James Conlon, Neeme Järvi, and Masaaki Suzuki; pianists András Schiff, Mitsuko Uchida, Lang Lang, Evgeny Kissin, and Richard Goode; singers Anna Netrebko, James Morris, and Angel Blue; and composers John Harbison and Wynton Marsalis. All either declined to comment or ignored the query.

Company managers were just as tight-lipped. The Met's Peter Gelb refused an interview; the Philadelphia Orchestra's Matías Tarnopolsky, Jonathan Martin of the Cincinnati Symphony Orchestra, and Jeff Alexander of the Chicago Symphony Orchestra were also unwilling to speak. Simon Woods's assistant said that he was caught up in moving to New Jersey and thus unavailable. (A source said that he had been in New Jersey for months already.)

The music professionals who did speak to me, with few exceptions, required that they be referred to in so generalized a category that it would contain thousands of members. A former household name in classical music gave an anodyne interview, with one brief exception: an anecdote undercutting a black conductor's unchallenged reputation. A day later, his wife wrote me: "We have just been informed that an interview has taken place between yourself and [former household name]. We request that you delete any comments made by [the name]. While we appreciate your enthusiasm for your project, we must decline from [*sic*] any involvement, on or off the record."[19]

Perhaps some of the star musicians who refused to comment think that the racial assault on classical music is not worth taking seriously. Emanuel Ax, who did go on the record, laughed good-naturedly when told of Ewell's Beethoven evaluation. "That is a wonderful quote," he said. "This movement is not a danger to anyone."[20] Ax is wrong. One need only look to the syllabi in literature departments today which, compared with those from forty years ago, show the devastation that the unopposed march of identity politics wreaks on the transmission of greatness.

Other music professionals understand the danger. One educator warns: "If conservatories start admitting by race and ethnicity, close them down. As soon as standards are modified, the game is over. Mediocrity is like carbon monoxide: you can't see it or smell it, but one day, you're dead." Woke music administrators are relativizing excellence as a white Western concept. Mention "quality" in a meeting of performing arts managers, and you may be accused of "sending the wrong message." The aforementioned music educator scoffs at that dodge. "We should face the facts. Excellence is easily identified. There are hundreds of thousands of composers; the world knows one hundred. Conservatories audition student conductors for fifteen minutes, but you can detect their caliber in the first ten seconds."[21]

Some Juilliard professors have taken early retirement rather than risk conflict with the identity-obsessed mob. The striving for excellence is now secondary, says Juilliard violin professor Earl Carlyss. "It is terrifying when politics takes precedence over quality."[22]

Conventions of scholarship are under attack as well. The distinguishing feature of Western classical music, which allowed an unparalleled transformation of style over seven centuries, is that it is written down, unlike most other world music. Notation allows us, miraculously, to hear what people were playing in the fifteenth century. But music departments are under pressure to eliminate the requirement that students can read scores, since such a requirement is purportedly exclusionary (that is, it has a disparate impact). Anti-racist musicologists are jettisoning another basic norm: source documentation. New York University musicologist Matthew Morrison scoffs at "Western (colonial) notions of 'documentation,'" as he put it in a November 2020 tweet. In his study of black people, Morrison wrote, he doesn't "put everything on paper. Some stuff is meant to be kept and transferred orally (and ritually)."[23]

In other words, ask Morrison for his written sources, and you may be accused of racism. It is a "colonial impulse" to "desire to . . . have access to everything," Morrison warns fellow academics and potential fact-checkers.[24]

Morrison is no fringe character. He has held fellowships at Harvard, King's College London, the American Musicological Society, the Mellon Foundation, the Library of Congress, and the Tanglewood Music Center. He has served as editor-in-chief of *Current Musicology*. And he represents the future.

The betrayal of the music guardians is not unique. Other individuals entrusted with preserving Western civilization are abdicating their responsibility, too, either actively colluding with the forces of hate or passively allowing those forces to conquer their field.

The National Archives and Records Administration, founded to preserve the country's historical records, declared itself guilty of systemic racism in April 2021. The Archivist's Task Force on Racism, which produced the April report, denounced the Capitol Rotunda for lauding the "wealthy White men" who participated in the nation's founding while "marginalizing BIPOC, women, and other communities."[25] Task force members included the directors of the John F. Kennedy Presidential Library and the Jimmy Carter Presidential Library.

Every humanities subject is being hollowed out with similar charges. Under the logic of the current moment, any tradition that comes out of Europe is racist because its contributors will have been overwhelmingly white. It matters not that the demographics of Europe until the last fifty years made that racial composition inevitable. Balinese gamelan music, the Chinese opera, Indian classical music, and the Nigerian talking drum have been as racially monolithic, without falling afoul of the diversity monitors. Only Western civilization is under attack for its traditional racial homogeneity.

The poisoning of classical music is heartbreaking enough. But unless more people fight back against the race war and defend our inheritance, we are going to cancel both a country and a culture.

Chapter Five

MAKING BEETHOVEN WOKE

———

The activists advocating a racial proportionality approach to musical performance are not satisfied with impugning the past; they want to rewrite it as well. Recent treatment of Beethoven demonstrates the revolutionary character of their movement.

For decades, opera directors in Europe and the United States felt licensed to revise operas to conform to their political agendas, even before Black Lives Matter hit the arts scene. These directors did so through wildly incongruous stagings that updated an opera's plot to modern times and introduced progressive totems that would have been unfathomable to the opera's original creator. Such directorial interventions left the libretto intact, however. Now even that cordon sanitaire between the structure of a work and an interpreter's political preferences has been breached.

In February 2022, the Metropolitan Museum of Art in New York City hosted a production of Beethoven's opera *Fidelio*, produced by Heartbeat Opera. The opera is an Enlightenment paean to freedom and to marital love. In Beethoven's version of the opera, a wife disguises herself as a male prison guard to free her husband from a Spanish fortress; at the Metropolitan Museum of Art, *Fidelio* became a Black Lives Matter critique of mass incarceration. In the Met's *Fidelio*, a BLM activist (the updated husband from Beethoven's *Fidelio*) had been writing a doctoral dissertation on the Thirteenth Amendment and investigating corrupt "fascists" in the criminal-justice system. In retaliation, racist cops shoot him, and a racist warden of a super-maximum prison throws him into solitary confinement. The activist's wife, unable to persuade any lawyers to take up her husband's case pro bono, goes undercover as a female correctional officer in her husband's prison. This change from a male to a female disguise allows for a pleasingly homoerotic revision to the plot. In the original opera, a prison guard's daughter falls in love with the new "male" employee, echoing Lady Olivia's fruitless infatuation for the disguised Viola in Shakespeare's *Twelfth Night*. In the Met Museum's *Fidelio*, the prison guard's daughter is a lesbian; her black father encourages his daughter to court the new black female assistant. Of all the production's revisions, this paternal matchmaking is the most counterfactual, given black attitudes toward homosexuality, especially among the working class.[1]

In the current political and artistic environment, *Fidelio* was a Black Lives Matter manifesto waiting to happen. What made the Met Museum's production noteworthy was that the revision did not occur exclusively through the staging; Heartbeat Opera rewrote the spoken dialogue as well. (That dialogue was delivered in English, while the arias and ensembles remained in their original German.) The activist's wife complains that the "*real* conspiracy" was not the one for which her husband was detained but rather the "suppression of immigrants and people of color" in the US. The super-maximum prison contains people "whose only mistake was being poor and black." The imprisoned activist rails against his black jailer: "You are complicit in a corrupt system that oppresses our people. I see in you a field Negro." The white prison warden reveals the depths of his racism by announcing that if the activist *really* "wanted to help his community he would tell them to stop burning down their neighborhoods and to pull up their bootstraps." Such an invocation of personal responsibility is—in the revisionist's mind—a surefire sign of white supremacy. None of these lines are related to the original libretto.

The only reason the Metropolitan Museum of Art mounted *Fidelio* was the Black Lives Matter gloss. Without it, the museum's leadership would have had no interest in the work. The production provided the museum with a racial-justice twofer, however, since opening night featured a post-performance discussion between five "social justice advocates" on how to dismantle "current systems of incarceration through the abolitionist movement."[2] The Eric H. Holder Jr. Initiative for Civil and Political Rights at Columbia University sponsored the discussion. Such a panel may have once seemed tangential to the mission of an art museum; in the post–George Floyd era, such racial-justice advocacy has become central to curating and programming.

Heartbeat Opera did preserve one aspect of the original *Fidelio*: the arias and ensembles were, by and large, textually intact, if sometimes compressed or cut to shorten the running time. The sublime quartet "Mir ist so wunderbar" was reduced to a trio, due to the elimination of a character who would have complicated the lesbian subplot. The overture (Beethoven ultimately wrote four) and early arias were also cut, replaced by mechanical noise and a wordless enactment of a black male being gunned down.

On April 7, 2022, the Baltimore Symphony Orchestra, led by outgoing conductor Marin Alsop, took textual intervention one step further. A poem by Baltimore-based rapper Wordsmith replaced Friedrich Schiller's "Ode to Joy" in a performance of Beethoven's Ninth Symphony. Wordsmith explained his goals in the rewriting: to use "present-day social issues to highlight the need for positive reinforcement. Encouraging gender equality, cultural acceptance, and living a purpose-driven life are worldly topics I sought to shine a light on during the writing process."[3]

The result was a radical change of register. Instead of Schiller's opening stanza:

> Freude, schöner Götterfunken,
>
> Tochter aus Elysium,
>
> Wir betreten feuertrunken,
>
> Himmlische, dein Heiligtum!

[Joy, bright spark of divinity,

Daughter of Elysium,

Drunk with fire we tread

Thy sanctuary!]

We get:

Live and love with open mind let our cultures intertwine.

Dig deep down, show what you're made of, set the tone it's time
    to shine.

We must fight for equal rights and share some common courtesy.

While pursuing all your dreams spread your joy from sea to sea.

We are admonished not to "hate," which has a very particular referent
in the circles in which Wordsmith and his institutional patrons travel:

Brothers, sisters equally say:

"Together we can make hate history!"[4]

In Beethoven's excerpt for the Ninth Symphony, Schiller's poem
moves ecstatically in its final strophe into the heavens:

Ahnest du den Schöpfer, Welt?

Such' ihn über'm Sternenzelt!

Über Sternen muß er wohnen.

[World, do you know your Creator?

Seek Him in the starry canopy!

Above the stars must He dwell.]

Wordsmith concludes *his* "Ode to Joy" with a leaden admonition—a
Hallmark card version of a diversity training session:

Positive vibes for an ode to joy!

Rise, oh rise, be the voice of change,

We must show more empathy.[5]

Wordsmith's word-setting is as clumsy as his content is banal. He regularly pits the natural stress of a line against the musical meter, as in the setting of "Oh this is our chance to unite" (measures 281 and 282 of the revised score).

Leonard Bernstein conducted Beethoven's Ninth Symphony in Berlin on Christmas Day, 1989. The Berlin Wall had come down the previous month. To mark the liberation, Bernstein changed one word of Schiller's text: "Freude" (joy) became "Freiheit" (freedom). This substitution was regarded as so momentous as to put Bernstein momentarily on the defensive: "I feel this is a heaven-sent moment to sing 'Freiheit' wherever the score indicates the word 'Freude,'" he explained. "If ever there was a historic time to take an academic risk in the name of human joy, this is it, and I am sure we have Beethoven's blessing."[6] Bernstein's one-word interpolation was still being talked about long after the 1989 concert. The *New York Times* observed in 1998 that "Bernstein, who in life got away with nothing and everything, boldly changed freude, the joy in Schiller's 'Ode to Joy,' to freiheit, freedom."[7]

But now, the wholesale elimination of Schiller's ode, so integral to Beethoven's score, requires no justification at all. In fact, Wordsmith's replacement poem is just one of several commissioned by conductor Marin Alsop for what Alsop hoped would be an attention-getting tour "in partnership with ten orchestras at leading venues on six continents" in 2020.[8] (Alsop's so-called "All Together" tour, to mark the 250th anniversary of Beethoven's birth, was ultimately cancelled due to COVID-19 lockdowns.) In London, the poem "O Human" by British poet Anthony Anaxagorou was to have displaced Schiller. Where Wordsmith was clear, if trite, Anaxagorou was mannered and opaque. Listeners were urged to "Speak up those who've held the tremble." The poet asked rhetorically: "Can you see us hurtling forward/Tying bells like vows to skin?"[9] To which the answer can only be: "No, we can't!"

The most technically adept of the Schiller substitutes came from former US poet laureate Tracy K. Smith. Smith concluded her ode, planned for an abortive Carnegie Hall performance, with a plug for sustainability:

> Battered planet, home of billions,
>
> Our long shadow stalks your face.
>
> All we've fractured, all we've stolen,
>
> All we've sought blind to your grace.[10]

The rewritings go beyond Beethoven. On November 5, 2022, the Baltimore Symphony Orchestra performed Igor Stravinsky's *The Soldier's Tale*, with another new text by Wordsmith. Stravinsky's 1918 work pairs a seven-member instrumental ensemble with three non-singing actors. The actors narrate the story of a soldier persuaded by the devil to exchange his modest but beloved possessions for a deceptive promise of wealth. The score is a concentrated gem of modernism, with protean time signatures and rhythms, acid harmonies, and an eclectic range of musical influences, including klezmer music and ragtime. Wordsmith retold the story from the "perspective of a Black American soldier during the Vietnam War," as the publicity materials explained.[11]

These modern bastardizations have eighteenth- and nineteenth-century precedent. Singers notoriously inserted their preferred arias into opera scores, however unrelated to the opera at hand. Throughout much of the nineteenth century, publishers and conductors "corrected" Beethoven's symphonies, which violated academic rules of harmony. In Paris, Mozart's operas were rewritten to match French tastes in musical theater. The composer and critic Hector Berlioz described how a German composer "fixed" *The Magic Flute* for a Parisian performance:

> He tacked a few bars on to the end of the overture (the overture to *The Magic Flute*!), made a bass aria out of the soprano line of one of the choruses, likewise adding a few bars of his own composition; removed the wind instruments from one scene and put

them into another, altered the vocal line and the whole character of the accompaniment in Sarastro's sublime aria; manufactured a song out of the Slaves Chorus "O cara armonia"; converted a duet into a trio; and, as if *The Magic Flute* were not enough to sate his harpy's appetite, gorged himself on Titus and Don Giovanni. . . . After that, need one add that in the hands of this master the famous "Fin ch'han dal vino"—that explosion of licentious energy in which the whole character of the Don is summed up—duly reappeared as a trio for two sopranos and bass, singing, among other sweet nothings, the following lines:

Joy past all telling!

My heart is swelling!

How my lot is different from his![12]

Berlioz laid down his rule of artistic respect:

No, no, no, a million times no! You musicians, you poets, prose-writers, actors, pianists, conductors whether of third or second or even first rank, you do not have the right to meddle with a Shake-speare or a Beethoven, in order to bestow on them the blessings of your knowledge and taste.[13]

It took a century, but Berlioz's lonely crusade for fidelity to a composer's intentions was eventually victorious—at least with regard to the notes and words on the page, if not, in recent years, in regard to staging. It is not a cultural advance to return to artistic revisionism. (To be sure, topical jokes and references are sometimes inserted into operettas today, but those works occupy a different place in our culture.) Beethoven chose Schiller's "Ode," not Wordsmith's, for what would prove his final symphony. That is sufficient reason to keep the original pairing. But there is a more self-interested reason as well. In revising works to match contemporary sensibilities, we diminish, not expand, our human possibilities. No one would write Schiller's "Ode to Joy" today. That is precisely why it should be performed intact. Its

elevated rhetoric belongs to a lost aesthetic universe of romantic idealism, classical allusion, and exacting formal craft. It speaks to a
now-alien way of being in the world that we can nevertheless dimly
sense through close engagement with its language. Likewise, the
original text of *The Soldier's Tale* hearkens back to the unsettling
world of Russian folktales, with their mysterious strangers, impene-
trable forests, and diabolical traps. That folk literature expresses
what it was like to be human before Enlightenment science and the
conquest of nature; it captures primal fears that even now we may not
have transcended.

We are awash in opportunities to hear rappers and to condemn alleged police brutality. Our means for entering the past, however, are
finite and available only through works of art that have survived into
the present. It is narcissistic to demand that these precious vehicles of
bygone form and feeling be dragooned into speaking in our language,
about our contemporary concerns. And it is delusional to think that
junking Schiller for Wordsmith or Beethoven for Black Lives Matter will
increase the "diversity" of the classical music audience. Such substitu-
tions may please institutional funders, but the only thing that will bring
blacks regularly into the concert hall is prolonged engagement, starting
in school or at home, with classical music.

An advocate of rewritings like the All Together project might respond that no lasting damage has been done to the host works. The
next performance can revert to the work's original structure; many
future performances will do so. But each rewriting legitimates the
idea that understanding a foreign idiom, especially a rarified one,
asks too much of an audience. Such revisions imply that we should
not try to stretch beyond the boundaries of our circumscribed lives
into a radically different aesthetic milieu. Moreover, most are animated
by the hermeneutics of suspicion (philosopher Paul Ricoeur's term for
the demystifying impulse that took over the humanities in the late
twentieth century). They see in past works of art only oppression and

illegitimate privilege. Such deconstructive readings provide an excuse for ignorance and a pretext for prejudice. Even without that deconstructive agenda, however, rewriters and revisionists destroy the precious link between present and past that is the primary means of transmitting civilization and of keeping our minds open to beauty.

Chapter Six

CAN OPERA SURVIVE THE CULTURE WARS?

The rules for what amount of melanin is required for what type of role are changing at breakneck speed. In a little over a year, an arts group in Great Britain went from celebrated to pariah status for violating a new apartheid code.

In late February 2020, the Scottish Opera mounted a sold-out run of *Nixon in China*, John Adams's opera about President Richard Nixon's 1972 visit to Communist China. The reviews of the production were uniformly glowing: it was "entrancing," "gripping," one of the "most rewarding and thought-provoking evenings available in any theatre this year."[1]

In June 2021, the company proudly announced that its *Nixon* had been nominated for a South Bank Sky Arts Award.[2] Yet less than forty-eight hours later, the company withdrew from the nomination and issued a groveling apology for causing "offence."[3] It begged for "space" to learn from its errors.

What had changed between 2020 and 2021? The meltdown among global elites over systemic racism after the death of George Floyd. In this fevered, racialized atmosphere, the hapless Scottish Opera committed an offence that heretofore no one had known existed.

The company's transgression lay in casting white singers in the roles of Communist Party Chairman Mao Zedong and Chinese Premier Zhou Enlai, consistent with more than three decades of performance practice. The fact that a black baritone sang the role of President Nixon, a first for *Nixon in China*, earned the Scottish Opera no protection from accusations of racism.

"Yellowface in opera has to stop," commented British baritone Julian Chou-Lambert. "It's like blackface, but applied to East and South-East Asian characters. It's offensive and dehumanizing for ESEA people. Opera folks, please learn about this and do better."[4] A Scottish MP from the Labor Party, Sarah Owen, lamented the paucity of Asians in the production and the "exaggerated winged eye make-up."[5] She wondered ominously if *Nixon in China* had received taxpayer funding.

The company tried to defend itself by explaining that its production "intended to portray the character of Chairman Mao as old and in ill-health and in no way were we trying to change his ethnicity."[6] Not good enough. "There is clear photographic evidence," an obscure advocacy group called BEATS (British East & Southeast Asians in Theatre and on Screen) shot back, "that the practice of yellowface was employed on dancers in the production."[7]

Apart from Chou-Lambert (who runs BEATS) and MP Sarah Owen, there was no groundswell of outrage against the Scottish Opera and its arts nomination. Nevertheless, the company caved immediately to its detractors. It issued a statement of neo-Stalinist self-abnegation: "We are deeply sorry for the offence caused by the casting of our 2020 production of John Adam's [sic] *Nixon in China*. We are also sorry for any misrepresentation caused by the stage make-up." Though the company practices diversity in casting, "we accept there is a lot more work still to be done. . . . Once again, our heartfelt apologies to everyone, most especially our ESEA communities."[8]

If the Scottish Opera owes these "communities" an apology for "yellowface" and "whitewashing" (defined by BEATS as using non-Asian singers for Chinese roles), so do the creators of *Nixon in China* and nearly every director that has mounted the opera since its 1987 premiere in Houston, Texas.

It would be hard to come up with a more progressive team of collaborators than *Nixon in China*'s composer (Adams), inaugural director

(Peter Sellars), librettist (Alice Goodman), and original choreographer (Mark Morris). Peter Sellars reigned for years as the *enfant terrible* of opera, updating operas to modern times and left-wing politics, sometimes imaginatively, more often anachronistically. When Sellars ceased being an *enfant*, he continued being merely *terrible*. He opines regularly on social justice from the lectern and in his capacity as regisseur.

His *Nixon in China* staging, for example, was inspired by the Reagan White House, he said in a 1994 interview. Reagan and his cronies were "tearing the country apart," and "dividing profits among their close friends, slashing budgets, putting cities deeply in the hole," while distracting the country with photo ops.[9] In response, Sellars and librettist Goodman sprinkled elephant jokes throughout that first production.

The elephant imagery did double duty, referring not just to the GOP but also to operatic imperialism. Giuseppe Verdi's *Aida* was playing concurrently with *Nixon in China* at the Houston Grand Opera. According to Sellars, *Aida*, set in Ancient Egypt, raises questions about the "imperialist tradition" of grand opera. (It is now considered "imperialist" for a Western composer like Verdi to, in Sellars's words, say "'we are now doing an opera about Egypt.'" The term "cultural appropriation" was not yet in currency when Sellars offered these comments, but the concept is the same.) Since many in *Nixon in China*'s audience would also have seen *Aida* the night before or after, the *Nixon* collaborators were, he said, "quite consciously commenting" on what it means to move an opera plot into Egypt. (Here's an alternative explanation for what such a plot device means: a laudable interest in other cultures, however imperfectly represented or understood. *Nixon in China* apparently avoids such imperialism because it said, per Sellars, "'Chinese people had their story and their history, and you may know what it is, but it's happening.'" If Sellars's distinction between *Aida* and *Nixon in China* does not seem clear, do not blame yourself for a deficit of understanding.)

Despite Sellars's exquisite sensibilities about imperialism and cultural appropriation, it apparently never occurred to him or to his colleagues that they were committing a racial transgression by casting all-white singers for the original *Nixon in China* production. Within a few years of its Houston premiere, *Nixon in China* had been performed in Brooklyn, Amsterdam, Edinburgh, Bielefeld, Germany, Los Angeles, and Paris. Those casts, too, were virtually all white.

And when Adams, Sellars, and Mark Morris got together again in 2011 for the opera's premiere at the Metropolitan Opera in New York, the lead Chinese characters were once more all white. No one protested. Indeed, the *New York Times*'s lead classical music critic, Anthony Tommasini, singled out one of those white *Nixon in China* singers, Robert Brubaker, for capturing Chairman Mao's "authoritarian defiance and rapacious self-indulgence."[10] Today, as we saw earlier, Tommasini lambastes classical music for its racism; in 2011, he did not mention Brubaker's race.

That blindness to whitewashing continued into 2020. In its review of the Scottish Opera's *Nixon in China*, *The Guardian*, hardly a conservative mouthpiece, praised both Mark Le Brocq as Chairman Mao and Nicholas Lester as Zhou Enlai.[11]

A norm against "whitewashing" would make *Nixon in China* almost impossible to stage in the West, an anonymous source told the *Telegraph*. Finding enough Asian singers of requisite quality to fill the large roster of Chinese characters "in a country the other side of the world from China" would be "just too difficult."[12]

Nixon in China's creators would presumably have an interest in defending their work and its production history against a potentially fatal new casting restriction. They are keeping out of the fray, however. When I asked John Adams if he thinks that it is problematic to cast a white tenor as Mao Zedong, he declined to comment. Peter Sellars also refused comment, via an assistant.

And so it is left to the advocacy group BEATS to explain the nuances of yellowface and whitewashing. Why is it acceptable for a black singer to sing Nixon but not acceptable for a white singer to sing Mao or Zhou Enlai? I asked. The answer turns on whether a singer's skin color helps or hurts a political agenda.

"Casting a black singer (or other Artist of Colour: AoC) as a white historical personage can be progressive," the group responded, "as it works to balance out the historical and current exclusion of AoCs on stage, and the discrimination they have experienced, and continue to experience." But "casting a white actor in a specifically non-white role, such as a Chinese historical personage, is regressive, as it perpetuates the exclusion of ESEAs (East & South-East Asians) from the stage."[13]

But no singer is presently "excluded" from roles because of his race. Asians and blacks have sung leading white characters in Mozart, Rossini, Berlioz, Bizet, Verdi, Puccini, Wagner, and Offenbach in the world's major opera houses. If there are fewer Asian singers on opera stages than in the orchestra pit, that is because Asian involvement with Western classical music began with the string instruments. But training in Western opera techniques is catching up fast.

Staying current with "progressive" casting rules will require full-time study. Would it be acceptable for a black singer to play a Chinese character such as Mao? I asked BEATS. Not really. Here "pan-Asian casting" would be recommended. So artists of color may bump whites from white roles but different categories of AoCs should enjoy monopolies over their respective identity-defined characters.

For an organization intent on policing identity boundaries in art, BEATS is remarkably lax in defining those boundaries. A Korean or Japanese singer may perform Mao or Zhou Enlai, the advocacy group said in response to a further question—notwithstanding the large differences in culture and history between the Chinese, Koreans, and the Japanese.

In fact, all the groups that BEATS regards as interchangeable for the purpose of casting are wildly heterogeneous. Individuals from the following countries may substitute for each other in roles written for any particular nationality: "Brunei, Burma, Cambodia, China, East Timor, Hong Kong, Indonesia, Japan, Laos, Macau, Malaysia, Mongolia, North Korea, Philippines, Singapore, South Korea, Taiwan, Thailand, Vietnam and their diasporas."[14] Never mind that many of these peoples spent millennia subjugating and colonizing each other. Today, their most important characteristic is that they are not white, so someone from Brunei may play a Chinese Communist leader even though Brunei had almost no connection with either Imperial or Communist China. Someone from Brunei could also sing Madama Butterfly, even though Japan invaded and occupied Brunei during World War II. This conflation of distinct identities under one "Asian" umbrella is little different from the "Orientalist" tropes decried by Edward Said and his epigones.

BEATS's tolerance for Asian theatrical fungibility is already out-of-date, however. In April 2022, Filipino actors and activists protested a Hong Kong–made television series for casting a Chinese Canadian actress as a Filipino housemaid. "An actor who performs in brownface is suggesting that she can portray the inner character of a Filipina domestic worker by embodying her, by mimicking her skin color or speech patterns or hair texture," a professor who studies race and politics at a Hong Kong university told the *New York Times*.[15] Well, yes, such external trappings *are* part of the transformation that is acting. Thus do the enemies of the imagination worm their way into every artistic endeavor.

To see the future of the diversity crusade in the arts, one must look to the United States where casting directors henceforth will need a spectrometer to decide if a performer is sufficiently "colored" to fill a role.

At the moment when the Scottish Opera was self-destructing, *In the Heights*, a screen adaptation of Lin-Manuel Miranda's Broadway musical, landed in American movie theatres. It, too, had an immaculately progressive creative team, with Miranda writing the screenplay and Jon Chu directing. The movie, about New York's Dominican community, which is concentrated in Manhattan's Washington Heights, received generally favorable press.

Miranda's diversity credentials would seem unassailable, given his portrayal of the Founding Fathers as rap-emitting black and Hispanic citizens in the musical *Hamilton*. *In the Heights* used an all-Hispanic cast, thus obeying the rule that whites may not play people of color. But the diversity racket has moved beyond such blunt categories. One critic complained that the actors in *In the Heights* were not dark-skinned enough,[16] even though the proportion of dark-skinned actors among the lead characters—16 percent—matches the racial demographics of Washington Heights.[17]

A new offence was born, which may be dubbed "brownwashing." Miranda fell on his sword immediately. "In trying to paint a mosaic of this community, we fell short," he tweeted. "I'm truly sorry. I'm learning from the feedback, I thank you for raising it . . . I promise to do better in my future projects, and I'm dedicated to the learning and evolving we all have to do to make sure we are honoring our diverse and vibrant community."[18]

Every time arts leaders and institutions cave to racial pressure, they deal creativity another blow. The dumb literalism of today's censors is a frontal assault on the human imagination, which frees us from the constraints of time, place, and the boundaries of our own subjectivity. One of drama's most mesmerizing set pieces is an onstage actor putting on his makeup and costume, effacing one identity and taking on another right before our eyes. Ovid's *Metamorphoses* is a classic of erotic literature because transforming oneself into another being is an act of godlike power and seduction, whether of an amorous target or of an audience.

The next step in imaginative emasculation is obvious: only elderly actors can play King Lear, only hunchbacks can sing Rigoletto or play King Richard III, only fat people can play or sing Falstaff, since using stage makeup and body suits to transform non-old, non-handicapped, and non-fat actors into those roles represents ageism, fat-shaming, and ableism. Certainly no straight actor will ever be able to play a gay character, as Sean Penn has observed.[19] But then again, maybe only Falstaff should be able to play Falstaff, since surely between a fat actor and Falstaff himself there are significant differences of identity. The Argentinian author Jorge Luis Borges, who explored the uncertain boundary between fiction and reality, could have figured this puzzler out, but not the rest of us.

Ultimately, theatre itself may have to be segregated, since to claim that a white audience can identify with a black-themed work is another form of cultural appropriation. A recent play, lauded twice by the *New York Times*, asked white audience members to leave the theatre before the play's conclusion so that black attendees could experience undisturbed racial solidarity. (One account implies that this mandate was obeyed.[20])

Imaginative empathy—the ability to project oneself into someone else's shoes—has been a key to expanding liberty and toleration. The arts have played a crucial role in widening human understanding. Now, however, they are leading the way back into a world of tribal barriers and stunted experience.

Chapter Seven

THE REVOLUTION COMES TO JUILLIARD

In the fall of 2020, students at the Juilliard School staged a drama of their own oppression designed to further carve the artistic world into racial fiefdoms.

The school's administration had all but handed them their script. The Drama Division had just announced a series of "community meetings" to address "Equity, Diversity, Inclusion, and Belonging (EDIB) issues."[1] The school's growing cadre of diversity bureaucrats would discuss Juilliard's "anti-racism work." The head of the Center for Racial Healing would give a presentation. Workshops would address such topics as "race in rehearsal" and "voice and speech and race."[2] NYU theater professor Michael McElroy, one of the school's two external diversity consultants, would offer a three-day seminar in black musical culture.

These Drama Division meetings were part of Juilliard's broader effort to bring race into all its activities, including music and dance. Damian Woetzel, former principal dancer with the New York City Ballet, became Juilliard's president in July 2018 and proceeded to put increasing bureaucratic clout behind the concept that Juilliard has a racism problem. The school added diversity curricula and diversity audition requirements. It beefed up its system for reporting bias incidents. It mandated diversity workshops for faculty and students.

Those efforts picked up steam after the death of George Floyd. Within a week, Woetzel and the EDIB taskforce had sent out three schoolwide emails on the "work" Juilliard still needed to do to become an "anti-racist community."[3] The school sponsored a blacks-only "healing" space. It recommended that students and faculty read the books of Ta-Nehisi Coates, Robin DiAngelo, Ibram X. Kendi, and Michelle Alexander to understand systemic racism.

On June 11, 2020, Juilliard's provost, Ara Guzelimian, circulated a student petition. Lending an administration email account to a student communiqué violated school protocol, but the Juilliard Student Congress's "Call to Action" was important enough to justify the exception, Guzelimian explained in his cover letter.[4]

The Call to Action charged Juilliard with "systemic injustice." It demanded an end to the school's "almost completely Eurocentric" faculty, curriculum, and performances and a "complete in-person season featuring the works of BIPOC [Black, Indigenous, and People of Color] artists." It called on Juilliard to create #BreonnaTaylor and #George-Floyd scholarships in music, drama, and dance.

In early August 2020, the school's black drama students issued their own Letter of Demands. The Drama Division student body is roughly 50 percent black.[5] That percentage is unlikely to have arisen spontaneously. Blacks are 13 percent of the national population, and there is no indication that they disproportionately study drama in high school and college. Yet the black drama students' letter portrayed the Drama Division as nearly lethally bigoted. Its "racist environment is hazardous to BIPOC students' bodies," the letter charged. "Some students are silenced, broken, and limited by racism within the Drama Division . . . [They] have to endure harm and violence [and] sacrifice their physical and mental health every day in this institution."

It was against this backdrop of increasing racial hysteria that Michael McElroy's three-day "Roots to Rep" drama workshop was planned to take place. The workshop would combine history, research, and music to explore the journey of black people in this country, McElroy explained, with a specific emphasis on the way "the Negro spiritual . . . is the foundation of so many musical genres today." McElroy, who is himself black, asked students to prepare for the workshop by writing a paragraph about a key event in the history of black enslavement. The president of Juilliard's Black Student Union, Marion Grey, saw this requirement as identity-threatening, but she kept her objections to herself, she told *American Theater*, in order to test whether the school would "protect" her in the face of such a racial assault.[6] (A better reason for keeping her complaint quiet was that it was unhinged, even for the racial hothouse of Juilliard's Drama Division.)

On the workshop's first day, McElroy offered a trigger warning that the forthcoming audio exercise contained the "N word." Students could leave the Zoom session any time they wanted, McElroy said. The lesson began with an auditory recreation of the African slave trade. A march through the jungle was followed by a slave auction, with the auctioneer extolling a "fine Black pearl" who would raise her owner "a fine litter of pickaninnies." During this soundscape, the black students were texting each other about how "utterly broken" they were by the exercise, according to Grey, while white students and faculty, as well as a few black students, participated in the workshop without protest. Afterward, the white students recounted how moving the experience had been.

Grey then Zoomed an impassioned remonstrance about cultural appropriation and trauma. "I was like, 'There are wounds here, and you don't get to just explore someone's history and culture with them—that is earned, you don't just get that,'" she told the class, according to *American Theater*.

McElroy had offered this workshop numerous times before without provoking a similar meltdown. The slave-auction dialogue was taken from the widely aired miniseries *Roots*. The historical record contains no indication that *Roots* generated trauma when it was released in 1977. But Juilliard immediately terminated McElroy's workshop and went into crisis mode. The president and provost met with Grey and her black peers. The administration launched new investigations of racial issues. Grey was not impressed. Despite getting an audience with the school's top leadership, she did not feel "truly supported," she told *American Theater*. She was the victim of a "culture of silencing." Apparently Grey and her fellow students could not provide actual examples of such silencing, but that inability only proves how serious the silencing is. "Asking us the question, 'When have you felt silenced?' does not mean you will get an answer, especially when you're not in the practice of making space for the student's voice," she said.

After spurning months of administrative outreach, Grey ratcheted up the pressure. On April 21, 2021, she released a teary video (the current version of which has been shortened) decrying the racism of what she called "Slavery Saturday." "It's maddening to have your humanity so disrespected, to have something done to you that is so wrong. It is so wrong," she told the camera.[7] A petition accompanying the video demanded the decolonization of the Drama Division and the hiring of an outside consultant to analyze the "inequitable, anti-black, and racist structures and systems that are built into the architecture of the Juilliard culture." Grey claimed to be frightened that Juilliard would retaliate against her. "It's terrifying to put myself on the line but I know my worth. I know that a wrong has been done to me."

The chance that Juilliard would offer any opposition to Grey's video, much less retaliate against her for posting it, was zero. Two days after the video was released, Woetzel sent out a schoolwide email. He adopted every trope of threat and injury used by the black students: "I want to state unequivocally that this workshop was ill-conceived and should not have occurred in the manner that it did. I extend a heartfelt apology to the individuals who have been adversely affected by it." Tackling difficult topics is a responsibility of artists, Woetzel said, but Juilliard must do so "in a manner that respects and protects the members of our community." Woetzel called the auditory experience of enslavement "extremely distressing and problematic."[8]

Woetzel was implicitly accusing McElroy of putting Juilliard's black students at risk through an "ill-conceived" historical recreation. The school did not respond to an inquiry asking whether Woetzel had sought McElroy's perspective before calling his presentation "ill-conceived."[9] The school also refused to spell out what exactly was "problematic" about the exercise or what criteria Juilliard would use in the future to ensure that pedagogy "protects members of [the] community." (McElroy declined to be interviewed.)

The Dean of the Drama Division, Evan Yionoulis, apologized for the workshop, too, in an email appended to Woetzel's own. The workshop never should have happened, Yionoulis wrote, throwing McElroy under the bus as decisively as Woetzel had done. Yionoulis felt "remorse" for engaging McElroy and for not stopping the exercise once it was in progress, though it is not clear how the school could have known to do so. Yionoulis lamented the "trauma" caused by the workshop without explaining what that trauma was. The school will continue to try to "facilitate healing," Yionoulis said, but it also recognizes that it "cannot fully change the impact of what happened, nor . . . erase all that was experienced in that moment."

The Drama Division's response to the students' protests betrays the division's very reason for being. Their complaints rest on notions about history and dramatic art so crabbed that they would destroy freedom of imagination entirely if they were widely implemented. Grey would erect gatekeepers around historical truths. Favored victim groups could expound on that history at will; others would need to "earn" permission to do so. It matters not that any given historical presentation is accurate; it may enter the public arena only if it does not offend the feelings of those who claim to be oppressed by its recollection.

But Grey and her peers notwithstanding, there are no barricades in historical study. Anyone with a commitment to the ideal of historical truth may explore whatever aspect of the past he chooses. Whites don't get to bar blacks from studying "white" history, and they don't need permission from blacks to study "black" history. A Japanese historian does not need to "earn" the right to research the Habsburg Empire; an Italian may become an expert on the Incas. To string "Do Not Enter" signs around territories in the past will smother human knowledge.

The idea that the recreation of the auction violated Juilliard's duty to "protect" its students would rule out a large portion of dramatic art. Many American stage classics, whether *Long Day's Journey into Night*, *Death of a Salesman*, or *Who's Afraid of Virginia Woolf*, would be off limits, lest they "retraumatize" students from dysfunctional families. Francis Poulenc's opera *Dialogues of the Carmelites* should not be performed, lest those with aristocratic or monastic ancestors be shaken. Aristotle argued that tragedy provides catharsis through the reenactment and transcendence of suffering. But under Juilliard's definition, there should be no passion plays because they would retraumatize Christians.

The Left claims that American history teaching underplays slavery and other civil rights violations in favor of a triumphalist story of white supremacy. This claim is ludicrous. There is almost no nonracialized political history taught today, much less a whitewashed narrative of the City on the Hill. The focus is on marginalized groups and their mistreatment by white males. But if it were true that students are being kept in ignorance about America's past betrayals of its democratic ideals, a visceral recreation of enslavement would seem an ideal way to pierce that ignorance.

It is taboo to question claims of racism-inflicted disability, since such a challenge denies someone his subjective "truth." When it comes to race, subjective truth is now the only allowable truth. Nevertheless, the alleged psychic catastrophe occasioned by the audio recreation of the slave auction strains credulity.

The experience of slavery is as remote from Juilliard's black students as it is from Juilliard's white students. Neither group has any realistic expectations of being subjected to such treatment. Imaginative empathy is a good trait for drama students, but so are emotional distance and objectivity. How broad must the protective cone be? Should museums shut down displays of slave shackles and whips? If the alleged emotional devastation here is taken at face value, it is time to retire the strained conceit of "white fragility" and replace it with "black fragility." (Diversity consultant Robin DiAngelo coined the former term in 2011 to describe what she viewed as whites' hysterical reaction when confronted with their supposed racism, a hysteria manifest in defensive invocations of such allegedly white supremacist concepts as color-blindness, individualism, and objectivity.)

The black drama students' claim of being daily "broken" by the "harm and violence" they are forced to endure at Juilliard is equally unpersuasive. There are no racists at Juilliard, and the school's leaders should say so. No one—it should not need stating—is engaged in violence against black students. To the contrary, Juilliard is filled with liberal, well-meaning adults who want all their pupils to succeed. Far from being oppressed, all of Juilliard's drama students are fantastically privileged compared to actors in bygone centuries who picked up their thespian skills rattling around with a flea-bitten vaudeville or commedia dell'arte troupe.

The need to assert victimization at the hands of Western civilization is all-consuming, however. It has led Juilliard's drama students to opt for ignorance rather than knowledge and identity rather than imaginative freedom. Their August 2020 demands called for the elimination of all pedagogy that seeks to enhance an actor's ability to transcend his particular identity. "'Color-blind' casting" (scare quotes in the original) must end, replaced by "color conscious casting practices." No student of color should "be forced to leave behind their racial/ethnic identity when playing a role." If a BIPOC student is cast in a non-BIPOC role, the director must justify that choice and reflect that justification throughout the production. The school should not "center" the General American Dialect in its speech and voice classes; doing so is "discriminatory."

Leave aside for a moment the implications of these demands for dramatic art. They are self-constricting as well. At present, black actors have a monopoly on black roles, since no director today would think of casting a white actor as a black character, but blacks can also play white roles, as we saw with Scottish Opera's *Nixon in China*. Now, however, per the Juilliard students, if a black actor plays a traditionally white character, it must be as a black and the rest of the production must foreground that black identity. The musical *Hamilton* took this tack, but such color-focused dramaturgy would outlast its welcome in Shakespeare's history plays, say, where the idea of a hip-hop *Henry V* or *Richard III* would quickly grow stale.

The essence of the actor's art is the ability to embody a life radically different from his own and, in so doing, to take the audience outside of itself as well. It is not an erasure of an actor's self to learn the General American Dialect; that neutral voicing is merely the launching ground for a range of imaginative possibilities. Peter Francis James's kaleidoscopic reading of *Native Son* on Audible uses the General American Dialect for the narrative voice but adopts a stunning range of accents for the characters, each one providing insight into the novel's fatal drama. But for today's black activists, their identity is their greatest power and their greatest weapon, and so anything that seeks to subsume racial identity into something more abstract must be beaten back.

The August 2020 demands complained that BIPOC students have "few if any meaningful and authentic performance opportunities" because the curriculum is "disproportionately Eurocentric." "Authenticity" is now defined by whether a role conforms to an actor's skin color, not by the human truth an actor may attain within it. The demands do not tell us what ratio of "Eurocentric" to "non-Eurocentric" plays constitutes "disproportionality." The tradition of performing theatrical scripts written by individual playwrights is almost exclusively a Western phenomenon. African drama was ritualistic and participatory; there was little distinction between the dramatic players and the audience; the rituals were passed down orally, not via writing. So whatever Juilliard's ratio of "Eurocentric" scripts to "non-Eurocentric" scripts, it would likely not be disproportionate to the actual distribution of written plays in our cultural inheritance.

The Juilliard students use a different measure of proportionality, however: their own representation in the student body. Thus do admissions quotas everywhere determine the future curriculum.

Racial identity is also the key to evading color-blind behavioral standards. The drama students demand that every black student on probation for missing or being late to class be taken off probation and his record wiped clean, since Juilliard's attendance policies have a disparate impact on black students. Any white students on probation for missing class will stay under discipline. Juilliard's self-described "rigorous" class schedule is "deeply rooted in capitalist and white supremacist hegemony," according to the students. That schedule, too, should change to "prioritize the physical and mental health needs of the student body."

Black drama students have been pushing back on the school's classical tradition for the past ten years, according to a school observer. A drama-division graduate expressed a typical view. His "light" had been extinguished at Juilliard by having to study "about how great white authors are," he told *American Theater*.[10] This self-pity would have astonished the division's early leaders. James Houghton, a former director of the drama school, expressed his goals for the program: "I want to see actors and playwrights coming out of this school with an absolute passion and joy connected to the craft of theater-making."[11] That black students should feel oppressed by studying some of the greatest drama ever written shows how conclusively Juilliard has failed to articulate what were once its core values.

Juilliard's ferment is nothing compared with the theater world as a whole, however. During 2020's George Floyd riots, a manifesto appeared online: "We See You White American Theater" (We See You W.A.T.). Rambling and repetitious, the document justified its redundancies as a "reflection of the significance [of those repeated demands] to the constituents" and as "also due to the interdependent functioning of the theatrical ecosystem." Its inconsistent "tones and formatting styles" were designed to "retain our orality," a technique "designed to hold the multiplicity and urgency we lay claim to given the persistent devaluation of our voices." We See You W.A.T. insisted that "radical change on both cultural and economic fronts" was required to eradicate white supremacy.[12]

We See You W.A.T. contained the usual accusations of vicious mistreatment lodged against an immaculately progressive industry: "We have watched you exploit us, shame us, diminish us, and exclude us."

As with the Juilliard demands, no examples of such shaming and exclusion were provided. But the manifesto's peroration did attain a dramatic tension that had eluded the Juilliard students:

> We see you . . . you are all a part of this house of cards built on
> white fragility and supremacy. And this is a house that will not
> stand.
>
> This ends TODAY.
>
> We are about to introduce you . . . to YOURSELF.

That final sentence may have been puzzling, but the theater world
reeled anyway. Regional theaters have been falling all over themselves
trying to comply with the usual quota demands: casts, directors, and
artistic staff must be over 50 percent minority, according to the online
manifesto. There have been purges. In Philadelphia, the nonprofit
PlayPenn, which supports the development of new work, fired its associate artistic director after receiving allegations that the company
"was not meeting community members' expectations for racial and cultural competence," reported the *New York Times* in September 2020.[13]
In Georgia, the Serenbe Playhouse laid off its entire staff following allegations of racism.[14]

We See You W.A.T. demanded that half of Broadway shows should be
plays "written by, for and about BIPOC." Every new play scheduled for
the 2021–2022 Broadway season was by a black author. We See You
W.A.T. demanded that half of Broadway theaters should be renamed
after artists of color and that theaters forswear advertising in any press
outlet where the reporters and critics are less than 50 percent POC.
Those two demands have been slower to yield results.

One president of a regional theater describes the present moment.
She is self-consciously "bean-counting, trying to hit racial quotas with
plays and actors," even though the community the theater serves is
overwhelmingly white.[15] The theater's young employees "get all het up"
over any diversity shortcoming. "Why did you use a white this or a

white that?" they complain. The president asked the theater's financial chief if he could name one "cisgender" white male director the company had hired over the last three years. There were none. On Broadway there have been no straight white guys running things for years, the president observes. Gay white guys will be the next target.

This theater veteran knows forty to fifty theater professionals who have left the profession or are about to do so, "so toxic" has the environment become, in her words. Any alternative perspective or criticism becomes: "You do not respect us." If a voice coach observes that a student's voice is not coming from his core, the student will respond: "That is because I don't feel comfortable in class with you."

An arts consultant reports the "unspoken fear" of theater leaders: they will put on quota-filling plays, and no one will come. "I have talked to long time audience members who have no interest in seeing much of this new work," the main purpose of which is to indict white America, the consultant says.[16]

The Black Lives Matter movement in the arts is only nominally about "inclusion." In fact, it is about exclusion and the power that has motivated every revolutionary mob: the power of negation, the power to tear things down. This purportedly "inclusive" movement will result in a world of constricted imaginative possibility and stunted human growth.

A leader in the arts world, told of Juilliard's travails, observed: "This is a crucial time to stand up and call out what is an overly emotional and irrational attack on the best of what humanity has to offer."[17]

He would not allow me to reveal his name or affiliation.

Chapter Eight

THE SWAMPING OF SWAN LAKE

In late 2020, the *New York Times* published another installment in its running tally of alleged racism in the high arts, accusing the Staatsballett Berlin (Berlin State Ballet) not of treating a black ballerina differently because of the color of her skin, but of treating her *the same* as the white ballerinas. The search for racism requires just such rhetorical nimbleness.

Since the nineteenth century, dancers in a corps de ballet have applied white body paint in works, such as *Giselle* or *Les Sylphides*, that feature a supernatural element. The intent was to create an impression of ghostly creatures from beyond the grave who might doom any red-blooded prince who crosses them. The use of white makeup was not a statement about white supremacy: there were virtually no black dancers in Russian or Parisian ballet troupes at the time, against which a statement about skin color might be made. If one is looking for slurs, the body paint could be seen as anti-white, in its association of whiteness with death.

In 2018, the Staatsballett Berlin mounted *Swan Lake*, another ballet where white body paint has traditionally been used—in this case to increase the illusion that the dancers are swans. One of the company's ballet mistresses told the company's one black dancer, Chloé Lopes Gomes, to use the paint as well. Gomes says she told the ballet mistress, "I'll never look white," to which the mistress responded: "Well, you will have to put on more than the other girls."[1]

Two years after the fact, this incident dominated the front page of the *Times* arts section and was flagged on the front page of the paper itself—it was that important. The Staatsballett Berlin issued a groveling apology, taking responsibility for white society's alleged "structural racism." The company has promised to hire the usual phalanx of diversity trainers to provide mandatory anti-racism workshops. The organization will also examine its repertory for "outdated and discriminatory ways of performing" and will "re-evaluate" its "longstanding traditions," it says.[2]

The accusations and the self-prostration would have been the same had the scenario been flipped. If the ballet mistress had told Lopes Gomes: "Don't bother with the body paint. You're too black. It will never work," this, too, would have been characterized as discrimination. Racism today is an unfalsifiable proposition governed by the principle "heads I win, tails you lose."

Naturally, Lopes Gomes alleged another instance of bias: her contract was not renewed for the coming season. Never mind that eleven of her fellow dancers—all white—were also let go. If a white person is dismissed, not hired, or not promoted, it is assumed to be for cause. Under the logic of disparate impact, however, if a black person suffers a negative employment outcome, the only reason must be racism, as we saw in the Overview. Lopes Gomes offered no explanation for how her case differed from those of her eleven colleagues.

Until recently, classical ballet had been largely spared the revisionist destruction that hit the opera and theater stages years ago. Audiences could still see *Swan Lake* and *La Bayadère* as their choreographers and composers intended, with all the conventions and costumes of nineteenth-century fairy tale intact. To be sure, feminists have long agitated against the ethereal body type championed by choreographer George Balanchine. But the adolescent politicizing that has been inflicted on defenseless operas had been mostly absent from the ballet stage. That immunity is ending. Expect to see classical ballets wrenched awkwardly into dumb shows about social justice.

If, that is, classical ballet is even allowed to continue. A leading English dance conservatory has issued the fatal judgement: classical ballet is, in the words of the school's head of undergraduate studies, "essentially an elitist form . . . built around particular white European ideas and body shapes."[3] Accordingly, in July 2022, the Northern School of Contemporary Dance in Leeds dropped ballet from its entrance auditions in the hope of increasing student diversity. For now, ballet will still be taught within the school, but it is likely under a death sentence. The Northern School of Contemporary Dance is in the process of decolonizing its curriculum, as it puts it, and ballet offends too many progressive norms to survive intact. Besides its white European roots, ballet accentuates masculine and feminine ideals, as embodied in its choreography and costuming: females dance in toe shoes (*en pointe*) while male dancers, shod in flat ballet slippers, lift the ballerinas and perform the most gravity-defying leaps (think: Rudolph Nureyev and Mikhail Baryshnikov). Ballet's hyper-masculinity and hyper-femininity are a large part of the art form's seductiveness but such sex differentiation is a disaster from a gender-fluid point of view.

The progressive denial of biological reality will be tested if, as part of the fight against oppressive gender stereotypes, female dancers try to hold male dancers over their heads the same way male dancers hold ballerinas. Perhaps the trans phenomenon will come to the rescue and allow ballet companies to claim that their "female" dancers lift male dancers with as much ease as the reverse.

The Leeds analysis will spread. And when the inevitable attacks on other ballet companies come, their leaders will fail to defend their art form, just as classical music leaders have failed to defend theirs. Referring to the *Swan Lake* body paint controversy, a former director of the Paris Opera Ballet rejected the aesthetic justification for artistic conventions. To defend an artistic tradition (such as white body paint) on the ground that it is seeking a stage illusion is, in his words as paraphrased by the *Times*, "not a valid argument in a context in which one race had oppressed another."[4] But classical ballet has nothing to do with racial oppression; such an idea was simply not what its creators were trying to express. If the relevant "context" for all European art is the West's alleged centuries-long assertion of white supremacy, then every Western artistic tradition must be overthrown, since there was never a moment when that "context" was allegedly not in play. (The inter- and intra-racial brutality, the lethal misogyny and homophobia of the Left's favored victim groups have no such cancel power over those groups' artistic output, of course.)

Narcissism is the operative trait of today's victims, who think that everything is about them. It is not. Identity politics projects its obsessions onto an aesthetic realm that in many cases is alien to our worldview. Visual and kinetic uniformity in a corps de ballet was an aesthetic ideal; it had nothing to do with race. Yet that uniformity must now fall so that no individual ballet dancer feels that her precious diversity currency is devalued.

Contaminating our artistic inheritance with the poison of identity politics is no way to build new audiences or strengthen our traditions. It merely gives ignorant young people another reason to reject something precious and sublime.

Chapter Nine

THE DEMISE
OF THE DOCENT

Disparate impact analysis treats any institution in which the racial demographics do not match the population at large as presumptively racist. Entire traditions, whether in the humanities, music, or scientific discovery, have been reduced to one fatal characteristic: whiteness. And now the anti-white crusade is targeting a key feature of American exceptionalism: the spirit of philanthropy and volunteerism.

In 2012, the Art Institute of Chicago posted a tribute to its volunteer museum educators. "Our docents are incredible," read the Facebook post. "'To walk through the galleries and see children, led by docents, jumping up and raising their hands to talk is to see the work of the museum at its best,'" the entry continued, quoting then–Institute Director Douglas Druick.[1]

At that time, the Art Institute was still seeking to expand its docent corps. "We Want You! (To Become a Docent)," announced a contemporaneous article in the museum's newsletter. The article emphasized the program's rigor: becoming a docent "was no small task," the museum advised, involving a competitive admissions process and written, supervised research on the museum's collections.

Less than a decade later, in September 2021, the Art Institute shut down its docent program entirely and told its participants that they would no longer be allowed to serve the Institute in a volunteer capacity. Henceforth, six salaried, part-time employees would replace the more than eighty unpaid educators.[2] The docents were told to clean out their lockers; as a consolation prize, they were offered a two-year complimentary membership to the museum.[3]

Had the docents been delivering subpar performances? Had the Institute discovered an incurable flaw in their training? No, it had noticed that they were overwhelmingly white. And that, in 2021, constituted a sin almost beyond redemption, whether found in an individual or in an institution.

The Art Institute of Chicago is not the first museum to turn on its docent program. But it is the most consequential. The Institute's docent saga is a case study in what happens when museums and other cultural organizations declare their mission to be anti-racism. The final result, if unchecked, will be the cancellation of a civilization.

Chicago's Art Institute, founded in 1879 as both a museum and an art school, emerged from the post–Civil War wave of museum-building. Successful businessmen from San Francisco to Boston created grand receptacles for European art in the spirit of democratic elitism, believing that history's masterpieces should be available to all. The Institute's original holdings consisted almost entirely of plaster casts of Greek and Roman sculpture, reflecting the centuries-long view that the classical world represented the pinnacle of artistic achievement in the West. Soon, however, Chicago's Gilded Age benefactors began donating a more sweeping range of works, starting with a bequest of forty-four predominantly Barbizon School oil paintings from the widow of Henry Field, brother of the Marshall Field & Company founder. More than four dozen classics of Impressionism and Postimpressionism came the Institute's way in 1925 and 1926. Non-Western traditions started filling out the collections as well; the largest gift in the Institute's history, from civic leader Martin Ryerson in 1933, included Asian art among Old Master paintings, textiles, and decorative arts.

Philanthropists underwrote the nearly continuous expansions of the Institute's 1893 Beaux-Arts building on Michigan Avenue to accommodate the growing holdings. Today, the Institute constitutes one of the finest repositories of global art on the American continent; one small corridor, containing exquisite pastel portraits by Martin Quentin de la Tour, Chardin, and other ancien régime artists, alone warrants a visit.

The Institute's docent program grew out of a particularly fertile period in American volunteerism: the 1950s, which saw the creation of hundreds of new civic associations, many organized and run by women. In 1951, a group of public-minded women from Chicago and its suburbs offered to help the Institute raise capital during an emergency-fund drive; they were so successful that the museum incorporated their organization into its administrative structure.[4] The newly created Woman's Board next tackled children's art education. The board proposed a corps of volunteer educators, despite the prevailing view in the museum world that only professionals should instruct the public, including children, about art. Ironically, it would be the head of the Woman's Board who would deliver the docents' death sentence seventy years later.

Barbara Wriston, sister of Citibank Chairman Walter Wriston, created the first docent curriculum in 1961. She insisted on "standards," she later said.[5] Students attended curatorial lectures, read widely in the museum's library, and wrote papers proposing ways to communicate art-historical concepts to children. The eighteen-month program, run with "military" discipline, according to an inaugural trainee, was the virtual equivalent of an MFA; graduates followed up with ongoing study of art history and pedagogy.

The question of "inclusion" arose early. By the end of the 1960s, the Institute's staff was grappling with how to make the museum more "accessible" to Chicago's poor communities.[6] The museum began a series of targeted outreach efforts, such as Spanish-language programming and an urban professionals' group to serve as ambassadors to black neighborhoods. The Woman's Board provided framed reproductions of the Institute's art, carefully chosen for diversity, to all Chicago public and parochial schools, along with resources for teachers.

The museum's most important outreach was simply the docent tours themselves, which brought thousands of public-school students into the museum to experience its wonders. Though the selection of the docents was color-blind, docent training was expanded to include months of diversity awareness on the assumption that black and Hispanic children required a special method of delivery and approach to art. The docents formed their own diversity and inclusion committee and presented activism-themed lectures in the pitch for "relevance."

Meantime, universities had started "problematizing" art museums and their contents as a means through which white males maintain their alleged privilege. In 1992, the dean of the Institute's affiliated art school wrote that art raises questions about "who gets to write, to speak, . . . to frame and interpret reality, [and] to position their text as part of the cultural mastertext."[7] Academic theorists cast museums as tools of exclusion and art as a mask for power. It took a while for this demystifying reflex to migrate from academia into the very bloodstream of art museums, but by the second decade of the new century, curators and museum directors nationwide had become fluent in deconstructive rhetoric, which they directed at their own institutions. The death of George Floyd only accelerated the trend.

The Art Institute is emblematic of this conversion, by which the impulse to share culture becomes culpable and tainted by whiteness. In good show-trial fashion, Art Institute leaders confess to the "biases and inequities of [their] history and the present." They are particularly exercised by the failure of their predecessors to embrace Black Lives Matter values. "Firmly rooted in Eurocentric tradition, the founding objectives of our institutional history did not consider gender, ethnic, and racial equity," laments the Art Institute's website. But no museum founder considered "gender, ethnic, and racial equity," beyond a generalized aim to make beauty widely available to a democratic citizenry.

Not good enough. Today's Art Institute accuses itself of sins of commission, not just of omission. The museum has long "centered certain stories while marginalizing and suppressing others."[8] The Institute, in this telling, did not just focus initially on those artists and traditions that its founders knew best and that they viewed as central to America's cultural legacy; it actively sought to silence other artists and traditions out of a racist, colonialist impulse. Despite the Institute's assertions, there is no evidence of such malign intent on the part of the founders or their successors.

The artists' names carved across the exterior of the Institute's original building are an especially fertile source of self-flagellation. The thirty-five individuals are part of a Who's Who of Western art and architecture, starting with Praxiteles and Phidias from classical Greek times, proceeding through the early and high Renaissance (including Fra Angelico, Brunelleschi, Ghiberti, da Vinci, Michelangelo, and Veronese) and into the Baroque (Rubens, Van Dyck, Velázquez, and Rembrandt). The roll call extends into the eighteenth century (Reynolds and Gainsborough) and ends with early-nineteenth-century Romanticism (Turner).

No such list can be exhaustive, and one can always quibble with the choice of this, rather than that, potential member. These thirty-five creators are nevertheless justifiably nominated as paragons of human achievement, each having broken into unexplored realms of representation. Yet if landmark preservation laws allowed, the Institute would have sandblasted the names off its entablature by now. The frieze is an "unsustainable formulation," current Art Institute Director James Rondeau said during a 2019 lecture, "in the context of our mission today."[9] Why? Because it presents "exclusively white Western European male artists." (In his zeal to apologize for the founders' "profoundly limited" art-historical aspirations, Rondeau overlooked the ninth-century Japanese court painter Kose Kanaoka, who also occupies a place on the frieze.) The museum's equity statement amplifies Rondeau's dissatisfaction: "The omission of artists of color, especially Black artists, as well as female, Indigenous, and non-Western artists, is glaring."

Only someone with an adolescent approach to reality would reduce, say, Giotto, Dürer, and Murillo (also members of the frieze), to the common denominator of "whiteness" and "maleness"—preposterously unilluminating categories for artists with such different styles and sensibilities. The absence of any historical awareness on the part of frieze critics is equally "glaring," to borrow a phrase, especially coming from an art museum. There were no known indigenous artists whom the Institute's founders could have or should have memorialized; American Indian art was anonymous, produced within a collective-craft tradition.

As for black and female artists, whom do the Institute's equity enforcers think the 1893 frieze should have included? There were a few pre-twentieth-century black painters, and their works deserve wider exposure. Henry Ossawa Tanner's Portrait of the Artist's Mother (1897), for example, is a haunting psychological study, sharing the muted palette of Whistler and Tanner's sometime-teacher Thomas Eakins. The Institute presciently bought a religious work from the artist in 1906, notwithstanding the callous discrimination that Tanner and his contemporaries experienced. But it would be ludicrous to equate any such black artists with Botticelli, Raphael, and Titian (also commemorated on the frieze), if for no other reason than their lack of historical influence.

Female artists have been more numerous, and much effort has gone into elevating them to the creative pantheon. The Baroque painter Artemisia Gentileschi is a particular target for promotion. But however accomplished her work, only gender equity could justify inducting her into the highest ranks.

Identity, however, is now the driving force in the Art Institute's collecting practices. Rondeau bragged in his 2019 speech, delivered at the Des Moines Art Center, that the first two trans artists had now entered the collection, as well as an indigenous artist who addresses "nonbinary, gender, and sexual identity" in his work.

Sometimes such equity bingo produces a dilemma. In April 2019, the Institute purchased two nineteenth-century silk portraits embroidered by an Italian princess, Maria Isabella Albertini de Medici di Ottaiano, based on a design by a male painter. Rondeau's assistant advised him that when flogging the purchase for equity and inclusion points, he should omit the "princess" descriptor.[10] History, it seems, does not conform to contemporary moral classification schemes.

The self-abasement common in the post–George Floyd era is actually a form of self-aggrandizement. Individuals and institutions blame themselves for inequalities for which they have no responsibility in order to claim a current impact that they do not possess. The Art Institute has issued an acknowledgment of the "adverse consequences" for Chicago's black neighborhoods of its "exclusionary past." This acknowledgment is posturing. The sources of the area's problems lie elsewhere. Nothing on the outside or inside of the Institute hurt Chicago's South Side. The creation of Fragonard's surprisingly proto-Expressionist *Portrait of a Man in Costume* and its 1977 gifting to the Institute, say, stripped no one of opportunity. To claim the opposite requires believing that anything made by a white person over the last 2,000 years is implicated in the West's lapses of compassion and equal rights. By that logic, every African work in the Institute's collection must also be condemned for the genocidal tribal warfare practiced by African cultures and for the corruption that continues to depress Africa's economic development.

The Institute's "land acknowledgments,"[11] now inserted at the beginning of every public pronouncement, are equally self-aggrandizing. "Our building is located on the traditional unceded homelands of the Council of the Three Fires: the Ojibwe, Odawa, and Potawatomi Nations; this region has been a center for Indigenous people to gather, trade, and maintain kinship ties since long before our Michigan Avenue building was constructed in 1893," reads the Art Institute's Equity page. The Institute's statement implies that the three nations are still gathering on Michigan Avenue, or perhaps would do so but for the building's footprint. In fact, the tribes were long gone by the time construction began; the Institute is not responsible for their disappearance, nor is Western art.

Asserting such an impact allows the Institute and its funders to position themselves as essential to the anti-racism crusade, however—a much more exciting function than curating beauty—and now, crucially, the only way to attract foundation support. And so the Institute has rede-fined its mission. The Institute will create an "antiracist culture" in the US and internally, proclaims the museum's statement of values. That respon-sibility can never be discharged; it is "intersectional and ongoing."[12] Translation: diversity consultants may feed at our trough indefinitely.

It would be enough to preserve history's treasures and to teach vis-itors to understand those treasures' place in the evolution of human expression. An art museum's comparative advantage lies in its art-his-torical expertise, not in any supposed capacity for racial justice "work." It should be a place apart, a sanctuary for aesthetic contemplation. But cultural authority today comes from one of two sources: the assertion of victimhood or the acknowledgment that one is oneself a victimizer. It is not open to the Institute to take the first course, given the race and sex of its founders. That leaves the vigorous assertion of racial guilt as the second-best means of retaining cultural capital.

In the years leading up to the docent sacking, the Institute deepened its self-directed exorcism rituals. Upon ascending to the directorship from his position as the Art Institute's chief curator of modern and con-temporary art, Rondeau volunteered himself for a three-day training in how to dismantle the systems of racism that hold back "ALAANA" (Af-rican, Latinx, Asian, Arab, and Native American) individuals in the arts; Rondeau labeled the pedagogy "cathartic," "eye-opening," and "deeply moving."[13] The museum's senior staff was put through the same ca-tharsis. The Institute hired an equity consultant to assess its "structural and systemic issues of identity." Hundreds of staff took off two days of work for another "incredibly powerful" (in Rondeau's words) workshop in systemic racism. And in March 2021, the Institute hired the anti-racism advocate who would become the docents' nemesis.

The press release announcing Veronica Stein's employment as the new Woman's Board executive director said much about anti-racism and little about art. Stein had previously worked at a foundation that provides arts-informed programming to youth in Chicago's hospitals. She shifted that programming "toward antiracist, trauma-informed modules."[14] Her priorities throughout her career have been the design of "culturally responsive programming and anti-racist curricula," priorities that the Institute shares, she said approvingly.

It was Stein who finalized and delivered the docent termination plan. Replacing the docents with paid educators "responds to issues of class and income equity," she wrote them on September 3, 2021. Stein and the Institute imply that there exists a significant group of would-be tour guides who cannot pursue their dream of educating the public about art because they lack the "financial flexibility" to participate. This proposition is speculative at best. The Institute is trading a corps of nearly one hundred highly trained and enthusiastic volunteers for six part-time staffers. The number of tours on offer will plummet. But it is better not to offer a tour to children at all than to do so in a way that fails to redress "class and income equity."

The Institute's chairman, Robert Levy, offered a different explanation in a *Chicago Tribune* op-ed. The docents constituted "barriers to engagement," he wrote. The Institute was choosing to "center . . . our students across Chicago—as we take this unexpected moment to rethink, redraw and iterate." Sacking the docents was an example of the "[c]ritical self-reflection and participatory, recuperative action" that is required for the Institute to remain relevant to "changing audiences."[15]

This euphemistic phraseology, too, requires translation. Put simply, the Institute terminated the docents because they were, as Rondeau put it in Iowa, "99 percent white females." "Centering" Chicago's students means not subjecting them to the trauma of learning about art from white females volunteering their time and energy. (Rondeau's "99 percent" estimate was too high, but the hyperbole was born of shame and frustration.)

The Art Institute has thus reinforced the consensus among the nation's elites that racial divides should be deepened rather than dissolved. Using white docents to serve "urban schools," Rondeau said in Iowa, creates a "disconnect between the voices [that students] hear for interpretation and the population we're trying to serve." Never mind that the docents were connecting to students through the language of art and perception. Their voices are irredeemably white, and thus a barrier to engagement.

Of course, this imaginative apartheid only works one way. No one would dare suggest that a black person can't teach white students. But it is unobjectionable to say that whites are not competent to teach blacks.

It may be the case that inner-city Chicago students see whites, especially older bourgeois whites, as alien. But white middle-class females in the early twentieth century taught immigrants who did not look like them the fundamentals of American history and literature, helping them to assimilate into American culture. That instruction did not harm the immigrants. An encounter with the bourgeois world of accomplishment and manners could constitute a lifeline to Chicago's inner-city children, compared with the oppositional underclass norms too prevalent in urban schools and families. Teaching them to expect color-coding and to view its absence as oppressive, by contrast, will prepare them for a life of resentment and excuse-making.

The new, paid educators will be chosen for their anti-racist credentials, not for their ability to present art as a means of expanding one's knowledge of what it means to be human. They must have previous experience facilitating "anti-racist" programming and be "equity-focused," according to the Institute's job announcement. A minimum of two years' experience "working with people who identify as ALAANA" is a must. Once on the job, the new hires will deploy "anti-racist museum teaching," develop "anti-racist pedagogy," and offer "anti-racist student experiences." One might think that students visiting the Institute were entering KKK territory, rather than a welcoming environment eager for their presence.

The overt white culling that doomed the docents is becoming more frequent across the cultural landscape.

In June 2020, the Crocker Art Museum in Sacramento, California, bragged about its own "progress" in culling its docent corps: down from

85 percent white in 2017 to 76 percent white in 2019. Given the inarguable truth, as Crocker put it, that "museums are the legacy of Western colonialism, serving as the products of straight, able-bodied, white, male privilege," reducing the number of white docents was essential to ensuring that Crocker could serve as a "safe space to talk about systemic inequality and inequity."[16] Addressing "inequality and inequity" is now so obviously a function of an art museum as to require no explanation. A board member of several New York art venues reports: "Museums can't hire a white person today; everyone's looking to hire blacks."[17]

In 2015, a Mellon Foundation survey found that 84 percent of curators, conservators, educators, and other professionals in art museums were white. Four percent were black, and 3 percent were Hispanic.[18] These racial ratios were universally regarded as scandalous and "damning," in the words of *Art News*.[19] The Mellon survey did not disclose the number of graduate degrees in art history going to minorities each year, the bare minimum of information needed to determine if museums were discriminating against qualified minority candidates.

The fatal taint of whiteness is taking down not only the contents of our cultural legacy but also its means of transmission. Museum directors are openly disparaging the philanthropy, past and present, that makes their organizations and their jobs possible. Upon the 150th anniversary of the Metropolitan Museum of Art, Director Max Hollein lamented the "inherent noblesse oblige of the founders' ambitions," reports James Panero in *The New Criterion*. The Met, according to Hollein, is connected to the logic of "what is defined as white supremacy."[20] James Rondeau views his board as his biggest obstacle to transforming the Art Institute into an anti-racist vehicle. The board's leadership, he told his audience at the Des Moines Art Center, was not "responding powerfully" to the "narratives" of oppression embraced by the museum's paid staff. Rondeau was quick to worry about disrespect— not toward his own board but toward that of his host. "No offense to the trustees at the Des Moines Arts Center; I'm sure you're better than . . . " he trailed off. "I mean I have powerful affinity groups on my board that are invested [in this work] but it's just that if I'm speaking to my board like I'm speaking to you, it's like a giant . . . " Rondeau trailed off again.

The contradiction between museum directors' social-justice pronouncements and their position as beneficiaries of the artistic and philanthropic traditions that they now disparage can reduce them to incoherence. Rondeau was asked in Iowa about his relationship to under-resourced ethnic museums in Chicago. His response was a non sequitur: there's "like this weird kind of, weird concentration of capital that we represent, it's like we're kind of fundamentally not an equitable proposition. Like, I've got 40 Monet paintings. It's weird you know, it's just, it's weird. Like there's a, you know. And we're in the business of kind of doing all this social-justice work and then just yesterday we, I, presided over buying like Pauline Bonaparte's rock crystal casket for baby clothes [Pauline was the sister of Napoleon Bonaparte] for 1.5 million it was like sha-a-a-a . . . like super-rich, weird. We're in the business of these, there's seven [crystal caskets] in the world, like we, so we do have this weird Jekyll and Hyde thing going where we're trying to do this work, but we're in the business of, like, I got a lot of gold, you know, it's just stuff."

To the extent that this statement can be deciphered, it seems to suggest that the very fact of owning a collection is now a source of discomfort, though not enough to lead to voluntary resignation from this "super-rich, weird" concentration of capital. Those benefactors whose donations created the Art Institute might find it disconcerting to hear their gifts referred to as "just stuff."

The new anti-racism mission of museums is not an outgrowth of the democratic impulse that inspired those institutions—it is its repudiation. In 2018, Alice Walton, art benefactor and heiress to the Walmart fortune, told Rondeau that she wanted to give him a "ton of money," by his recounting, to loan some of the Institute's unexhibited holdings to poor rural communities in America. Rondeau was contemptuous. "I don't want to get into your business, *Alice*," he told her, with a sneering emphasis, "but I'm not sure poor rural communities in America need

Toulouse-Lautrec. I'm not sure that that's what they're asking for. But this kind of art for the people, like, eat your Shakespeare, look at beautiful paintings, you will be ennobled, not so much. I don't, you know, I don't think that that methodology is sufficiently sophisticated even though we're seeing it still operable."[21] Rondeau then hit Walton up for a contribution to Chicago's ethnic museums that "struggle to keep their doors open." What is the difference between the poor rural communities that don't need the Art Institute's art and the hoped-for audiences of Chicago's ethnic museums that deserve Walton's money? The former are predominantly white; the latter are not.

The persistent denigration of our cultural institutions and their supporters as bearers of oppressive white privilege is taking its toll. During an equity and inclusion session for the board of the Whitney Museum of Art in October 2021, board member Laurie Tisch observed that it was a "tough time to be a not-for-profit leader. People are tiptoeing around every issue . . . afraid of every word coming out of their mouth being sliced and diced."[22] Organization heads have been taken down; it may be difficult to attract the next generation of leadership, she added.

It will be even more difficult to attract the next generation of art lovers. Identity politics poisons its host. As with classical music, instructing potential audiences that an art form is repressive will only give them another reason to maintain their ignorance. And yet museum directors are doubling down on just such a message; the Metropolitan Museum of Art engages humanities professors to "challenge" the Met's "history and collections"—as if such challenges are not already pouring forth spontaneously from the academy.

There is no counterpart to American philanthropy, not even in other Western nations. In the absence of royal patrons for the arts, wealthy Americans created institutions that would pass on our inheritance, confident that there was something worth preserving in that inheritance. Now the anti-racism crusade erodes that belief by the day. Voluntarism was already on the decline before the racial-justice movement.[23] Good luck finding volunteers and donors if some of the most generous of them are told that their whiteness brands them as pariahs and that the American and Western past is defined by white oppression. In 2012, the top 1 percent of donors gave 43.5 percent of all individual donations.[24] Impugn their identities and their "super-rich, weird" capital, and non-profits might have considerably less "gold" with which to pursue their social-justice ambitions. Following the docent sacking, letter writers to the *Chicago Tribune* announced that if the Institute can do without its volunteers, it must not need financial contributions either.

Western civilization is not about whiteness; it is a universal legacy. The guardians of that civilization, however, portray it as antithetical to racial justice because of its demographic characteristics. They are impoverishing the world.

Chapter Ten

MUSEUMS APOLOGIZE FOR ART

Like the Art Institute of Chicago, the Metropolitan Museum of Art has redefined itself as an anti-racist "agent of change." In July 2020, director Max Hollein and CEO Daniel Weiss announced that the museum will henceforth aim to overcome the racism still perpetrated by our "government, policies, systems, and institutions."[1]

What such a political mandate means for an art museum may seem puzzling, but two ongoing exhibits at the Met (as of early 2023) provide an answer. They suggest that the museum will now value racial consciousness-raising over scholarship and historical accuracy. Double standards will govern how the museum analyzes Western and Third World art: only the former will be subject to demystification, while the latter will be accorded infinite curatorial respect. The Met will lay bare European art's alleged complicity in the West's legacy of oppression, while Third World violence and inequality will be kept off stage.

The first show, *In Praise of Painting: Dutch Masterpieces at The Met*, arranges the Met's own seventeenth-century Dutch canvases in thematic categories, such as still life and landscape. (Some of the exhibit's thematic categories, such as "Contested Bodies," so mimic academic rhetoric as to be all but inscrutable in their meaning.) Highlights of the show include Franz Hals's portrait of *Paulus Verschuur*,[2] a bravura performance of spontaneous brushwork and psychological acuity that captures the Rotterdam merchant's modern irony, and Johannes Vermeer's *A Maid Asleep*,[3] which anticipates Paul Cézanne in its treatment of decorative pattern and geometry.

The Dutch Baroque formed the cornerstone of the Met's first holdings; subsequent bequests created one of the world's great assemblages of Rembrandt, Hals, Vermeer, and their peers. The anti-racist museum, however, understands that it is not just Western art that needs deconstructing; the collecting and donating of art does too. Thus, the commentary accompanying *In Praise of Painting* wearily notes that "of course" there are "blind spots in the story these particular acquisitions tell. Colonialism, slavery, and war—major themes in seventeenth-century Dutch history—are scarcely visible here."[4] It is hard to know who is more at fault, in the Met's view: the artists or the art lovers who collected their work. Few seventeenth-century Dutch paintings depict "colonialism, slavery, and war," and, of those, fewer still approach the technical mastery of the Dutch canon. *In Praise of Painting* contains a Brazilian landscape by Frans Post that shows members of an Indian tribe gathered in a clearing.[5] The painting is included in the exhibit as a synecdoche for a Dutch colony in northern Brazil; its interest is purely ethnographic. What other paintings about "colonialism, slavery, and war" do the curators think the Met should have acquired? Amsterdam's Rijksmuseum recently mounted a self-flagellating show called *Slavery*,[6] intending to atone for Holland's former holdings in Indonesia, New Guinea, and elsewhere. Even the royally endowed Rijksmuseum assembled few canvases with colonialism subject matter; as a second-best solution, the museum's wall texts and catalogue attributed luxury items in portraits and still-lifes to slavery and racism.

In Praise of Painting adopts that strategy as well. "Still life paintings pictured the bounty provided by newly established Dutch trade routes and the Republic's economic success, while omitting the human cost of colonial warfare and slavery," the accompanying wall text points out. The curators did not reveal how a still-life painter should portray the "human cost of colonial warfare and slavery." As even the curators admit, a still life by definition focuses on "things without people." The

Dutch masters, who brought the nascent genre to peak gorgeousness, may have delighted in the dragonfly translucence of grapes and the somber radiance of silver and cut glass; they may have taught us to see beauty in a kitchen's bounty. Not good enough. They should have anticipated twenty-first-century concerns about racial justice and revised their subject matter accordingly.

The museum's benefactors receive a feminist whack as well. "Only one picture painted by an early modern Dutch woman has entered the collection over the course of nearly 150 years," the curators scold. Which Jacob van Ruisdael or Gerard ter Borch would the curators forego for a painting chosen on identity grounds? There simply weren't as many females as males painting in the seventeenth century. Today, there are; women have unfettered access to art schools and galleries. The Met's founders bought its female-painted Dutch Baroque canvas—a towering arrangement of peonies, tulips, roses, and marigolds—in 1871.[7] Sexism did not prevent that addition to the museum's original holdings, but sexism, we are to believe, prevented follow-up purchases.

Having been instructed to see oppression behind portraiture and to hear silenced voices in tableaux of oysters and lemons, the chastened Met visitor may wend his way to *The African Origin of Civilization*, another show drawn from the Met's own collections. He would find himself back in a world of prelapsarian innocence, where art, if not the collecting of it, is unencumbered by a debunking impulse, and where the culture that gave rise to that art is accepted on its own terms, not measured against present values.

The African Origin of Civilization pairs artefacts from ancient Egypt with those from modern (from the thirteenth-century A.D. forward) sub-Saharan Africa to demonstrate their alleged "shared origins," as the Met puts it, and to "recenter" Africa as "the source of modern humanity and a fount of civilization." A timeline runs around the walls noting significant moments in African history, such as the receipt of Grammy awards by pop stars from Benin and South Africa.

The show is based on the writings of Senegalese historian Cheikh Anta Diop (1923–1986). Diop held that ancient Egypt was black, that ancient Egypt and modern sub-Saharan Africa are part of a unified black civilization, and that this black African civilization, not Greece or Rome, is the source of Western civilization. The exhibit opens with a covertly doctored quote from Diop: "The history of Africa will remain suspended in air and cannot be written correctly until African historians connect it with the history of Egypt." (More on that doctoring below.) The exhibition "pay[s] homage" to Diop's "seminal" 1974 book, *The African Origin of Civilization: Myth or Reality*, the Met explains.[8]

So who was this "Senegalese scholar and humanist," as the Met describes him? Diop came from an aristocratic Muslim background in Senegal. In the 1950s, he participated in Paris's anti-colonial student groups. Diop's research aims were unapologetically political. He hoped to accelerate Africa's independence movements by "reconquer[ing] a Promethean consciousness" among the African peoples, he wrote in *The African Origin of Civilization*. Such a task would be impossible so long as the proposition that ancient Egypt was a Negro civilization "does not appear legitimate."[9]

In Diop's telling, in prehistoric times, black Africans moved into the Nile Valley from the south, merged with the blacks already living there, established the ancient Egyptian dynasties, then migrated back across the Sahara into the south. The less demanding conditions those black Egyptians found south of the Sahara discouraged the further development of science and engineering that had begun under the pharaohs. "The Negro became progressively indifferent towards material progress," Diop writes.[10] Rather than pursuing scientific knowledge, the southern Africans concentrated on perfecting their political arrangements. Those political structures were and have remained superior to those of the West, in Diop's view. Africans also far exceeded the Europeans in the "social and moral order," which was on the "same level of perfection" as their political order.

Scientific progress may have come to a standstill back in sub-Saharan Africa, but the gains made in black Egypt during the Pharaonic period,

Diop argues, were so great as to serve as the basis for all subsequent developments in the West. "[T]hat Black world is the very initiator of the 'western' civilization flaunted before our eyes today," Diop alleged in *The African Origin of Civilization*.[11] "Pythagorean mathematics, the theory of the four elements of Thales of Miletus, Epicurean materialism, Platonic idealism, Judaism, Islam, and modern science are rooted in Egyptian cosmogony and science."

Diop's intellectual history is as shaky as his demographic claims. Leave aside for the moment the question of whether Egypt was black. Greco-Roman science and philosophy were different enterprises from Egyptian learning. The Egyptians developed the calendar, the calculation of time, and some medical cures in the second millennium B.C. Their funerary architecture attests to their engineering skills. But the Egyptian numeration system did not provide the basis for Western mathematics. And though the Greeks admired Egyptian accomplishments, the principle of grounding scientific conclusions on logic and empirical evidence—the hallmark of Western science—began with Aristotle, not with the Egyptian dynasties.

As for Diop's arguments regarding ancient Egypt's black racial identity, they rest on Old Testament myth, cherry-picked images of Egyptian sculpture, a reference to "black" Egyptians by Herodotus, and a few alleged similarities between Egyptian and African words. According to DNA analysis from the Max Planck Institute in Germany, mummies from the New Kingdom were most closely related to peoples of the Levant (Turkey, Iraq, and Lebanon, among other countries). Modern Egyptians share just 8 percent of their genome with central Africans.[12] As small as that share is, it is much more than that between ancient Egyptians and central and southern Africans; that common 8 percent developed only over the last 1,500 years. The ancient Egyptians, notorious xenophobes, did not believe themselves related to the peoples of the south, with whom their relations were often imperialistic.[13]

The original Diop quote with which the Met opened its *African Origin* show, before the Met doctored it, was more explicit about Diop's racial agenda. The actual sentence reads: "The history of *Black* Africa will remain suspended in air and cannot be written correctly until African historians *dare to* connect it with the history of Egypt" (emphasis added).[14] The Met removed the words in italics, underplaying the Afrocentric angle and smoothing over Diop's own acknowledgment of how outside the mainstream his scholarship was.

Contrary to the Met's designation of Diop as "influential," his scholarship has remained outside the mainstream. His oeuvre is a marginal presence in African and Egyptian studies, except in the most fervent bastions of Afrocentrism, such as Temple University's Department of Africology and African American Studies (which also offers a course on Ebonics). Frank Snowden, a Howard University classicist, showed definitively in 1989 that Diop, in Snowden's words, "distorts his classical sources," including Herodotus.[15] Oxford University Press's *African History* (2007) notes that Diop's theories have been "convincingly rejected by archeologists and historians on empirical grounds."[16] Kwame Anthony Appiah called Diop an example of "romantic racialism."[17] Contemporary scholarship on Africa emphasizes, irony of ironies, the diversity of cultures on the continent, not their alleged pan-African unity.

For the Met to build an entire show around Diop's discredited theories shows how much today's anti-racist museums privilege political considerations over scholarly ones. After the doctored Diop quote, the Met's wall texts pile on their own Diopian inaccuracies. "Studied by the Greeks, ancient Egypt remained the paradigm of 'classical' antiquity and the cornerstone of Western representation until the early twentieth century," the Met writes. (What motivates the scare quotes here is unclear, besides a desire to "problematize" any possible Eurocentric perspective.)

This statement is astonishing. Ancient Egypt was not the "paradigm" of classical antiquity; classical antiquity, by definition, was ancient Greece and Rome. The Renaissance was ignited by the rediscovery of Greek and Latin texts, not of Egyptian stelae. For the next several centuries, European humanists pored over Greek and Roman philosophy, literature, and art for inspiration regarding what a civilization could achieve. Egyptian thought played no discernible role in that development, if for no other reason than that knowledge of how to read hieroglyphs disappeared in the early centuries of the common era and remained a mystery through the early nineteenth century. The characteristic features of the West—democracy, citizenship, experimental science, the rule of law—have their roots in Greece and Rome, not in the Ancient Near East or Africa. Yet a final wall panel in *African Origin* reinforces the show's initial distortions: Africa played a "generative role in shaping foundational institutions" worldwide, the Met asserts. This claim is untrue regarding ancient Egypt and even more untrue regarding modern Africa.

The Met should be on firmer ground regarding the arts, but its claim that ancient Egypt remained the "cornerstone of Western representation until the early twentieth century" is as inaccurate as its claim about "paradigmatic" Egyptian antiquity. Certainly ancient Greece and Rome had cultural contact with Egypt. Greek Kouroi and decorative motifs from the Archaic period show Egyptian influence; the Doric shaft, as well as the very idea of monumental public architecture, may derive from Egypt's funerary districts. Roman emperors brought obelisks and other Egyptian artifacts back to Rome. But the full-blown Classical style of the Parthenon went far beyond any Egyptian antecedents, and artists from the Renaissance forward took Greek and Roman sculpture and architecture as their models, not Egyptian sculpture and architecture. The nineteenth-century Empire style, with its sphinxes, caryatids, and winged lions, is an exotic sideshow in the larger scheme of "Western representation."

Given the shaky theoretical foundations of *The African Origin of Civilization*, it's no surprise that the show fails on purely visual, as well as on historical, terms. The paired Egyptian and sub-Saharan African objects are supposed to buttress the show's thesis of the "shared origins" and cultural continuity between ancient Egypt and modern Africa. Instead, the pairings undermine that thesis at nearly every turn.

A limestone sculpture[18] of a man and woman standing next to each other from 2575 to 2465 B.C. (the golden age of Egypt's Old Kingdom) is paired with a wooden carving[19] of a man and woman seated next to each other from early-nineteenth-century Mali. The Egyptian male has his arm around the female's shoulder and his hand over her breast; the female has her arm around the male's waist. The African male has his arm around the female's shoulder and his hand extending toward her breast. Apart from the number and the sex of the figures in each pair and their apparent connubial relationship, nothing unites them. The softly modelled Egyptian sculpture aspires to realism; the female's belly, pelvis, and thighs press through her sheath dress. The Malian sculpture is abstract, symbolic, and angular; it would be difficult to distinguish the male from the female were it not for a quiver on the male's back and a baby on the female's. It would have been as relevant, in art historical terms, for the Met to have thrown Jan van Eyck's Arnolfini Portrait into the grouping as to pair these wildly dissimilar works.[20]

The curatorial gloss on the Malian sculpture claims that its "precision" and "exacting bilateral symmetry" suggest a "mathematical equation." Such scientistic rhetoric is ubiquitous throughout the show. A cracked lump of earth with a hump rising from its middle has been "composed by a specialist with precision," explains the text accompanying a twentieth-century "power object" from Mali.[21] The power object's form is "deliberately indeterminate," says the Met, and is made up of an "exacting combination" of millet, alcoholic beverages, expectorated kola nuts, and the "blood of sacrificial offerings" (more on sacrificial offerings below). That exacting combination constitutes "esoteric knowledge," per the Metropolitan Museum of Art. If the knowledge that went into this power object lies at the root of Western science, as Diop would have it, it is a miracle that the West conquered a host of once-lethal infectious diseases and unlocked the genome.

The Met paired the twentieth-century Malian power object with the museum's iconic turquoise hippopotamus from Middle Kingdom Egypt.[22]

Perhaps the power object is meant to be a hippopotamus itself; even so, nothing formally connects the two works. Antoni Gaudí's Casa Batlló in Barcelona comes more readily to mind than the Egyptian faience when viewing the power object.

The artifacts in *The African Origin of Civilization* are exempt from the political standards that *In Praise of Painting* establishes, though the Met's founders and benefactors came in for the usual drubbing. Those patrons' "profound bias" explains the late arrival (1982) of sub-Saharan works into the Met's collection, as well as the priority placed on the Western tradition in the Met's early decades. But the Met's initial emphasis on Western art was perfectly appropriate, given the museum's role as a transmitter of America's cultural inheritance. Art museums in non-Western countries, where they exist, would likewise foreground their national inheritance. It is unlikely that African museums contain Rococo fêtes galantes or Hudson River School landscapes.

Regarding the African works themselves, the exhibit's organizers forgot all about the "war, colonialism, and slavery" that so haunted the curators of *In Praise of Painting*. The African show contains no sculptures depicting Africans enslaving each other, a practice that long antedated European arrival on the continent. The exhibit's timeline of Africa notes the start of the Transatlantic slave trade in 1528 but ignores the kidnapping, coercion, and brutality with which rulers in West African kingdoms like Dahomey and Oyo produced the human subjects of that trade.

War has been a constant in sub-Saharan Africa. The Ashanti Empire (now Ghana) enslaved members of vanquished tribes when it did not murder them ritually. The Zulu state in southern Africa unleashed the "Mfecane" (the crushing) against Sotho-speakers and other Nguni societies starting in the late eighteenth century. Highlander Abyssinians conquered and colonized Somalis, Oromos, and assorted small chieftains from the late sixteenth century to the early twentieth century. The *African Origin* curators do not decry the African artifacts' inattention to such matters.

A brass plaque from the court of Benin shows a warrior chief in a helmet, holding a sword and surrounded by soldiers and attendants, smaller in size to indicate their inferior status.[23] The plaque commemorates the triumphs of Oba Esigie (the ruler of the Benin kingdom) over what the curators discreetly term "internal and external power dynamics." What became of those internal critics and external enemies is not represented on the plaque, nor did the Met note the absence of any reference to their fate.

The exhibition is silent on the tradition of human sacrifice in Africa. Asante kings offered human sacrifices as protection against enemies. This backward practice is not a historical relic. In recent years, police inspectors and doctors in Uganda have reported on children and women sacrificed[24] by witch doctors to improve the fortunes[25] of their clients.

None of the ritual objects in the *African Origin* show was created by a female, or we would have heard about it. Yet the Met condemned its own sexism for failing to collect more female Dutch Baroque painters. Power objects are owned and handled exclusively by Malian males, a privilege which undoubtedly gives those males even more power with respect to females. Nineteenth-century British explorer Sir Richard Francis Burton described female genital mutilation in his 1856 travel memoir, *The First Footsteps in East Africa*.[26] That reality was left out of the show, which adopts the Diopian view of Africa's matriarchal equality and harmony.

New York Times art critic Holland Cotter parroted the Met's conceit regarding women's equality in Africa in his rave review of the *African Origin* exhibition. The male-female carving from Mali balances out "gender-based hierarchies of size," Cotter claimed approvingly. In the Egyptian pair, the male is a "head taller than his mate," whereas in the African carving the "figures are almost equal in height and their features matched with delicate, near-mathematical precision." (The curators' mathematical equation imagery has proven infectious.) Cotter even marveled at the mathematical precision with which the "attributes that define" the Malian couple's roles in life are carved—the "quiver of arrows strapped to the man's back and the bundled baby the woman carries on hers." Had someone suggested that Western females were defined by childbearing, the cries of "patriarchy" would be deafening. Yet sex-based role definition was more implacable in African tribal societies; there likely were no female wood carvers in the seventeenth century whose works the Met's founders could have collected.

If the *In Praise of Painting* and *African Origin of Civilization* exhibitions point to the future of curation at the Met and other "anti-racist" museums, Cotter's review reveals the media pressure accelerating that future. He calls on the "profoundly conservative" Met to "politicize the art historical narrative," as if such politicization were not already a done deal. Cotter repeats the Met's self-criticism about its collecting and display practices, blaming "antiquated, racist Western distinctions" for the Met's traditional installation of Egyptian and African art in separate museum wings.

That wing for African and other Third World art was undergoing renovation when *African Origin* opened. It will surely follow Cotter's template for a "politicized" art narrative. (The December 2021 groundbreaking ceremony for the renovation, attended by the crème de la crème of New York's Democratic leadership, included a prayer to the ancestors and a curator singing an Aboriginal song, perhaps a first for the Met.)

Expect the new wing to emphasize, as Cotter puts it, "the degree to which much of the art of sub-Saharan Africa . . . is inherently, and often forthrightly, about ethics, about the workings of social justice; about right living, personally, socially, and spiritually; about the quest for balance in the natural world."[27] The *Times* critic finds such a commitment to ethics and social justice in a late-nineteenth-century "power figure" from the Congo, which has been recently placed in another wildly incongruous pairing in the Graeco-Roman wing.[28] Power figures—stubby, stylized versions of the human form—are the objects of magical thinking. A human nganga (or "spiritual specialist" in the inevitably glorified translation) fills a cavity in the power figure's belly with seeds, relics, resins, and plant fibers. These "powerful medicines," as the Met dutifully puts it, are believed to have the capacity to settle disputes and punish wrongdoers. A stone placed in a power figure's receptacle may allegedly result in the pelting of one's enemies or one's own protection from being pelted. The nganga's clients lick nails and blades that are pounded into the power figure to seal its efficacy through their saliva. The power figure will then mete out destruction or divine protection as appropriate.

This is not "ethics," "social justice," or just plain "justice"—it is superstition, akin to a belief in astrology or the healing power of crystals. The power figure operates transactionally—I, the client, give something to a magical charm or its overseer and hope to get something in return. Rational argument and the rule of law are not involved. Nor is the concept of rights, which are uniquely a product of Western political thought. "Social justice," with its emphasis on group, rather than individual, rights, may be a distortion of the Western notion of justice, but it derives from that tradition.

Nevertheless, Holland Cotter maintains that it is the West that "badly" needs instruction in ethics, social justice, and right living. The best source for those ideas, he writes, is in the arts of black Africa, unmatched for "head-turning, eye-locking beauty." Cotter's ignorance about the origin of the concepts—such as equality and tolerance—with which the woke Left bashes the West is typical. And that ignorance now increasingly governs our leading cultural institutions. Whether art museums or classical music organizations, those institutions have sacrificed their comparative advantages—connoisseurship, scholarly knowledge, and devotion to the highest expressions of culture—in favor of a partisan political program that distorts both present and past.

■   ■   ■

University art history departments helped spawn "anti-racist" museum practices. Academic art history started characterizing anything historically "white" or European as suspect decades before that approach surfaced in museum exhibits and personnel policy. Those academic art history departments once regarded themselves as the guardians of a tradition, but they, too, have betrayed their role, just like classical music leaders and museum directors. The fate of a storied art history course at Yale University demonstrates this break from the past.

For decades, Yale offered a two-semester introductory sequence on the history of Western art. The fall semester spanned the ancient Middle East to the early Renaissance; the spring semester picked up from the High Renaissance through the present. Many Yale students were fortunate enough to take one or both of these classes while the late Vincent Scully was still teaching them; I was among those lucky students. Scully was a titanic, galvanizing presence, combining charismatic enthusiasm with encyclopedic knowledge. When the lights went down in the lecture hall, the large screen behind him, on which slides were projected, became the stage on which the mesmerizing saga of stylistic evolution played out. How did the austere geometry of Cycladic icons bloom into the full-bodied grandeur of the Acropolis's Caryatids? Why were the rational symmetries of the Greek temple, blazing under Mediterranean light, replaced by the wild vertical outcroppings of the Gothic cathedral? What expressive possibilities were opened up by Giotto's fresco cycle in the Arena Chapel?

Such questions, under Scully's tutelage, became urgent and central to an understanding of human experience. Trips to the Yale Art Gallery supplemented his lectures, where it was hoped that in writing about an object in the collection, students would follow John Ruskin's admonition that the "greatest thing a human soul ever does in this world is to see something, and tell what it saw in a plain way."[29] I chose to analyze Corot's *The Harbor at La Rochelle*, being particularly taken by the red cap of a stevedore, one of the few jewel colors in a landscape of silken silvers and transparent sky blues.

By 1974, when I enrolled at Yale, its faculty had long since abdicated one of its primary intellectual responsibilities. It observed a chaste silence about what undergraduates needed to study in order to have any hope of becoming even minimally educated; curricular selections, outside of a few broad distribution requirements, were left to students, who by definition did not know enough to choose wisely, except by accident. So it was that I graduated without having taken a single history course (outside of one distribution-fulfilling intellectual history class), despite easy access to arguably the strongest American history faculty in the country. Scully's fall semester introductory art history course has been my anchor to the past, providing visual grounding in the development of Western civilization, around which it is possible to develop a broader sense of history.

But now, the art history department has junked the entire two-semester sequence. Given the role that these two courses have played in exposing Yale undergraduates to the joys of scholarship and knowledge, one would think that the department would have amassed overwhelmingly compelling grounds for eliminating them. To the contrary, the reasons given were either laughably weak or at odds with the facts.

The first reason was the most absurd: the course titles (Introduction to the History of Art: Prehistory to the Renaissance and Introduction to the History of Art: Renaissance to the Present). Art History Chair Tim Barringer apparently thought students would be fooled by those titles into assuming that other traditions don't exist. "I don't mistake a history of European painting for the history of all art in all places," he primly told the *Yale Daily News*. No one else would either. But if the titles were such a trap for the Eurocentric unwary, the department could have simply added the word "European" before "Art" and been done with it. (Barringer, whose specialties include post-colonial and gender studies as well as Victorian visual culture, had been teaching the doomed second semester course—a classic example of the fox guarding the henhouse.)

Barringer also claimed that it was "problematic" to put European art on a pedestal when so many other regions and traditions were "equally deserving of study." The courses that would replace the surveys would not claim to "be the mainstream with everything else pushed to the margins," he told the *Daily News*. Leave aside for the moment whether the European tradition may legitimately form the core of an art history education in an American university. The premise of Barringer's statement—that previously European art was put on a pedestal and everything else was pushed to the margins—is blatantly false. The department requires art history majors to take two introductory-level, one-semester survey courses. Since at least 2012, the department has offered courses in non-Western art that can fulfill that requirement in lieu of the European surveys. Those classes include Introduction to the History of Art: Buddhist Art and Architecture; Introduction to the History of Art: Sacred Art and Architecture; Global Decorative Arts; The Politics of Representation; and The Classical Buddhist World. No one was forced into the two Western art courses.

Nor would anyone surveying the art history catalogue think that Yale was "privileging" the West, as they say in theoryspeak. That catalogue is awash in non-European courses. In addition to the introductory classes mentioned above, the department also offers Japan's Classics in Text and Image; Introduction to Islamic Architecture; The Migrant Image; Sacred Space in South Asia; Visual Storytelling in South Asia; Aztec Art & Architecture; Black Atlantic Photography; Black British Art and Culture; Art and Architecture of Mesoamerica; The Mexican Cultural Renaissance, 1920–1940; Painting and Poetry in Islamic Art; Aesthetics and Meaning in African Arts and Cultures; Korean Art and Culture; African American Art, 1963 to the Present; Art and Architecture of Japan; Textiles of Asia, 800–1800 C.E.; and Art and Politics in the Modern Middle East, among other courses. The Western tradition is just one among many. Nevertheless, Marisa Bass, the director of undergraduate studies in the department, echoed Barringer's accusation of Eurocentrism. The changes recognize "an essential truth:

that there has never been just one story of the history of art," Bass told the *Daily News*. But Yale does not tell just one story of the history of art. Department leaders have created a parody of their own department simply in order to kill off the Western survey courses.

Another reason those Western survey courses must be sacked is that it is impossible to cover the "entire field—and its varied cultural backgrounds—in one course," as the *Daily News* put it. If this statement means that the span of time covered in each of the one-semester Western art classes is too large, the non-Western survey courses are as broad or broader. Chinese Painting and Culture covers sixteen centuries. Power, Gender, and Ritual in African Art covers nearly two millennia. Introduction to the History of Art: Buddhist Art and Architecture covers seven centuries. Introduction to the History of Art: Sacred Art and Architecture covers several millennia. None of these courses is facing extinction.

Barringer promised that the replacement surveys will subject European art to a variety of deconstructive readings designed to pull that tradition down from its alleged pedestal. The new classes will consider Western art in relation to "questions of gender, class, and 'race,'" he told the *Daily News* in an email, carefully putting scare quotes around "race" to signal his adherence to the creed that race is a social construct. The new courses will discuss the involvement of Western art with capitalism. Most intriguingly, the relationship between Western art and climate change will be a "key theme," he wrote.

Barringer's proposed deconstruction of Western art illustrates a central feature of modern academia: the hermeneutics of suspicion applies only to the Western canon. Western academics continue to interpret non-Western traditions with sympathy and respect; those interpreters seek to faithfully convey the intentions of non-Western creators and to help students understand what makes non-Western works great. So, while the replacement European art survey courses would, in Marissa Bass's words, "challenge, rethink, and rewrite" art historical narratives, the department will not be cancelling its Buddhist art and architecture class due to the low representation of female artists and architects, nor will it "interrogate" (as High Theory puts it) African arts and cultures for their relationship to genocidal tribal warfare, or Aztec art and architecture for their relationship to murderous misogyny and human sacrifice.

In the replacement European survey courses, however, Tim Barringer will ask students to nominate a work of art that has been left out of the curriculum or textbook, in order to challenge long-held views of art history. Barringer is looking forward to seeing how students will "counteract or undermine" his own narratives about Western art, he wrote in an online syllabus note.[30] Will students in Painting and Poetry in Islamic Art be asked to nominate an excluded artwork? Unlikely. The idea that a Yale undergraduate knows enough to "counteract or undermine" the expertise of Islamic scholars would be seen as ludicrous. Only with regard to the Western tradition are ignorant students given the power to countermand what was once the considered judgment of the scholarly profession.

Students exert pressure over what gets taught not just through explicit pressure but also through their mere existence, if they possess favored identity traits. The "diversity of today's student body" guides the art history department's curricular thinking, department leaders explained in a statement on the cancelled survey courses. But the ephemera of students' race and sex have no bearing on the significance of the past. The sublimity of Chartres Cathedral, a focal point of Scully's fall semester course, transcends the skin color of the latest round of freshmen. If the University of Lagos suddenly received a large influx of students from Idaho, that would not change how Yoruba bronzes would be taught or interpreted. It is only in the West where scholarship and pedagogy are held hostage to some students' demographic profile, as we noted regarding the Juilliard Drama Division.

Yale has cancelled other landmark courses on identity grounds. For decades, English majors were required to take a yearlong course called Major English Poets. I had the privilege of taking that course as well in

1974. We read Chaucer, Edmund Spenser, John Milton, Alexander Pope, and William Wordsworth, among others—authors whose stylistic achievements and influence over British literature are incontestable. No one at the time thought to complain about the race or gender of these literary giants. We were—remarkably—simply allowed to wallow in the glories of their language and to enter the vast imaginative realms they created.

But that course was defenestrated from its gateway status for English majors in 2017, following a student petition griping preposterously that a "year spent around a seminar table where the literary contributions of women, people of color, and queer folk are absent actively harms all students, regardless of their identity. . . The Major English Poets sequences creates a culture that is especially hostile to students of color."

Rather than push back against this ignorant nonsense, members of Yale's English faculty validated its premise. Professor Jill Richards announced that it was "unacceptable that the two-semester requirement for all majors routinely covers the work of eight white, male poets."[31] But Medieval and Elizabethan England simply did not have black poets writing in the English language, a pattern that continued through the Augustan and Romantic periods. Females were only slightly more represented, but none of them had the influence of the course's focal authors.

Never mind. Yale upended its requirements for the major, making Major English Poets optional and creating new introductory courses— such as Anglophone literature (i.e., Third World literature in English)— to take in its stead. Whatever the merits of that latter body of work, it plays only the most recent and marginal of roles in the English literary tradition. (Jill Richards, who specializes in global modernism, gender and sexuality, citizenship, human rights, critical legal theory, revolution, social movements, cinema, avant-gardes, and young adult literature, is another example of the *trahison des clercs*; terrifyingly, despite her contempt for "white, male poets," she teaches the now-optional Major English Poets.)

Yale's lust for curricular cancellations has picked up steam since Major English Poets lost its required spot in the English major. The art history department appears to have eliminated the Western art introductory courses on its own initiative, without the pretext of a student petition or other agitation. The only possible ground for doing so is a hatred of the Western tradition, since the axed courses were voluntary and surrounded by numerous non-Western alternatives. Barringer did not respond to an email asking for a preview of the mysterious relationship between Western art and climate change. He also chose not to reveal whether African, Asian, and South American art will now be "problematized" along with Western art.

The one-sided subjection of Western civilization to the petty tyranny of identity politics will only worsen. Yale is one of four universities to have received a $4 million grant to infuse the theme of race into every aspect of humanities teaching and scholarship. Brown, the University of Chicago, and Stanford are the other recipients of that Andrew W. Mellon Foundation bequest. (The Mellon Foundation, once a supporter of apolitical humanities scholarship, has been captured by the identitarian Left.) Race, Yale announced in its press release about the Mellon grant, is critically important and indisputably central to the humanities.[32]

Actually, it is not. The humanities are about matters far more compelling than the trivialities of race, which in any case we are supposed to believe is not even real. For centuries, poets, painters, novelists, and architects sought to express essential truths about the human condition. Race may have played a role in a few classic works, such as *Othello* or *The Heart of Darkness*, but it was hardly "central" to the entire tradition. Those who seek to make it so do so in the pursuit of political grievance, not scholarly accuracy.

Some students know better, however. Once word got out about the curtain call for the two introductory Western art courses, students stampeded to enroll. Though the courses were not in fact a required gateway into the study of art history, it would have been perfectly appropriate to make them so. The primary obligation of education is to pass on a particular civilization's cultural inheritance with love and gratitude. Yale, like nearly every other college today, has lost the will to do so. It has therefore negated its very reason for being.

Chapter Eleven

AN ART MUSEUM CANCELS ART

The Metropolitan Museum of Art has mounted an exhibit which, were its curatorial philosophy widely adopted, would spell the end of art and of art museums. The art press greeted the show ecstatically, as a sign of the Met's new direction. This prognosis is undoubtedly correct.

The exhibit, *Fictions of Emancipation*, is built around an 1873 sculpture, *Why Born Enslaved!*, by the brilliant French sculptor Jean-Baptiste Carpeaux. The marble bust portrays a black woman, bound by a rope, looking over her left shoulder with a piercing expression of defiance, incredulity, and contempt.

Why Born Enslaved! has been understood since its creation as an antislavery work. The Met, however, knows better, now that it has been reborn as an "anti-racist" institution. *Fictions of Emancipation* argues that the Carpeaux bust "visualizes longstanding European fantasies about the possession of and domination over the bodies of Black people." Far from carrying an antislavery message, *Why Born Enslaved!* "fetishizes violence and submission," according to the Met.[1] And Carpeaux was not the only artist to give an aesthetic gloss to racial oppression, while seeming to oppose it; *Fictions of Emancipation* portrays abolitionist art more widely as a fig leaf for Western colonialism and white supremacy.

Arriving at this reading of the Carpeaux statue and of similarly themed works requires the deconstruction of virtually every aspect of artistic creation. An artist's use of live models, the preparation of preliminary sketches, the representation of the nude, and the selling and buying of art—all are revealed by the Met as ploys used by the white European power structure to oppress people of color. That reading also requires jettisoning a museum's reason for being—the loving application of connoisseurship to the treasures of the past—and replacing it with a political agenda.

The Met's first engagements with *Why Born Enslaved!* provided no hint of the revisionist readings to come. In 1997, a donor gave the museum a terracotta version of the bust dating from 1872. In announcing the gift, the Met described Carpeaux as a "liberal romantic" whose "humanitarian sentiments" were manifest in the museum's new sculpture. The museum was still in the business of stylistic explication rather than ideological denunciation, so it noted the influence of Carpeaux's most important master in the bust's "Michelangelesque sideward turn."[2]

In 2014, the Met assembled a magisterial Carpeaux retrospective, introducing many Americans to this stunningly gifted artist for the first time. The show, *The Passions of Jean-Baptiste Carpeaux*, included some of Carpeaux's most psychologically piercing busts, along with his tormented self-portraits and flamboyantly kinetic paintings. The exhibit traced the artist's hard-fought rise, from son of a stonemason in provincial northern France to premier sculptor of the Second Empire. Carpeaux's fountains, pediments, and bas-reliefs contributed exuberant beauty to the public-works projects then transforming Paris; tantalizing fragments from these monumental commissions were included in the 2014 show. (*Why Born Enslaved!* was an offshoot of one of those commissions: the Fountain of the Observatory in the Luxembourg Gardens.) *The Passions of Jean-Baptiste Carpeaux* also marked the sculptor's harrowing end, dying in agony at age forty-eight after a botched operation for cancer had pierced his bladder.

The Passions of Jean-Baptiste Carpeaux exhibited the Met's terracotta version of *Why Born Enslaved!* Even as late as 2014, the museum could still discuss the work in sympathetic terms. The bust's early success was due to the "beauty of the woman's expression and the powerful emotion to which it gives rise," the catalogue suggested. Art historian Laure de Margerie wrote in a catalogue essay that the bust "partook of the prolonged enthusiasm generated by the abolition of slavery in France in 1848 and in the United States in 1865."[3]

In 2019, the Met bought the marble version of *Why Born Enslaved!* The acquisition announcement revealed how much had changed in the museum's curatorial philosophy. The announcement alerted future viewers of the bust to look out for patriarchy and white privilege: "It is critical to reckon with the power imbalance enacted when a white male artist transposes the body of a black woman into an emblem of enslavement." Though the statue had heretofore been interpreted (including by the Met) as "an expression of Carpeaux's stance against slavery," the museum was no longer taken in. In fact, the bust was a "disturbing fantasy of aestheticized bondage—the transformation of human carnage into erotically-charged drama," the acquisition announcement explained.[4] Had Carpeaux anticipated and acted upon the Met's objections to *Why Born Enslaved!*, he never would have created the bust in the first place. Sadly, however, the work does exist. So the Met's anti-racist curators have adopted a second-best solution to its damaging effects: cancel the work symbolically.

The new guard at the Met—Sarah Lawrence, recently named curator in charge of the Department of European Sculpture and Decorative Arts; Elyse Nelson, a new assistant curator in the same department; and director Max Hollein—was just warming up.

The museum immediately started planning an exhibit around the marble *Why Born Enslaved!* that would serve as a corrective to what the staff now viewed as the impossibly mystified *Passions of Jean-Baptiste Carpeaux*. The new show was intended to "critically engage with issues of imperialism and colonialism that are present in that bust that were not addressed in that [earlier Carpeaux] exhibition," Elyse Nelson told *ARTnews*.[5]

Then the George Floyd race riots broke out in the summer of 2020. It became even more important to insulate the Met against any possible charge of curatorial white privilege. So the museum belatedly engaged an associate professor of writing at Columbia University, Wendy Walters, to serve as co-curator with Nelson. Walters has received the usual fellowships which rain down upon intersectional academics, but her closest involvement with art museums at that point had been limited to an obsession with white paint. White paint irritates Walters, especially on the "walls of educational spaces," so she is writing a book on its "social and cultural implications," as she put it in an interview.[6]

Qualification enough, since *Fictions of Emancipation* is all about whiteness—white supremacy, white colonialism, white subjugation, and white scientific ignorance. What it is not about is art—about seeing what makes *Why Born Enslaved!* great and what makes Carpeaux's style singular.

The first of Carpeaux's many sins is to have portrayed the inhumanity of slavery. It turns out that if a white artist depicts a black slave, he participates in subjugation himself. That is because such a depiction suggests, according to the Met, that slavery is the primordial condition of blacks. Elyse Nelson and Wendy Walters explain in their catalogue introduction: The "enduring visual culture of abolition and emancipation" posits that "Black persons must first have been enslaved in order to be free."[7] A wall label in *Fictions of Emancipation* notes disapprovingly that Carpeaux's interpretation of the "injustice of enslavement remains embodied in a bound woman."

This claim regarding emancipationist art is nonsense. Portraying a black slave by no means implies that blacks can only be free if they are first enslaved. To arouse people to act against a wrong, a wise rhetorician portrays that wrong in as heart-wrenching a way as possible. To raise money for hunger relief, Oxfam does not show chubby, smiling children; it shows dull-eyed semi-corpses. Resettlement charities display desperate refugees. The medical school movement White Coats for Black Lives stages die-ins, in which medical students lie on the ground in sympathy with the black victims of fatal police shootings.

Those protesters are not saying that all blacks are dead or that being dead is a necessary component of being black.

Fictions of Emancipation is equally scathing toward other abolitionist works. British porcelain entrepreneur Josiah Wedgwood was a fierce anti-slavery campaigner. His firm created an iconic medallion in the 1780s that depicted a black man kneeling on one knee, shackled hands raised in supplication. The inscription reads: "Am I not a man and a brother?" This image was widely reproduced on rings, broaches, tableware, and cologne bottles. The *Fictions* curators see in the cameo only triumphant white supremacy. "The beseeching Black figure cemented associations between Blackness, slavery, and subservience," explains an accompanying wall text. A catalogue essay by Iris Moon, an assistant curator in the Met's European sculpture department, complains that the "paternalistic" Wedgewood medallion made it "impossible to picture the liberation of Blackness without seeing simultaneous scenes of subjection."[8] This charge against the Wedgwood medallion is as nonsensical as the charge against the Carpeaux bust. While liberation from slavery does presuppose that there is something (i.e., slavery) from which the slave is to be liberated, it does not presuppose that the slave's natural condition is slavery.

The Met's anti-white supremacy theorists have a problem, however. Black artists have portrayed enslaved blacks and white artists have portrayed enslaved whites. White artists have also created gorgeous portraits of unchained blacks.

Concurrent with *Fictions of Emancipation*, the National Gallery of Art in Washington, DC, ran a show called *Afro-Atlantic Histories*. That exhibit shared the Met's revisionist agenda, aiming to unmask art history and art museums as an "enduring apparatus of imperialism and colonization," in the words of its main organizer.[9] Yet it contained a canvas that, under the Met's new compositional rules, would also suggest that blacks' natural condition is slavery. *Into Bondage,* by Aaron Douglas, a leading figure in the Harlem Renaissance, shows shackled figures walking through palm leaves to an ocean shore, their heads hung low, while two boats wait on the horizon. A female raises her chained hands to the sky;

a shackled male lifts his eyes to a shining star. Douglas gets away with this otherwise-taboo iconography because the acceptability of imagery now depends on the skin color of the person deploying it.

Western art portrayed white slaves before and after the transatlantic slave trade got underway. Ancient Greek columns incorporated images of white slaves captured at war. Michelangelo sculpted a series of captive white figures, including a bound, nearly nude white male subsequently named the *Rebellious Slave.* The Palazzo Pitti in Florence and the Palazzo Ducale in Mantua, among other Renaissance and Baroque palaces, contain sculpted white slaves in their ceiling friezes. Carpeaux's contemporary, Ernest Christophe, sculpted a nude shackled female, *Slave,* in 1851, her torso bent over her knees, her face buried in long tresses. Neoclassical American sculptor, Hiram Powers, created a life-size *Greek Slave* in 1843, inspired by the Greek Revolution against the Turks. White artists have been as willing to represent whites as slaves as they were to represent blacks as slaves, suggesting that the impetus in the latter case is not one of racism.

The Met's next critique of *Why Born Enslaved!* erases, in one stroke, a foundational component of Western art: the nude. The garment of Carpeaux's captive has fallen below one of her breasts. This partial nudity turns the work into racist soft porn, according to the Met. Assistant curator Elyse Nelson describes *Why Born Enslaved!* as "an eroticized object for visual consumption" that gives form to "colonialist fantasies about the physical possession and containment of black women's bodies."[10] This curatorial Puritan is aghast at the "visual display of so much flesh," which suggests, in Nelson's words, optical reference to the slave market and auction block.[11] A wall text echoes Nelson's outrage at "so much flesh." Carpeaux's bust allows us to accept that the "Black female body can still be collected and consumed, be gazed at, desired, despised, dissected, and distorted by all."

The curators' willful ignorance is breathtaking. Since the classical period, the West's greatest artists have portrayed the unclothed human body. This artistic lineage includes Lucas Cranach the Elder,

Durer, Mantegna, Michelangelo, Botticelli, Titian, Raphael, Giorgione, Rembrandt, Rubens, Velázquez, Watteau, Boucher, Ingres, David, Géricault, Goya, Courbet, Renoir, Degas, Matisse, Rodin, Klimt, Picasso, and Henry Moore, among thousands of other artists.

Starting at least from the Kouroi of Archaic Greece, nudity has been especially central to sculpture. In 1859, Carpeaux abandoned a project portraying two characters from a French novel because the motif did not contain "enough nudity for a sculptor," he explained at the time.[12] Those two characters were white.

Cancel the nude and you cancel art itself. Nearly 100 percent of those nudes throughout history have been white. Their state of undress has been far more revealing, and often far more "eroticized," than the single unsheathed breast in *Why Born Enslaved!* If that one black breast teaches us that the black female body can still be "desired, despised, dissected, and distorted by all," those thousands of white breasts should carry that meaning too. In fact, far from being a mark of contempt, the solo naked breast in *Why Born Enslaved!* places the work in the tradition of heroic rebellion, recalling as it does the naked double breasts of Delacroix's *Liberty Leading the People.*

A wall text claims that the Carpeaux bust is part of the nineteenth century's "representation, commodification, and fetishization of Black females and the disproportionate amount of attention aimed at their bodies." This verbiage is pure Black Studies boilerplate, unmoored from historical reality. There was actually little representation of "black females" and "their bodies" in the nineteenth century or any previous century—unsurprisingly, given the racial demographics of Europe. The art-historical Left can't get its story straight regarding the black nude. While the Met decries the "disproportionate" attention directed against the black female body, a feminist art historian blames racism for the "paucity of images of the black female nude in the history of Western 'high' art."[13] In reality, the representation of black females that did exist employed the opposite "binary" (to use academic jargon) more than the one lambasted by the Met: it was the white female who was nude and paired with a clothed black female, as in Manet's *Olympia* or Felix Vallotton's enigmatic *La Blanche et La Noire*.

Hiram Powers's *Greek Slave* was a life-size, full-frontal nude. If the one breast of *Why Born Enslaved!* represents "fetishization" and "commodification," the *Greek Slave*'s two breasts, with bonus genital area, should be off the charts for fetishization and commodification. Yet the Met curators ignore Powers's *Greek Slave* entirely, even though the museum owns a porcelain reproduction of the statue.[14] It is quite conceivable that Met curators no longer know what is in the museum's collections.

Having taught viewers to see the nude as racial oppression, the Met takes on the creative process itself. Nelson is scandalized by the fact that Carpeaux changed the formal elements of *Why Born Enslaved!* a number of times. Apparently, an artist is supposed to arrive at his composition immediately and make no changes. This bizarre "no experimentation" rule would also torpedo a vast portion of our artistic inheritance. Sketches and maquettes often prove more compelling than the finished work, at least to the modern sensibility.

But if an artist simply *must* change his composition, he can at least do so in an anhedonic state of mind. Nelson gripes that the preliminary versions of *Why Born Enslaved!* indicate a "certain pleasure taken by the artist" in the "creative possibilities provided by his subject."[15] That "sense of pleasure" is no less apparent in the "sensuous play between rope and body" in the finished version of *Why Born Enslaved!*, Nelson observes. But what Nelson belittles as voyeuristic racial oppression is simply a manifestation of Carpeaux's supreme ability to portray in marble tensile pressure on flesh, a capacity arguably matched only by Bernini. Nelson would presumably have preferred an inept representation so that Carpeaux might not have had any grounds for artistic satisfaction.

Nelson's grudging acknowledgement of the "sensuous play" between rope and body is the closest the Met comes in *Fictions of Emancipation* to an aesthetic evaluation of the bust. The exhibit is silent about the work's psychological subtlety. It has nothing to say about its artistic genealogy. It passes over the ambiguous, inscrutable expression on the woman's face, seemingly caught in a fleeting moment in time.

What the Met *does* see is that the model for the bust is unnamed. Nelson complains that the "name and biography" of Carpeaux's model remain unknown.[16] A wall text reinforces this complaint: though "real people posed" for the artists in the show, the "names and biographies of these individuals were disregarded or lost, their likenesses recast into exoticized symbols." This theme of suppressed identity was parroted by the art press. *ARTnews*'s review of *Fictions of Emancipation* recycles the Met's complaint: the identity of Carpeaux's model remains unknown, clucks the reviewer in dismay.[17]

And unknown was the identity of the vast majority of models who have sat for artists over the centuries, unless the artist was creating a commissioned portrait. The few models whose names we do know, we know due to research into an artist's working (and often romantic) life, and only rarely to the works themselves. What is the "name and biography" of the white male who sat for Carpeaux's massive composition, *Ugolino and His Sons*? We don't know, beyond Carpeaux's reference, in an 1858 letter, to a "seaman of rare beauty" whom he had spotted in Rome.[18] What street urchin sat for Carpeaux's Neoclassical *Fisherboy with a Seashell*? We don't know. Who were Vermeer's, Veronese's, and Fragonard's white models? We don't know.

And yet a young newcomer to art who visited *Fictions of Emancipation* with his high school class would come away with the impression that Carpeaux and the other artists in the show were engaged in the unprecedented erasure of their black models' identities, violating a long-standing artistic tradition out of racial contempt. That wildly incorrect understanding has been deliberately created by the Met's curators, our supposed guides to the history of art, and it will only increase black students' sense of victimhood and animosity toward the Western cultural tradition.

Any anti-racist enterprise worth its salt must take aim at the idea that race exists. Even if Carpeaux had not portrayed someone in bondage, if he had named his model and provided a long biographical note about her, if he had draped every available inch of his subject's neck and shoulders in heavy wool, he still would have buttressed Western racism by having created an identifiably black figure. Carpeaux's bust and its original title, *Négresse*, "reinforce the fallacy of racial difference," according to a wall text. The Met's curators, by contrast, understand that race is just a social construct. (This most inviolate of all academic credos conflicts with the fact that race is genetically marked, and that its genetic markers correlate with individuals' identification of their own and of others' race.)

The Met wields the "fallacy of racial difference" to kneecap another artist in the show: Charles-Henri-Joseph Cordier. A contemporary of Carpeaux's, Cordier specialized in sculpting non-Europeans, a genre known at the time as "ethnographic sculpture." Cordier's intentions were explicitly egalitarian and humanistic. "My genre," he wrote, "has the freshness of something new, a revolt against slavery . . . widening the circle of beauty by showing that it existed everywhere." Beauty is not the "province of a privileged race," Cordier asserted, it is universal.[19] If Cordier's manifesto would seem to be unpromising material for demonstrating the ubiquity of white supremacy, one does not understand the determination of the Met's anti-racists.

The Cordier busts included in *Fictions of Emancipation* are sensual, dignified, and brooding. A slender, long-necked woman whom the critic Théophile Gautier named *Venus Africaine* has been caught in a moment of meditation, her half-lidded eyes downcast, her lips slightly parted. Cordier described his goal as creating an ideal "type in which is united all the special beauty of the race that I am examining."[20] Yet though aiming for an "ideal type," his busts convey a stronger sense of character than the bland Neoclassical sculpture of the time, such as Powers's *Greek Slave*.

The nobility of Cordier's busts speaks for itself. The Met fights back with verbal descriptions of the sculptures that try to make Cordier out to be a knuckle-dragging Klan member. Cordier's subjects "exhibit thick and fleshy lips; broad, flat noses; [and] coarse locks of hair,"[21] writes James Smalls, chair of the Department of Visual Arts, and professor of Gender, Women's and Sexuality Studies; Africana Studies; and Language, Literacy, and Culture, at the University of Maryland, Baltimore County. No viewer not already wedded to an ideological program would use such language to characterize Cordier's compositions. To be sure, we recognize the subjects as black, not because of Cordier's racism but because of his realism. Proponents of the race-as-social-construct conceit are enraged that human beings continue to identify each other's race accurately.

The ban on portraying blacks as blacks (and whites as whites) only applies to white artists, however. For an actual example of "thick and fleshy lips" and a "broad, flat" nose, one need only turn to a 2014 work lauded by a Met curator. *A Subtlety, or the Marvelous Sugar Baby*, by Kara Walker, is an airplane-hangar-sized sphinx made out of polystyrene foam. *The Marvelous Sugar Baby* has a nose four times as long as it is high and flat as a pug's; the *Sugar Baby*'s blimp-like lips protrude beyond every other feature of her face. Met sculpture curator Iris Moon praises the *Sugar Baby* but is silent about its simian features. If pressed, Moon would presumably explain that Kara Walker is ironizing white racism.

A bust by contemporary painter Kehinde Wiley, celebrated in another catalogue essay, also eludes the Met's ban on racial representation. Wiley's *After La Négresse* shows a man with a tattooed head in a Lakers jersey; his lips are full, his jaw protruding, and his shoulders muscular. We immediately recognize him as black. Is Wiley racist, or just the viewer? The Met's curators slam Charles-Henri-Joseph Cordier for embellishing his Ethiopian subjects with African ornament. But Wiley can dress his young black male in a Lakers jersey and get away with it because Wiley is black and thus exempt from the Met's racial rules. Wiley can also conceal the name and biography of his model without being accused of racial oppression.

A final link in the chain of creation must be broken if the Met's war on the European tradition is to succeed: the art market. If a white artist tries to sell his art, he is engaged yet again in white supremacy, according to the Met. At the time of *Why Born Enslaved!,* Carpeaux had barely escaped bankruptcy, having invested huge sums of his own money into creating a sculpture for the Paris Opera House. Economic difficulties hounded Carpeaux throughout his life; he sometimes had to auction off his works at bargain basement prices. Carpeaux created *Why Born Enslaved!* with the hope of sale—just as nearly every other post-Gothic artist has done. But according to Nelson, that commercial end undercuts any abolitionist meaning that a naïve viewer may attribute to the bust. Since the work "was designed to meet consumer desire," Nelson writes, it should be seen as a vehicle for "colonialist fantasies about the physical possession and containment of Black women's bodies."[22]

The art press ran with the Met's anti-commercial theme. *New York Times* art critic Holland Cotter dismissed any abolitionist motivation for Josiah Wedgewood's anti-slavery medallion, since it, too, entered the stream of commerce. Once the medallion was offered for sale, it became merely a "commodified emblem of Black abjection and white paternalism," Cotter writes in his review of the *Fictions* show.[23]

These coddled curators and critics are detached from reality. Absent ecclesiastical or aristocratic patronage, an artist's only mechanism for survival is the market. Perhaps these snobs imagine that artists should rely on Ford, Rockefeller, and Andrew Mellon foundation support (though good luck to any heterosexual white male artist seeking such philanthropic backing today).

Contemporary black artists possibly *could* live on grants alone in the post–George Floyd era. They market their works anyway—and the Met lauds them for their branding creativity. Kehinde Wiley, creator of *After La Négresse,* has an entire "Kehinde Wiley Shop" online where he peddles his "exclusive, limited-edition designs," such as a $395.00 silk scarf, described by the shop as "made from Italian silk twill with the image printed on both sides and . . . presented in a monogrammed rigid box, wrapped in branded tissue paper."[24]

Caitlin Meehye Beach, an assistant professor of art history and an affiliated faculty of the African and African American Studies department at Fordham University, notes admiringly in her catalogue essay that Wiley's *After La Négresse* comes "packaged in a glossy black cardboard box printed on one side with a high-contrast photo." The box seems "as much a part of the work of art as the sculpture itself," Beach writes breathlessly, unoffended by such commodification of culture.[25]

The Met castigates white artists' commercial motives as inimical to positive ideological content. Black artists get to hawk the hell out of their works while still claiming moral virtue. According to Beach, Wiley is not seeking to get rich with his Kehinde Wiley Shop; he is critiquing white supremacy. His marketing of *After Le Négresse*, box and all, simply "brings the question of bodily objectification into the contemporary moment," and makes a "forthright statement on the nature of art objects as consumable goods."[26]

White artists need not embrace penury, however. They *may* enter the stream of commerce without reproach if they are on the correct political side. If the Met's curators and essayists have ever objected to Shepard Fairey's wildly profitable Barack Obama silk screen, the record does not reflect it. Holland Cotter may scoff at sales of the Wedgewood medallion, but he is silent about the flood of Black Lives Matter–branded hoodies, hats, shirts, jewelry, and accessories available on Amazon. The *New York Times* admiringly covered the marketing of anti–Vladimir Putin T-shirts during the Ukraine war. And the curators of *Fictions* have not forsworn a cut of the profits from the Met's gift shop, where never-ending catalogues offer $250 Egyptian-themed necklaces and $38 Van Gogh tote bags.

Shattering the market nexus for non-Met-approved art requires going after the demand side as well. The wife of Emperor Napoleon III, Empress Eugénie, purchased a version of *Why Born Enslaved!* in 1869. She thus became complicit in the work's whitewashing of the colonial impulse. Curator Nelson sneers that "Eugénie stood to benefit from the political posturing that [the bust] enabled." The Left, as we know, would never engage in "political posturing." Yard signs announcing a house against hate and for science are acts of political sacrifice, not posturing. Ditto the Met's land acknowledgments—not cost-free virtue signaling but difficult decisions with real-world consequences. Nelson further demystifies Eugénie's purchase of the Carpeaux work as an effort to "protect her reputation as a virtuous empress devoted to charitable causes." The corporations that funneled billions into Black Lives Matter shell organizations in the weeks after George Floyd's death were not seeking to burnish their anti-racist credentials with the media and activists but were disinterestedly seeking alleged racial justice.

One work alone in the *Fictions* exhibit escapes the Met's opprobrium. The museum's treatment of that work is the most striking example of how the Met has abdicated its responsibility for education and connoisseurship. Edmonia Lewis was a nineteenth-century American neoclassical sculptor of black and American Indian descent. Her *Forever Free*, from 1867, depicts a male and female of indistinct age and relationship. The life-size male stands with his left arm raised and a broken shackle on his wrist. He is bare-chested and wearing what look like boxer shorts. The man's right hand rests on the shoulder of a kneeling supplicant female in a long frock; her hands are clasped in petition—or perhaps in thanks. The female's scale is so much smaller than the male's that it is difficult to know if she represents a child or the man's diminutive wife. While the male's tightly curled hair buttresses the assumption that he is black, the female's hair is long and wavy, her features too nondescript to provide a further clue as to her race.

Forever Free is patently inferior to the other works in *Fictions of Emancipation.* The composition is static; the figures are expressionless, their faces blank masks, without a trace of individuality. It is not just the scale between the two figures that is inconsistent; the anatomical proportions within each figure are also out of alignment. Their feet are gargantuan; the female's foot is as large as the male's, despite her miniature head and vastly reduced overall size compared to the male's colossal body. Lewis's modelling of muscle and bone is elementary.

And yet, the Met curators treat this work as the only masterpiece in the exhibit. The figures are "imbued with power, dignity, and spirituality—human traits they share with their creator," expounds a wall text. If Carpeaux possessed any such "human traits," a visitor to the show would never know. Though *Fictions of Emancipation* is nominally about Carpeaux, it provides little biographical background outside of the bare minimum to allegedly establish his supposed complicity with colonialism. Carpeaux's battles with excruciating pain and illness—recorded in haunting self-portraits—his artistic and financial struggles, and his personal losses are all ignored while Lewis's "determination to sculpt" is lauded for its bravery.

The Met's enthusiasm for the one "black"-created work included in the show is all the more striking, since *Forever Free* violates the proscriptions that damned more artistically compelling works. Despite the vacuity of the pair's expressions, Lewis presumably used live models for the composition. We do not know their names or biographies. Elyse Nelson claims that Carpeaux ignored the "personhood" of his subject in favor of a "racial type." This is curatorial malpractice. The subject of *Why Born Enslaved!* is particularized; we feel that we know the movement of her soul. Lewis's figures, by contrast, are generic.

The Met was scandalized that the white artists in *Fictions of Emancipation* portrayed recognizable blacks, thus fueling the fiction that race exists. But its commentators do not flinch from presuming the male in *Forever Free* to be black, thus confirming the reality of race. One commentator, Harvard University researcher Adrienne Childs, cheerfully concludes that the female is of mixed race. The Met scorned the supplicant gestures in white-created abolitionist works. The female in *Forever Free* is beseeching someone or something. She gets a pass, however.

The most shameless application of racial double standards comes from *New York Times* critic Holland Cotter. In January 2022, Cotter reviewed the Met's *African Origin of Civilization* show (which anticipated *Fictions of Emancipation* in its contempt for historical accuracy and aesthetic honesty. *See* Chapter Ten.) Cotter had criticized an ancient Egyptian sculpture of a man and a woman for making the "man...dominant." The Egyptian male was a "head taller than his mate, his left arm [was] around her shoulder; his hand cover[ing] her breast," Cotter wrote.[27]

Cotter should be concerned, then, about *Forever Free*'s "gender-based hierarchies," as he put it in his earlier review. Not only is the female three-quarters the scale of the male, she is on her knees, her head barely reaching up to the male's crotch, and under his protective paw.

Cotter solves the double standard problem elegantly: he simply excises the female out of the composition. Lewis's sculpture "offers an exultant vision of Black male agency in the figure of a man standing tall and waving broken chains skyward," Cotter writes. One would never guess from his description of the work that the man was "standing tall" next to a female. If we didn't know Cotter's sympathies, we might suspect him of misogyny.

The art museum was once considered a place apart, where visitors seeking beauty could see the world through more perceptive eyes than their own. British critic William Hazlitt marveled in 1824 at the newly opened National Gallery in London: "We are abstracted to another sphere; we breathe empyrean air; we enter into the minds of Raphael, of Titian, of Poussin, of the Caracci, and look at nature with their eyes; we live in time past, and seem identified with the permanent forms of things."[28] An art museum, Hazlitt wrote, "calls forth the most intense desires of the soul." A former curator at the Louvre Museum, Germain Bazin, compared the viewing of art to a "sort of trance uniting spectator and masterpiece."[29]

The Metropolitan Museum of Art is obliterating that ideal. The making and collecting of art—when done by white artists and white collectors—is now a culpable act for which the museum must atone. The Met's collections have "imperialist origins," its buildings occupy "stolen lands," and its galleries are dedicated to "pervasive narratives of white supremacy," notes Chief Sculpture Curator Sarah Lawrence.

The Met's European sculpture collection in particular is "embedded within a pernicious history of colonization," writes Lawrence, and "requires redress."[30] If there is beauty anywhere in those culpably "Eurocentric" galleries, you would never know it from the Met's spokesmen and scholars.

The Met used to acquire art because it was exquisite and because it expanded our understanding of artistic influence and evolution. In the 1998 bulletin of recent acquisitions, former Met Director Philippe De Montebello shared his enthusiasm for "an especially engaging addition to our Egyptian bestiary, a rare and good-sized alabaster hippopotamus head"; shards of some Greek vases, the "power and expressiveness" of which "transcend their fragmentary quality"; a "spectacular" harvest of drawings; and one of Caravaggio's "most moving late tenebrist paintings."[31]

Such enthusiasm is in short supply today. The Met now acquires white-created art as if it were taking castor oil. The Met purchased *Why Born Enslaved!*, writes Lawrence, to fulfill a "commitment to broaden the narratives told in our galleries." The bust is a "prompt to acknowledge issues of race and empire."[32]

"Narratives," not seeing, drive the Met today. Director Max Hollein writes in his catalogue essay that the *Fictions* exhibit grows out of the Met's campaign to redress "institutional narratives by bringing race to the forefront of our discussion of 5000 years of art."[33] Race was irrelevant for probably 99 percent or more of the works created during those 5000 years, which will not stop the Met from imposing its anti-Western template upon them.

Museumgoers don't need a "prompt to acknowledge issues of race and empire." They are surrounded by such "issues" every day. To use a work as dazzling in its technical accomplishment as *Why Born Enslaved!* to pummel viewers for their white supremacy is a misallocation of resources. Banal sources like the *New York Times* and CNN provide such pummeling without any artistic skill at all.

But the artist is no longer a source of transcendence or insight. The Met worries that visitors might think that Carpeaux offers a glimpse of the human spirit rebelling against bondage. Worse, visitors might even think that Carpeaux and other artists have portrayed blacks with empathy and understanding, thus leaping over the color line so necessary for today's racial activism. So the Met nervously advises viewers that Carpeaux is "only able to convey his perception of a world about which he has only an idea." This gratuitous put-down is a meaningless truism. No human being has unmediated access to the world outside of his perceptions, as Plato, Locke, Kant, and other philosophers have understood. But human beings do differ in their capacity to imagine and communicate a broader range of experience than their own; traditionally we have turned to artists for just that superior capacity.

The works in *Fictions of Emancipation* refute on their face the "narrative" that the Met imposes on them. Subjugation of enemy peoples is not what sets the West apart from the rest of the world. Cruelty toward the "Other" has characterized virtually all human societies, and still does in many parts of the world today. Traditional attitudes toward foreigners in non-Western countries like China and Japan, or toward lower-caste Hindus in India, or toward blacks among African Arabs,[34] have been condescending, to put it mildly.

Only the West developed whole disciplines devoted to understanding non-Western cultures.[35] Some of those disciplines may have originally been handmaidens to conquest.[36] But European interest in difference, manifest in Herodotus and Xenophon's observations about Asia, preceded colonialization and outlasted it. The Met should mount a show of non-Western portrayals of the Other. It would have a hard time locating works displaying as much respect for their subject as Carpeaux's bust of a Chinese man, whose glance conveys mysterious depths of feeling, or Jean-Léon Gérôme's resplendent warrior Bashi-Bazouk (both included in the *Fictions* show). Non-Western representations of the "Other," often sanctioned and promoted by the state, routinely descend into caricature.

The Met should also try to mount an exhibit of African art calling for an end to Africa's essential and profiteering role in internal and external slave trades. Its crusading curators might discover that the trait of fierce self-criticism has not been equally distributed among the world's civilizations.

Fictions of Emancipation is a barometer of hate. Only hate toward Western civilization could drive the repudiation of art historical knowledge required to arrive at the show's analyses. Only hate could drive so casual a disregard for consistency in the application of aesthetic and moral standards. The curators started with their conclusion: the West is unremittingly white supremacist, even (or especially) when it appears to be fighting against white supremacy. Then they manufactured evidence to support that conclusion, evidence provided solely by parroting the tired nostrums of academic theory. Give the Met credit for aiming high. If it can portray abolitionist art as a smoke screen for slavery, it can portray anything in Western history as a pretext for oppression—and it will do so.

This hate is a betrayal of the Met's civilizational responsibilities. For a century-and-a-half, donors gave it art that responds to our yearning for sublimity and that teaches us to see beauty in the everyday. Now the museum wants to expose the alleged racist subtexts of those works. The distortions entailed by that demystifying project will take down art itself.

Chapter Twelve

ABSTAINERS

Not all members of the arts world capitulate to phony racial grievance, however.

Conductor and violinist John McLaughlin Williams, whom we met in Chapter Four, for example, has a question for advocates of de-blinding orchestral auditions: "Why hold an audition at all? Why not just send in a head shot?"[1]

Williams's contempt for the racialization of classical music is not the only thing that sets him apart from today's classical music establishment. His voracious musical curiosity has led him on a quest that few other conductors have dared.

Ever since he was a child growing up in Washington, DC, Williams has been fascinated by the vagaries of musical fate. He would pore over a music encyclopedia, reading about once-popular composers who have since been forgotten. *Why don't we hear them now?* he wondered. As a student at the New England Conservatory of Music, he haunted the library stacks, perusing scores that are no longer played.

That passion for the musical unknown resulted in an important project of historical reclamation. Williams has recorded works from a group of neoromantic American composers from the first half of the twentieth century, including Nicolas Flagello, Arnold Rosner, George Frederick McKay, and Henry Kimball Hadley—the latter of whom Williams calls the first rock star of classical music. These once-prominent musicians have fallen into near-total oblivion, despite constituting a key chapter in American musical history. Their compositional style violated the emerging modernist orthodoxies, Williams says. "They were hated by a younger generation of composers who fled to the university and wrote books."

Williams's discography alone distinguishes him from his colleagues. Most conductors, Williams observes, have been "astoundingly unoriginal in their programming, constantly replaying old pieces in which they have nothing to say, rather than finding some vital work that could use their advocacy."[2] Performing the 217th Beethoven or Mahler symphony cycle is a much surer commercial bet.

Orchestral musicians are often little better than conductors in their musical conservatism. Many "labor under the philosophically false premise that if they haven't heard of [a work], it can't be any good," Williams jokes.

An additional fact about Williams's career is noteworthy in the current moment: the majority of the composers whom he has championed have been white. His recordings—featuring a black conductor leading the National Symphony Orchestra of Ukraine in the performance of obscure American works—epitomize the universality of classical music and constitute a profound rebuttal to the constricting vision of today's racial arbiters.

"I never gave race any thought and never used it in my career," Williams says. As a violin student, he had as his role models Jascha Heifetz, Nathan Milstein, and Zino Francescatti. His color blindness was an inheritance from his family. His parents—both accomplished pianists—met as music students at Howard University. Williams grew up hearing Chopin nocturnes and études, Bach partitas, and Beethoven sonatas on the family piano. Did it matter that those composers were white males? "It never came up," he answers. Williams's parents also played William Grant Still, Ulysses Kay, and other black composers. But they acknowledged the greatness of the musical canon. "It's why we play these things. All great ideas that have ever been born in the world were meant for everyone. It's the reason I have a car and can get vaccines."[3]

The conductor's family epitomizes the tradition of black bourgeois striving, courageously maintained in the face of widespread discrimination. His maternal grandfather, John C. McLaughlin, returned severely injured from military service in France during World War I. Though the veteran McLaughlin had not finished grammar school, he went on to earn a master of science degree in agricultural economics from Cornell University. He became a dean at the North Carolina Agricultural and Technical College, while serving on dozens of philanthropic boards. Williams's paternal grandfather was one of the few black officials in the Defense Department. Both sets of grandparents passed on a love of classical music to their children. Williams's father aspired to a career as a classical pianist but was blocked by prejudice. Though he rarely talked about his experiences with discrimination, Williams says, they took a deep psychic toll on him, leading to depression and drinking.

Yet despite this personal tragedy, Williams is able to distinguish the present from the past. The classical music industry was "racist in the day but not now by any means," he says. Though he disagrees with the reflexive charge of discrimination, he understands its origin: history makes it almost impossible for "black people to believe that any reverse in fortune or progress is not rooted in racism, because in the past, it always, always was."[4]

Williams leaves race out of the narrative when describing his own classical music career. As a twelve-year-old, he soloed as a violinist at the Kennedy Center in concerts for DC's schoolchildren; a backstage photo after one of those concerts shows a smiling and self-possessed young Williams shaking First Lady Pat Nixon's hand, surrounded by Betty Ford and the wives of Nixon cabinet officials.

Though Williams eventually landed a coveted concertmaster seat at the Virginia Symphony, the repetitiousness of the repertoire wore on him. The only way he could build on his passion for lost music was to be at the front of the orchestra, not within it, he concluded. He walked away from his concertmaster position and, in 1994, enrolled in the Cleveland Institute of Music's conducting program. Happily, around that time, the Naxos record label had launched an American Classics series, featuring forgotten American works. Williams's encyclopedic knowledge of that repertoire was a perfect fit, and he began rolling out a series of recordings with the label.

His choice of music as a violin soloist has been as iconoclastic as his conducting repertoire. British composer Sir Arnold Bax is rarely, if ever, performed in the United States. Williams encountered some of Bax's symphonic scores during his library sleuthing. They were a "revelation," he says: "Strong, biting, hard-edged music of struggle, yet tinged with the wistfulness of one who has known loss. I was hooked."[5] Ever the contrarian, Williams became "really interested" in Bax's violin concerto after reading a negative assessment of the work. He tracked down the music in the Library of Congress and gave the concerto its US premiere in 1990—fifty-two years after it was written—soloing on the violin with the Pro Arte Chamber Orchestra of Boston.

Williams's masterful performance, available on YouTube, digs into Bax's complicated syncopations with rhythmic flair and suavely shapes the concerto's melodic lines.

Williams is scathing about the introduction of identity politics into music. "It will be the death of quality," he warns. "It will breed resentment from musicians who have worked all their lives to achieve perfection." An orchestra's primary reason for being is to make the best music it can with the best musicians available, according to Williams; social justice is not its comparative advantage. "It's ridiculous to pursue 12 percent black representation in orchestras," he told me. "It's an unrealistic expectation, given the deliriously difficult level of competition now, especially from Asians." Moreover, programming and hiring by race will not bring blacks into the concert hall over the long-term unless those black audiences have an underlying interest in the music.

Williams is not optimistic about resistance to the quota lobby, however: "It will take an administration inured to being called a racist." Unfortunately, "nothing scares these organizations more" than that charge. "The accusers don't have to prove anything. It's like Soviet-style confessions: the accused is guilty no matter what he actually did."[6]

Ironically, the prejudice that Williams has encountered as a musician is not racial but political. He was a candidate for a significant recording project until the family of the composer whose music he was to record learned of Williams's purported conservative leanings. (The composer was no longer alive.) In a long missive explaining the family's decision, the project's producer recounted his own shock upon discovering in the early 2000s that Williams had backed George W. Bush. That dismay paled in comparison with the producer's horror in hearing that Williams occasionally wrote in support of Donald Trump on Facebook. "I have to say, I can't begin to imagine how you rationalize/justify this to yourself—it is beyond my ability to comprehend. This is partly because I haven't encountered a soul who supports Trump, other than perhaps the local pizza guy." The composer's family was encased in the same political bubble: "In all honesty," the producer wrote, "everyone's immediate reaction was that they could never work with someone who would associate himself with and defend that individual."[7]

Williams responded passionately:

> I cannot find words to express how disappointing it was to read your [email]. . . . I have always accepted that people will disagree about many things and yet when it comes to work—to music—I have no problem at all working with anyone. It is the American Way to agree to disagree and to do so civilly without harm to life, limb, or livelihood. That was a major part of The Founders' purpose: to enable disagreement, dialogue, and a smooth, non-violent transfer of power. That has been forgotten by an unhealthy chunk of the population. . . . It shouldn't matter what I think or who I support politically; when it comes to music, we have always wanted the best result.

One of Williams's former teachers, reading the composer's account of the exchange on Facebook, responded that he, too, would deny work to someone sharing Williams's political orientation.[8] This teacher, not Williams, is most representative of the classical music industry today.

Williams has not backed down from expressing views that put him at odds with much of that establishment, however. On the Fourth of July 2021, he posted on Facebook: "Happy Birthday to the greatest country the world has ever known. It is a place where the humblest and most common can achieve the highest and most respected places in society through dint of hard work, determination, and a willingness to take risks. Our core documents were sagaciously designed to encompass everyone, and they do despite those who tried to prevent it."[9]

■ ■ ■

Tulsa Opera also took an unexpected stand against victim politics in a dispute with composer Daniel Bernard Roumain.

Roumain has made a good career leveraging his skin color. He writes pieces with titles like "i am a white person who ____ Black people."[10] He argues that orchestras should "focus on BLACK artists exclusively" (capitalization in the original). He has solicited funding for a work written "EXCLUSIVELY for BIPOC [black, indigenous, and people of color] members of ANY orchestra."[11]

When a percussionist on Roumain's Facebook page suggested that such a work would be divisive, Roumain told him to "speak less and try to listen and learn and understand more." BIPOC musicians "FACE racism everyday" from their white orchestral colleagues, Roumain added. In fact, Roumain argues, white musicians' contracts should be term-limited as reparations for "decades of benefitting from orchestral racism."[12] Roumain's racial-justice profile has earned him a seat on the boards of the League of American Orchestras and the Association of Performing Arts Presenters, as well as a faculty position at Arizona State University. He has been commissioned by Carnegie Hall and is working on film, TV, and opera scores.

He likely seemed a natural choice, then, to write a piece to commemorate the centennial of a race riot in Tulsa. That explosion of violence,

from May 31, 1921, to June 1, 1921, followed a still-undetermined incident between a nineteen-year-old black male and a seventeen-year-
old white female. Tulsa officials tried to protect the male from a possible lynching; armed black residents circled the jail where the teen was
being held as another line of defense. Gunfire broke out around the jail,
killing ten whites and two blacks. In retaliation, white rampagers looted
and set fire to hundreds of homes and businesses in the black section
of Tulsa called Greenwood. Entire neighborhoods were reduced to
ashes, leaving thousands homeless. A 2001 report by the Tulsa Race
Riot Commission confirmed twenty-six black and ten white deaths
from the riots;[13] unofficial estimates put the death toll at several
hundred. Many more were wounded.

Tulsa Opera planned a concert called *Greenwood Overcomes* as part
of the city's riot centennial events. Eight black opera singers, accompanied on the piano by Metropolitan Opera assistant conductor Howard
Watkins (discussed in Chapter Four), would perform the works of
twenty-three living black composers. Tulsa Opera commissioned four
new works for the concert, the first commissions in its history.

Roumain received one of those commissions, and it was a peach:
writing a short aria for mezzo-soprano Denyce Graves. Graves's Metropolitan Opera debut as Carmen in 1995 received rousing acclaim,
drawing international attention to her full-bodied vocal tone and smol-
dering stage presence. She would be the biggest star of the Tulsa
concert; any composer would jump to have her perform his work.

Roumain titled his aria for Graves "They Still Want to Kill Us," referring, he explained, to "the murder of Breonna Taylor and George
Floyd," deaths that provide evidence of the "bloodlust sown deep within
the American psyche."[14] Roumain's titles are his calling card, into which
he puts his greatest effort, he says—arguably an unusual emphasis for
a composer; once he comes up with the name of a piece, the musical
writing comes easily, he says.

Roumain also wrote the aria's lyrics, which begin with brief phrases
about the rampage and end with:

They still want to kill us.

God Bless America

God Damn America.[15]

Before Roumain composed the piece, Graves had sent him possible texts as an example of what might appeal to her. This was not it. Graves balked at the aria as written. "I don't have trouble with strong lyrics," she explained in a written statement. "As a Black woman I am a huge supporter of all Black Lives, Black expression, and creativity." But the aria's concluding words did not "line up with my personal values," she wrote. She could not "find an honest place to express the lyrics as they were presented."[16]

Tulsa Opera's artistic director, composer Tobias Picker, suggested that Roumain rewrite the final line, perhaps to "God Help America."[17] Roumain refused to make any changes, and Graves declined further involvement with the piece. Picker reached out to other singers on the program; they were also reluctant to sing the work, Picker says. Tulsa Opera cancelled the Roumain piece and paid him his fee.[18]

If Tulsa Opera was caught off guard by the content of "They Still Want to Kill Us," it should not have been. Roumain was also invited to participate in another group composing project called *America/beautiful*, which premiered on July 4, 2021. The purpose of *America/beautiful*, according to organizer Min Kwon, is to remind us that "there is still so much beauty in this country of ours."[19] Roumain's contribution was called "America, NEVER beautiful." He explained the title: "I don't want to be complicit in the horrors of white America, so, as a composer, I will do all that I can to remind us all just how much America has not, is not, and may not ever really be beautiful.... This country has created horrors for so many, that the title reflects how I feel, and the music is an expression of anger and rage and sorrow."[20]

Roumain's response to the cancellation of "They Still Want to Kill Us" was also predictable: he went immediately to work playing the race card, finding a receptive audience in the classical music press. Welcome to "Life in Black America," he tweeted.[21] The cancellation of his aria was the "height of racist and discriminatory practice," he told *New York*'s Vulture website.[22] The decommissioning of "They Still Want to Kill Us" echoed the racist tragedy that the concert was meant to commemorate, he said. The Black Opera Alliance announced that it was "saddened and disturbed" by Tulsa Opera's decision.[23]

Roumain was particularly exercised that Picker was involved in trying to reach a compromise. Picker is white. No matter that Graves was the one who rejected the piece and that Howard Watkins was just as instrumental as Picker in the abortive negotiations. The entire incident, in Roumain's view, reflected what happens when a white male runs a classical music organization. Roumain told Tulsa Public Radio that it "hurt" to have Picker suggest possible revisions. Picker's whiteness is emblematic of the racism of an institution with "far too many white males in charge," Roumain said. And Picker's suggested revisions didn't speak to "what happened on Jan. 6, what happened in Ferguson, what happened in Charlottesville . . . what happened in Atlanta."[24]

Roumain expanded on his theme in a statement to *Opera Wire*:

The Tulsa Opera has revealed why the operatic field continues to be seen as racist and divisive. When a Black composer must endure the intrusions of a white composer—within a work and a festival built around the death and artistry of Black people—but insists on his words and his way, what are we to think and do? I say we don't bend, or break, or subject ourselves to their ideas. . . . I don't think asking a white man to be the Artistic Director around an event honoring the murder of hundreds of Black men, women, and children—by a mob of white men—was the right choice. . . . When these types of poor administrative choices happen, they often times lead to these types of artistic and moral dilemmas.

It was Graves who refused the final line and Roumain who "insist[ed] on his words and his way." But in his racial monomania, Roumain effaces Graves's agency and transfers it to a white man, even though Picker was just a go-between.

The concert organizers were astonished by Roumain's racial gloss. The "desire to change the text was not a race issue," Watkins told *Opera Wire*.[25] It was "reverse racist, and a bit offensive actually" for Roumain to denounce Picker, he said, given that Picker's opera company was seeking to uplift black composers.[26]

Picker, moreover, is a far cry from the white reactionary of Roumain's nightmares. Tulsa Opera hosted the American debut of a transgender Heldenbaritone—formerly male, now "female"—who in 2019 sang the title role in Tulsa's *Don Giovanni*, creating a sexual hall of mirrors that would delight the most cutting-edge gender studies professor. Picker's own opera about one of the first recipients of sex-reassignment surgery will be premiered in 2023.

Roumain equates being asked to rewrite a line of text with having one's home burned down by a mob. The comparison is not only hyperbolic but also unhistorical. For centuries, composers have chafed under the operatic star system. Sopranos, castrati, and tenors often insisted on replacing arias that the harried composer had written expressly for their voice with an aria from an unrelated opera, likely by a different composer, that they believed would better showcase their talents. Broadway and film composers have likewise had to watch impotently as their favorite music ends up on the cutting-room floor.

In this case, Denyce Graves was not even behaving like the prototypical diva; her reluctance to sing "They are Still Killing Us" grew out of a philosophical difference. She was asking for just one line of revision rather than for the sacking of the entire work.

Roumain quickly appealed for funding to premiere the aria in a different venue. A "consortium of loving Partners in Creation,"[27] as he put it, came through, including Opera Philadelphia, Apollo Theater, the Fine Arts Center at the University of Massachusetts Amherst, Joe's Pub, Stanford Live, and the University Musical Society at the University of Michigan.[28] A video of the work was produced and released on May 25, 2021, to commemorate the one-year anniversary of the death of George Floyd.[29] Mezzo-soprano J'Nai Bridges, a leader in opera's Black Lives

Matter movement, sang the piece in Central Park, while sometimes-puzzling images, such as a document on felon disenfranchisement in the 2014 midterm elections, flashed across the screen.

The video suggested an additional reason why Graves may have balked: "They Still Want to Kill Us" is lousy music. The piano accompaniment consists of New Age-y broken triads and cliché-ridden chord progressions. The melodic line is negligible; Roumain struggles to fit words to music, awkwardly cramming lines of text, such as "In that elevator everything changed," into inadequate musical space. A composer speculates that had the score risen to "some purpose that could dramatically support" the "God damn America" exhortation, there may not have been a problem. "Graves is canny enough to understand that she cannot say publicly that this just sucks," the composer observes. "Although I do believe that she was not in sympathy with the tone and thrust of the text, she also knows well what good music is. This ain't it."[30]

Tulsa Opera's *Greenwood Overcomes* may have been the first time that Roumain has not gotten his way. In the summer of 2020, Roumain had been complaining on Facebook about the lack of racial proportionality in orchestras. A retired principal violist from the Detroit Symphony Orchestra offered to tutor minority musicians in audition techniques if Roumain would secure introductions. The offer went nowhere, apparently because the violist, Alexander Mishnaevski, was not sufficiently sensitive to the black struggle in the eyes of Roumain and his Facebook followers.

Later that year, when Roumain announced his commission from the New Jersey Symphony for "i am a white person who ____ Black people," Mishnaevski let rip with a Facebook post accusing Roumain of racial divisiveness and musical mediocrity. The post was so intemperate that one can only surmise that the Russian-born Mishnaevski, despite five decades in the US, remains naïve about America's racial landmines.

This one, of course, blew up. The Detroit Symphony Orchestra expressed its outrage at Mishnaevski's "racist comments" and immediately programmed "i am a white person who ____ Black people" for its next season. Mishnaevski would be banned from any future involvement with the orchestra. The New Jersey Symphony Orchestra condemned the "vile comment," which only underscores the need, it said, for all to "stand against racism and hatred, and the need for orchestras to amplify BIPOC voices." The symphony reiterated its "commitment to addressing racism that exists in our field" and declared, "Black Lives Matter."[31] Roumain wondered on Facebook why Mishnaevski was still receiving a "pension for being [a] racist."

A contemporaneous photo on the New Jersey Symphony Orchestra's website publicizing "i am a white person" showed smiling, elderly white people clustered around the composer, hanging on his every word. One imagines him explaining his status as a victim of their white privilege, an accusation they humbly accept. The NJSO audience will have many more opportunities to learn from Roumain about their white privilege, since in April 2021, he was named the orchestra's inaugural resident artistic catalyst, one of the many novel titles that have been pouring out of arts organizations desperate to diversify their organization chart.[32]

The "I am a white person" flap amplified Roumain's profile. But he may have avoided embarrassment in Tulsa. The *Greenwood Overcomes* concert contained musical riches.[33] The piano writing was sinuous and suave. The ecstatic accompaniment in Adolphus Hailstork's "My Heart to Thy Heart" (1954) recalled Rachmaninoff and Scriabin, while the syncopations in Tania León's "Mi amor es" (2016) brought Manuel Ponce to mind. Melanie DeMore's "Sending You Light" (1993) achieved a consoling catharsis in the tradition of Schubert's "Des Baches Wiegenlied," albeit with far more elementary musical means. Graves delivered DeMore's song as if speaking straight into the listener's heart. Jazz and Spanish idioms, filled with delicate harmonies, infused songs by David Bontemps, Quinn Mason, and Rosephanye Powell. The poetry, often lush and surreal, whether by Langston Hughes or Gwendolyn Bennett, was smoothly set to the scores.

"They Still Want To Kill Us" would have been out of place at *Greenwood Overcomes*, its musical level overmatched and, though not disqualifying, its tone discordant. Surprisingly, love songs predominated on the program, followed up by anthems of hope and uplift. The only piece about the Greenwood massacre itself was an excerpt from an opera by Anthony Davis, *Fire Across the Tracks: Tulsa 1921*, commissioned by the Tulsa Opera. "There Are Many Trails of Tears," in a jazzy style occasionally bordering on atonalism, recounts the alleged aerial firebombing of Greenwood. The narrator's father was enslaved by the Chickasaw, which may explain why the libretto claims that the father "lived in peace." The aria ends with electronic whisperings and clickings offstage, invoking the aerial firebombing. (That air raid, reported as fact in the media's centennial coverage, is contested; the 2001 Tulsa Race Riot Commission found little support for the claim.[34])

The enthusiastic audience for *Greenwood Overcomes* was predominantly white and middle-aged, judging by the concert video, just like Roumain's audience at the New Jersey Symphony Orchestra. This demographic, scorned by the Black Lives Matter movement, is more likely to turn out for black-themed programs than blacks themselves. Roumain seeks color-coded boundaries around artistic expression and historical commemoration. This neo-segregationism is not just a blow against human understanding; it is also commercially suicidal.

Roumain tried to get in the last word, playing the victim to the end. "I love Tulsa Opera," he told Vulture. "The question is, does Tulsa Opera still love me? And if they're going to say that they can't say the words 'God damn America,' well, what does 'God bless America' really mean for them?" Tulsa Opera undoubtedly still does "love" Roumain and will be happy to commission him again. The significance of the episode, however, is that the company is still standing, despite having refused to cave in to a racial hustle. In a world of increasingly craven arts organizations, that, too, is worth commemorating.

■ ■ ■

Tulsa Opera has not been the only opera company to refuse to buckle. Long Beach Opera (LBO)—which would seem even less likely than Tulsa Opera to resist racial pressure tactics—also stood firm. Celebrated by music critics for its "provocative" programming and stagings,[35] Long Beach Opera commissioned *The Central Park Five*,[36] for example, an opera about the allegedly wrongful convictions of five minority teens for a near-fatal beating and rape of a white jogger in New York's Central Park in 1989. Anthony Davis, composer of *Fire Across the Tracks: Tulsa 1921*, mentioned previously, wrote the score.

Every decision taken by Long Beach Opera happens, in Executive Director Jennifer Rivera's words, through the lens of "'equity, diversity, inclusion and representation.'"[37] Hiring a white male is a last resort. "'I really did not want to hire a white man'" as the opera's new artistic director, Rivera told the *Los Angeles Times* in February 2021. Nevertheless, Rivera gritted her teeth and hired the disturbingly undiverse James Darrah anyway, since there are "'very, very, very few opera directors of color,'" as Rivera explained.

Otherwise, Long Beach Opera has filled out its managerial ranks with "persons of color," conferring on them an ever-changing array of titles. It hired self-described "equity, diversity, and inclusion (EDI) practitioner" Derrell Acon in 2018 as manager of "community engagement and education." Acon was then promoted to "director of engagement and equity." He eventually became "associate artistic director and chief impact officer."[38]

In 2020, Long Beach Opera asked stage director Alexander Gedeon if he would serve as artist in residence. Gedeon could pick his title and decide on his responsibilities, the opera said. Gedeon joined the company and eventually denominated himself "minister of culture," a title reminiscent of the Nation of Islam.

While Acon was wearing the hat of director of engagement and equity, he nominated himself for the artistic director post. Not only did Long Beach Opera choose the white Darrah instead, but the other finalist for artistic director was also white—a red flag if ever there were one. Incredibly, in August 2021, Rivera followed up with another white male pick, choosing contemporary music impresario Christopher Rountree as the company's new music director.

By then, Acon and Gedeon were complaining about being left out of decision-making. They accused Artistic Director James Darrah of "shutting down" whenever Acon and Gedeon challenged company plans "through the lens of equity and inclusion," in the words of the *Los Angeles Times*. Darrah had had the temerity to propose a project allegedly featuring all-white collaborators. When Acon and Gedeon objected, Darrah allegedly went quiet. Acon, Gedeon, and the *Times* imply that Darrah's alleged refusal to "engage in the conversation," in the *Times*'s words, was a sign of white privilege. In fact, it was likely a sign of terror.

Gedeon launched the mandatory "unsafety" claim. "I don't actually feel safe, because even when I'm seeing a Black person given power, I'm then watching them precluded from it," he told the *Times*. Who knew that a cushy administrative job in a time of financial cutbacks in the arts was dangerous?

In 2022, a week before Long Beach Opera's 2022 season was to open, Acon and Gedeon resigned, lodging complaints of racial bias. The company hired an investigator, a human resources firm, and a mediator to look into the charges. *Mirabile dictu*, the investigator found no evidence of racial bias, and the company did not offer an apology. The company's press statement read: "While a great deal of the allegations listed here are extremely misleading, lacking in important context, simply false, or contain direct personal attacks, we feel that as an organization, continuing to publicly engage with the complaints of former employees is causing undue harm to our current employees and artists."

Composer Anthony Davis defended Long Beach Opera. Acon and Gedeon had undercut the June 2022 revival of *The Central Park Five*, Davis charged. After their resignations, a host of production staff and performers pulled out of the revival in solidarity with Acon and Gedeon. "I thought there were efforts on their part to undermine the project. And I felt that that was misplaced," Davis told the *Times*. "And

I felt that was destructive in terms of the bigger picture of what we want to accomplish in terms of people of color in opera." LBO has been one of the strongest advocates for "composers of color," Davis said. Another black composer, Shelley Washington, seconded Davis's assessment of the company.

Like Daniel Roumain, Gedeon and Acon played the race card to the end, including against other "POCs." LBO had used a familiar and "abhorrent" tactic to "pit Black people against other Black people to protect white structures," Acon told the *Times*. Also like Roumain, Gedeon and Acon are not hurting for other diversity gigs. Acon will continue serving as Opera Philadelphia's first Vice President of People Operations & Inclusion,[39] for example, a position he assumed in January 2022 while still at LBO.

When other arts companies face phony charges of racism, as most will in the post-Floyd age, they should ponder the examples of Tulsa Opera and Long Beach Opera. The moral of those sagas is: never apologize; never endorse a racial falsehood. If only the Scottish Opera, the Art Institute of Chicago, the Metropolitan Museum of Art, the League of American Orchestras, the Juilliard School, and so many other leading institutions had shown the same integrity.

PART III

LAW AND ORDER

Chapter Thirteen

A NEW CRIME WAVE

Disparate impact analysis has had its most concrete effect on the criminal justice system, where every disparity in arrest or incarceration rates is now attributed to racism. Prosecutors, legislators, and police chiefs are rolling back criminal penalties and enforcement to eliminate such disparities. The lessons of two decades of successful crime-fighting have been forgotten, with predictable results: spreading violence and predation.

New York City was the laboratory for the earlier successful anti-crime crusade. Former mayor Rudolph Giuliani presided over a 62 percent drop in major felonies from 1994 through 2001. That crime drop proved that violence was not an urban inevitability. Giuliani's successor, Michael Bloomberg, drove crime down further, through the 2008 recession and beyond. Both mayors set a benchmark for what was possible, preemptively discrediting any future mayor's excuse that crime was beyond his capacity to overcome. Many New Yorkers assured themselves that a return to the crime and squalor of early 1990s New York was unlikely.

That assumption about the permanence of the crime drop was wrong. New York City in 2020 experienced an unprecedented one-year increase in homicides and shootings.[1] Through late December 2020, the number of murders was up 41 percent from 2019[2] and 53 percent from 2018. Shooting victims were up 103 percent from 2019 and 109 percent from 2018; shooting incidents rose 95 percent and 104 percent over 2019 and 2018, respectively. In gang-ridden precincts, the spike was even more startling. In Brooklyn's Brownsville and Bedford-Stuyvesant neighborhoods, there were 170 percent more shooting victims in 2020 than in 2019 and 151 percent more shooting incidents. Murder was up 94 percent in these parts of Brooklyn.

It wasn't just gang areas that were afflicted. On December 29, 2020, a roving pack of young bicyclists in midtown Manhattan attacked a BMW, smashing a bike on top of the car and jumping on its windshield. The same group went after a cab minutes later. Office workers in the area have been chased by similar flash mobs.

The 2020 increase was actually worse than the annual numbers suggested. Street crime dropped from March 2020 to late May 2020 due to the coronavirus lockdown.[3] The 2020 increase incorporates that early crime drop. Measured from June to the end of 2020, the rise in violence would be even more extreme. And it continued. Carjackings surged 55 percent in 2021;[4] major felonies rose another 7 percent over 2020. Homicides were up 52 percent in 2021 over 2019 and shootings up 100 percent over 2019.

New York Mayor Bill de Blasio seemed almost blasé about this crisis. The reason for that passivity is the same as the reason for the crime increase itself: the dominance of disparate impact as the overriding policy concern among liberals and progressives. As long as disparate impact remains the primary focus of New York's leaders, the crime surge will continue.

De Blasio's early mayoralty suggested that the Giuliani-Bloomberg benchmark was, in fact, checking the default Leftism of New York's leadership class. De Blasio chose as his police commissioner William Bratton. Bratton had engineered the crime turnaround of the 1990s as Giuliani's first police commissioner. Selecting Bratton angered de Blasio's Left-wing base, which demanded a black or female commissioner (or, ideally, both). But de Blasio wanted maximal insurance against a crime increase, so he went with the sure bet. His next two commissioners were also white males, chosen for their likely ability to keep crime down, rather than for their race and sex. The Left was even angrier, but it could not overcome the power of the benchmark.

In 2020, though, something even more powerful than a concern for one's political legacy arose: the need to signal a commitment to fighting white supremacy. As we have seen throughout this book, racial disparities became the obsession of the nation's elites, whether in medical school student bodies and faculties, in concert halls, or on museum walls. The core concern of the disparate impact crusade, however, is policing and incarceration. This is not a new focus, but in 2020, it became ever more destructive of law and order.

For years, anti-police activists, academics, and liberal politicians have decried the overrepresentation of blacks in the criminal-justice system. Blacks make up less than 13 percent of the nation's adult population, but they account for about one-third of the combined federal and state prison rolls;[5] their per-capita rate of imprisonment is more than five times higher than the per-capita imprisonment rate of whites.[6] Racism on the part of cops and prosecutors is the only permissible explanation for that disparity; acknowledging the vastly higher black crime rate is taboo. (The black incarceration rate is driven by convictions for violent crime—not, as popular lore has it, by convictions for drug offenses; 61.9 percent of black prisoners in state facilities, which house the vast majority of the nation's prisoners, were serving time for a violent offense in 2018, compared with 48.3 percent of white state prisoners. By contrast, a larger percentage of white prisoners than of black prisoners was serving time for drug offenses: 16.3 percent of white prisoners versus 12.7 percent of black prisoners.[7] Virtually all drug prisoners are drug traffickers, even when their conviction is for the more easily proven "possession.") If, as anti-racism orthodoxy dictates, the real root causes of higher black crime—above all, family breakdown—may not be discussed, then the only way to reduce racial disparities in the criminal-justice system is to stop penalizing criminal behavior.

Such decriminalization efforts were ongoing in New York before 2020. The New York City Council and the New York State Legislature had lightened traditional penalties for a host of public-order offenses, such as public urination and public drinking. Bail was eliminated for misdemeanors and many felonies. The Manhattan and Brooklyn district attorneys competed for the most sweeping de-prosecution initiatives. Former Manhattan District Attorney Cy Vance announced that he would not prosecute turnstile jumping, calling it a crime of poverty. (Actually, it's a crime of arrogance, as a retired NYPD chief told me. Here is a challenge to Vance: find a turnstile jumper who does not possess a smart phone.) Not to be outdone, Brooklyn District Attorney Eric Gonzalez stopped sending most youthful gunslingers into detention, diverting them instead into poorly managed social services programs. Meanwhile, officers who put pressure on a resisting suspect's back or chest to subdue his violence could now be criminally charged.

These anti-racism initiatives were just warm-ups. The more frenzied dismantling of law enforcement began in mid-2020, triggered by the national riots over Floyd's death. As noted in Chapter One, the incident was universally treated as a manifestation of the lethal police brutality that blacks allegedly endure on a daily basis. Minneapolis was the first city to burn, and riots soon spread across the country. In New York City, caravans of looters smashed storefronts and made off with millions of dollars in luxury merchandise and dollar-store inventory alike; rioters burned police cars and attacked officers with bottles, bricks, cement blocks, and jagged metal pipes. Officers worked back-to-back shifts with no time to sleep; nearly 400 officers were injured. More than 200 police cars were vandalized. As darkness fell each night, the city cowered behind plywood barriers hastily erected over apartment building entrances and commercial storefronts.

De Blasio called the unrest "very justified" and asked the police to use a "light touch" because people are "undeniably angry for a reason."[8] Not surprisingly, the violence continued unabated, finally pushing the mayor to impose an 8 p.m. curfew, the city's first since World War II.[9] Manhattan D.A. Vance was not cooperating. Vance would not be prosecuting curfew violations and other riot-related offenses, like disorderly conduct and resisting arrest, his office announced.

The capitulation continued. On June 15, Police Commissioner Dermot Shea announced that he was dismantling the undercover units tasked with getting armed felons off the streets. This abdication was being done in the name of serving the "community"—code for avoiding disparate impact. The so-called anti-crime units were among the last NYPD entities that forthrightly used their constitutional power to stop, question, and sometimes frisk individuals engaged in criminally suspicious behavior—a legal tactic, contrary to what New York's political class believes. Shea labeled the tactic "brute force."[10]

It is true, as was widely reported after Shea's announcement, that anti-crime officers were involved in a disproportionate number of police shootings. What was not reported was how low that number of shootings was. In 2019, there were twenty-five incidents in which NYPD officers intentionally shot criminal suspects, the second-lowest number of officer-involved shootings since records began to be kept nearly fifty years ago. Fifty-four members of the NYPD were involved in those twenty-five shooting incidents, of which nineteen—or 35 percent— were from anti-crime units. By comparison, the roughly 600 anti-crime officers made up 1.6 percent of the total NYPD sworn force. Those twenty-five shooting incidents resulted in eleven civilian fatalities— also a historically low number. All the civilians killed by NYPD officers in 2019 appeared to be threatening officers with potentially lethal force; seven had loaded guns.[11]

To put those twenty-five citywide shooting incidents in perspective: in 2019, the 36,397 members of the NYPD responded to more than 6.4 million calls for service. More than 64,000 of those calls involved weapons.[12] Twenty-five shootings and eleven fatalities are remarkably few, given the size of New York and of the NYPD. The NYPD's per-capita use of force is significantly below that of many other departments facing comparable population demographics.

For example, from 2015 to 2020, the Houston police, a department of 5,400 officers, killed an average of eight people a year.[13] The NYPD, nearly seven times the size of Houston's force, killed an average of nine people a year from 2010 to 2019. In 2018, the NYPD killed five people.[14] The Houston rate, if translated to the NYPD, would mean an average of close to fifty-six civilian fatalities a year.

That anti-crime officers were overrepresented among officers involved in shootings says nothing about whether they were trigger-happy or prone to excessive force. Confronting armed, violent, and resisting suspects was virtually their job description. The likelihood of an officer's use of force is a function of how often he interacts with violent suspects. Three percent of anti-crime officers discharged their weapons at suspects in 2019; that number, too, suggests restraint rather than brutality.

Shea should have lauded the anti-crime officers for their professional contributions to "community" safety, rather than decommissioning them. Disbanding the units signaled that the department was "no longer in the arrest business," noted former Police Commissioner Ray Kelly.[15] That message was heard. Shootings jumped 205 percent in the two weeks after Shea's announcements, from thirty-eight incidents over those two weeks in 2019 to 116 incidents in 2020. Gunshot injuries rose 238 percent. June 2020 became the most violent month, in terms of gunfire, in twenty-four years.[16] Suspects knew that their chances of getting stopped with a gun had dropped enormously.

NYPD officers also got the message. In the month following the disbanding of the anti-crime units, narcotics arrests fell 85 percent, gang detectives made 90 percent fewer arrests, subway and housing arrests fell by comparable amounts, and gun arrests dropped 67 percent.[17] Through early December, arrests citywide were down 36 percent, though gun arrests had started rebounding.[18] Too late: the increased gun arrests couldn't keep up with the increase in guns on the street, and the year ended with close to a 100 percent surge in gun violence in December.[19]

When proactive policing and public-order enforcement are universally denounced as racist, officers do less of those activities. When crime rises as a result, officers are charged with racism as well. Now, as shootings surged, the NYPD was accused of indifference to the "community." Then–Brooklyn Borough President Eric Adams, formerly a fierce internal critic of the department's stop tactics, complained that his constituents were not getting the police response that they deserved. (Adams is now mayor.) The police had allegedly not cracked down on illegal dice games and loud music at night, following resident complaints. But had officers tried to end those illegal dice games and loud music, they would have subjected themselves to complaints about their oppression of minority communities. Moreover, Brooklyn District Attorney Eric Gonzalez would have thrown out any summonses or arrests for such low-level quality-of-life problems anyway, so why should officers bother in the first place?

Chair of the city council's public-safety committee, Donovan Richards (now Queens borough president), has complained about the "systemic racism inherent in certain enforcement tactics."[20] Yet here was Richards, a month after the disbanding of the anti-crime units, complaining that "communities are being held hostage by the cops and the robbers at the same time."[21] The cops allegedly engaged in such extortion by not delivering precisely the proactive enforcement that Richards previously called a "systemic wrong." When crime goes up, it is easier to lash out at the cops than to acknowledge the social ecology of crime—it thrives in an environment with neither informal social controls such as strong families nor formal controls such as police presence.

New York's slide into lawlessness is mirrored nationwide. The year 2020 saw the largest percentage increase in homicides in US history—29 percent.[22] The shooters were just getting started. New homicide records were set in 2021 in Philadelphia, Columbus, Indianapolis, Rochester, Louisville, Toledo, Baton Rouge, St. Paul, Portland, and elsewhere.[23] The violence continued into 2022. January 2022 was Baltimore's deadliest in nearly fifty years, with thirty-six people killed, compared to thirty-five in 1973, when the city's population was much larger.[24]

The local and the national crime increases have the same cause: making the avoidance of disparate impact the guiding principle of law enforcement. Given the vast disparities in crime commission, law enforcement will inevitably fall heaviest on blacks. But crime, too, falls heaviest on blacks. In order to protect law-abiding minority residents, officers have to operate more intensively in minority areas. There is no middle ground. Shooting victims were nearly 74 percent black in 2020 and less than 2 percent white. In New York City, blacks made up over 72 percent of all known shooting suspects in 2020, though they are only about 23 percent of the city's population.[25]

Non-Hispanic whites made up a little over 1 percent of all known shooting suspects, though they are about 34 percent of the city's population. Those suspect identifications come from the victims of, and witnesses to, shootings—overwhelmingly minority themselves. Police do not wish these facts into existence; they are the reality of urban crime. The data mean, however, that the police *cannot* respond to shootings without being called into minority neighborhoods and being given the description of a minority suspect, if anyone is cooperating with the police. Given those disparities, it should be no surprise that blacks made up 56.6 percent of all stop subjects in 2020; the only surprise is that whites made up over 9 percent of stop subjects, which is higher than their participation in street crime would predict.[26]

New Yorkers elected Eric Adams mayor in 2021 on his promise to restore order to the city. His ability to do so will require him to face down the very disparate impact arguments that he himself once weaponized. As a rabble-rousing NYPD officer and subsequently as a politician, Adams accused the New York Police Department of racist policing because its stop activity had a disparate impact on blacks. If the NYPD goes back to more aggressive proactive policing, the number of officer interactions with suspects will increase. Those interactions will inevitably be disproportionately with black subjects, given the demographics of crime.

Adams would perform an enormous public service if he repudiated disparate impact thinking. Such repudiation will require telling the truth about black crime, which no elected official has been willing to do. As New Yorkers grapple with brutal above- and below-ground shootings, stabbings, and subway crime, the need for such candor never appeared greater.

Chapter Fourteen

THE ROAD TO ANARCHY

Traffic enforcement, too, has a disparate impact. Police critics are thus predictably calling for its curtailment, using the death of Daunte Wright in 2021 as a pretext.

On April 11 of that year, police from Brooklyn Center, Minnesota, stopped the twenty-year-old Wright for an expired vehicle registration. The officers discovered that Wright had an open warrant for failing to appear in court on charges of illegal gun possession and fleeing from arrest. After getting out of his car, Wright fought with the cops and lunged back into the driver's seat when they attempted to arrest him on the outstanding warrant. Officer Kim Potter reached for her taser but mistakenly grabbed her pistol instead. She fired one lethal shot. (Potter was convicted of manslaughter and sentenced to prison in February 2022.)

Wright's death was caused by his own actions and those of the arresting officers. But politicians and commentators blamed the laws Wright violated in the first place. "No one should die over a traffic stop," New York City Councilman Brad Lander said.[1] Yale legal scholar James Forman Jr. and a law student wrote in the *Washington Post* that "having expired tags or temporary plates" must be added to the list of activities that can "shatter Black lives"[2]—never mind that Wright's abortive arrest was not for expired tags but for failing to answer to gun charges.

New York State Attorney General Letitia James proposed that New York City police cease routine traffic stops. Urban League President Marc Morial told CNN that police departments should discontinue the "discredited broken windows of 1990s policing," including traffic enforcement.[3] Since 2020, Seattle, Virginia, Pittsburgh, Philadelphia, and Berkeley, California, among other jurisdictions, have banned officers from making stops for many traffic offenses.[4]

But it is precisely high-crime areas that most need traffic enforcement. The National Highway Traffic Safety Administration, an office of the Transportation Department, has a program based on the "nexus of crashes and crime."[5] For decades, research has found that neighborhoods with the highest rates of fatal accidents also have the highest rates of violent crime. In other words, criminals violate traffic laws as routinely as they violate other laws, and those criminals and bad drivers are disproportionately black. When the police pay inadequate attention to traffic violations, it further sends the message that people "may break the law with impunity," according to a 2000 study.[6]

In Oakland, California, nearly 60 percent of fatalities and serious injuries occur on only 6 percent of the city's streets, overwhelmingly in minority neighborhoods.[7] Blacks in Oakland are twice as likely as whites to die or be severely injured in traffic incidents, and black pedestrians are three times as likely to die, according to an Oakland equity study. The reason is reckless driving by minority drivers.

Yet Oakland police were ordered to decrease their traffic involvement sharply following a Stanford study accusing them of racial profiling. The result has been growing disorder. In March 2021, Councilman Loren Taylor reported his constituents' sense of a "general lawlessness and a lack of accountability for driving however you want to in the city." An Oakland officer backs him up: "It's like the Wild West of driving out there. There is a really a very small line of defense before utter chaos ensues and I think we are there."[8] Traffic deaths were up 22 percent in Oakland in 2020. Most of the victims were black.

Milwaukee, Wisconsin, has documented the inverse correlation between car stops and nonfatal shootings, robberies, and car thefts. When traffic enforcement declines, those crimes increase, says former Police

Chief Edward Flynn. It is a truism of policing that "criminals are bad drivers," Flynn says. "They don't follow traffic laws or update their vehicle registration. Years ago, I learned that expired inspection stickers were the quickest way to find a warrant fugitive."[9]

A social scientist who has observed Cincinnati's Over-the-Rhine neighborhood says that "survival in the inner city involves more than avoiding violent encounters. It also involves learning how to cross a road without being killed or seriously injured by a car. Narrow streets are traversed at high speed, without regard for the children who play there."[10]

If blacks are stopped more for speeding or red-light running, the only allowable explanation is officer bias—or in the case of traffic cameras, machine bias. Oak Park, Illinois, saw the usual post–George Floyd spike in carjackings and drive-by shootings; its police chief proposed installing license plate readers to control illegal behavior. In March 2022, the Village Board voted down the proposal on racial equity grounds. Forty percent of drivers stopped by Oak Park police are black, a Village Trustee alleged (Oak Park is less than 20 percent black, though the composition of its roads, which feed into Chicago, is unknown). The cameras would only exacerbate such bias, the Village Board concluded.[11]

The California legislature has rejected speeding camera proposals on the grounds that minority drivers would be unfairly penalized, even though those proposals were intended to save minority lives.[12] The possibility that blacks on average speed more is outside the bounds of civil discourse. It has now become unacceptable to study driving behavior; before that taboo became ironclad, however, several large-scale analyses confirmed that blacks speed at higher rates than whites.[13]

Traffic enforcement dropped in Minneapolis and other cities following the George Floyd riots as officers disengaged from proactive policing. Traffic fatalities nationally rose nearly 7 percent in 2020[14] and another 10.5 percent in 2021[15]—the largest increase since the National Highway Traffic Safety Administration began tracking in 1975. Banning uniformed traffic enforcement outright would further endanger the people the reformers claim to be protecting.

In September 2020, a North Minneapolis high school principal begged for more road arrests after one of her school's students was killed in a drive-by. "We are literally in a city that is completely and entirely out of control," said Mauri Melander Friestleben in a self-made video. "I can see outright laws getting broken, traffic laws, people driving outright through red lights, speeding, going sixty to seventy miles per hour. We got kids on skateboards getting hit by cars."[16] Yet the police do nothing, she said. Like cops throughout the US, they have been bludgeoned into passivity by the idea that any policing with disparate impact is racist.

Chapter Fifteen

ON DOUBLE STANDARDS

———

Many Americans are so accustomed to being called racist for being white that they don't even notice the insult. Witness the reaction to Joe Biden's first speech as president-elect.

The address was universally hailed as a long-overdue call to overcome division. While praise from CNN and the *New York Times* was to be expected (CNN: "President-elect Joe Biden seeks to unite nation with victory speech";[1] the *New York Times*: "Mr. Biden renewed his promise to be a president for all Americans in a polarized time"[2]), conservative pundits lauded Biden's calls to "put away the harsh rhetoric" as well. *Wall Street Journal* columnist William McGurn called the speech "Lincolnesque." Biden's unity message was "exactly what the country needed to hear," McGurn wrote.[3] *Daily Wire* podcast host Ben Shapiro also took Biden's call for reconciliation at face value; indeed, Shapiro found the speech so Pollyannaish as to be risible. (*Daily Wire* is the publisher of this book.)

Yet Biden's remarks were anything but unifying. Among the "great battles of our time" that Biden has now been called to fight, he said, was the still unaccomplished goal of "root[ing] out systemic racism in this country."[4] That "systemic racism" is presumably underwritten by millions of white Americans who continue to prevent "racial justice," in Biden's words. They are the ones who represent what Biden called "our darkest impulses," locked in "constant battle" with our "better angels." It was time—finally—for those better angels to prevail, Biden said.

This indictment of white Americans was a constant theme during the Democratic presidential primaries. In an August 2019 press briefing,

Biden claimed that racism was a "white man's problem visited on people of color." "White folks are the reason we have institutional racism," he said.[5] In a January 2019 speech, Biden had announced: "We have a lot to root out, but most of all the systematic racism that most of us whites don't like to acknowledge even exists."[6] On Friday, November 6, 2020, the day before the press declared Biden the president-elect, he was still hammering the racism theme. He had a "mandate" to eliminate "systemic racism," he announced, prefiguring his victory speech the next day.

Throughout the election season, the Democratic contenders and mainstream media paired denunciations of white Americans' racism with the claim that Donald Trump was the racially divisive candidate. But in those now-iconic examples of Trump's alleged racism, the president was referring to attitudes and behaviors that he deemed antisocial or anti-American. The few times Trump used explicit racial categories were dwarfed by the constant and unapologetically anti-white statements coming from the press, the Democratic field, and academic opinion writers.

Calling whites racist is not racially divisive, however, in establishment thinking; referring to "law and order" is. This rhetorical rule reflects the fact that elite whites have internalized the idea of their own racism. Decades of ever more exacting civil rights legislation and litigation, billions of dollars of transfer payments, and the deployment of racial preferences throughout business and academia matter little to this white racism conceit. It is now simply assumed that whites will be accused of bigotry and that they will meekly hang their heads and pack themselves off to white privilege remediations. If the tables were turned—if there were routine denunciations of black racism—there would be an uproar.

Perhaps the targets of the racism accusation don't take it personally. If the problem is "systemic," then any given individual seems absolved from responsibility for the fact that racial justice in America allegedly remains unrealized. After all, the very term "systemic racism" was coined to overcome the fact that it is hard to find actual individuals in positions of even moderate power who discriminate on the basis of race. The reality is the opposite. It is hard to find an institution today that does not go out of its way to prefer minority groups if at all possible.

But while the "systemic racism" notion may seem to take individuals out of the equation, they are, in fact, essential to the idea. The character of our institutions does not arise in a vacuum; those institutions are sustained by individuals. The connection between the system and the individuals within it is made often and explicitly enough. A November 2020 column by a *New York Times* in-house opinion writer singled out "white people" for having voted as a majority for Trump. These whites are either racist or willing to accommodate racists, according to the columnist, and their vote was a "cause for profound and pervasive grief."[7]

The Trump vote in part represented a rebellion against this double standard: accusing whites of racial sins they no longer commit is not "divisive," but criticizing actual behavior like rioting or drive-by shootings is. That rebellion was inarticulate and inchoate—and it has been sidelined for now.

A striking example of such double standards took place in March 2021, as Miami Beach endured anarchic behavior from an influx of spring break tourists. Shootings and street brawls triggered stampedes. People hit one another with bar glasses and chairs. More than one hundred guns were confiscated. Officers trying to disperse large, illegally gathering crowds were assaulted with rocks and bottles. Commercial property was destroyed. Restaurant customers walked away from their meals without paying. At least one hotel shut down its food service, unable to protect its employees and patrons. Police made over 350 felony arrests and twice as many misdemeanor arrests. And in the most serious crime, two spring breakers from North Carolina drugged a twenty-four-year-old woman from Pennsylvania and raped her while she was passed out, according to the confession of one.[8] The two assailants left her semi-nude and unconscious in her hotel room, stealing her phone and wallet for good measure. Apparently confident in their immunity from the law, they used her credit cards throughout Miami

Beach for subsequent purchases. A few hours after the two rapists walked out of her hotel room, hotel staff found her dead there.

It is a virtually inviolate rule that if police crack down on disorder involving black people, the *New York Times* will accuse the police of racism. This rule held regarding the Miami Beach festivities. The *Times* covered the chaos only to criticize city officials' antiblack bias. Faced with rising mob mayhem, Miami Beach's mayor declared an 8:00 p.m. curfew for Saturday, March 19. It was universally ignored. The streets were impassable; thousands of people stuck around. The city declared a state of emergency. Police officers in riot gear tried to disperse the crowd with pepper balls, to minimal effect.

To the *Times* and its sources, the only possible reason for the city's response to the "by and large, nonviolent" partying was that the participants were black. ("By and large, nonviolent" recalls the media's response to the arson and looting of 2020: "mostly peaceful," a phrase that translates to "violent.") The chair of the Miami-Dade Black Affairs Advisory Board, Stephen Hunter Johnson, told the *Times*: "I think people see these large crowds of young Black people, and there is anger and the sense that something must be done." In fact, the city had allowed the chaos to grow for days. The "sense that something must be done" was the result of the crowds turning the city into what one tourist from Baltimore called a "war zone"—quite an assessment from the resident of a city with one of the nation's highest per capita homicide rates.[9]

Johnson also complained that "similar partying by white tourists" on South Padre Island in Texas had not brought a similar police crackdown. But the South Padre Island spring break festivities involved no gunplay, rampages, theft, or assault. As a local outlet reported: "People were drinking, dancing, playing volleyball, and just having a good time on the beach."[10]

The president of the Miami-Dade NAACP, Daniella Pierre, told the *Times* that Miami Beach needed to project a "more welcoming attitude toward Black visitors. . . . it felt like you looked at the group and treated them like they were here to do you harm." But it was the actual harm being done that brought out the quasi-military response, not vice versa. To the mainstream media, police crackdowns on riots are always the cause of riots, even if the temporal sequence belies that logic.

Miami Beach's Democratic Mayor, Dan Gelber, rejected the claim of racial bias: "We did not target race; we targeted conduct," he told the *Times*. "What we have experienced the last month has been frightening."

The most striking aspect of the *Times's* coverage, however, was not its blame-shifting treatment of the downtown anarchy but rather its lackadaisical response to the hotel rape and subsequent death. This is the same paper that put nearly every allegation of unwanted sexual innuendo on the part of New York Governor Andrew Cuomo on the front page; that pioneered the media #MeToo beat; that staffs a gender desk to cover misogyny, sexism, and violence against females; and that treats the drunken college hookups that women later regret as rape. Yet when confronted by an actual rape of someone too incapacitated to consent, and who actually dies afterward, the *Times* buries the incident as a minor detail in what it characterizes as a predominantly peaceful gathering.

In the fourth paragraph of the story, the *Times* acknowledged that "there has been some violence; in perhaps the most serious case, two male visitors are accused of drugging and raping a woman who later died." But we hear no more about the incident until much later in the story: "In the case of the woman who died, the police have arrested two North Carolina men on charges of drugging and raping her and stealing her credit cards. The woman, a 24-year-old from Pennsylvania, was later found dead in her Miami Beach hotel room."

And that is all. No outrage. No calls for protests and legislation against male violence. If the perpetrators had been white, this incident would be a front-page story about the lethal misogyny of spring break partyers. If the perpetrators had been white and the victim black, the incident would be a front-page story about lethal white supremacist misogyny, followed by widespread protests. But since the alleged perpetrators are black and the victim was white, the incident can, by definition, contain no racial element and is barely worth mentioning.

These double standards now predominate. Elite "anti-racists" absolve blacks from responsibility for their actions. All crime is the result of racism, if such crime is even acknowledged. This patronizing attitude is today's real racism, and it guarantees that the bourgeois behavioral gap—the cause of lingering socioeconomic disparities—will continue. (Bourgeois values include respect for authority and the law, hard work, self-discipline, and deferred gratification.) No one in a position of elite authority is sending the message that society expects blacks to live by the same standards as other groups (even if those other groups abide by such standards imperfectly). Instead, we are unwinding every objective standard of conduct and achievement—whether it's the criminal code or academic proficiency requirements for school and employment—if enforcing that standard has a disparate impact on blacks.

Consider in this light the media's color-coded parenting standard. On April 19, 2021, McDonald's CEO Chris Kempczinski suggested in a text to Chicago's mayor that the parents of two children recently killed in Chicago's gang activity had "failed those kids."[11] Kempczinski's text became public in November 2021, prompting widespread accusations of racism and calls for his resignation. Kempczinski confessed to his white privilege and apologized profusely for holding parents responsible for the fate of their children.

When the parents are white, the rules are flipped. On December 3, 2021, a district attorney in Michigan filed involuntary manslaughter charges against the parents of Ethan Crumbley. The fifteen-year-old Crumbley allegedly killed four fellow students during a shooting rampage at his Oxford, Michigan, high school on November 30. The prosecutor based her indictment of Crumbley's parents on the fact that they had allowed Ethan to access a legally purchased handgun and ought to have known that the boy was primed to kill his classmates. The press, Democratic politicians, and gun-control advocates greeted the homicide charges against the Crumbley parents with ecstatic approbation.

The reactions to the Kempczinski text message and to the Crumbleys' indictment illuminate society's different expectations for minority parents and white parents. When black juveniles perpetrate street violence, the press and public officials almost never ask: where were the parents? The less involved a black parent is in his child's life, the less society expects of him. These double standards may have a benign intent, but they enable a cultural dysfunction whose lethal effects are far more widespread than those of school shootings.

Kempczinski made his ill-fated suggestion of parental responsibility after seven-year-old Jaslyn Adams was gunned down by her father's gang rivals. Jaslyn and her father, Jontae Adams, were parked in a McDonald's drive-through lane on Chicago's West Side on April 18, 2021, when two gunmen jumped out of a car and unleashed at least forty-five shots at their car. Jaslyn was struck six times and died; Jontae was seriously wounded. Jontae Adams, a convicted heroin dealer, knew that his gang's enemies were out for his blood. The day before the shooting, he tweeted: "Opps probably downstairs waiting on me."[12]

A few weeks before Jaslyn Adams's murder, thirteen-year-old Adam Toledo was out running the streets at 2:30 a.m. with a fellow gang member. Both Toledo and his associate Ruben Roman were armed. ShotSpotter technology picked up eight rounds of gunfire from the pair; two calls to 911 also reported the shots. Toledo and Roman fled from the responding officers; the officer who chased Toledo down an alley shouted at him to "stop it" or "drop it [i.e., the gun]."[13] In an almost instantaneous succession of events, Toledo wheeled toward the officer with his gun in his hand, then unexpectedly dropped the weapon and put his hands up. A fraction of a second later, the officer shot him once, fatally. In March 2022, Cook County State's Attorney Kim Foxx concluded that there was no basis for criminally charging the officer who killed Toledo, despite public pressure to bring an indictment.

A day after the Jaslyn Adams murder, Chicago Mayor Lori Lightfoot visited the McDonald's headquarters. Kempczinski thanked Lightfoot via text message for her visit and added: regarding the "tragic shootings

... both at our restaurant yesterday and with Adam Toldeo ... Both the parents failed those kids, which I know is something you can't say. Even harder to fix."[14]

Kempczinski would pay the price for saying the unsayable. After activists obtained the text message in November, a coalition including Color of Change and Showing Up for Racial Justice released an open letter to the CEO: "Your text message was ignorant, racist and unacceptable coming from anyone," the letter read, "let alone the CEO of McDonald's, a company that spends big money to market to communities of color and purports to stand with Black Lives."[15] McDonald's employees and race advocates protested outside the company's headquarters and demanded reparations. US Representative Bobby Rush joined calls for Kempczinski to resign. A McDonald's worker told a local TV station that Kempczinski was "putting the blame on parents for the violence in the streets. He can't relate because he is wealthy."[16] Jaslyn Adams's mother, heretofore a cipher, emerged from her obscurity to vent her anger: "How dare you judge me! ... You come from privilege. You can't speak about me."[17]

Lightfoot's office joined the denunciations: "Victim shaming has no place in this conversation," a press release read. ("Victim shaming" is a euphemism for ascribing moral agency to a favored victim class.)

Kempczinski went into penance mode. He held "listening sessions" with franchise owners, employees, and corporate managers. He repeatedly accused himself of racial insensitivity. "Not taking the time to think about this from their viewpoint was wrong, and lacked the empathy and compassion I feel for these families," Kempczinski said in one message.[18] "This is a lesson that I will carry with me." A few days later, Kempczinski announced: "My texts to the Mayor of Chicago were wrong—plain and simple. I am truly sorry and I know I have let you down. I also know this has conflicted with our values—values that you have all worked so hard to embody across the business."[19]

Kempczinski was right the first time around. Had thirteen-year-old Adam Toledo not been gangbanging at 2:30 a.m., had he been in bed or at the very least at home and out of trouble, he would be alive today. His parent (in this case, the usual single mother) was responsible for keeping him off the streets. Did Toledo's mother know he had a gun? And if not, should she have known? Those questions may not be asked.

Jontae did come under fleeting criticism for his role in Jaslyn's death. In May 2021, Chicago radio host Leon Rogers asked Adams how, if he knew that he was a target of gang rivals, he could have made the decision to "move around with that baby girl, knowing there is possibly someone out there who wants to hurt you?" Adams danced around the question: "My daughter wanted McDonald's. I tried to Uber McDonald's," he responded. "As far as my actions or my past, maybe it had something to do with it. But I was a father the day my daughter died. . . . I don't remember gang-banging. I don't remember what led to it."

Chicago Tribune columnist Dahleen Glanton issued an even more definitive accusation of parental negligence: "Gang-banging and parenting don't mix. Those who engage in gang activity should have to make a choice—either give up gang life or forfeit the ability to be a good dad. . . . When a bullet meant for [the father] kills a child, he becomes an unwitting accomplice in the murder."[20]

Glanton and Rogers are black, so their criticism of Adams flew under the radar, leaving just Kempczinski to bear the wrath of the race activists.

Contrast the response to Kempczinski with the public attitude toward Ethan Crumbley's parents. Even if one agrees with the indictment holding them criminally responsible for their son's murder rampage, one can still notice that parents of a different race are treated as nonexistent. The Crumbleys' very presence in their son's life and their responsiveness to the authorities made them available as a target of criminal liability.

On the day of the shooting, a teacher noticed a drawing Ethan had made of a semi-automatic handgun pointing at the words "the thoughts won't stop help me."[21] The Crumbleys had recently bought Ethan a semi-automatic pistol for Christmas. Following interception of the note, school officials summoned Ethan's parents to school. They promptly showed up but declined to take Ethan home because they both worked and didn't want to send him to an empty house. Had Ethan's parents been from the inner city and not shown up at all, no media figure would have objected.

While at Ethan's school, his parents did not search his backpack for the pistol. The media seized on this failure to search as another sign of criminal negligence. That charge, too, is predicated on the Crumbleys' responsiveness to the initial call. We could ask the same question of parents whose children are out on the streets every night, obviously up to no good—why aren't *they* monitoring their children's access to guns?

One can maintain that Ethan Crumbley's intercepted note provided clear warning of his homicidal intent and is sufficient evidence to deem his parents legally responsible for the four deaths. (Ethan's school counsellors, however, who observed his behavior for nearly two hours after the note was found, also concluded that he posed no risk to himself or others.) If Ethan's note is a basis for his parents' criminal liability, many other parents are also on notice that their children are toting around guns. Urban youth routinely post videos flaunting illegal firearms and other contraband. One such video, obtained by Wisconsin Public Radio, shows "three young women dancing and laughing while pointing a semi-automatic weapon at the screen."[22] Have their parents confiscated and locked up *their* gun by now, and if not, why not?

The gun Ethan used was bought legally by the Crumbleys. Juvenile gangbangers usually get their guns illegally. Complying with gun laws would thus seem to make a parent more susceptible to prosecution than a parent who ignores his child's illegal acquisition.

In 2021, there were thirty-four shooting incidents on school property in the US, including the Crumbley rampage (a shooting incident defined as an outbreak of gunfire in which at least one person was wounded).[23] Twelve students (including Crumbley's four victims) were killed; another fifty-three people were injured. In 2022, through May 28, there were twenty-seven school shootings, including the May 24 massacre in Uvalde, Texas. Two educators and nineteen elementary school children were killed in Uvalde.[24]

Contrary to popular perception, the majority of those shooting incidents had black perpetrators and black victims. Many involved gang activity. Those shootings were thus of no interest to the press. No one asked how the gunmen got access to their weapons or where their parents were. Contrast the twelve student deaths nationally in 2021 with urban street violence. In Chicago alone, at least twenty-seven children aged fifteen and younger were killed in shootings in 2021, according to the *Chicago Sun-Times*.[25] More than one hundred children were shot. The national toll of drive-bys on children is considerably higher and entirely off the media's radar screen.

School shootings with white perpetrators and white victims are even rarer than school shootings generally, but they get all the attention. They are irrelevant to the US homicide toll, which the FBI put at 17,815 in 2020.[26] White-on-white school shootings receive disproportionate attention partly because the media value white life more than black life (except in those few instances involving a white shooter and black victim). But saturation coverage of the handful of white-on-white school shootings is also essential to establishing the myth that whites with legal guns, especially those from Red states, are the biggest criminal and terror threat today. Never mind that black males between the ages of fourteen and seventeen commit lethal gun violence at over ten times the rate of white and Hispanic teen males combined.[27]

Parental inattention and irresponsibility account for a large percentage of urban youth victimization, as well as of youth crime commission. On Labor Day weekend of 2021, a fourteen-year-old boy in Chicago was shot while standing on a sidewalk at around 3 a.m. by someone who emerged from a car and fled the scene. That same weekend, a seventeen-year-old boy in Chicago was shot in the back while sitting in a car at about 2 a.m. During the weekend of September 25 in Chicago, a seventeen-year-old boy was shot in a mass shooting with four victims at 1:40 a.m. Like Adam Toledo, had they been at home rather than running the streets after midnight, they would likely be alive today. They were victims waiting to happen, and had they not been shot, they may have been in line to commit a similar drive-by themselves. No one called their parents to account.

Many daylight shootings are also predictable. On September 21, 2021, a fifteen-year-old boy was standing in a strip mall near his South Side high school in Chicago when two people fired at him; after he fell, the shooters continued to unload twenty shots into his body. That boy's gangster-style death was all but inevitable; his father was killed in a drive-by in 2020. Neither parent kept the teen from gang life and away from guns.

On Saturday night, December 4, 2021, anarchic flash mobs swarmed downtown Chicago's Magnificent Mile. A bus driver was lured out of his bus and savagely beaten by two teens; two officers were injured trying to control the crowds; a twelve-year-old girl was shot in the back. The bullet ruptured her kidney and spleen. The girl's mother claims she had no idea that her daughter was in downtown Chicago that night and that once the daughter arrived back home on Sunday night, neither she nor her daughter knew that the daughter had been shot. A fifteen-year-old boy was also shot less than three hours later during the same night.

The country turns its eyes away from this mayhem and the social dysfunction that it represents, terrified that both situations are beyond any solution. The media follow strict rules of concealment: the race of black perpetrators may not be mentioned; the race of white perpetrators is always relevant. On December 2, 2021, a felon stabbed an Italian computer science student to death in Manhattan's Riverside Park; minutes later, he stabbed an Italian tourist. The *New York Times* buried the story on page A16 and remained silent about the race of the suspect and his victim.[28] Above the *Times* story was an article about jury selection in the manslaughter trial of the Minnesota police officer who fatally shot Daunte Wright in April 2021 after mistaking her gun for a Taser. The *Times* carefully laid out the racial configuration: "Ms. Potter, who is white," and "Mr. Wright, who was Black."[29] Likewise, the suspects in the 2021 murders of two Chinese graduate students at the University of Chicago have no race, as far as the media is concerned.

Coverage of the killing of six holiday celebrants at a Wisconsin Christmas parade on November 21, 2021, by a man who plowed his car into the crowd, faded out after the police released the suspect's identity; Darrell Brooks is black (and on the record as anti-white). Had a white person (let alone one with such a trail of racial animosity) driven into a Martin Luther King Day celebration, the round-the-clock coverage would have lasted for weeks.

As with the Miami mayhem coverage, such double standards help no one. Society should have a color-blind norm of parental responsibility and of the duty to obey the law. If the Crumbley parents are found guilty of involuntary manslaughter, there are many more parents out there whose passivity in the face of likely lawlessness deserves equally strict scrutiny.

Racial double standards apply to violence against the police as well.

The coverage of the January 6, 2021, assault on the US Capitol by angry Trump supporters contained an iconic moment: CNN anchor Don Lemon wept at video footage of a police officer being crushed in a door by the mob. (The officer suffered headaches for the following week.)

If Lemon has cried over previous or subsequent attacks on officers, an informal search of the record does not reveal it. The rest of the media were similarly—and uncharacteristically—moved by the January 6 assaults. The *New York Times* and other outlets ran long reports on the emotional trauma experienced by the Capitol defenders, none of whom was lethally injured in the attacks. In what might be a first in modern media history, the lieutenant who killed the unarmed Ashli Babbitt was even given a sympathetic interview on NBC, after half a year of media inattention to the seemingly unjustified shooting. The interracial aspect of that officer-involved killing (black officer, white victim) was not deemed noteworthy, unlike officer-involved killings where the races are reversed.

On December 16, 2021, Police Officer Keona Holley was assassinated, sitting alone in her patrol car at 1:30 a.m. in southern Baltimore. Travon Shaw, thirty-two, a violent felon awaiting trial on a gun possession charge, shot her from behind, according to his accomplice—striking

Holley twice in the head, once in the leg, and once in the hand.[30] A week after the ambush, Holley was removed from life support and died, leaving behind four children and a stricken police force.

A bystander filmed the aftermath of the shooting and posted the video on Instagram. He can be heard urging viewers not to report the assault, since the police harass members of the community.[31]

Much of the media seem to have taken his advice. The *New York Times* did not cover the murder, though it published in the interim several long features on police shootings and alleged police racism. The *Baltimore Sun* and the *Washington Post* did report on the incident, but elsewhere, the coverage was thin to nonexistent.

And yet the murder of police officers is, on a per-capita basis, a far more significant problem than fatal officer shootings of civilians. And the killing of police officers by black civilians is a far more significant problem than the killing of unarmed blacks by police officers. In 2021, seventy-three police officers were killed by criminals.[32] Using the 2019 national headcount of 697,195 sworn officers[33] (a conservative estimate, given the officer exodus from police departments that began after the 2020 race riots), ten officers per 100,000 officers were feloniously killed through November.

In 2021, eight unarmed black people were slain by police officers, according to the *Washington Post*.[34] Those eight unarmed black people represent .00001 percent of the nation's nearly 47 million self-identified blacks, or 1/100th of one person killed by a cop per 100,000 blacks.

Historically, black males have made up over 40 percent of cop-killers nationwide, though black males are 6 percent of the population.[35] Conservatively estimating that 40 percent of the cop-killers in 2021 were black, twenty-nine officers were killed by a black suspect in 2021, for a rate of over four cops per 100,000 officers killed by black civilians. A police officer is about 400 times as likely to be killed by a black suspect as an unarmed black is to be killed by a police officer.

Murders of police officers were up 59 percent in 2021 compared with 2020, a year that already saw surging anti-cop violence in the wake of the George Floyd race riots.[36] Like the assassination of Baltimore Officer Holley, those killings get almost no attention from the national media, since they occur disproportionately as part of the daily gun violence that afflicts inner cities and that is, as we have seen, also beneath media notice.

Yet such officer killings strike at the very heart of our civilization. A society that looks away when law enforcement is attacked is a society that is heading for anarchy. The crime wave of the last few years suggests that we are well on our way to just such a disintegration of law and order.

Chapter Sixteen

A GRIM—AND IGNORED—
BODY COUNT

Anti-cop riots convulsed Philadelphia in October 2020, part of a stream of such violence since early summer 2020. That October round of looting and assault broke out after the fatal police shooting of Walter Wallace Jr. on October 26. That shooting appeared justified. The twenty-seven-year-old Wallace had been threatening his mother with a knife, resulting in two previous 911 calls that day. When the police arrived, he ignored repeated requests to drop the knife as he approached the officers. The officers had not been equipped with Tasers, which would have provided an alternative to the use of their guns.[1] (That March, Wallace had stabbed the mother of his children and threatened to "shoot you and that house up."[2] His record included eighteen previous arrests for robbery, assaults on cops, aggravated assault, terroristic threats, and domestic abuse. As was usual in such cases, he was on the streets anyway, thanks to the disparate impact attack on incarceration.)

Responding to the shooting, then–presidential candidate Joe Biden tweeted his sympathy "for all those suffering the emotional weight of learning about another Black life in America lost." Wallace's life "mattered," the candidate wrote.[3] To be sure—but Biden was referring here exclusively to the loss of black life at the hands of the police, which he, the rest of the Democratic Party, and the mainstream media have portrayed as a national epidemic, growing out of the country's systemic racism. In fact, fatal police shootings constitute a smaller fraction of black homicide deaths than they do white and Hispanic homicide deaths. In 2020, a little over 2 percent of black homicide victims were killed by a cop, compared with 9 percent of combined white and Hispanic homicide victims who were killed by a cop.[4]

Police departments should work incessantly to minimize the number of times officers feel compelled to use deadly force, but police shootings are not the main problem afflicting urban black communities; criminal violence is. Wallace's life mattered, yes—but so did the lives of the dozens of black children killed in drive-by shootings since Floyd's death. The Democratic and media establishments were virtually silent about those shootings, even amid their skyrocketing numbers.

A sampling of just some of those 2020 incidents, including non-child cases, in the four months leading up to Wallace's shooting:

On October 23, a three-year-old boy was shot twice in Southwest Philadelphia.[5]

In Baltimore, Maryland, a twelve-year-old boy was shot on October 21; the man standing next to him was killed. That same afternoon, a sixteen-year-old boy was killed, and the twelve-year-old boy with him was shot. The sixteen-year-old was the fifth teenager killed in Baltimore over the previous two weeks.[6]

On October 13, a thirty-five-year-old probation officer who was eight months pregnant was fatally shot in the back outside of her home on the Far South Side of Chicago.[7]

On October 10, a sixteen-year-old boy turned Lake Shore Drive in Chicago into a "shooting gallery," according to the police, shooting out the eye of a nineteen-year-old girl in a nearby car.[8]

On October 8, a fifty-one-year-old bus driver in Baltimore repri-manded a couple for getting on his bus without paying. The female grabbed the driver's backpack and ran off. The bus driver gave chase; the male opened fire and continued pumping bullets into the driver as he lay on the ground, killing him.[9]

In Sacramento, a nine-year-old girl was killed on October 3 during a family gathering in a park. Her six-year-old cousin and aunt were also shot. Two hours later, a seventeen-year-old crashed into a pole after being fatally shot. Shortly thereafter, a seventeen-year-old girl was shot.[10]

On October 2, a fourteen-year-old girl was shot from a passing car in the West Englewood section of Chicago while standing on a sidewalk. The thirty-five-year-old man standing next to her was killed.[11]

On September 26, a fifteen-year-old boy was fatally shot in the head on the Far South Side of Chicago.[12]

A three-year-old boy in Orlando, Florida, was fatally shot in the head while playing in his living room on September 22, when a passing car sprayed bullets at the front door and windows of the home. The day before, a fourteen-year-old boy in the same neighborhood was killed with a shot to his head while he was sitting on his front porch. A fifteen-year-old next to him was critically wounded.[13]

On September 21, a one-year-old boy in Kansas City, Missouri, was killed when someone walked up to the car in which he was riding and riddled it with bullets. The victim, Tyron Patton, was among the thirteen children who had been killed in shootings through late September in Kansas City.[14]

Five people were shot on September 19 when two cars sped down a street on the South Side of Chicago, spraying bullets across a sidewalk, onto a porch, and inside a home. That same day, a gunman opened fire on a group of men in West Englewood before escaping down an alley. Four people were hit.[15]

A fifteen-year-old girl was shot to death in St. Louis on September 14.[16]

That same day, gunfire broke out on Michigan Avenue in downtown Chicago; the suspects fled in a car then crashed into three other cars.[17]

On September 12, a man on house arrest for a gun case opened fire on a family he had just met on the West Side of Chicago. He killed two people and wounded another three.[18]

On September 11, a fourteen-year-old boy was killed in a drive-by shooting in Northeast Baltimore, part of a burst of violence that killed twelve people and wounded another forty-five over six days.[19]

On September 10, a female mail carrier on the Far South Side of Chicago was fatally shot in the head, abdomen, legs, and buttocks by occupants of a car speeding down the street.[20]

On September 9, an eleven-year-old girl in Bethlehem, Pennsylvania, was shot in the face answering a knock on the back door of her home.[21]

A six-year-old boy was shot on September 7 at the annual J'Ouvert party that opens the West Indian Day Parade in Brooklyn (both the party and parade had been officially cancelled, to no avail.) Five other people were shot that night in what is a long-standing West Indian Day Parade tradition of deadly weapons violence.[22]

Also on September 7, a young girl and three adults in a car were seriously wounded in a drive-by shooting on the South Side of Chicago.[23]

A seven-year-old girl was killed on August 29 while at a family birthday party in South Bend, Indiana; the assailants shot from a passing car.[24]

On August 31, an eleven-year-old girl was shot in the hip in Wilmington, Delaware, while playing outside in the morning.[25]

On August 22, a twenty-five-year-old woman was killed with a bullet to her head in the Bronx. On the same day, a thirty-three-year-old man near West Burnside Avenue and Loring Place was shot in the arm, an eighteen-year-old was shot in bother of her legs, and a thirty-two-year-old man was shot in the leg in a Brooklyn.[26]

On August 19, a nine-year-old boy was shot in the lower back on the West Side of Chicago when gunmen got out of a car and started shooting at a group of men on a sidewalk. The boy's mother was also hit in the back.[27]

On August 18, a four-year-old girl in Asbury Park, New Jersey, was shot outside an apartment complex.[28]

On August 17, a nine-year-old was shot in the head in a car on the South Side of Chicago.[29]

On August 16, a forty-six-year-old man at a vigil in Brooklyn for a man killed two days before was fatally shot twice in the head.[30] A day earlier, a man in Canarsie, Brooklyn, was shot in the face, one of three shootings within fifteen minutes. The day before, four people were killed, including an off-duty corrections officer at a party in Queens, and another eleven people wounded, bringing that week's shooting toll in New York City to fourteen fatalities and seventy-six wounded.[31]

On August 12, a fourteen-year-old boy was fatally shot in the back of the head in his St. Louis neighborhood, found near a street curb.[32]

On the morning of August 11, an eleven-year-old girl was shot in the head in an SUV in Madison, Wisconsin; two days later, her family took her off of life support.[33]

The weekend of August 8, three children were victims of shootings in Philadelphia.[34]

On August 9, twenty people were shot a block party in Southeast Washington, DC, killing a seventeen-year-old boy.[35]

On August 5, a six-year-old girl in West Philadelphia was shot while playing outside her home.[36]

On August 1, a seven-year-old boy was shot in the head while sitting on his family's front porch in West Philadelphia. A shoot-out had broken out when a man drove onto the street and unloaded his weapon at a group of people standing outside. The boy died two days later.[37]

On August 1, a nine-year-old was fatally gunned down on the near North Side of Chicago while playing with friends. The gunman had fired into a parking lot at a group of males standing nearby. As of August 1, the number of shooting victims ten or younger in Chicago was three times that of 2019, according to the *Chicago Tribune*.[38]

On July 31, a seventeen-year-old in Chicago was killed on a sidewalk in a case of friendly fire. His companion had started shooting at a passing car.[39]

On July 22, one-year-old Ace Lucas was killed in his bed in Canton, Ohio; his twin brother sleeping next to him was wounded.[40]

On July 14, nine-year-old Devonte Bryant was killed with a shot to his head in New Orleans; a thirteen-year-old boy and a fifteen-year-old girl were hit in the same shooting.[41]

On July 12, a one-year-old boy in a stroller was killed by a shot to the stomach at a cookout in Bedford-Stuyvesant, Brooklyn; three men were also hit. That same night, a twelve-year-old boy was shot in Brooklyn's Crown Heights section and a fifteen-year-old boy was shot in Harlem.[42]

On July 8, a twelve-year-old boy was killed inside his home in a drive-by shooting in Wadesboro, North Carolina.[43]

On July 5, a six-year-old boy was fatally shot in a drug hot-spot home in Northeast Philadelphia.[44]

At least six children were killed in drive-bys nationally over the Fourth of July 2020 weekend. Eight-year-old Secoriea Turner was in a car with her mother in Atlanta trying to inch past a barricade illegally erected by Black Lives Matter protesters. Two people opened fire on the car. Michael Goodlow III, age four, was fatally hit in the head on July 4 in St. Louis. In Hoover, Alabama, a gun battle broke out between three males in a mall. Royta De'Marco Giles Jr., eight years old, was caught in the crossfire and killed; other bystanders were wounded. In Galivants Ferry, South Carolina, a four-year-old boy was killed. In Southeast Washington, DC, Davon McNeal, eleven, ran toward his aunt's house to get a cell phone charger and was killed in gunfire between a group of five males. In Chicago, Natalia Wallace, seven, was playing in a yard when three males exited a car and opened fire at a group standing on the street. Wallace was fatally hit in the head. A fourteen-year-old boy was also killed playing basketball on the Fourth of July. In San Francisco's Bayview district, a six-year-old boy was shot and killed.[45]

On July 2, two girls, ages eleven and twelve, were killed in a drive-by shooting at a birthday party in Delano, California.[46]

On June 30, a three-year-old girl was shot while playing in the front yard of her Englewood, Chicago, home.[47]

On June 29, four-year-old LeGend Taliferro was killed while sleeping in his father's apartment in Kansas City.[48]

On June 27, in the Englewood section of Chicago, one-year-old Sincere Gaston was killed in his mother's car driving home from a laundromat.[49]

A three-year-old girl was shot on June 22 playing outside her home in Chicago Lawn.[50]

On June 20 in Chicago, three-year-old Mekhi James was killed in his father's car. A thirteen-year-old, a sixteen-year-old, and a seventeen-year-old were also fatally shot that day.[51]

On June 19, a twenty-three-year-old woman who was eight months pregnant was killed in her car in Southwest Baltimore. Her three-year-old daughter was also killed. Both were left in the car for fourteen hours.[52]

In South-Central Los Angeles alone, nine children under the age of ten were shot in the first nine months of 2020, and forty children under the age of eighteen. In Philadelphia, as of early August 2020, eleven children had been fatally shot, six of those victims under the age of ten. One in ten shootings victims in Philadelphia had been children.[53]

At least seventeen children were killed in St. Louis, Missouri, through the summer of 2020. St. Louis hospitals treated 114 children, including an infant, for gunshot wounds through October 8 of that year, according to the *Washington Post*.[54] The average age of drive-by victims in St. Louis is dropping, and the wounds are more serious due to gangbangers' increased firepower. The number of homicides in black St. Louis neighborhoods rose 800 percent over the summer, from one every four days to two a day. "It's like it's no big deal. They've accepted homicides, too," the mother of two males killed in 2014 told the *St. Louis Post Dispatch* in September 2020.[55]

The killers have not been identified in many of these shootings, despite ample witnesses, because of the ghetto code against "snitching" and cooperating with the police. The anti-cop rhetoric that paints the criminal justice system as racist because of its disparate impact on blacks breeds the anti-snitching ethic. The foregoing list of shootings, without parallel in any other American demographic, explains why law enforcement has a disparate impact on blacks.

In a sample of twenty-seven big cities, including Los Angeles, San Francisco, Boston, Milwaukee, Nashville, and Louisville, homicide rates rose an average of 37 percent in June 2020.[56] Yet when the Department of Justice announced a federal crime task force after the June 29 murder of LeGend Taliferro in Kansas City to help cities fight the rising violence, many local politicians and activists denounced the effort as merely a pretext to retard police reform.[57]

These drive-by shootings happened virtually exclusively in black neighborhoods, taking a toll on black children that would be inconceivable if white children were involved. Likewise, if even a handful of black children had been killed by whites, the uproar over white supremacy would dwarf anything seen to date.

Instead, since the black children's assailants are overwhelmingly black themselves, the country changes the subject, lest it be accused of a taboo attention to black crime.

Anti-cop activists and many academics claim that racial crime disparities are simply a product of racist police deployment. Cops are over-saturated in black neighborhoods, the activists argue (ignoring the pleas for help from community residents). Once there, officers discover the same crimes that go undetected in white communities.

But the bodies don't lie. Blacks between the ages of ten and thirty-four die of homicide at thirteen times the rate of whites, according to the Center for Disease Control (CDC), thanks to comparably high rates of violence.[58] If whites were being mowed down in drive-by shootings, we would have heard about it.

Yet in a bizarre non sequitur, as the corpses piled up and the cultural breakdown fueling the shootings bled out into riots, looting, and an open season on police officers, the national conversation in the mainstream media and among Democrats focused exclusively on white supremacy. The white psyche has been prodded and parsed and declared universally racist. College-educated whites have been packing themselves off to anti-white privilege trainings and confessing their racism in public-apology sessions, even as the evidentiary basis for that ubiquitous white racism charge has become increasingly fantastical.[59] The elite consensus has been unbroken: the only problem worth paying attention to in the black community is the supposedly lethal effects of white bigotry.

While he was president, Donald Trump's pronouncements about law and order were at the center of this discourse, portrayed as nothing more than that ubiquitous left-wing trope, a "racist dog whistle." Coverage of Trump's September 1, 2020, visit to Kenosha, Wisconsin, following days of rioting there, was particularly illustrative.

"More Than Ever, Trump Casts Himself as the Defender of White America," ran the headline on a *New York Times* front-page article by Peter Baker, the paper's erstwhile full-time Trump basher.[60] "Not in generations has a sitting president so overtly declared himself the candidate of white America," Baker asserted.

What were those overt declarations? Trump's "defending the police and condemning demonstrations during which there have been outbreaks of looting and violence," in Baker's formulation. Apparently, only whites would care about looting and violence. Black business owners, who have been devastated by the anarchy, either don't exist in the *Times*'s world or are presumed to care more about the fight for racial justice that such looting is understood to represent.

Baker sneered at Trump's mention of Kenosha as another Democratic-run city that Trump "claimed" had been troubled by "rioting, looting, arson, and violence"—as if such turbulence were just a racist fiction. The documentary evidence suggested otherwise. A caption on a photograph of Trump's visit in the *Washington Post* read: "President Trump tours an area affected by civil unrest in Kenosha,"[61] using the now-mandatory euphemism for rioting. That "unrest" had the force of an aerial bombing raid, as the photo showed, leaving in its wake blocks of rubble, twisted steel girders, and sagging brick walls close to collapse.

Brian Klaas, the global opinions contributor of the *Washington Post*, wrote that, by invoking law and order, Trump assumed that people could be scared into voting "based on fear of minorities."[62] *Washington Post* columnist Eugene Robinson called the Kenosha visit "nothing less than undisguised white supremacy."[63] The *Los Angeles Times* wrote that Trump's mention of law and order was perceived "as drawing on familiar racist tropes."

This equation between a concern with law and order and white racism involves the mainstream media and progressive politicians in some difficulties, however. It is they who hear any conservative or Republican reference to crime as a veiled reference to black crime. But the progressive Left denies that street violence is disproportionately black. Why, then, is it so sure that anyone talking about violent street crime is talking about blacks, especially when, as the *Los Angeles Times* put it, Trump himself "does not explicitly mention white sub-urbanites or Black city dwellers"?[64] Perhaps the Left knows something about crime which it is not letting on.

If it is fact, not fiction, that violent street crime today is almost exclusively a minority phenomenon, then it would appear that one simply may not speak about it. That proscription injures law-abiding residents of high-crime areas most of all—people like the aunt of a child victim in St. Louis, who told the *Washington Post* in October 2020: "I live in fear of living in St. Louis. I feel trapped."[65] Such citizens beg for more police protection and see the police as the only thing standing between them and anarchy.

The psychoanalysis of "white pathologies," as a headline on a September 2020 *New Republic* article by critical race theorist Kimberle Williams Crenshaw put it, has gone beyond whites' unseemly obsession with law and order.[66] Whites also have a hallucinatory idea that the Left thinks of them as racists. A September 2020 Peter Baker article suggested that Trump was in effect "reaching out to a subset of white voters who think the news media and political elites see Trump supporters as inherently racist." Now where would they get that idea?

Yet at the same time, Baker ironized Trump's rejection of the "notion that America has a problem with systemic racial bias." The reader is expected to guffaw at such a patent Trumpian falsehood. So it turns out that the news media do think that America has a problem with "systemic racial bias." That subset of white voters to whom Trump was allegedly reaching out was reading elite opinion correctly. But if there were any doubt, Baker quotes Ibram X. Kendi, arguably the most sought-after and highly-paid anti-bias guru, who has been cleaning up since the Floyd death. Trump was "relying on manipulating the racist fears of white voters to win them over," Kendi said.[67] And those white voters were doubly racist, because they thought that Kendi thought of them as racist.

The insistence on white racism entails some determined overlooking of facts. A June 22, 2020, news article in the *New York Times* titled

"White Americans Say They Are Waking Up to Racism" quoted a professor of African-American Studies at Emory University, Carol Anderson. "What kind of nation is this, that can be comfortable with a police officer kneeling on someone's neck for eight minutes and 46 seconds?" Anderson asked.[68]

It must have taken Anderson considerable effort to have overlooked the universal outpouring of outrage prompted by the death of George Floyd. As we have seen, manifestos against systemic racism tumbled out of large corporations and small start-ups; out of banks, law firms, and restaurants; out of symphony orchestras, music conservatories, and theater groups; out of universities, elementary schools, and tutoring companies; out of foundations, government offices, and union halls. Any institution that did not immediately issue a denunciation of systemic racism found itself in the hot seat and had to scramble to make amends.

An assistant professor of African-American Studies at Northwestern University, writing in the *New York Times*, decried white America's "inability to recognize [blacks'] humanity—the disdain, disregard and disgust for our existence."[69] In fact, the United States has spent billions of dollars since the 1960s trying to lift blacks out of poverty through welfare payments, food stamps, housing vouchers, Medicaid, and racial set-asides in government contracting. White philanthropists, many of them Republicans, pour millions into educational programs for inner-city children. The United States is in the process of dismantling a host of color-blind criminal-justice practices that are essential to keeping law-abiding citizens safe simply because they have a disparate impact on blacks. Businesses have been trying for decades to hire and promote as many blacks and Hispanics as possible. If they fail to reach proportional representation of underrepresented minorities in their workforce, it is not due to lack of effort but to the yawning academic skills gap that leads to a severe shortage of competitively qualified candidates.[70]

The vast majority of white Americans are decent, well-meaning people who yearn for a post-racial country and don't give a damn about race. White Republicans have had one love affair after another with black politicians and public figures—Colin Powell, Alan Keyes, Condoleezza Rice, Allen West, Herman Cain, Ben Carson, Tim Scott, Burgess Owens, Herschel Walker, Winsome Sears, Wesley Hunt, Kathy Barnette, and others. Some voted for Barack Obama. What matters to those Republicans is not someone's skin color but whether he is perceived as sharing their values. When I speak on policing, I have been told repeatedly by white listeners that hearing the data on disproportionate black crime makes them "uncomfortable." This feeling is not the response of a white supremacist; it is the response of someone who is in the dark about racial disparities in criminal offending or who wishes that those disparities would go away in the service of racial harmony and equality.

The taboo on honesty about street crime and the dysfunction behind it is of recent vintage. In late September 2020, the *Los Angeles Times* issued a front-page public apology for its alleged history of racism, followed up by a series of articles detailing that purported racism. Its opening apology focused on a July 12, 1981, *Times* story on the growing phenomenon of itinerant gangs from Watts, California, driving miles across the Los Angeles freeways to commit robberies and burglaries in the wealthy parts of West LA. The article was heavily reported and statistically grounded, giving a disturbing portrait of multigenerational gang culture, a world otherwise completely out of sight and out of mind in most of Los Angeles's sprawl.

The offending story did not claim that gang culture represented all of South Central Los Angeles. It profiled several black business owners who had succeeded through hard work and self-discipline, but who were themselves victimized by unchecked lawlessness. One man, whose store had been bulldozed by gang members after he refused to take back an already-opened bottle of apple juice, opined that the predatory young males in his community were being held back by their fear of society, their inability to defer gratification, and the welfare system's penalizing of two-parent families. It is the Left that seems to think that such bourgeois blacks do not exist, or, if they do exist, that they could not possibly want strong law enforcement.

Nevertheless, the present-day editors at the *Los Angeles Times* repudiated the story because, they said, it "reinforced harmful stereotypes" about "Black and Latino Angelenos."[71] The editors pointed to no errors or exaggerations. The subjects spoke for themselves, describing a nightmare world of violence, welfare dependency, male exploitation of female sexual partners, drug use, and an entitlement mentality regarding crime. If those first-person accounts conformed to a stereotype, it is because those stereotypes are based on truth. What is harmful is not the stereotype but the behavior that gives rise to it.

Putting a lid on such reporting is not a public service. It allows the mainstream world to continue suppressing a reality that public policy has failed to improve.

In the 1990s, it was still possible to acknowledge that there were cultural problems in the inner city that were holding people back. The debate around welfare reform was based on that premise. Sociologist Elijah Anderson could still elucidate the conflict between "street culture" and the "decent" people in the ghetto and could still call interpersonal violence the biggest problem facing the inner city.[72] Today, the only allowable discourse is about white supremacy. The behavior of blacks is off limits.

Meanwhile, the anarchy that has become a regular feature of American cities since the summer of 2020 has continued and remains all but ignored by the media. The October 2020 rioting in Philadelphia barely registered on the national consciousness. In two days of mayhem, liquor stores, dollar stores, sneaker stores, banks, clothing stores, and restaurants were looted and torched, and thirty officers were injured, mostly with rocks and other projectiles, though a female officer suffered a broken leg when a pick-up truck ran over her.[73] At least five people were killed on the second day of rioting and another thirteen were shot.[74] Multiple ATM machines were blown up with explosives[75] and a dozen police vans were stolen. An Amazon truck was stolen and crashed. A thousand people showed up at one suburban mall and stripped stores wall to wall. The enterprising had brought hand carts to carry washing machines and other large appliances to their cars and trucks. People broke into the roof of a Walmart and destroyed the sprinkler system; as the store flooded, they continued lugging clothes, watches, and sneakers out the side and back doors. The frenzy of theft was so great that there were traffic jams of getaway cars in the strip mall parking lots. The looting had a recursive quality, with looters looting looters. A man tried to take a shopping cart already filled up with baby goods and was shot at from a passing car; one bullet hit a fifteen-year-old female looter nearby.[76] Another looter who had taken an Uber to a Snipes sneaker store was shot in the leg when he tried to intervene in an argument between fellow looters. A gunman tried to hijack a getaway car in the parking lot of a Checkers restaurant, shooting the car owner in the leg.[77]

Many of the plundered businesses had just reopened after their inventories and physical plants were destroyed by the June Floyd riots. More than eighty pharmacies were ransacked for drugs, many numbering among the more than 150 pharmacies plundered in June.[78] In the June rioting, a black pharmacist on Girard Avenue lost all his medications and a 600-pound safe. Neighboring residents, almost all black and Hispanic, who had depended on his store for their diabetic-control and blood-pressure drugs were out of luck.

But according to critical race theorist Kimberle Williams Crenshaw, "consternation over the loss of goods" in rioting is nothing more than fear of "marauding Black masses undermining white people's well-being," just another example of "violence-enabling pearl-clutching about looming social disorder."[79] Crenshaw, too, is apparently unable to imagine black proprietors whose livelihoods are destroyed by unchecked barbarism.

Chapter Seventeen

MASS SHOOTINGS, HATE CRIMES, AND RACE

On May 15, 2022, an eighteen-year-old white supremacist massacred ten black shoppers in a Buffalo, New York, supermarket. The rampage was a horrifying reminder of this nation's white supremacist past. Because of that history, which took far too long to move beyond, white acts of terror have an elevated significance. Vigilance against any revival of the centuries-long cruelty that preceded the civil rights revolution is appropriate.

But the Buffalo massacre, however heartbreaking, was not representative of American violence today. It was not representative of how blacks die. Nevertheless, the media and Democratic politicians turned it into the very emblem of America's alleged racial hate. And in so doing, they increased the black alienation that is tearing the country apart.

The day after the slaughter, President Biden called on Americans to "address the hate that remains a stain" on the country's soul.[1] Those stained by hate were not named by race, but the reference was clear.

Two days later, Biden gave a longer speech in Buffalo about the attack. In Biden's telling, white Americans are at best indifferent to the racist slaughter of their fellow black citizens. "We need to say as clearly and forcefully as we can that the ideology of white supremacy has no place in America. None," Biden insisted. Biden seemed to believe that his exhortations and moral clarity were the only forces impeding a slide back toward Jim Crow and the reign of the KKK: "I promise you. Hate will not prevail. And white supremacy will not have the last word. . . . We can't allow . . . these hate-filled attacks . . . to destroy the soul of the nation." We can't allow this violence, the president intoned, to "be the story of our time." To "confront the ideology of hate requires caring about all people"—something that whites, in their silent complicity with racist rampages, apparently fail to do.[2] (The name "White House" will eventually have to go, in this purging of allegedly racist symbols.)

Biden's recurring suggestions that white hate crimes are America's dominant reality is racial propaganda. Whites are not the biggest source of hate crime and interracial violence in the US; blacks are. From 2016 to 2020, blacks nationally were twice as likely to commit a hate crime as whites, according to FBI data, among hate-crime suspects whose race and ethnicity were known.[3]

Local data tell the same story. In New York City, from 2010 to 2020, blacks were 2.42 times as likely as whites to commit a hate crime, among hate-crime suspects whose race and ethnicity were known.[4] Blacks in Los Angeles committed anti-Asian hate crimes at 4.8 times the rate of whites in 2021, according to internal LAPD data.[5] Blacks in LA committed anti-gay hate crimes at seven times the rate of whites, and anti-Semitic hate crimes at 2.4 times the rate of whites, among hate-crime suspects whose race and ethnicity were known. Blacks committed anti-trans hate crimes at 2.5 times the rate of Hispanics; there were no white suspects in anti-trans hate crimes in LA in 2021.

Biden, the mainstream media, and Democratic politicians claim that demographic angst is driving whites to paroxysms of violence. As Biden himself said in 2015, an "unrelenting stream of immigration, nonstop," was eliminating the white majority population share.[6] If whites were lashing out against this immigration-fueled shift in US culture, you would think Los Angeles would experience a particularly disproportionate level of white-committed hate crimes, since whites are only 28 percent of the LA population and Hispanics are 49 percent. But that is not the case. Blacks committed anti-Hispanic hate crimes in Los Angeles at 13.5 times the rate of whites in 2021.[7]

The media and race activists seize on absolute numbers of hate-crime victims to argue that blacks are the target of disproportionate violence from whites. This is statistical sleight of hand, based on disparate population shares. Take a hypothetical population of eighty whites and twenty blacks, for example, where, for the sake of illustration, blacks commit hate crimes against whites at a 100 percent rate and whites commit hate crimes against blacks at one-quarter that rate. Blacks would commit twenty anti-white hate crimes, and whites would commit twenty antiblack hate crimes. Every black would be victimized by a hate crime because of the smaller black population, not because of disproportionate white offending.

In the US, blacks commit the vast share of non-lethal interracial violence between blacks and whites that is not classified as a hate crime: 88 percent, according to the Bureau of Justice Statistics.[8] The brutal beatings and carjackings that have become even more routine in the aftermath of the 2020 race riots could well have racial animus behind them. The authorities treat black-on-white crime as unremarkable, however, and rarely look into motive. Authorities almost always scrutinize white-on-black crime, rare as it is, for a hate enhancement, precisely because it is so rare.

Maintaining the fiction of white hate-crime dominance takes work. Video evidence relentlessly shows that blacks are the predominant torturers of frail elderly Asians. In Dallas, Texas, Asian businesses experienced a wave of drive-by shootings starting in April 2022 and stretching into May, with bullets being fired into Asian-owned establishments from a passing car.[9] On May 11, a man entered an Asian-run hair salon in Dallas and fired off at least thirteen rounds, hitting three people, one in the lower back. The victims survived this attempted mass murder only because of the shooter's poor aim. Police believe the assailant is connected to the previous drive-bys.[10] Had he been white, his shooting spree would have been an international story. Because he was black, it was barely covered outside of Dallas. There has been no hand-wringing about black hate.

Teenage bullying is racially lopsided. On November 22, 2021, four white female Catholic school students were riding a city bus home in the Bronx.

Two black male teenagers started taunting them and were joined by three black girls who beat up the white girls.[11] Riders of mass transit in cities across the country know the dynamic and keep their heads down.[12]

Had the races on the Bronx bus been reversed, the incident would have been a national scandal—think: the Covington Catholic hate-speech hoax.[13] (The mainstream media obsessively portrayed Nick Sandmann, a student from Covington Catholic High School in Kentucky, as having racially harassed a Native American man in 2019; CNN and NBC have settled Sandmann's hundred-million-dollar libel suits for undisclosed sums.[14])

The problem facing blacks today is not whites; it is black criminals. In his May 17 speech from Buffalo, Biden scolded his white listeners for their apparent apathy: "We have to refuse to live in a country where Black people going about a weekly grocery shopping can be gunned down by weapons of war deployed in a racist cause."[15] Biden may not have noticed, but sorrow and outrage over the attack were universal.

Furthermore, awful as the Buffalo massacre was, it was almost sui generis. White supremacist shootings like the Buffalo massacre are so rare that they do not show up statistically in the tidal wave of black homicide victims between the ages of ten and thirty-four. Blacks going about their quotidian chores in inner-city areas do have reason to fear, but the threat is not from white supremacists. It is from other blacks.

On Thursday, May 19, 2022, a group of Baltimore City Council members denounced a level of violence in the city that they called "beyond comprehension."[16] On Tuesday, May 10, a gunman had opened fire with an assault rifle at midday, spraying more than sixty bullets onto the street. He killed a twenty-five-year-old male and injured three other people. There was another mass shooting hours later.[17] Two days later, a pregnant woman and her fiancé were shot and killed in a car outside their home. The seven-month-old fetus, delivered prematurely, was fighting to survive. The next day, Friday, saw two other homicides in the city: an 18-year-old killed in East Baltimore and a man found dead inside a vacant house in the Carrollton Ridge neighborhood. Three other males were injured in separate shootings that Friday across the city, including a young man shot in the chest and seriously injured in South Baltimore.[18]

A fifty-one-year-old resident of Baltimore told the *Baltimore Sun* after another mass shooting: "It's like a norm now."[19] Residents tear police tape down and "carry on like nothing happened," he said. The man, a former gangbanger, said he has been afraid to leave his house at night, but now that fear extends to broad daylight.

The day of the Buffalo massacre, Saturday, May 14, a nine-year-old boy was fatally shot in an apartment building in Skokie, Illinois; a six-year-old was wounded in the same shooting.[20] The Wednesday before, May 11, in the West Englewood neighborhood of Chicago, a drive-by shooting from one car to another struck a six-year-old boy, an eleven-year-old boy, a twenty-one-year-old woman, and a twenty-four-year-old man.[21] On Tuesday, May 10, in Chicago's Back of the Yards neighborhood, assailants emerged from a stolen Mazda and started spraying gunfire. They killed a nineteen-year-old with a bullet to the head and injured four other teenagers. The shooters took off, crashed the Mazda, and fled on foot. Investigators recovered three guns from the car and at the scene.[22] Members of a crowd assaulted police officers who tried to administer first aid to the victims, another manifestation of the anti-cop hatred that disparate impact ideology cultivates. Gunfire broke out in the same area a few hours later.[23]

The typical mass shooter in America is not a white supremacist. He is black and either retaliating for a previous shooting or impulsively reacting to a current dispute. In 2020, more than two dozen blacks were killed every day—more than all white and Hispanic homicide victims combined—even though blacks are only 13.6 percent of the population.

Fervent government pronouncements about soaring white supremacy are notable for their absence of data, as *The Federalist* has pointed out.[24] A much-trumpeted Anti-Defamation League study, "Murder and Extremism in the United States in 2021," classified white-on-white crimes as "white supremacist" if committed by a white supremacist; the vast majority of what the ADL labelled "white supremacist homicides" were non-ideological (and constituted at most .001 percent of murders nationally over the ten-year reporting period), according to a Real Clear Investigations study.[25]

The press invokes the Christchurch shooting in New Zealand, the 2019 shootings in El Paso, Texas, and at a San Diego, California, synagogue, and the 2016 gay nightclub attack in Orlando, Florida, to buttress the "rampant white supremacy" narrative. All were repugnant crimes resulting in tragic losses of life. But they are not, thankfully, an epidemic. Moreover, the Christchurch shooting was not even on American soil, and the Pulse nightclub attack in Florida was not an instance of "homophobia," but was rather a "taste [of] Islamic state vengeance," in the ISIS-inspired shooter's words.[26] On the other hand, the November 2021, Waukesha Christmas parade massacre, the April 2022 Brooklyn subway shooting, the 2016 cop assassinations in Dallas and Baton Rouge, among other shootings, are officially forgotten.

Democrats, the media, and academia nevertheless exploited the Buffalo atrocity. The Domestic Terrorism Prevention Act of 2022, passed by the House of Representatives in 2022, would have provided a powerful tool for suppressing opposing viewpoints by falsely characterizing them as white supremacy.[27] Though there is no shortage of government officials already investigating domestic terrorism, the bill would have created three new offices in the Department of Homeland Security, the Justice Department, and the FBI tasked with assessing white supremacist and neo-Nazi threats in the US and inside public agencies. (The act will need to be reintroduced in another Congress in order to become law.)

A Democratic congresswoman laid out the chain of reasoning that these new bureaucracies would use to characterize "white supremacist" terror groups: "America has a racism problem. America has a hate problem, and America has a domestic terrorism problem," said Texas Representative Veronica Escobar.[28] Expect the government to adopt the college campus definitions of "racism" and "hate": any political position with which the Left disagrees. If you don't think that children should have their innocence stripped from them by premature knowledge of sexuality, you are filled with hate. If you think that a country has a right to determine who crosses its border, you are filled with hate. If you think that college admissions and faculty hiring should be based on academic merit, you are filled with hate. If you think parents should have a role in deciding whether their children are castrated, you are filled with hate.

The media and Democratic politicians tied the Buffalo atrocity to conservative discourse opposed to mass illegal immigration from Third World countries. Glenn Greenwald has laid out the definitive rebuttal of efforts to blame ideas for violence committed by individuals who share some of those ideas.[29] Someone who makes an argument without advocating violence cannot be held responsible for murder possibly influenced by that argument without destroying freedom of speech, Greenwald argues.

As a legal and political matter, Greenwald's free-speech absolutism is unequivocally correct. Yet his robust assertion of the bright-line distinction between speech and action fails to capture our intuition about the power of language and ideas. To be sure, we connect repugnant acts to speech in direct proportion to the degree to which we find that speech repugnant. The Left blamed Great Replacement theory for the Buffalo massacre; law-and-order conservatives instinctively feel that the demonization of the police since 2015 has contributed to increased cop killings.[30]

President Biden and the elite establishment tell blacks, nonstop, that they are under lethal threat from whites, and that it is white supremacists who pose the greatest threat to their safety. "Buffalo attack ignites safety worries for Black Angelenos," read a headline in the print *Los Angeles Times*.[31] New York Representative Jerrold Nadler, a sponsor of the Domestic Terrorism Prevention Act, said, "Democrats are taking the fight straight to the . . . violent extremists that are terrorizing minority institutions."[32] This message is heard and absorbed, however lacking in a factual basis. A *Washington Post*-Ipsos poll found that 75 percent of black Americans were very or somewhat worried that they or someone they love will be attacked because of their race. A respondent interviewed by the *Post* says that he was "apprehensive at stoplights, imagining a White man getting out and shooting him in his car."[33]

The false claim that we are living through an epidemic of racist shootings of black men by police officers led to the crime wave of 2015 and 2016, when homicides logged the largest two-year increase in half a century. That earlier crime wave was triggered by the police shooting of Michael Brown in Ferguson, Missouri, and the false "Hands up, don't shoot!" narrative. In the face of race riots and public cop-bashing, officers backed off of proactive policing in what I called the Ferguson Effect.[34] The George Floyd anarchy has been worse, though its causes are the same. It's not hard to imagine that the equally false claim that we are living through an epidemic of white supremacist shootings of blacks could escalate America's violence into something approximating a race war.

■   ■   ■

Mass shootings in Boulder, Colorado, and Atlanta, Georgia, in 2021 further revealed how invested the Democratic establishment is in the white-hate narrative. Both shootings produced the usual gloss: white Americans are the biggest threat facing the US. That interpretation was reached, in the case of the Boulder shooting, on the slimmest of evidence, and in the case of the Atlanta shooting, in the face of contradictory facts.

On March 22, 2021, a body-armor-wearing gunman started firing at shoppers in the parking lot of a King Soopers supermarket in Boulder; he entered the store and continued shooting inside. Ten people were murdered, including a Boulder police officer, Eric Talley, who had run into the line of fire. Social media lit up with gloating pronouncements that the shooter was a violent white male and part of what Vice President Kamala Harris's niece declared (in a since-deleted tweet) to be the "greatest terrorist threat to our country."[35] (Video of the handcuffed shooter being led away by the police appeared to show a white male.) When the shooter's identity was revealed as Ahmad Al Aliwi Al-Issa, a Syrian-American, and his tirades against the "Islamophobia industry" were unearthed, that line of thought was quietly retired and replaced with the standby Democratic response to mass shootings—demands for gun control.

But the false narrative about the Atlanta spa shootings had legs. It represented a double lie—first, that the massacre was the product of Trump-inspired xenophobic hatred, and second, that whites are the biggest perpetrators of violence against Asians. The most striking aspect of these untruths is the fact that they were fabricated in plain sight and in open defiance of reality. Given the enduring hold of the Atlanta story on mainstream discourse, it is worth examining in some detail.

On March 16th, 2021, twenty-one-year-old Robert Aaron Long allegedly opened fire at three Atlanta-area massage parlors. Six of his eight victims were Asian.[36] The analysis was instantaneous and universal—the shootings were the product of anti-Asian hatred, whipped up by Trump's criticism of China for allegedly unleashing the coronavirus on the world. Protests broke out across the country against the scapegoating of Asians. Protest signs read, "I am not a virus"; "Asians are not viruses, racism is!!"; "End white supremacy now!"; "All of us against racism."

An organizer of a protest in Alhambra, California, told the *Los Angeles Times*: "I think it's important for Black and Asian communities to work together on this because at the end of the day, it's about dismantling white supremacy and speaking out against white racism."[37] The *New York Times* ran front-page story after front-page story linking the Atlanta murders to anti-Asian COVID-19 propaganda; CNN and MSNBC went into programming overdrive about the alleged wave of Trump-inspired xenophobia. On March 21, MSNBC anchor Alex Witt suggested that we should be concerned about the prospect of more white supremacist violence over the summer.[38]

At Emory University in Atlanta, Kamala Harris announced that America faces many internal "foes" (read: Trump's followers, who have bought into what she called his "scapegoating [of] Asian-Americans"). The attacks showed yet again, Harris said, that "racism is real in America, and it has always been. Xenophobia is real in America, and always has been. Sexism, too." Speaking alongside Harris, President Joe Biden returned to his 2021 inauguration theme—that hate is embedded in Americans' hearts. "We have to change our hearts. Hate can have no safe harbor in America. It must stop." Because hatred is so rooted in our history, Biden said, it is "so often met with silence . . . But that has to change, because our silence is complicity."[39]

The problem with this interpretation was that there was no evidence to support it. Long told the police that he had targeted the three Atlanta spas to purge himself of his lust and his addiction to pornography. This explanation was wholly credible. All three establishments had been linked to prostitution, and Long had frequented at least two of them. Customer reviews of the massage parlors attested to their provision of sexual services.[40] Long said nothing about Asian responsibility for the coronavirus. Indeed, if he were upset by a supposed connection between Asians and the pandemic, one would expect him to have avoided close contact with Asians. By all accounts, Long was tormented by an inability to control his sexual thoughts and behavior, which he believed to be a violation of his Christian faith. He also said nothing about hatred of Asians per se. Long appeared to have targeted presumed sex workers who happened, given the demographics of the massage trade in Atlanta, to be Asian. Long intended to target a business in Florida next that made pornography, he told police.[41] The employees there were unlikely to be Asian.

The uncontradicted evidence for Long's motivation and the absence of evidence for a white supremacist impulse were no impediment to the narrative. Anyone who doubted that narrative was complicit in white supremacy. Reuters was reprimanded on social media for the headline: "Sex addiction, not racial hatred, may have driven suspect in Georgia spa shootings." The news organization's revised attempt—"Motive in Georgia spa shootings uncertain, but Asian-Americans fearful"—earned it no absolution.[42] "We don't let mass casualty shooters diagnose themselves," sniffed a terrorism expert at Georgia State University.[43] Needless to say, had Long told the police that he was seeking revenge on Asians for COVID-19, his self-diagnosis would have been taken as definitive proof.

Both Harris and Biden obliquely referred to the question of motive while dismissing its relevance. "Whatever the killer's motive, these facts are clear," Harris said. "Six out of the eight people killed on Tuesday night were of Asian descent." Biden was similarly unconcerned about the relationship between Long's intentions and the atrocity's significance: "Whatever the motivation, we know this: Too many Asian-Americans have been walking up and down the streets and worrying."[44]

But in stigmatizing and punishing hate crimes, motive is the entire issue. If Long were not exacting revenge for the coronavirus, there is no basis for characterizing the shootings as hate crimes and for lambasting uninvolved Americans for sharing Long's hatred in their "hearts." And if the fact that 75 percent of Long's victims were Asian turned the shootings into an anti-Asian hate crime, then the fact that 100 percent of Ahmad Al Aliwi Alissa's victims in Boulder were white should turn that shooting into an anti-white hate crime.

Nowhere was the compulsion to buttress the meme about white supremacist violence clearer than in the treatment of the actual street violence that Asians have long suffered. Before the Atlanta shootings, there had been a recent string of attacks on elderly Asians, especially in California's Bay Area.

On January 28, 2021, eighty-four-year-old Vicha Ratanapakdee was walking in his driveway in San Francisco. A nineteen-year-old male barreled into him, knocking him to the ground. The male, Antoine Watson, was accompanied by a twenty-year-old female.[45] Two days later, Ratanapakdee died of his injuries. In March, an elderly woman was beaten during a robbery in broad daylight in Daly City, California. The attacker stripped her of her belongings and started to leave, before re-turning to club her again.[46] In San Jose, California, on February 5, a sixty-four-year-old Vietnamese grandmother was getting into her car after withdrawing $1,000 in cash in advance of the Lunar New Year. Two males yanked open the car door, grabbed the woman's purse, keys, and phone, and fled.[47]

On January 31, 2021, a ninety-one-year-old man was walking gingerly along an Oakland sidewalk when a young male in a hoodie came up behind and pushed him to the ground. As the man's head hung over the curb into the street, the assailant calmly continued his walk.[48] A sixty-year-old man and a fifty-five-year-old woman were attacked in Oakland's Chinatown by the same assailant. Seventy-five-year-old Pak Ho was robbed and killed while taking his morning walk near Oakland's Lake Merritt in March.[49] He hit his head on the sidewalk and was taken off life support for brain trauma shortly thereafter. On February 3, a seventy-one-year-old grandmother was walking across an Oakland sidewalk toward her apartment when a young man dashed up and knocked her to the ground. A second male ran up and danced around as the first pulled the woman's purse from her prone body, breaking the strap. Both males then ran off with the booty.[50]

On February 23, three nineteen-year-olds and a twenty-year-old walked into a San Francisco laundromat where a sixty-seven-year-old man was sitting. They kicked him to the ground, dangled him upside down by his legs, twisted him back and forth and beat him while they rifled through his pockets. Finally, they found his wallet and walked out the door.[51] In January 2019, an eighty-eight-year-old great-grandmother, Yik Oi Huang, went missing. When her son searched the park next to her home, he saw what he thought was a pile of old clothes next to a recycling bin. It was his mother, beaten so brutally that she was unrecognizable and choking on her own blood. Her pants were down, and her belly exposed. The eighteen-year-old suspect had gone on to burglarize her home, stealing jewelry and house keys before fleeing the area. Huang died a year later.[52] On March 18, 2021, a man allegedly yelled "you motherfucking Asian!" as he knocked a sixty-eight-year-old Sri Lankan unconscious on a New York subway.[53] In March 2020, four teenage girls assaulted a fifty-one-year-old woman on a bus in the Bronx, hitting her with an umbrella and accusing her of spreading the coronavirus.[54] Here was a perfect example of Trump-inspired COVID-19 xenophobia, if only the girls had been a different race.

In fact, the suspects in all of these cases were black; as with the Dallas attacks noted earlier, the news reports rarely mentioned that detail. Had the suspects been white, their race would have led each news report, as it did for Atlanta killer Robert Aaron Long. A former member of the Oakland Police Department's robbery undercover suppression team tells me that this racial pattern of attack and its lack of coverage is long-standing. No one cares about Asian robbery victims, he says. "We used to follow around elderly Asians, waiting for the bad guys to start circling. This has been one of my long-term frustrations. They are pretending to care now but ironically blaming it on white supremacy"— even though the suspects in Asian robbery attacks are almost exclusively, in this cop's experience, black.[55]

The data support that officer's observation. In New York, blacks are over six times as likely to commit a hate crime against Asians as whites, NYPD records show. In 2021, blacks made up 52 percent of all suspects in anti-Asian attacks in New York City, even though blacks are less than 22 percent of the city's population. Whites made up 12 percent of all suspects in anti-Asian attacks in 2021 in New York City but account for 32 percent of the city's population.[56]

Inner-city animus against Asian small business owners is also long-standing, as the 1992 Los Angeles riots and the 1990 Big Apple grocery boycott in New York City recall. The predominantly black character of the attacks on elderly Asians may be euphemistically acknowledged in only one context: disparate impact. Racial justice advocates oppose a law enforcement response to those attacks because, the *New York Times* explained, going to the police would have a disparate impact on "Black and Latino communities."[57] Actors Daniel Kim and Daniel Wu offered a $25,000 reward to anyone who helped find the assailant in the January 31 assault on the ninety-one-year-old man and two other Asians in Oakland.[58] *Teen Vogue* contributor Kim Tran criticized them both for failing to understand "why it's problematic to offer 25k for information about a Black man in Oakland."[59] In response to a polite objection, she added: "this looks a lot like a bounty on a Black person funded by Asian American celebrities."[60]

According to *Time* magazine, the reward underscored the problem of how to "tackle anti-Asian violence without relying on law enforcement institutions that have historically targeted Black and brown communities."[61] Neither *Time* nor Kim Tran explicitly said that anti-Asian violence is predominantly black—we are left to infer that for ourselves.

The disparate impact framework treats the government response to antisocial behavior as the problem, not the behavior itself. A supervising attorney with the Racial Justice Unit at Legal Aid in New York City told the *New York Times*: "I've rarely seen people who are more socially privileged be the ones accused of hate crimes. Often what you end up seeing is people of color being accused of hate crimes."[62] Maybe that is because those are the people disproportionately committing hate crimes. But that possibility must not be granted. Biden chastised the country for its silence about anti-Asian violence. The reason for that silence, however, is that blacks are the primary drivers of this violence. Acknowledging these assaults only became acceptable when there was a white perpetrator, even if his motive did not fit the story being told.

Two other strategies have emerged for ducking the racial reality of anti-Asian violence. The first is denial. Claire Jean Kim, a professor of political science and Asian-American studies at the University of California, Irvine, told *Slate* that she was asked by Asian reporters if black people are going after Asians. Those reporters had apparently seen the videos. Kim pushed back against what is patently obvious. "I kept asking them, *What's the evidence? Are there other videos?* There was a rush to judgment about these cases *all* being about Black people going after Asians, and when you think about the tendency in American society to criminalize Black people, it's a problem to reach for that frame and apply it before the evidence warrants it" (emphasis in original).[63] A COVID-xenophobic frame was applied to Long before the evidence warranted it, but never mind.

The second strategy is to change the subject. In her *Slate* interview, Claire Jean Kim complained that focusing on the "Asian-Black thing" takes "attention away from the larger structures of power in which they're embedded." A racial justice educator, Bianca Mabute-Louie, warned about focusing on interracial (i.e., black-Asian) conflict, since doing so would deflect from recognizing that "racism is a result of white supremacy," as *Time* put it. It turns out that white supremacy has been bashing frail Asians over the head, not black criminals.

White supremacy is also apparently getting whites beaten up. As noted previously, blacks commit 88 percent of all interracial violence between whites and blacks.[64] Yet on March 22, 2021, CNN ran a special entitled "Afraid: Fear in America's Communities of Color," as if whites were putting US minorities at risk.[65] The move to blame white supremacy for black-perpetrated attacks on Asians results in a strange linguistic divide. Press reports refer to activists condemning "anti-Asian racism" and fighting anti-Asian "hate."[66] The intended referent in such observations is whites. But the actual referent is blacks.

The lie about white supremacist violence is not innocuous. It forms the basis of the Biden administration's policy in national security and in a host of domestic welfare programs. It is the pretext for Big Tech and Big Media's silencing of speech. And the shamelessness with which that lie is constructed grows more brazen by the day. It must be fought with facts before it irrevocably alters our culture.

Chapter Eighteen

THE CHAUVIN TRIAL AND ITS AFTERMATH

America's cities did not burn on April 20, 2021, the day a jury convicted Minneapolis Police Officer Derek Chauvin on all three counts of murder and manslaughter. But the terrified preparations in Minneapolis and elsewhere in anticipation of the George Floyd verdict—the razor wire and barricades around government buildings, the activation of the National Guard, the declaration in Minnesota of a "peacetime emergency," the fortified police presence, the curfews, the cancellation of school, the boarded-up businesses—raised serious questions about the rule of law in the United States. Had the jury acquitted or hung, the ensuing riots would likely have made the conflagrations of 2020 look like a Girl Scout campfire.

This likely outcome was evident long before Congresswoman Maxine Waters told Minneapolis protesters to "stay on the street" and "get more confrontational" if Chauvin were not found guilty of murder.[1] The precedent of 2020, the ensuing twelve months of wildly inaccurate rhetoric about white supremacy, and the recent looting in Brooklyn Center, Minnesota, over a fatal police shooting made such rioting a virtual certainty. That inflammatory rhetoric poured forth from every institution in the country—from the presidency, Congress, corporations, law firms, banks, tech companies, academia, and the public school system. The mainstream media pounded home the narrative about unchanging black oppression. And even after the verdict, the press and the White House doubled down on the systemic racism conceit, despite the coordinated effort to convict among Minnesota's public officials and the state's most prestigious members of the private bar.

Going forward, it is an open question whether any police officer can receive a trial free from mob pressure, should he be prosecuted for use of lethal force.

The Chauvin jury may have pondered not just the destruction of American cities following any acquittal but its own safety. The *Minneapolis Star-Tribune* had published profiles of jury members minus their names during closing arguments in the trial.

Contrary to the prosecution's assertions, this was not an entirely open-and-shut case. The defense had arguably raised reasonable doubt about whether Floyd died of a Fentanyl overdose, aggravated by his preexisting heart disease and the stress of the arrest, and about Chauvin's requisite intent to cause serious bodily harm. Floyd had been complaining about not being able to breathe before he was put facedown on the ground under Chauvin's knee. The medical examiner had said that, had Floyd been found dead at home in the same condition, the cause of death would have been identified as a drug overdose.[2] The speed of the verdict and the absence of any questions to the judge may suggest that the jury had a broader set of issues on its mind than exclusively the evidence before it. Further complicating the process, as jury selection was underway, the city of Minneapolis had awarded civil damages to Floyd's family. In short, the criminal justice system did not behave like an institution shot through with antiblack bias.

Yet President Joe Biden took the occasion of the conviction to recycle his favorite "white supremacy" themes. Floyd's murder "ripped the blinders off for the whole world to see the systemic racism . . . that is a stain on our nation's soul; the knee on the neck of justice for Black Americans; the profound fear and trauma, the pain, the exhaustion that Black and brown Americans experience every single day," Biden said from the White House. The "summer of protest" had sent the message, according to Biden: "Enough. Enough. Enough of the senseless killings."

Biden was not referring to the senseless killing of seven-year-old Jaslyn Adams, who had been gunned down in a Chicago McDonald's two days earlier. (*See* Chapter Fifteen.) He was not referring to the four dozen black children who were killed in 2020 in their beds, front porches, back porches, at barbecues and family birthday parties, and in their parents' cars. He was not referring to the dozens of blacks killed every day in drive-by shootings.

Biden, rather, was referring to a phantom idea: that blacks have to "worry about whether their sons or daughters will come home after a grocery store run or just walking down the street or driving their car or playing in the park or just sleeping at home."[3] This would be an accurate statement if it referenced the terrorism of neighborhood gangs and their stupefyingly mindless retaliatory shootings. It is a falsehood, however, when directed at the police.

Yet immediately after the verdict, Barack Obama repeated the same fiction, one that he had, in fact, pioneered during his presidency: that black Americans rightly "live in fear" that their next encounter with law enforcement will be their last. Minnesota Lieutenant Governor Peggy Flanagan's tweet that Minnesota is a place where it is not safe to be black (because of the police)[4] is an equal betrayal of the truth.

The idea that blacks are frequently and disproportionately gunned down by the police is an optical illusion created by selective media coverage. If the press chose to ignore police shootings of blacks and focus exclusively on police shootings of whites (which are twice as numerous), Americans would think that they are living through an epidemic of racially biased police shootings of whites. A 2016 case from Dallas involving a white man named Tony Timpa[5] almost exactly adumbrated the Floyd arrest and death, but almost no one has heard of Tony Timpa.

The Minneapolis verdict will not change the poisonous narrative about a racist criminal-justice system. That narrative ensures that encounters between black suspects and the police will remain fraught. Black suspects will continue to resist arrest, increasing the chance that officers will escalate their use of force. If a suspect death ensues, more riots will follow.

Americans should be deeply concerned about the future of the rule of law.

■   ■   ■

About a month after the Chauvin verdict, Al Sharpton and civil rights attorney Benjamin Crump led a march in downtown Minneapolis in advance of the first anniversary of George Floyd's death on May 25.

Messrs. Sharpton and Crump didn't visit North Memorial Health Hospital, where two recent victims of the post-Floyd violence were on life support. On April 30, 2021, Ladavionne Garrett Jr., ten, was riding in a car with his parents when a gunman opened fire. A bullet pierced Ladavionne's head; doctors put him in a medically induced coma and removed part of his skull to relieve swelling on the brain. (Ladavionne spent the next six months in the hospital; a year after the shooting he remained unable to walk or talk. The shooting remained unsolved for lack of witness cooperation.[6]) On May 15, nine-year-old Trinity Ottoson-Smith was jumping on a trampoline at a friend's house when bullets fired from a passing car struck her in the head. She was also in critical condition at North Memorial, in the room next to Ladavionne's.[7] Trinity died on May 28, 2021.

Nineteen children in Minneapolis had been shot by that point in 2021, an increase of 171 percent over the same period in 2020.[8] Their relatives wondered where the protesters were. "Why ain't nobody mad about a 10-year-old, my grandson, fighting for his life?" asked Sharrie Jennings, Ladavionne's grandmother, at a May 17, 2021, mayoral event. "Because a cop didn't shoot him, is that why?" Jennings warned of "a deadly summer" for kids if the mayor and police chief don't "step up."[9] Later that day, Aniya Allen, six, was caught in a shoot-out between rival gangs while in her mother's car. She died on May 19.[10]

Minneapolis homicides between January 1, 2021, and the second week of May were up 108 percent compared with the same period in 2020; shootings were up 153 percent, and carjackings 222 percent.[11] The Minneapolis crime increase began after Floyd's death and never let up—nor has the assault on law enforcement that began with the arson destruction of the Third Precinct building on May 28, 2020. Officers are routinely punched, kicked and hit with projectiles. In May 2021, officers were maced and pelted with rocks and debris while trying to disperse disorderly crowds.[12]

After Floyd's death, the Minneapolis City Council called for the abolition of the police department and its replacement with a "new transformative model for cultivating safety."[13] Abolition didn't happen—a ballot initiative that would have dismantled the Minneapolis Police Department and set up a new Department of Public Safety, run by social workers, was rejected by city voters. But "some folks" in the community got the message anyway that "they have a sort of open season on their enemies," said Alicia Smith, the executive director of the Corcoran Neighborhood Organization.[14]

Attrition was accomplishing the same goal as defunding. Officers' "morale and mission" were destroyed by the failure to defend the Third Precinct and to prevent the torching and looting of businesses during the May 2020 riots, newly retired Lieutenant Kim Voss wrote in a February 2021 op-ed.[15] The rank and file had been exiting the department in droves, leaving it severely understaffed.

On the one-year anniversary of Floyd's death, the area around what is now called George Floyd Square remained burned-out and desolate, isolated within a civilian-enforced, police-free zone. Earlier that year, a local barbecue shop owner told the *Star Tribune*: "I am afraid. I am frustrated. I am mentally ill right now."[16] City Council member Alondra Cano told the paper she hears from senior citizens who sleep in the bathtub to avoid being shot at night and whose bus routes for picking up medications and groceries have been disrupted by the autonomous zone. The Floyd family pledged $500,000 of its $27 million wrongful-death settlement from the city to black business owners at George Floyd Square. That won't compensate the barbecue shop owner and his neighbors if diners and shoppers still have to dodge bullets and employees are still getting carjacked.

Of the at least one hundred homicide victims in Minneapolis in the year after Floyd's death, only one had been killed by a cop. The victim was a suspected gunrunner who had tried to run over officers before shooting at them through his car window, causing them to return fire.[17] There is little evidence that the Minneapolis Police Department systemically violates blacks' civil rights. A black Minneapolis resident is 480 times as likely to be shot by a criminal as by a cop, according to former Police Chief Medaria Arradondo.[18] Yet a day after the Chauvin verdict, Attorney General Merrick Garland announced a civil rights investigation into the Minneapolis Police Department, part of the Biden administration's reinvigorated efforts to subject local police departments to federal control. If history is any guide, the resulting consent decree in Minneapolis will cause crime to increase further. The victims will, as always, be disproportionately black. Eighty-three percent of shooting victims in Minneapolis were black in 2021, though blacks are less than a fifth of the city's population. Messrs. Sharpton and Crump have no answers to that dilemma, so they ignore it.

While police need to train relentlessly in de-escalation and sound tactics, they are not the problem in minority communities; criminals are. As long as the police are demonized and scapegoated, law-abiding residents of high-crime neighborhoods will continue to live in fear and wonder why no one protests when their loved ones are murdered by gangs with guns. And as long as the disparate impact of law enforcement on blacks is portrayed as evidence of racism, those law-abiding residents will not get the protection they deserve.

SAVING MERITOCRACY, SAVING A CIVILIZATION

In August 2022, the National Cancer Institute, a branch of the National Institutes of Health, notified its cancer research centers that their understanding of scientific merit needed revision. The institute confers Outstanding Investigator Awards on scientists deemed most likely to make a breakthrough in the understanding of cancer. The prestigious seven-year grants allow the recipients to pursue high-risk lines of inquiry that may not pan out but that promise huge scientific returns if they do.

The awards invest in the very best of the very best, an oncologist told me. But past recipients suffer from a fatal flaw: they are not proportionally diverse. So the National Cancer Institute's deputy director appealed to the cancer centers to nominate from a "broader pool" of candidates than in the past. Doing so will help to "diversify the cohort of OIA investigators," the deputy director explained in an email to center leaders.

The deputy director did not clarify which aspects of scientific merit were to be discarded in order to achieve this broader pool of nominees. But such discarding would, in fact, be required, since no one had alleged that the previous nomination process had considered anything other than merit, or that bias on the part of cancer center directors had prevented deserving black and Hispanic researchers from being nominated.

I asked the cancer researcher: when would white and Asian male scientists fight back? How much longer would they continue to allow their hard work and accomplishments to be disparaged and sidelined?

His response, sent by email, explains why the disparate impact crusade has heretofore been unstoppable:

> We value our jobs
>
> We need our jobs
>
> Our peers will turn on us
>
> Speak out, lose job forever, be quickly forgotten and abandoned
>
> I admire the bravery of those who speak out but they are being exterminated and will systematically be exterminated until they are all gone
>
> The system will have to rot from within and be reinvented, which will take 50-100 years.[1]

The costs of opposing the evisceration of standards, in other words, outweigh the benefits for anyone not driven by a transcendent (if self-destructive) commitment to principle. This cost-benefit calculus means that disparate impact orthodoxy will continue to tear down excellence absent a means for protecting dissenters from retaliation.

The consequences of prolonging the disparate impact regime extend beyond any particular sacrifice of standards for any particular position or job. The National Cancer Institute's Outstanding Investigator Awards show why. The official organs of science may disparage merit. (A headline in the August 19, 2022, issue of *Science* magazine is typical in this regard: "The Myth of Meritocracy in Scientific Institutions: Inaccurate Ideas about Objectivity and Merit Perpetuate Biases and Inequality in Academia."[2]) But most working scientists know better. A scientist's peers can tell within seconds of his opening his mouth whether he knows what he is talking about, a medical researcher tells me. When unworthy individuals are advanced into the upper echelons of a scientific organization, the credibility of the entire enterprise collapses, according to the researcher: the "best and the brightest will not enter a field that has been degraded in that fashion."

It is, therefore, urgent that the disparate impact charade end. Some prominent academics—the "public intellectuals" beloved of the liberal press—could blow the whistle on the diversity crusade without risking their careers. They know that the presumption of racial proportionality is based on multiple fictions, and yet they have been silent.

It thus falls to the rest of us to fight. One possible solution to the fear factor is a membership organization dedicated to the unapologetic defense of color-blind standards of achievement and behavior. It would relentlessly provide the data that explain the lack of racial proportionality in meritocratic institutions and in the criminal justice system. If one of its members were punished for opposing the latest application of disparate impact analysis, the organization would come to his defense with facts. Ideally, there would be enough strength in numbers to avoid its members being cancelled.

This hope may strike some as overly optimistic in the age of ruthless left-wing hegemony. The Great Barrington Declaration, a science-based statement of fact opposing COVID-19 lockdowns, had thousands of signatories—yet some of those signatories lost jobs, opportunities to work on grants, and teaching assignments at universities around the world. This is all the more reason why member organizations, not just statements signed by individuals, may prove vital in the future.

While disparate impact thinking has leapt beyond the law, its legal infrastructure should be cut out from under it anyway. A sympathetic White House could change the federal regulations that have allowed executive branch agencies to impose disparate impact liability on employers, schools, the police, and landlords. A sympathetic Congress could pass legislation clarifying that traditional civil rights statutes ban actual discrimination, not disparate impact. If the White House and Congress drag their heels, an organization dedicated to the defense of merit could pursue litigation to remove the disparate impact standard from statutes and regulations. Opposition to anti-racism pedagogy in schools has proven a winning electoral strategy. Politicians wanting to take the next step in moving America away from the tyranny of diversity ideology should campaign on restoring legitimacy to color-blind norms of achievement and behavior, whether in STEM or in law enforcement.

Racial etiquette does not demand a denial of reality. It demands that every individual be treated fairly, with courtesy and respect. But the reality remains that a dysfunctional inner-city culture is hindering black progress. That culture belittles academic achievement as "acting white." It is indifferent to life, as the dozens of drive-by shootings that occur daily in American cities attest to. It is cruel, as shown by the regular beatings and stomping of elderly Americans, many of them Asian. It is entitled, as the lootings that have become a plague on retail business reveal.

America turns its eyes away from this pathological culture and blames itself for phantom racism. We pretend that the reason for the lack of proportional representation in institution after institution is racist measures of achievement rather than vast academic and behavioral gaps. As a remedy for this alleged racism, we create double standards of accomplishment and behavior. But double standards help no one. They are condescending, and they are lethal. The crime wave that began after the death of George Floyd claimed thousands of additional lives, mostly black, and there is no end in sight to the spreading anarchy. The redefinition of excellence in the medical profession, in engineering, and in other STEM fields will prove lethal as well.

Unless the criminal justice system goes back to enforcing the law without fear of disparate impact, vigilantism will rise, as law-abiding Americans lose faith that the state will protect their lives and property. White and Asian flight from "diverse" cities and communities will accelerate. And the willingness of non-elite Americans to acquiesce in the fiction that they are white supremacists may eventually give out. Ideally, that vanished acquiescence would lead to an overdue defense of the Western heritage and of color-blind standards. It may, however, result in a country violently divided along racial lines.

A new generation of black voices is speaking the truth about achievement and behavior gaps—Kendall and Sheila Qualls, Brandon Tatum, Carl

Jackson, Candace Owens, and others. They are not making excuses for black underperformance. They are not calling for bans on the *words* "rioting" and "looting" (bans already adopted by many press outlets); they are calling for a cessation of rioting and looting *themselves*. These nonconformists know that Jews, Asians, and other previously discriminated-against groups eventually trounced the rest of America by exceeding standards, not by demanding that standards be lowered on their behalf. These emerging leaders should be elevated at every opportunity.

Western civilization contains too much beauty and grandeur, too much achievement, and too much innovation—from advances in the sciences to the blessings of republican self-government—to be lost without a fight. It *will* be lost, however, if disparate impact continues to be our measure of injustice.

NOTES

INTRODUCTION: A CULTURAL REVOLUTION

[1] Griggs v. Duke Power Co., 401 U.S. 424 (1971).

[2] Heather Mac Donald, "Undisciplined: The Obama Administration Undermines Classroom Order in Pursuit of Phantom Racism," *City Journal*, Summer 2012, https://www.city-journal.org/html/undisciplined-13485.html.

[3] Andrew L. Sandler and Kirk D. Jensen, "Disparate Impact in Fair Lending: A Theory without a Basis & the Law of Unintended Consequences," Banking & Financial Services, electronically reprinted from February 2014, https://buckleyfirm.com/sites/default/files/Disparate_Impact_in_Fair_Lending.pdf.

[4] The United States Department of Justice, "Justice Department Settles Employment Discrimination Allegations Against City of Austin," June 9, 2014, https://www.justice.gov/opa/pr/justice-department-settles-employment-discrimination-allegations-against-city-austin.

[5] Zachary Halaschak, "Two Major Real Estate Search Engines Nix Crime Data in Racial Equity Push," *Washington Examiner*, December 14, 2021, https://www.washingtonexaminer.com/restoring-america/equality-not-elitism/economy/two-major-real-estate-search-engines-nix-crime-data-in-racial-equity-push.

[6] Cary P. Gross and Ezekiel J. Emanuel, "The Missing Part of America's Pandemic Response," *The Atlantic*, June 5, 2022, https://www.theatlantic.com/ideas/archive/2022/06/nih-covid-vaccine-research-studies/661182/.

[7] "Racial Disparities in NIH Funding," National Institutes of Health, last updated August 15, 2022, https://diversity.nih.gov/building-evidence/racial-disparities-nih-funding.

[8] Harmeet K. Dhillon (Dhillon Law Group), email message to Gabriela Lopez (President, San Francisco Board of Education), March 18, 2021, https://www.sfchronicle.com/file/800/4/8004-20210318_Ltr_SF_BOE.pdf.

[9] David K. Li, "San Francisco School Board Eliminates Academic Admission Standards for Renowned School," NBC News, February 10, 2021, https://www.nbcnews.com/news/asian-america/san-francisco-school-board-eliminates-academic-admission-standards-renowned-school-n1257161.

[10] Ricardo Cano and Nanette Asimov, "New Data Shows Shift at Lowell High School: More Students Given Failing Grades after Admissions Change," *San Francisco Chronicle*, May 25, 2022, https://www.sfchronicle.com/sf/article/Lowell-High-admissions-17196603.php.

[11] Brandon L. Wright, "Attacking Gifted Education Is Bad Policy and Bad Politics," Thomas B. Fordham Institute, December 2, 2021, https://fordhaminstitute.org/national/commentary/attacking-gifted-education-bad-policy-and-bad-politics.

[12] Michael Burke, "University of California Sticks with Test-Free Admissions, Won't Replace SAT and ACT with New Standardized Test," EdSource, November 18, 2021, https://edsource.org/2021/university-of-california-sticks-with-test-free-admissions-wont-replace-sat-and-act-with-new-standardized-test/663870.

[13] Teresa Watanabe, "UC Set to Drop Major Admissions Tests," *Los Angeles Times*, accessed August 21, 2022, https://enewspaper.latimes.com/infinity/article_share.aspx?guid=15acddb7-4a62-440c-a972-8f4d9ad6e204&utm_source=veooz&utm_medium=referral.

[14] Frederick Douglass, *The Life and Writings of Frederick Douglass*, vol. II ed. Philip S. Foner (International Publishers Co., Inc., New York, 1950), "The Meaning of July Fourth for the Negro," accessed August 21, 2022 on PBS.org, https://www.pbs.org/wgbh/aia/part4/4h2927t.html.

[15]Tema Okun, "White Supremacy Culture Characteristics," *White Supremacy Culture* (blog), accessed October 16, 2022, https://www.whitesupremacyculture.info/characteristics.html.

[16]Fuller, Timothy, ed. *The Voice of Liberal Learning: Michael Oakeshott on Education* (Yale University Press, 1989), https://doi.org/10.2307/j.ctt1xp3tm1.

OVERVIEW: THE BIAS FALLACY

[1]Evan Hill, et al., "How George Floyd Was Killed in Police Custody," *New York Times,* published May 31, 2020, updated January 24, 2022, https://www.nytimes.com/2020/05/31/us/george-floyd -investigation.html.

[2]Fred de Sam Lazaro and Alison Thoet, "Medical Examiner Doubles Down on Original Autopsy Finding, Labels Floyd's Death a Homicide," PBS, April 9, 2021, https://www.pbs.org/newshour/show /medical-examiner-doubles-down-on-original-autopsy-finding-labels-floyds-death-a-homicide.

[3]Liz Hoffman and Susan Pulliam, "Wall Street Knows It's Too White. Fixing It Will Be Hard.," *The Wall Street Journal,* July 2, 2020, https://www.wsj.com/articles/wall-street-knows-its-too-white -fixing-it-will-be-hard-11593687600.

[4]Patrick Thomas, "A Decade-Long Stall for Black Enrollment in M.B.A. Programs," *The Wall Street Journal,* June 17, 2020, https://www.wsj.com/livecoverage/protests-george-floyd-death-2020 -06-17/card/ef6HsWrXh617mw14PxYy.

[5]Sam Dean and Johana Bhuiyan, "Why Are Black and Latino People Still Kept Out of the Tech Industry?," *Los Angeles Times,* June 24, 2020, https://www.latimes.com/business/technology /story/2020-06-24/tech-started-publicly-taking-lack-of-diversity-seriously-in-2014-why-has -so-little-changed-for-black-workers.

[6]Meg James and Daniel Hernandez, "L.A. Times Faces Painful Reckoning Over Race in Its Staff and Pages," *Los Angeles Times,* published June 24, 2020, updated June 25, 2020, https://www.latimes.com /entertainment-arts/business/story/2020-06-24/los-angeles-times-black-lives-matter-diversity.

[7]Sudip Parikh, "AAAS CEO Statement on #ShutDownSTEM and Black Lives Matter," June 9, 2020, https://www.aaas.org/news/aaas-ceo-statement-shutdownstem-and-black-lives-matter.

[8]American Mathematical Society (@amermathsoc), "2/2 We Recognize This Will Require Fundamental Change. The AMS Is Developing a Plan to Reckon with Our Own History of Racist Behavior and to Address Systemic Inequities That Exist in Our Mathematics Community. We Look Forward to Sharing Our Action Plan with You Soon," Twitter, June 11, 2020, https://twitter.com /amermathsoc/status/1271171913327484931.

[9]Nitin, "Standing and Acting Together for Racial Justice," Harvard Business School, June 7, 2020, https://www.hbs.edu/news/articles/Pages/standing-acting-together-for-racial-justice.aspx.

[10]Mike Laws, "Why We Capitalize 'Black' (and Not 'White')," *Columbia Journalism Review,* June 16, 2020, https://www.cjr.org/analysis/capital-b-black-styleguide.php.

[11]Dean and Bhuiyan, "Why Are Black and Latino People Still Kept Out of the Tech Industry?"

[12]Thomas, "A Decade-Long Stall for Black Enrollment."

[13]April Joyner and Arriana McLymore, "Analysis: For Black Founders, Venture Funding Remains Elusive Despite New Funds," Reuters, February 22, 2021, https://www.reuters.com/article/venture -capital-funding-diversity-idINKBN2AM12X.

[14]Sam Dean, "222 L.A. Tech Companies Pledged to Improve on Diversity. Have They Made Any Progress?," *Los Angeles Times,* July 15, 2020, https://www.latimes.com/business/technology /story/2020-07-15/la-fi-tn-pledgela-diversity-annenberg-efforts.

[15]Ginia Bellafante, "WNYC Employees Demanded Diversity. They Got Another White Boss.," *New York Times,* July 3, 2020, https://www.nytimes.com/2020/07/03/nyregion/wync-audrey-cooper -staff-revolt.html.

[16]Dean and Bhuiyan, "Why Are Black and Latino People Still Kept Out of the Tech Industry?"

[17]Patrick Thomas, "What Does Being an Ally Look Like? Companies Offer Training in Support of Black Colleagues," *The Wall Street Journal*, July 12, 2020, https://www.wsj.com/articles/what -does-being-an-ally-look-like-companies-offer-training-in-support-of-black-colleagues -11594602000.

[18]Rachel Sandler, "EEOC Probing Whether Facebook Has Committed Systemic Racial Discrimi- nation in Hiring," *Forbes*, published March 5, 2021, updated March 6, 2021, https://www.forbes .com/sites/rachelsandler/2021/03/05/eeoc-probing-whether-facebook-has-committed-systemic -racial-discrimination-in-hiring/?sh=2727bb77715f.

[19]Elizabeth Dwoskin, "Complaint Alleges That Facebook Is Biased Against Black Women," *The Washington Post*, July 3, 2020, https://www.washingtonpost.com/technology/2020/07/02 /facebook-racial-bias-suit/.

[20]Johana Bhuiyan, Sam Dean, and Suhauna Hussain, "Black and Brown Tech Workers Share Their Experiences of Racism on the Job," *Los Angeles Times*, June 24, 2020, https://www.latimes.com /business/technology/story/2020-06-24/diversity-in-tech-tech-workers-tell-their-story.

[21]Nicole Taylor, "Black Employees, Don't Sign Away Your Right to Speak Out," *New York Times*, June 23, 2020, https://www.nytimes.com/2020/06/23/opinion/nda-racism-separation-agreements .html?searchResultPosition=8.

[22]Bhuiyan, Dean, and Hussain, "Black and Brown Tech Workers Share Their Experiences."

[23]James and Hernandez, "L.A. Times Faces Painful Reckoning Over Race."

[24]Megan Zahneis, "This Professor Was Denied Tenure. Was Race a Factor?," *The Chronicle of Higher Education*, June 30, 2020, https://www.chronicle.com/article/this-professor-was-denied -tenure-was-race-a-factor.

[25]Hoffman and Pulliam, "Wall Street Knows It's Too White."

[26]James and Hernandez, "L.A. Times Faces Painful Reckoning Over Race."

[27]Kim Severson, "A Powerful, and Provocative, Voice for Southern Food," *New York Times*, May 9, 2017, https://www.nytimes.com/2017/05/09/dining/southern-food-john-t-edge-profile.html.

[28]Kim Severson, "A White Gatekeeper of Southern Food Faces Calls to Resign," *New York Times*, last updated July 1, 2020, https://www.nytimes.com/2020/06/29/dining/john-t-edge-southern -foodways-alliance.html.

[29]Tim Carman, "John T. Edge to Remain Director, While Southern Foodways Alliance Maps a More Inclusive Future," *The Washington Post*, September 2, 2020, https://www.washingtonpost.com /news/voraciously/wp/2020/09/02/john-t-edge-to-remain-director-while-southern-foodways -alliance-maps-a-more-inclusive-future/.

[30]The Black Caucus of the L.A. Times Guild, "Letter to Patrick Soon-Shiong from the L.A. Times Guild's Black Caucus," L.A. Times Guild, June 23, 2020, https://latguild.com/news/2020/6/23 /letter-from-la-times-guild-black-caucus.

[31]Bellafante, "WNYC Employees Demanded Diversity."

[32] Jon Campbell, "LaFontaine Oliver, Veteran Public Radio Executive, Named Next CEO of New York Public Radio," Gothamist, October 4, 2022, https://gothamist.com/news/lafontaine-oliver -veteran-public-radio-executive-named-next-ceo-of-new-york-public-radio.

[33]Sheryl Sandberg, "Supporting Black and Diverse Communities," Meta: Newsroom, June 18, 2020, https://about.fb.com/news/2020/06/supporting-black-and-diverse-communities/.

[34]Richard Nieva, "Google Says It Will Increase Diversity in Leadership 30 Percent by 2025," CNET, June 17, 2020, https://www.cnet.com/tech/tech-industry/google-says-it-will-increase-diversity -in-leadership-by-30-percent-by-2025/.

35"NEAP Report Card: Mathematics," The Nation's Report Card, accessed July 9, 2022, https://www.nationsreportcard.gov/mathematics/nation/achievement/?grade=12.

36"The NAEP Mathematics Achievement Levels by Grade," National Center for Education Statistics, accessed September 8, 2022, https://nces.ed.gov/nationsreportcard/mathematics/achieve.aspx#grade12.

37"Intended Meaning of NAEP," National Center for Education Statistics, accessed November 7, 2022, https://nces.ed.gov/nationsreportcard/guides/.

38"NEAP Report Card: Reading," The Nation's Report Card, accessed July 9, 2022, https://www.nationsreportcard.gov/reading/nation/achievement/?grade=12.

39"Black Students' Scores on the ACT Test Continue to Fall and the Racial Gap Widens," *The Journal of Blacks in Higher Education*, filed in Research & Studies on October 18, 2021, https://link.edgepilot.com/s/cac9f5e6/iL_33mwo30iytS8-hs7UdA?u=https://www.jbhe.com/2021/10/black-students-scores-on-the-act-test-continue-to-fall-and-the-racial-gap-widens/.

40Richard Reeves and Dimitrios Halikias, "Race Gaps in SAT Scores Highlight Inequality and Hinder Upward Mobility," The Brookings Institution, February 1, 2017, https://www.brookings.edu/research/race-gaps-in-sat-scores-highlight-inequality-and-hinder-upward-mobility/.

41"Fast Facts: SAT Scores," National Center for Education Statistics, accessed October 15, 2022, https://nces.ed.gov/fastfacts/display.asp?id=171.

42"A Snapshot of the Individuals Who Took the GRE General Test," ETS, accessed November 18, 2022, https://www.ets.org/pdfs/gre/snapshot.pdf, 6-7.

43Llana Kowarski, "What Is a Good GRE Score for Graduate School Admissions? Experts Say What Qualifies as a Good GRE Score Depends on the Grad School You Want to Attend.," U.S. News & World Reports, July 16, 2018, https://www.usnews.com/education/best-graduate-schools/articles/2018-07-16/what-is-a-good-gre-score-for-graduate-school-admissions; "Average GRE Scores."

44"GRE Scores for Engineering Programs (Average and Good) Required," Student Progress, accessed November 18, 2022, https://www.studentprogress.org/gre/scores-for-engineering/#:~:text=A%20GRE%20score%20above%20320,GRE%20score%20for%20engineering%20schools.

45Letter from Brian Nord, "How Long Should We Wait?," Particles for Justice, Strike for Black Lives, June 10, https://www.particlesforjustice.org/letter.

46Kelly Kang, "Survery of Earned Doctorates," National Science Foundation, accessed November 18, 2022, https://ncses.nsf.gov/pubs/nsf21308/data-tables.

47Kelly Kang, "Data Tables: Doctorate Recipients from U.S. Universities: 2017," National Science Foundation, accessed October 14, 2022, https://ncses.nsf.gov/pubs/nsf19301/data.

48L. Rafael Reif, "Letters to the MIT Community: Addressing Systemic Racism at MIT," Massachusetts Institute of Technology, July 1, 2020, https://president.mit.edu/speeches-writing/addressing-systemic-racism-mit.

49Reeves and Halikias, "Race Gaps in SAT Scores Highlight Inequality and Hinder Upward Mobility."

50"The Widening Racial Scoring Gap on Standardized Tests for Admission to Graduate School," *The Journal of Blacks in Higher Education*, accessed July 16, 2022, https://www.jbhe.com/news_views/51_graduate_admissions_test.html.

51Richard Sander and Robert Steinbuch, "Mismatch and Bar Passage: A School-Specific Analysis," Bar Passage Rate, submission to the *Journal of Legal Education*, August 2018, https://images.law.com/contrib/content/uploads/documents/292/Mismatch-and-Bar-Passage-JLE-submission.pdf.

52Richard Sander, "The Racial Paradox of the Corporate Law Firm," *North Carolina Law Review* 84, (2006): 1755-1822.

53"The BCG Attorney Search 2020 State of the American Lateral Law Firm Market Report," BCG

Attorney Search, https://www.bcgsearch.com/article/900050539/The-BCG-Attorney-Search -2020-State-of-the-American-Lateral-Law-Firm-Market-Report/.

[54]"Profile of GMATTM Testing 2021," Graduate Management Admission Council, February 2022, https://www.gmac.com/-/media/files/gmac/research/gmat-test-taker-data/profile-of-gmat -testing-north-america-ty2021.pdf.

[55]"Diversity Insights Black/African American Candidates," Graduate Management Admission Council, May 2021, https://www.gmac.com/-/media/files/gmac/research/diversity-enrollment /2021/gmac_diversity_insights_african-americans.pdf.

[56]"The 15 Highest GMAT Scores at Business Schools," *The Economist*, accessed November 18, 2022, https://www.economist.com/whichmba/mba-rankings/gmat-score.

[57]"The Widening Racial Scoring Gap on Standardized Tests for Admission to Graduate School."

[58]Thomas, "A Decade-Long Stall for Black Enrollment in M.B.A. Programs."

[59]Based on author's calculation.

[60]Nitin, "Standing and Acting Together for Racial Justice."

[61]"Race & Justice News: One-Third of Black Men Have Felony Convictions," The Sentencing Project, October 10, 2017, https://www.sentencingproject.org/news/5593/.

[62]Michelle J.K. Osterman, et al., "Births: Final Data for 2020," *National Vital Statistics Reports* 70, no. 17, (2022), https://dx.doi.org/10.15620/cdc:112078.

[63]Giulia McDonnell Nieto del Rio, "University of California Will No Longer Consider SAT and ACT Scores," *New York Times*, May 15, 2021, https://www.nytimes.com/2021/05/15/us/SAT-scores-uc -university-of-california.html.

[64]Katie Langin, "'GRExit' Gains Momentum as Ph.D. Programs Drop Exam Requirement," *Science*, (2022), https://www.science.org/doi/epdf/10.1126/science.adg0520.

[65]Chacour Koop, "Smithsonian Museum Apologizes for Saying Hard Work, Rational Thought Is 'White Culture,'" *Miami Herald*, July 17, 2020, https://www.miamiherald.com/news/nation -world/national/article244309587.html.

[66]Peggy McGlone, "African American Museum Site Removes 'Whiteness' Chart after Criticism from Trump Jr. and Conservative Media," *The Washington Post*, July 17, 2020, https://www .washingtonpost.com/entertainment/museums/african-american-museum-site-removes -whiteness-chart-after-criticism-from-trump-jr-and-conservative-media/2020/07/17/4ef6e6f2 -c831-11ea-8ffe-372be8d82298_story.html.

[67]"Retiring 'Work Hard. Be Nice.' as KIPP's National Slogan," KIPP: Public Schools, July 1, 2020, https://www.kipp.org/retiring-work-hard-be-nice/.

CHAPTER ONE: Medicine's Racial Reckoning

[1]"Organizational Strategic Plan to Embed Racial Justice and Advance Health Equity: 2021-2023," American Medical Association, June 2021, https://www.ama-assn.org/system/files/2021-05/ama -equity-strategic-plan.pdf.

[2]"Systemic Racism: Science Must Listen, Learn and Change," *Nature* 582, 147 (2020), doi: https:// doi.org/10.1038/d41586-020-01678-x.

[3]Alan Weil, "An Editor's View of Race, Racism, and Equity," *Health Affairs* (2020), https://doi.org /10.1377/forefront.20210125.123273.

[4]Stanley Goldfarb, *Take Two Aspirin and Call Me by My Pronouns: Why Turning Doctors into Social Justice Warriors Is Destroying Medicine* (Bombardier Books, New York, 2022), 155.

[5]LaShyra Nolen, Anna Goshua, Orly Nadell Farber, and Max Jordan Nguemeni Tiako, "Cheers and Jeers as Med School's Step 1 Test Becomes Pass/Fail," STAT, February 14, 2020, https://www .statnews.com/2020/02/14/cheers-and-jeers-as-med-schools-step-1-test-becomes-pass-fail/.

[6]Katherine Chretien, "The Step 1 Exam Is Going Pass-Fail. Now What?," Association of American Medical Colleges (AAMC), January 11, 2022, https://www.aamc.org/news-insights/step-1-exam-going-pass-fail-now-what.

[7]Dowin Boatright, et al., "Racial Disparities in Medical Student Membership in the Alpha Omega Alpha Honor Society," *JAMA Intern Med* 177, no. 5 (2017): 659-665, https://doi.org/10.1001/jamainternmed.2016.9623.

[8]Goldfarb, *Take Two Aspirin and Call Me by My Pronouns*, 167.

[9]Goldfarb, *Take Two Aspirin and Call Me by My Pronouns*, 170.

[10]Daniel Low, et al., "Racial/Ethnic Disparities in Clinical Grading in Medical School," *Teaching and Learning Medicine: An International Journal* 31, no. 5 (2019): 487-496, https://doi.org/10.1080/10401334.2019.1597724.

[11]Nolen, Goshua, Farber, and Tiako, "Cheers and Jeers as Med School's Step 1 Test Becomes Pass/Fail."

[12]Robin Klein, MD MEHP, et al., "Association Between Resident Race and Ethnicity and Clinical Performance Assessment Scores in Graduate Medical Education," *Academic Medicine* 97, no. 9 (2022): 1351-1359, https://doi.org/10.1097/ACM.0000000000004743.

[13]Stanley Goldfarb (@one1iron), "Association Between Resident Race and Ethnicity and... :Academic Medicine... 3 Possible Explanations Provided. All Are Due to External Agents. Could It Be They Were Just Less Good at Being Residents?," Twitter, May 22, 2022, https://twitter.com/one1iron/status/1528308342128623616.

[14]Jennie-O (@JennLeigh84), "Might Be the Most Garbage Human I've Seen with My Own Eyes.," Twitter, May 24, 2022, https://twitter.com/JennLeigh84/status/1529093523449909249.

[15]Marianne Incmikoski, Chair's message to faculty, trainees, and staff, May 25, 2022.

[16]Lala Tanmoy Das, "The MCAT Should Be Optional," Inside Higher Ed, June 8, 2020, https://www.insidehighered.com/admissions/views/2020/06/08/mcat-should-be-optional-opinion.

[17]Tanmoy Das, "The MCAT Should Be Optional."

[18]"MCAT Psychology and Sociology: Everything You Need to Know," Shemmassian Academic Consulting, accessed July 16, 2022, https://www.shemmassianconsulting.com/blog/mcat-psychology-and-sociology.

[19]Mark J. Perry, "New Chart Illustrates Graphically the Racial Preferences for Blacks, Hispanics Being Admitted to US Medical Schools," American Enterprise Institution (AEI), June 25, 2017, https://www.aei.org/carpe-diem/new-chart-illustrates-graphically-racial-preferences-for-blacks-and-hispanics-being-admitted-to-us-medical-schools/.

[20]Perry, "New Chart Illustrates Graphically the Racial Preferences for Blacks, Hispanics Being Admitted to US Medical Schools."

[21]"Medical School Chance Predictor: What Are Your Odds of Getting into Medical School?," Prospective Doctor, updated for 2022, https://www.prospectivedoctor.com/medical-school-chance-predictor-2/.

[22]"Early Assurance Programs," Icahn School of Medicine at Mount Sinai, accessed July 16, 2022, https://icahn.mssm.edu/education/medical/md-program/early-assurance.

[23]Susan Snyder and Jason Laughlin, "Penn's Medical School Formalizes Its Partnership with HBCUs in Pursuit of Greater Diversity," *The Philadelphia Inquirer*, updated July 21, 2022, https://www.inquirer.com/news/penn-medical-school-diversity-black-hispanic-20220721.html.

[24]Dwight Davis, et al., "Do Racial and Ethnic Group Differences in Performance on the MCAT Exam Reflect Test Bias?," *Academic Med* 88, no. 5 (2013): 593-602, doi: 10.1097/ACM.0b013e318286803a.

[25]MCAT External Request Team, email message to author, June 3, 2020.

[26]Norman C. Wang, MD MS, "Diversity, Inclusion, and Equity: Evolution of Race and Ethnicity

Considerations for the Cardiology Workforce in the United States of America From 1969 to 2019," *Journal of the American Heart Association* 9, (2020), (retracted August 2020), https://doi.org /10.1161/JAHA.120.015959.

[27]Seyi Bolorunduro MD MPH (@seyi_dr)," @ABCardio1 @DrQuinnCapers4 @ajaykirtane @drbrowncares @uche_blackstock No Surprise This Is Published in 'Our' Heart Journal. This Is D Popular Thinking That Defines Systemic Racism. The Assumption Among Many Academics That Blacks in Ds Specialty Implies a Decline in Standards," Twitter, August 2, 2020, https://twitter.com/seyi_dr/status/1290122833914339331?s=20.

[28]Sharonne Hayes MD (@SharonneHayes), "Rise Up, Colleagues! The Fact That This Is Published in "Our" Journal Should Both Enrage & Activate All of Us #BeAntiracist @DrJMieres @biljana_ parapid @gina_lundberg @DrLaxmiMehta @KBerlacher @HeartBobH @hvanspall @robertshor @MayraGuerreroMD #RetractRacitsts," Twitter, August 2, 2020, https://twitter.com/Sharonne Hayes/status/1290047712239419393.

[29]Crystal Phend, "Anti-Affirmative Action Paper Blows Up on Twitter," Medpage Today, published August 4, 2020, updated August 10, 2020, https://www.medpagetoday.com/publichealthpolicy /medicaleducation/87903.

[30]"AAMC Response to the American Heart Association's Statement, 'Wang Paper Is Wrong,'" Association of American Medical Colleges (AAMC), August 7, 2020, https://www.aamc.org /news-insights/press-releases/aamc-response-american-heart-association-s-statement-wang -paper-wrong.

[31]Katie Berlacher (@KBerlacher), "He Was Removed as EP PD as Soon as This Was Known. FTR. I Am PD of Gen Cardiology Fellowship at @PittCardiology - Will Say Again: We Stand United for Diversity Equity and Inclusion. And Denounce This Individual's Racist Beliefs and Paper.," Twitter, August 3, 2020, https://twitter.com/KBerlacher/status/1290248892580130816?s=20.

[32]Barry London MD, PhD, "Diversity, Equity, and Inclusiveness in Medicine and Cardiology," *Journal of the American Heart Association* 9, no. 17, (2020), https://doi.org/10.1161/JAHA.119 .014592.

[33]"Retraction to: Diversity, Inclusion, and Equity: Evolution of Race and Ethnicity Considerations for the Cardiology Workforce in the United States of America From 1969 to 2019," *Journal of the American Heart Association* (JAHA), 9, no. 20, originally published August 6, 2020, https://www .ahajournals.org/doi/10.1161/JAHA.119.014602.

[34]Allison Dunn, "Federal Judge: Cardiologist Can Proceed with Claim That Pitt Removed Him from Leadership Post over Affirmative Action," *The Legal Intelligence*, April 7, 2022, https://www.law .com/thelegalintelligencer/2022/04/07/federal-judge-cardiologist-can-proceed-with-claim -that-pitt-removed-him-from-leadership-post-over-affirmative-action-article/.

[35]"Me, Biased? Recognizing and Blocking Bias," (Zoom webinar, FOCUS on Health & Leadership for Women, May 3, 2022), https://www.focusprogram.org/events-1/me-biased-recognizing-and -blocking-bias.

[36]"Leadership Workshops & Research Seminars," FOCUS on Health & Leadership for Women, accessed July 16, 2022, https://www.focusprogram.org/leadership-workshops-research-semin.

[37]Heather Mac Donald, "Are We All Unconscious Racists?," in *The Diversity Delusion: How Race and Gender Pandering Corrupt the University and Undermine Our Culture* (New York: St. Martin's Press, 2018), 87-113.

[38]"Anti-Racist Transformation in Medical Education," Icahn School of Medicine at Mount Sinai, accessed July 16, 2022, https://icahn.mssm.edu/education/medical/anti-racist-transformation.

[39]Dr. Jonassaint, WebEx information forwarded by unnamed source to author, Medicine Grand Rounds 2022 (EGCG007), May 12, 2022.

[40]Stanford Department of Pediatrics, "Standford Peds Grand Rounds: Creating Native American

Pathways to Diversity the Healthcare Workforce," November 18, 2022, YouTube video, 56:42, https://www.youtube.com/watch?v=TfZm_ZwXov4.

[41] William A. Jacobson, "The National Alarm Should Be Sounding Over the Racialization of Medical School Education," Legal Insurrection, May 16, 2022, https://legalinsurrection.com/2022/05/the -national-alarm-should-be-sounding-over-the-racialization-of-medical-school-education/.

[42] "New and Merging Areas in Medicine Series: Diversity, Equity, and Inclusion Competencies," AAMC, accessed December 5, 2022, https://www.nas.org/storage/app/media/New%20Documents /deicrosscontinuumcompetenciesandglossaryuncorrectedincompleteproof-1-1.pdf.

[43] "Year Three – MS3," UCLA David Geffen School of Medicine, accessed July 16, 2022, https:// medschool.ucla.edu/education/md-education/curriculum/heals-curriculum/year-three-ms3.

[44] "Systemic Racism: Science Must Listen, Learn and Change," *Nature* 582, no. 147 (2020), doi: https://doi.org/10.1038/d41586-020-01678-x.

[45] Chelsea Long, "Few Black, Hispanic, and Native Researchers Are Getting Published," *The Chronicle of Higher Education*, April 25, 2022, https://www.chronicle.com/article/few-black-hispanic-and-native -researchers-are-getting-published?utm_source=Iterable&utm_medium=email&utm_campaign =campaign_4147121_nl_Daily-Briefing_date_20220426&cid=db&source=ams&sourceid=.

[46] Interview with author, April 29, 2022.

[47] Interview with author, May 3, 2022.

[48] Lawrence A. Tabak, "Overview of FY 2023 Presidents Budget," National Institutes of Health (NIH), accessed July 16, 2022, https://officeofbudget.od.nih.gov/pdfs/FY23/br/Overview%20 of%20FY%202023%20Presidents%20Budget.pdf.

[49] "ADVANCE: Organizational Change for Gender Equity in STEM Academic Professions," National Science Foundation, accessed July 16, 2022, https://www.nsf.gov/pubs/2020/nsf20554 /nsf20554.htm#toc;.

[50] Francie Diep, "Can $1.5 Billion Help Diversify the Sciences?," *The Chronicle of Higher Education*, May 26, 2022, https://www.chronicle.com/article/can-1-5-billion-help-diversify-the-sciences.

[51] Jeffrey Mervis, "Can Happy Labs Increase Diversity? Major Funder Bets Big on Young Scientists," *Science* (2022), https://doi.org/10.1126/science.add1848.

[52] "Freeman Hrabowski Scholars Program" HHMI, accessed October 20, 2022, https://www.hhmi .org/programs/freeman-hrabowski-scholars.

[53] Howard Bauchner, "Structural Racism for Doctors – What Is It?," accessed August 21, 2022, podcast, MP3 audio, 0:45, https://jamanetwork.com/journals/jama/pages/audio-18587774.

[54] Crystal Phend, "'No Physician Is Racist'? Twitter Calls Foul on JAMA Podcast," MedPage Today, published March 5, 2021, updated March 11, 2021, https://www.medpagetoday.com/public healthpolicy/ethics/91511.

[55] CHE Team, "Structural Racism in Medicine and Health Care," Johns Hopkins Center for Health Equity, March 22, 2021, https://www.healthequityhub.com/center-news-announcements-blog /structural-racism-in-medicine-and-health-care.

[56] "AMA Announces Transition in JAMA Editorial Leadership," American Medical Association, June 1, 2021, https://www.ama-assn.org/press-center/press-releases/ama-announces-transition-jama -editorial-leadership.

[57] Usha Lee Mcfarling, "After Accusations of Structural Racism at JAMA, a Black Health-Equity Advocate Is Named the Journal's Editor," STAT, April 11, 2022, https://www.statnews.com /2022/04/11/after-accusations-of-structural-racism-at-jama-a-black-health-equity-advocate-is -named-the-journals-editor/.

[58] Mcfarling, "After Accusations of Structural Racism at JAMA, a Black Health-Equity Advocate Is Named the Journal's Editor."

[59]Kavita Vinekar, M.D., M.P.H., "Pathology of Racism – A Call to Desegregate Teaching Hospitals," *N Engl J Med* 385, no. 40 (2021), doi: 10.1056/NEJMpv2113508.

[60]Michael O. Mensah, M.D., M.P.H., "Majority Taxes – Toward Antiracist Allyship in Medicine," *N Engl J Med* 383, no. 23 (2020), doi: 10.1056/NEJMpv2022964.

[61]Zinzi D. Bailey, Sc.D., M.S.P.S., et al., "How Structural Racism Works – Racist Policies as a Root Cause of U.S. Racial Health Inequities," *N Engl J Med* 384, (2021): 768-773, doi: 10.1056/NEJMms2025396.

[62]"Race and Medicine," *The New England Journal of Medicine*, accessed July 16, 2022, https://www.nejm.org/race-and-medicine.

[63]"The Science of Overcoming Racism," Special collector's edition, *Scientific American* 30, no. 3 (2021), https://www.scientificamerican.com/magazine/special-editions/2021/special-editions-volume-30-issue-3s/.

[64]Sabrina Strings and Lindo Bacon, "The Racist Roots of Fighting Obesity: Prescribing Weight Loss to Black Women Ignores Barries to Their Health," *Scientific American*, 332, no. 1, (2020): 26-27, https://www.scientificamerican.com/article/the-racist-roots-of-fighting-obesity2/.

[65]"Criminal Injustice: Mass Incaceration in the United States," Special issue, *Science* 374, no. 6565 (2021), https://www.science.org/toc/science/374/6565.

[66]Sean Joe, "Analyzing Mass Incarceration," *Science* 374, no. 6565 (2021): 237, doi: 10.1126/science.abm7812.

[67]"On Gun Violence, the United States Is an Outlier," IHME, published March 25, 2021, updated May 31, 2022, https://www.healthdata.org/acting-data/gun-violence-united-states-outlier.

[68]"2019 Reading Trial Urban District Snapshot Report Baltimore City, Grade 4, Public Schools," The Nation's Report Card, accessed July 16, 2022, https://www.census.gov/quickfacts/fact/table/baltimorecitymaryland, US/PST045221; "2019 Reading Trial Urban District Snapshot Report," The Nation's Report Card, 2019, https://nces.ed.gov/nationsreportcard/subject/publications/dst2019/pdf/2020016xm4.pdf.

[69]Email message to author, May 2, 2022.

[70]Email message from researcher's colleague to author, May 20, 2022.

[71]Gina Kolata, "Targeting the Uneven Burden of Kidney Disease on Black Americans," *New York Times*, May 17, 2022, https://www.nytimes.com/2022/05/17/health/kidney-disease-black-americans.html.

[72]"Understanding African American and Non-African American eGFR Laboratory Results," National Kidney Foundation, accessed July 16, 2022, https://www.kidney.org/atoz/content/race-and-egfr-what-controversy.

[73]"Filtering Bias Out of Kidney Testing," Penn Medicine News, Winter 2021, https://www.pennmedicine.org/news/publications-and-special-projects/penn-medicine-magazine/winter-2021/filtering-bias-out-of-kidney-testing.

[74]Nicole Karoll, "A Story in USA TODAY Sparked Oprah Winfrey's New Documentary on – and Battle Against – Racial Bias in Health Care," *USA TODAY*, April 29, 2022, https://www.usatoday.com/story/opinion/2022/04/29/oprah-winfrey-documentary-color-of-care-racial-bias/9573034002/.

[75]Alan Weil, "An Editor's View of Race, Racism, and Equity," *Health Affairs: Forefront*, (2020), doi: 10.1377/forefront.20210125.123273.

CHAPTER TWO: How 'Diversity' Subverts Science

[1]Francis S. Collins, et al., "Affirming NIH's Commitment to Addressing Structural Racism in the Biomedical Research Enterprise," *Cell* 184, no. 12 (2021): 3075-3079, https://doi.org/10.1016/j.cell.2021.05.014.

[2]"Intramural Research Program Personnel Demographics (End FY20)," National Institutes of Health

(NIH): Office of Intramural Research, accessed July 16, 2022, https://oir.nih.gov/sourcebook /personnel/irp-demographics/intramural-research-program-personnel-demographics-end-fy20.

3Kelly Kang, "Survey of Earned Doctorates: Data Tables," National Science Foundation, accessed July 16, 2022, https://ncses.nsf.gov/pubs/nsf21308/data-tables.

4Travis A. Hoppe, et al., "Topic Choice Contributes to the Lower Rate of NIH Awards to African -American/Black Scientists," *Science Advances*, 5, no. 10, (2019), doi: 10.1126/sciadv.aaw7238.

5Collins, et al., "Affirming NIH's Commitment to Addressing Structural Racism in the Bio-medical Research Enterprise."

6"Building Diverse Teams," National Institutes of Health (NIH), accessed October 21, 2022, https://commonfund.nih.gov/bridge2ai/enhancingdiverseperspectives.

7"Department of Health and Human Services: Part 1. Overview Information," National Institutes of Health (NIH): Grants & Funding, accessed July 16, 2022, https://grants.nih.gov/grants/Annotated _FOA.pdf.

8"Inclusion Across the Nation of Communities of Learners of Underrepresented Discoverers in Engineering and Science (NSF INCLUDES)," (Program Solicitation NSF 22-622), National Science Foundation, accessed September 10, 2022, https://www.nsf.gov/pubs/2022/nsf22622 /nsf22622.htm?WT.mc_ev=click&WT.mc_id=&utm_medium=email&utm_source=govdelivery.

9 "Inclusion Across the Nation of Communities of Learners of Underrepresented Discoverers in Engineering and Science (NSF Includes)," National Science Foundation, accessed July 16, 2022, https://www.nsf.gov/pubs/2020/nsf20569/nsf20569.htm.

10"About the National Science Foundation," National Science Foundation, accessed September 10, 2022, https://nsf.gov/about/.

11Francis S. Collins, MD, PhD, "Time to End the Manel Tradition," National Institutes of Health, June 12, 2019, https://www.nih.gov/about-nih/who-we-are/nih-director/statements/time-end-manel-tradition.

12Alessandro Strumia, "Why Are Women Under-Represented in Physics?," *Quillette*, April 16, 2019, https://quillette.com/2019/04/16/why-are-women-under-represented-in-physics/. *See also* "National Hiring Experiments Reveal 2:1 Faculty Preference for Women on STEM Tenure Track" Wendy M. Williams and Stephen J. Ceci, Proceedings of the National Academy of Sciences (PNAS), Vol. 112, No. 17, pp 5360-5365.

13"Research Supplements to Promote Diversity in Health-Related Research (Contacts, Submission Dates and Special Instructions) PA-21-071," National Institutes of Health (NIH): Grants & Funding, released April 20, 2020, https://grants.nih.gov/grants/guide/contacts/Diversity-Supp_contacts.html.

14"Fund for Help NYC," NYCDetectives, accessed July 16, 2022, https://www.nycdetectives.org /wp-content/uploads/2020/05/Contact-Tracer-Job-Description.pdf.

15Hannah Sparks, "China's AI Attorney Claims to Prosecute Crimes 'with 97% Accuracy,'" *New York Post*, December 27, 2021, https://nypost.com/2021/12/27/chinas-ai-attorney-prosecutes -crimes-with-97-accuracy/.

16"CHIPS and Science Act of 2022, Section-by-Section Summary," U.S. Senate Committee on Com-merce, Science, & Transportation, accessed September 10, 2022, https://www.commerce.senate .gov/services/files/1201E1CA-73CB-44BB-ADEB-E69634DA9BB9.

17Fredrick Hess, "Gifted Education Is Under Attack," *Forbes*, December 6, 2021, https://www .forbes.com/sites/frederickhess/2021/12/06/gifted-education-is-under-attack/?sh=3ca375e850ee.

18Howard Blume, "Will Your Gifted Child Take Calculus? Maybe Not Under California's Reimagined Math Plan," *Los Angeles Times*, May 20, 2021, https://www.latimes.com/california/story/2021 -05-20/california-controversial-math-overhaul-focuses-on-equity.

19"PISA Results Published in Dec 2019: Which Countries Score the Highest and Why?," School In

Reviews, February 8, 2020, https://schoolinreviews.com/pisa-results-published-in-dec
-2019-which-countries-score-the-highest-and-why/.

[20]Graham Allison, et al., "The Great Tech Rivalry: China vs the U.S.," Harvard Kennedy School:
Belfer Center for Science and International Affairs, December 2021, https://www.belfercenter.org
/sites/default/files/GreatTechRivalry_ChinavsUS_211207.pdf.

[21]Douglas Belkin and Sha Hua, "China's Universities Rise in World Rankings as American Schools
Continue to Falter," *The Wall Street Journal*, October 12, 2022, https://www.wsj.com/articles
/american-universities-continue-to-falter-in-world-rankings-china-rising-11665535646.

[22]"Asmeret Asefaw Berhe: Director of the Office of Science," Department of Energy, accessed July
16, 2022, https://www.energy.gov/person/asmeret-asefaw-berhe.

[23]"Professor Berhe Nominated to Lead Federal Office of Science," University of California, Merced,
April 22, 2021, https://news.ucmerced.edu/news/2021/professor-berhe-nominated-lead-federal
-office-science.

[24]Asmeret Asefaw Berhe, "Soil Biogeochemistry: Equity," University of California, Merced, accessed July 16, 2022, https://aaberhe.com/equity/.

[25]"About PPFP," University of California: President's Postdoctoral Fellowship Program, accessed
July 16, 2022, https://ppfp.ucop.edu/info/about-ppfp/index.html.

[26]Email message to author, May 4, 2021.

[27]Email message to author, May 4, 2021.

[28]"Information about PIER Plans," U.S. Department of Energy, accessed October 14, 2022, https://
science.osti.gov/grants/Applicant-and-Awardee-Resources/PIER-Plans/Information-about-PIER
-Plans.

[29]Colleen Flaherty, "Victim, or Astronomy's Icarus?," Inside Higher Ed, November 4, 2021, https://
www.insidehighered.com/news/2021/11/04/astronomer-withdraws-paper-amid-concerns.

[30]John Kormendy, "Metrics of Research Impact in Astronomy: Predicting Later Impact from Metrics
Measured 10-15 Years after the PhD," Internet Archive Wayback Machine, compiled October 28,
2021, https://web.archive.org/web/20211028230225/https://arxiv.org/pdf/2110.14115.pdf.

[31]J.E. Hirsch, "An Index to Quantify an Individual's Scientific Research Output," *PNAS* 102, no. 46
(2005): 16569-16572, https://doi.org/10.1073/pnas.0507655102.

[32]Viviana Acquaviva (@AstroVivi), "And I Stayed Calm Until Now But Here Are The Two Things I
Want To Shout Out: One, All These Metrics Plainly Ignore That Success Depends On Environment.
You Just Took Any Tiny Steps We Are Making Towards Equity And Threw Them Out Of The
Window. 8/," Twitter, October 28, 2021, https://twitter.com/AstroVivi/status/1453753649566523394.

[33]László Molnár (@lacalaca85), "And This Is Why Studies Like These Should Be Left To, Or At Least
Consulted With Relevant Humanities Experts. They Might've Told Them How Small Biases Add
Up And Lead To Less Female Postdocs, Less Female Tts, Then Less Female Profs, Then No Female
Nobels. But He Didn't.," Twitter, November 1, 2021, https://twitter.com/lacalaca85/status
/1455301379908591628.

[34]László Molnár (@lacalaca85), "And Then Says That Underrepresentation Shouldn't Be Fixed By
'Simply' 'Filling Up' Academic Positions To Societal Ratios, But Only With Women (And Minorities) Who Match The Success Rate Of The Majority (I.E., Men). I Get The Feeling He Has No Idea
How The Leaky Pipeline Works.," Twitter, November 1, 2021, https://twitter.com/lacalaca85
/status/1455299938942922756.

[35]Caroline Morley (@AstroCaroline), "My Colleague John Kormendy Has Withdrawn His Recently-
Posted Paper On Publication Metrics In Astronomy. The Book Is "On Hold." He Has Posted An
Apology... I Hope We Can Continue The Work, Here At UT & Broadly, To Improve The Field And
Do Science Inclusively.," Twitter, November 1, 2021, https://twitter.com/astrocaroline

/status/1455265972470878208.

36László Molnár (@lacalaca85), "What He Did Was A Bunch Of Old People From A Bunch Of Western Us Rate Some Whatever Selection Of People (Two Thirds From US Us), Who Graduated 20-30 Years Ago, And End Up Favoring Those Who Have More Citations More. And Now Insert That Saying About Good Intentions.," Twitter, November 1, 2021, https://twitter.com/lacalaca85/status/1455301950879195136.

37Kormendy, "Metrics of Research Impact in Astronomy: Predicting Later Impact from Metrics Measured 10-15 Years after the PhD."

38Brian P Schmidt (@cosmicpinot), "As an Unintended Consequence Of This Article, I Hope Our Field Can Be More Reflective of Our Hiring Practices, and the Inequitable Gatekeeping that Occurs into Astronomy to This Day. I Am Sorry For My Involvement.," Twitter, October 28, 2022, https://twitter.com/cosmicpinot/status/1453938013818392580.

39Interview with author, November 2, 2021.

40Flaherty, "Victim, or Astronomy's Icarus?"

41John Kormendy, email message to friends and colleagues, June 29, 2022.

42Chelsea Harvey, "Nominees for a Science Award Were All White Men-Nobody Won," Scientific American, October 22, 2021, https://www.scientificamerican.com/article/nominees-for-a-science-award-were-all-white-men-nobody-won/.

43John Kormendy, email message to friends and colleagues, June 29, 2022.

CHAPTER THREE: The Crusade Against Classical Music

1"League Issues Statement Protesting Racial Injustice, Suspends Public Events for Blackout Tuesday," The Hub, June 3, 2021, https://hub.americanorchestras.org/todays-news/page/2020-6-3?1646777348.

2"Confronting Anti-Black Racism in American Orchestras," Hartford Symphony Orchestra, accessed July 16, 2022, https://hartfordsymphony.org/confronting-anti-black-racism-in-american-orchestras/.

3"Equity Commitment," Seattle Opera, accessed on July 16, 2022, https://www.seattleopera.org/about/commitment-to-equity/.

4"Opera Omaha," Opera Omaha, accessed July 16, 2022, https://operaomaha.org/content/home/we-will-listen.pdf.

5Zachary Woolfe and Joshua Barone, "Musicians on How to Bring Racial Equity to Auditions," New York Times, September 10, 2020, https://www.nytimes.com/2020/09/10/arts/music/diversity-orchestra-auditions.html.

6"Lift Every Voice," LA Opera, accessed July 16, 2022, https://www.laopera.org/discover/la-opera-on-now/lift-every-voice/.

7Lauren Michelle, "Our Participation with Racism in Opera," Lauren Michelle Soprano, July 16, 2020, http://www.laurenmichelle.org/new-blog/2020/7/16/6go4vxvjesamocxjmwa0gnr5pe4566.

8"A Message from Damian Woetzel and Christina Salgado," Juilliard, June 1, 2020, https://www.juilliard.edu/news/146526/message-damian-woetzel-and-christina-salgado-june-1-2020.

9Steven Laitz, email, September 9, 2020.

10Alex Ross, "Black Scholars Confront White Supremacy in Classical Music," The New Yorker, September 14, 2020, https://www.newyorker.com/magazine/2020/09/21/black-scholars-confront-white-supremacy-in-classical-music/amp.

11Anthony Tommasini, "To Make Orchestras More Diverse, End Blind Auditions," New York Times, published July 16, 2020, updated August 6, 2021, https://www.nytimes.com/2020/07/16/arts/music/blind-auditions-orchestras-race.html.

[12]Joshua Barone, "Opera Can No Longer Ignore Its Race Problem," *New York Times*, updated September 23, 2020, https://www.nytimes.com/2020/07/16/arts/music/opera-race-representation.html?action=click&module=RelatedLinks&pgtype=Article.

[13]Michael Andor Brodeur, "That Sound You're Hearing Is Classical Music's Long Overdue Reckoning with Racism," *The Washington Post*, July 16, 2020, https://www.washingtonpost.com/lifestyle/style/that-sound-youre-hearing-is-classical-musics-long-overdue-reckoning-with-racism/2020/07/15/1b883e76-c49c-11ea-b037-f9711f89ee46_story.html.

[14]Nate Sloan and Charlie Harding, "How Beethoven's 5th Symphony Put the Classism in Classical Music," *Vox*, updated Spetember 16, 2020, https://www.vox.com/switched-on-pop/21437085/beethoven-5th-symphony-elitist-classism-switched-on-pop.

[15]"Let's Reload the Canon," PressReader, September 3, 2020, https://www.pressreader.com/uk/bbc-music-magazine/20200903/281891595653205.

[16]Chris White, "Beethoven Has a First Name: It's Time to 'Fullname' All Composers in Classical Music," *Slate*, October 24 2020, https://slate.com/comments/culture/2020/10/fullname-famous-composers-racism-sexism.html.

[17]Jenna Ross, "Radio Host Garrett Mcqueen Agitates for Change While Elevating Black Artistry," *Star Tribune*, July 6, 2020, https://www.startribune.com/radio-host-garrett-mcqueen-agitates-for-change-while-elevating-black-artistry/571643792/.

[18]"Call for Papers: Notes Special Issue on Race and Music Libraries," Music Library Association News, accessed July 16, 2022, https://wp.musiclibraryassoc.org/call-for-papers-notes-special-issue-on-race-and-music-libraries/.

[19]Philip Ewell, "Beethoven Was an Above Average Composer—Let's Leave It at That," *Music Theory's White Racial Frame: Confronting Racism and Sexism in American Music Theory* (blog), April 24, 2020, https://musictheoryswhiteracialframe.wordpress.com/2020/04/24/beethoven-was-an-above-average-composer-lets-leave-it-at-that/.

[20]Ewell, "Beethoven Was an Above Average Composer—Let's Leave It at That."

[21]Philip Ewell, "Music Theory and the White Racial Frame," *MTO* 26, no. 2 (2020), doi: 10.30535/mto.26.2.4.

[22]"Get Involved," SPHINX, accessed August 17, 2022, https://www.sphinxmusic.org/get-involved.

[23]Woolfe and Barone, "Musicians on How to Bring Racial Equity."

[24]"NAAS Recommended Audition and Tenure Guidelines," National Audition for Alliance Support, January 15, 2021, https://static1.squarespace.com/static/602d7bac7cb8834f84ebcef0/t/60f1e593a5d32b6e4ddb2409/1626465683788/NAAS+Recommended+Audition+and+Tenure+Guidelines+v.+01.15.21+%28Watermarked%29.pdf.

[25]"The Next Normal: Arts Innovation and Resilience in a Post-COVID World," The Peabody Institute of The Johns Hopkins University, February 10, 2021, https://peabody.jhu.edu/wp-content/uploads/2021/03/Next-Normal-Transcript-Music-Leadership-Panel.pdf.

[26]Julia Jacobs, "Metropolitan Opera to Lock Out Stagehands as Contract Talks Stall," *New York Times*, December 7, 2020, https://www.nytimes.com/2020/12/07/arts/music/met-opera-lockout-stagehands.html.

[27]Lee Abrahamian, email message to author, November 6, 2020.

[28]"The Met Appoints Marcia Sells as Its First Chief Diversity Officer," The Metropolitan Opera press release, January 25, 2021, https://www.metopera.org/about/press-releases/the-met-appoints-marcia-sells-as-its-first-chief-diversity-officer/.

[29]Lee Abrahamian, email message to author, November 11, 2020.

[30]Peter Crimmins, "Philadelphia Orchestra Makes Diversity and Equity Executive Priorities," WHYY PBS, October 23, 2020, https://whyy.org/articles/philadelphia-orchestra-makes-diversity

-and-equity-executive-priorities/.

31Michael Monks, "CSO to Add First Diversity and Inclusion Officer," WVXU, August 19, 2020, https://www.wvxu.org/arts/2020-08-19/cso-to-add-first-diversity-and-inclusion-officer.

32Tommasini, "To Make Orchestras More Diverse, End Blind Auditions."

33Javier C. Hernández, "Asians Are Represented in Classical Music. But Are They Seen?," *New York Times*, updated July 30, 2021, https://www.nytimes.com/2021/07/21/arts/music/asians-classical -music.html.

34Tommasini, "To Make Orchestras More Diverse, End Blind Auditions."

35Email message to author, December 30, 2020.

36"Juilliard Student Racial-Ethnic Demographics," College Factual, accessed November 18, 2022, https://www.collegefactual.com/colleges/the-juilliard-school/student-life/diversity/chart-ethnic -diversity.html.

37Former Juilliard administrator, email message to author, January 13, 2023.

38Interview with author, February 7, 2021.

39Interview with author, December 28, 2020.

40Interview with author, January 9, 2021.

41Interview with author, December 4, 2020.

42Interview with author, December 21, 2020.

43Interview with author, January 3, 2021.

44Zachary Wolfe and Joshua Barone, "Black Artists on How to Change Classical Music," *The San Juan Daily Star*, July 20, 2020, https://issuu.com/thesanjuandailystar/docs/jul-20-20.

45"Americanizing the American Orchestra," Report of the National Task Force for the American Orchestra: An Initiative for Change, June 1993, https://americanorchestras.org/wp-content/uploads /2021/01/americanizing-the-american-orchestra.pdf.

46Jeremy Reynolds, "Equality or Equity: Orchestral Auditions Should Be More 'Blind,' Not Less," *Pittsburgh Post-Gazette*, July 25, 2020, https://www.post-gazette.com/news/insight/2020/07/26 /Orchestra-blind-audition-New-York-Times-diversity-argue/stories/202007240112.

47Interview with author, November 10, 2020.

48Interview with author, February 7, 2021.

49Interview with author, March 4, 2021.

50Interview with author, November 6, 2020.

51"Jonathon Heyward Named Baltimore Symphony Orchestra Music Director, Becomes First Black American Conductor to Lead Major U.S. Symphony," WEAA, July 22, 2022, https://www.weaa.org/ show/two-way-talk/2022-07-22/baltimore-symphony-orchestra-names-29-year-old-jonathon -heyward-music-director.

52Beth Wood, "Classical Composer Carlos Simon Uses Music to Express Frustration and Anger, Giving Way to Hope," *The San Diego Union-Tribune*, February 21, 2021, https://www.sandi egouniontribune.com/entertainment/classical-music/story/2021-02-21/classical-composer -carlos-simon-uses-music-to-express-frustration-and-anger-giving-way-to-hope.

53Celina Colby, "Handel and Haydn Society and Castle of Our Skins Celebrate Black Musicians," *The Bay State Banner*, April 25, 2019, https://www.baystatebanner.com/2019/04/25/handel-and -haydn-society-and-castle-of-our-skins-celebrate-black-musicians/.

54"Manhattan School of Music Announces Its Inaugural Rosterof Artist Scholars, an Influential Group of Black Artists, Activists, Educators, and Administrators," *Africlassical* (blog), October 29, 2020, https://africlassical.blogspot.com/2020/10/.

55 "#BlackVoicesMatter: The Legacies of Blackface Minstrelsy, Confederacy Nostalgia, Technology, and Music on Black Lives 2020," Manhattan School of Music, November 9, 2020, https://www .msmnyc.edu/performances/blackvoicesmatter-the-legacies-of-blackface-minstrelsy -confederacy-nostalgia-technology-and-music-on-black-lives-2020/.

56 Joseph Striplin, interview by Peter Whorf, 90.9 WRCJ, December 9, 2020, https://soundcloud .com/wrcj909fmhd1/striplin-final.

57 Terry Barnes, "African-Americans Striving to Break Classical Barriers," *Billboard*, October 24, 1992, https://books.google.com/books?id=2REEAAAAMBAJ&pg=PA1&lpg=PA1&dq=Terry+Bar nes,+%E2%80%9CAfrican-Americans+Striving+to+Break+Classical+Barriers,%E2%80%9D+ Billboard,+October+24,+1992,&source=bl&ots=KvNlc_Lz_f&sig=ACfU3U2Y5MerSPPF8eI6 bz4Cs_10V2vHLg&hl=en&sa=X&ved=2ahUKEwjBncbG1_b6AhXvj2oFHUQnD10Q6AF6BAgJEA M#v=onepage&q=Terry%20Barnes%2C%20%E2%80%9CAfrican-Americans%20Striving %20to%20Break%20Classical%20Barriers%2C%E2%80%9D%20Billboard%2C%20October %2024%2C%201992%2C&f=false

58 Interview with author, December 4, 2020.

CHAPTER FOUR: Scapegoats and the Rise of Mediocrity

1 Heather Mac Donald, "A Glorious Refuge from Identity Politics," *City Journal*, December 27, 2019, https://www.city-journal.org/manhattan-school-of-music.

2 "Brevard Alumna Dona Vaughn Creates Vocal Scholarship," Brevard College, accessed July 17, 2022, https://brevard.edu/brevard-alumna-dona-vaughn-creates-vocal-scholarship/.

3 Howard Watkins, September 20, 2020.

4 Interview with author, February 13, 2021.

5 Concerned student, August 10, 2020, comment on petition, "Immediate Removal of Dona Vaughn from the Manhattan School of Music Faculty," https://www.change.org/p/james-gandre -immediate-removal-of-dona-vaughn-from-the-manhattan-school-of-music-faculty.

6 Interview with author, December 10, 2020.

7 "Symposium on Philip Ewell's 2019 SMT Plenary Paper," *Journal of Schenkerian* Studies 12, (2019): 125-214, https://www.scribd.com/document/471711685/Journal-of-Schenkerian-Studies-responses.

8 "Executive Board Response to Essays in the Journal of Schenkerian Studies Vol. 12," Society Music Theory: Announcements, July 2020, https://societymusictheory.org/announcement/executive -board-response-journal-schenkerian-studies-vol-12-2020-07.

9 Jackson v. Wright et al, No. 4:2021cv00033 - Document 41 (E.D. Tex. 2021).

10 Lisa Mullens, "Exploring the Life of Chevalier de Saint-Georges, The 'Black Mozart,'" WBUR-FM, August 19, 2019, https://www.wbur.org/hereandnow/2019/08/19/black-mozart-chevalier-de-saint -georges.

11 Interview with author, November 6, 2020.

12 Interview with author, December 28, 2020.

13 Richard Fairman, "Boston and Birmingham Orchestras Seek a Wider Audience through Streaming," *Financial Times*, November 23, 2020, https://www.ft.com/content/2df74ceb-8bd5-4ce2-ad64 -3c0816212341.

14 Helen Walker-Hill, "Black Women Composers in Chicago: Then and Now," *Black Music Research Journal* 12, no. 1 (1992): 1-23, https://www.jstor.org/stable/779279.

15 Alex Ross, "Black Scholars Confront White Supremacy in Classical Music," *The New Yorker*, September 14, 2020, https://www.newyorker.com/magazine/2020/09/21/black-scholars-confront -white-supremacy-in-classical-music/amp.

16 "Symposium on Philip Ewell's 2019 SMT Plenary Paper."

[17]Tom Service, "Let's Reload the Canon," PressReader, September 3, 2020, https://www.press reader.com/uk/bbc-music-magazine/20200903/281891595653205.

[18]"El Sistema," Up Beat NYC, accessed October 23, 2022, https://upbeatnyc.org/el-sistema/.

[19]Email message to author, November 19, 2020.

[20]Interview with author, December 4, 2020.

[21]Interview with author, November 6, 2020.

[22]Interview with author, November 10, 2020.

[23]Matthew D. Morrison (@DrMaDMo), "In My Study of Black People and Our Music, I Don't Reveal All or Put Everything on Paper. Some Stuff Is Meant to Be Kept and Transferred Orally (and Ritually). I Trust That Process As Much As I Do Western (Colonial) Notions of 'Documentation,'" Twitter, November 1, 2020, https://twitter.com/drmadmo/status/1328884275102572546.

[24]Matthew D. Morrison (@DrMadMo), "The Desire to Feel Like You Have Access to Everything (I'm Thinking of Folks 'Interest' in All Aspects of Black Music/Study) is a Colonial Impulse," Twitter, November 17, 2020, https://twitter.com/drmadmo/status/1328836209074987010.

[25]"The Archivist's Task Force on Racism: Report to the Archivists," National Archives, April 20, 2021, https://www.archives.gov/files/news/archivists-task-force-on-racism-report.pdf.

CHAPTER FIVE: Making Beethoven Woke

[1]Sarah Nelson Glick and Matthew R. Golden, "Persistence of Racial Difference in Attitudes Toward Homosexuality in the United States," *JAIDS* 55, no. 4 (2010): 516-523, https://journals .lww.com/jaids/Fulltext/2010/12010/Persistence_of_Racial_Differences_in_Attitudes.16.aspx; F. A. Ernst et al., "Condemnation of Homosexuality in The Black Community: A Gender-Specific Phenomenon?," *Archives of Sexual Behavior* 20, (1991): 579-585, https://link.springer .com/article/10.1007/BF01550956; Timothy E. Lewis, "African American Gatekeepers or the Black Church?: Using Modified Grounded Theory to Explore the Debate on Black Homophobia 2022," *Journal of Homosexuality*, (2022), https://doi.org/10.1080/00918369.2022.2085935; Claire Gecewicz and Michael Lipka, "Blacks Are Lukewarm to Gay Marriage, but Most Say Businesses Must Provide Wedding Services to Gay Couples," Pew Research Center, October 7, 2014, https://www.pewresearch.org/fact-tank/2014/10/07/blacks-are-lukewarm-to-gay -marriage-but-most-say-businesses-must-provide-wedding-services-to-gay-couples/.

[2]"Heartbeat Opera's *Fidelio*," MetLiveArts, accessed July 17, 2022, https://www.metmuseum.org/-/ media/files/Events/Programs/MetLiveArts%20House%20Programs%202021_2022/Fidelio_ House%20Program.

[3]"All Together, a Global Ode to Joy: English Adaptation by Wordsmith," Baltimore Symphony Orchestra, Carnegie Hall, accessed July 17, 2022, https://www.carnegiehall.org/Educatio n/Programs/All-Together-A-Global-Ode-to-Joy/Texts-and-Translations/English-Baltimore.

[4]"All Together, a Global Ode to Joy: English Adaptation by Wordsmith."

[5]"All Together, a Global Ode to Joy: English Adaptation by Wordsmith."

[6]Sharon Kelly, "Bernstein's Legendary 'Ode to Freedom' Marking Fall of Berlin Wall, Out Now," uDiscoverMusic, https://www.udiscovermusic.com/classical-news/bernstein-beethoven-ode -to-freedom.

[7]Leslie Kandell, "MUSIC; Lots of Voices, Raised Constructively," *New York Times*, April 26, 1998, https://www.nytimes.com/1998/04/26/nyregion/music-lots-of-voices-raised-constructively .html.

[8]"Marin Alsop Appointed First-ever Music Director of the National Orchestral Institute + Festival: Trailblazing Conductor Will Innovate Programming, Conduct Multiple Concerts and Mentor Emerging Musicians," The Clarice National Orchestral Institute + Festival, accessed July 17, 2022, https://theclarice.umd.edu/noi/marin-alsop-announcement.

9"All Together, a Global Ode to Joy: English Adaptation by Anthony Anaxagorou," London Southbank Centre, Carnegie Hall, accessed July 17, 2022, https://www.carnegiehall.org/Education /Programs/All-Together-A-Global-Ode-to-Joy/Texts-and-Translations/English-London.

10"Poetry Friday: Tracy K. Smith's 'Ode to Joy,'" New York State Writers Institute: Center for the Literary Arts in New York State, August 27, 2021, https://www.nyswritersinstitute.org/post/poetry -friday-tracy-k-smith-s-ode-to-joy.

11Rune Bergmann and Wordsmith, "A Soldier's Tale and Romeo and Juliet," Baltimore Symphony Orchestra, https://my.bsomusic.org/overview/17600, accessed October 14, 2022.

12Hector Berlioz, *The Memoirs of Hector Berlioz: Translated and edited by David Cairns* (Everyman's Library Classics Series, 2002), 65.

13Berlioz, *The Memoirs of Hector Berlioz: Translated and edited by David Cairns,* 67.

CHAPTER SIX: Can Opera Survive the Culture Wars?

1Fiona Maddocks, "Nixon in China Review – A Gripping Human Drama," *The Guardian*, February 22, 2020, https://www.theguardian.com/music/2020/feb/22/nixon-in-china-scottish-opera -review-theatre-royal-glasgow-john-adams; "What the Critics Thought: Nixon in China Brings Political Opera to Life," Scottish Opera, March 5, 2020, https://www.scottishopera.org.uk/news /what-the-critics-thought-nixon-in-china-brings-political-opera-to-life/.

2Scottish Opera (@ScottishOpera), "What Amazing Company! We're Thrilled That Our 2020 Production Of NIXON IN CHINA (Our Last Full-Scale Show Pre-Lockdown) Has Been Nominated In The Opera Category Of This Year's South Bank Sky Arts Awards 😮. Read More >>" Twitter, June 9, 2021, https://twitter.com/ScottishOpera/status/1402630419149905921.

3Scottish Opera (@ScottishOpera), "A Statement From Scottish Opera Regarding Our South Bank Sky Arts Award Nomination For Our 2020 Production Of Nixon In China: @BeatsOrg @skytv," Twitter, June 11, 2021, https://twitter.com/scottishopera/status/1403332965900431361.

4Julian Chou-Lambert (@JulesC_L), "#Yellowface In Opera Has To Stop. It's Like Blackface, But Applied To East & South-East Asian Characters. It's Offensive And Dehumanising For ESEA People. Opera Folks, Please Learn About This And Do Better, Our Industry Is So Behind Here! #Yellowface #Opera #Orientalism," Twitter, June 9, 2021, https://twitter.com/julesc_l/status /1402746216551792640.

5Sarah Owen MP (@SarahOwen_), "This Is Disappointing @Scottishopera 1) Why Are There So Few ESEA People In This Production? 2) Why Do Cast Members Have Exaggerated Winged Eye Make Up On? Classic #Yellowface. 3) Has This Production Received Any Taxpayer Funding? 4) Why Does This Continue, Especially On Stage?," Twitter, June 11, 2021, https://twitter.com/sarahowen_ /status/1403289627834957824.

6Scottish Opera (@ScottishOpera), "A Statement from Scottish Opera Regarding Our South Bank Sky Arts Award Nomination for Our 2020 Production of Nixon in China."

7British East & South East Asians in the Screen & Stage Industry (BESEA), "What," *We Are Beats* (blog), accessed October 14, 2022, http://wearebeats.org.uk/.

8Scottish Opera (@ScottishOpera), "A Statement from Scottish Opera Regarding Our South Bank Sky Arts Award Nomination for Our 2020 Production of Nixon in China."

9Matthew Daines, "'Nixon in China': An Interview with Peter Sellars," *Tempo* 197, (1996): 12-19, https://doi.org/10.1017/S0040298200005143.

10Anthony Tommasini, "President and Opera, on Unexpected Stages," *New York Times*, February 3, 2011, https://www.nytimes.com/2011/02/04/arts/music/04nixon.html.

11Maddocks "Nixon In China Review – A Gripping Human Drama."

12Camilla Turner, "Nixon in China, the Opera Critics Loved, Engulfed in 'Yellow Face' Row," *The Telegraph*, June 13, 2021, https://www.telegraph.co.uk/news/2021/06/13/critically-acclaimed

-opera-yellow-face-row/.

13BEATS, email message to author, June 24, 2021.

14BeatsOrg Advocacy for #BESEAS (@BeatsOrg), "Thank You for Engaging. For Those Asking for the Context Surrounding This, Please See Our Statement in Full.," Twitter, June 12, 2021, https:// twitter.com/BeatsOrg/status/1403860205973164037.

15Tiffany May, "A Hong Kong Actress Wears Brownface. Cue Outrage and Shrugs.," New York Times, April 26, 2022, https://www.nytimes.com/2022/04/26/world/asia/brownface-barrack-okarma -1968-hong-kong.html.

16Felice León, "Let's Talk About In the Heights and the Erasure of Dark-Skinned Afro-Latinx Folks," The Root, June 9, 2021, https://www.theroot.com/lets-talk-about-in-the-heights-and-the-erasure -of-dark-1847064126.

17"Race and Ethnicity in Washington Heights, New York, New York (Neighborhood)," Statistical Atlas, access August 14, 2022, https://statisticalatlas.com/neighborhood/New-York/New-York /Washington-Heights/Race-and-Ethnicity.

18"Lin-Manuel Miranda Addresses Colorism in 'In The Heights' on Twitter: 'I Am Truly Sorry,'" Just Jared, June 14, 2021, https://www.justjared.com/2021/06/14/lin-manuel-miranda-addresses -colorism-in-in-the-heights-on-twitter-i-am-truly-sorry/.

19Gabe Kaminsky, "Sean Penn Blasts 'Soviet' Cancel Culture for Wrecking Hollywood with 'Gotcha Moments,'" The Federalist, July 9, 2021, https://thefederalist.com/2021/07/09/sean-penn -blasts-soviet-cancel-culture-for-wrecking-hollywood-with-gotcha-moments/.

20Maya Phillips, "In 'What to Send Up,' I See You, Black American Theater," New York Times, published July 6, 2021, updated July 8, 2021, https://www.nytimes.com/2021/07/06/theater/what-to -send-up-bam.html?smid=em-share.

CHAPTER SEVEN: The Revolution Comes to Julliard

1"A Message from President Woetzel," Juilliard, April 23, 2021, https://www.juilliard.edu/news /149411/message-president-woetzel.

2"EDIB Fall 2020 Report," Juilliard, January 20, 2021, https://www.juilliard.edu/news/148006 /edib-fall-2020-report.

3"A Message from Damian Woetzel and Christina Salgado," Juilliard, June 1, 2020, https://www .juilliard.edu/news/146526/message-damian-woetzel-and-christina-salgado-june-1-2020.

4The Office of the Provost, email message, June 11, 2020.

5Former Juilliard administrator, email message to author, January 13, 2023.

6Rob Weinert-Kendt, "A Teaching Moment for Juilliard," American Theatre, April 30, 2021, https:// www.americantheatre.org/2021/04/30/a-teaching-moment-for-juilliard/.

7Shelley (@shelley_fort), "Marion Grey Is an Actor I Love and Have Worked with Back in NYC. She's Currently a Student at Juilliard (Drama). This Story Breaks My Heart, but I'm Unsurprised. *TW*," Twitter, April 22, 2021, https://twitter.com/shelley_fort/status/1385365423638474753?ref_ src=twsrc%5Etfw%7Ctwcamp%5Etweetembed%7Ctwterm%5E1385383530155413512%7Ctwg r%5E%7Ctwcon%5Es3_&ref_url=https%3A%2F%2Fwww.comicsands.com%2Fjuilliard -student-slavery-exercise-trigger-2652801534.html.

8"A Message from President Woetzel."

9Heather Mac Donald, email message to Rosalie Contreras (Vice President of Public Affairs), May 13, 2021.

10Weinert-Kendy, "A Teaching Moment for Juilliard."

11Anna O'Donoghue, "A Conversation with James Houghton: Nurturing the Art of Theater," The Juilliard Journal, September 2007, http://journal.juilliard.edu/journal/conversation-james-houghton.

12"BIPOC Demands for White American Theatre," Squarespace, accessed August 14, 2022, https://static1.squarespace.com/static/5ede42fd6cb927448d9d0525/t/5f064e63f21dd43ad6ab3162/1594248809279/Tier2.pdf.

13Michael Paulson, "At Theaters, Push for Racial Equity Leads to Resignations and Restructuring," *New York Times*, August 19, 2020, https://www.nytimes.com/2020/08/19/theater/racial-equity-theater-resignations.html.

14Bo Emerson, "Serenbe Playhouse Staff Removed Amid Charges of Racism," *The Atlanta Journal-Constitution*, June 18, 2020, https://www.ajc.com/news/serenbe-playhouse-staff-removed-amid-charges-racism/vlCgkH7ADgDkwChQqAPiVI/.

15Email message to author, May 11, 2021.

16Email message to author, May 7, 2021.

17Email message to author, May 8, 2021.

CHAPTER EIGHT: The Swamping of *Swan Lake*

1Roslyn Sulcas, "Black Ballerina, Playing a Swan, Says She Was Told to Color Her Skin," *New York Times*, December 11, 2020, https://www.nytimes.com/2020/12/11/arts/dance/Chloe-Lopes-Gomes-Ballet.html.

2"Statement from the Artistic Director Addressing Issues of Racism at the Staatsballet Berlin," Staatsballet Berlin, accessed August 14, 2022, https://www.staatsballett-berlin.de/en/statement.

3Craig Simpson, "Woke Dance School Drops Ballet from Auditions As It Is 'White' and 'Elitist'," *The Telegraph*, July 16, 2022, https://www.telegraph.co.uk/news/2022/07/16/woke-dance-school-drops-ballet-auditions-white-elitist/.

4Sulcas, "Black Ballerina, Playing a Swan, Says She Was Told to Color Her Skin."

CHAPTER NINE: The Demise of the Docent

1The Art Institute of Chicago, "Our Docents Are Incredible. As Our Own Museum Director Douglas Druick Said On The Occasion Of The Docent Program's 50th Anniversary Last Year, 'To Walk Through The Galleries And See Children, Led By Docents, Jumping Up And Raising Their Hands To Talk Is To See The Work Of The Museum At Its Best.' Interested In Becoming A Docent? Learn More About The Program At One Of Three Information Sessions, Including One Tonight At 5:30.," Facebook, January 26, 2012, https://www.facebook.com/artic/posts/our-docents-are-incredible-as-our-own-museum-director-douglas-druick-said-on-the/284494074938464/.

2Christopher Borrelli, "Chicago's Art Institute Fired Its Volunteer Docents and Caused a Furor Heard Nationwide. The Fight Is Really about the Future of Museums.," *Chicago Tribune*, December 2, 2021, https://www.chicagotribune.com/entertainment/ct-ent-docents-art-institute-diversity-20211202-imwkcqnd3bghbn2smhpc7252wy-story.html.

3The Editorial Board, "Editorial: Shame on the Art Institute for Summarily Canning Its Volunteer Docents," *Chicago Tribune*, September 27, 2021, https://www.chicagotribune.com/opinion/editorials/ct-edit-art-institute-docents-firing-20210927-dfrho66bjba2bp27phz2yndwzu-story.html.

4Gregory Nosan, "Women in the Galleries: Prestige, Education, and Volunteerism at Mid-Century," *Art Institute of Chicago Museum Studies* 29, no. 1 (2003): 47–95. https://doi.org/10.2307/4113027.

5Gregory Nosan, "Women in the Galleries: Prestige, Education, and Volunteerism at Mid-Century," 66.

6Robert Eskridge, "Museum Education at the Art Institute, 1980-2003: Expansion, Diversity, Continuity," *Art Institute of Chicago Museum Studies* 29, no. 1 (2003): 73–96, https://doi.org/10.2307/4113028.

7Robert Eskridge, "Museum Education at the Art Institute, 1980-2003: Expansion, Diversity, Continuity."

8"The Art Institute of Chicago Commits to Advancing Racial Justice Now and in the Future.," Art

Institute of Chicago, accessed August 14, 2022, https://www.artic.edu/about-us/identity-and
-history/equity.

[9]"The Changing Role of Museums by James Rondeau," Des Moines Art Center, May 10, 2019,
https://desmoinesartcenter.org/art/resources/the-changing-role-of-museums-by-james-rondeau/.

[10]"The Changing Role of Museums by James Rondeau."

[11]"Land Acknowledgement," Art Institute of Chicago, accessed October 28, 2022, https://www
.artic.edu/about-us/mission-and-history/land-acknowledgment.

[12]"Mission," Art Institute of Chicago, accessed October 14, 2022, https://www.artic.edu/about-us
/identity-and-history.

[13]"The Changing Role of Museums by James Rondeau."

[14]"Museum Appoints Veronica Stein as the New Woman's Board Executive Director, Learning and
Public Engagement," *Artdaily*, accessed August 21, 2022, https://artdaily.cc/news/134062/Museum
-appoints-Veronica-Stein-as-the-new-Woman-s-Board-Executive-Director--Learning-and
-Public-Engagement#.YwJ6TezMJUJ.

[15]Robert M. Levy, "Op-Ed: The Art Institute – and Its Critics – Must Embrace Change," *Chicago
Tribune*, September 30, 2021, https://www.chicagotribune.com/opinion/commentary/ct-opinion
-art-institute-docent-change-response-20210930-himtjin2xne2jkkkb7hzz5xpra-story.html.

[16]Brian Hendershot and Mallorie Marsh, "Docent Diversity Initiative: Looking at 2020 and Beyond,"
Crocker Art Museum, June 1, 2020, https://www.crockerart.org/oculus/docent-diversity
-initiative-looking-at-2020-and-beyond.

[17]Interview with author, November 3, 2021.

[18]Roger Schonfeld, Mariët Westermann, and Liam Sweeney, "The Andrew W. Mellon Foundation
Art Museum Staff Demographic Survey," The Andrew W. Mellon Foundation, July 28, 2015,
https://mellon.org/media/filer_public/ba/99/ba99e53a-48d5-4038-80e1-66f9ba1c020e/awmf
_museum_diversity_report_aamd_7-28-15.pdf.

[19]Renaud Proch, "If Museums in the US Want to Be More Inclusive, They First Have to Recognize—
and Unlearn—Old Habits and Biases," Artnet News, June 25, 2020, https://news.artnet.com
/opinion/renaud-proch-ici-changing-museums-1889284.

[20]James Panero, "Unmaking the Met: On the Past, Present, and Future of the Metropolitan Museum of
Art," *The New Criterion*, 39, no. 4, (2020), https://newcriterion.com/issues/2020/12/unmaking
-the-met.

[21]"The Changing Role of Museums by James Rondeau."

[22]Whitney Museum of American Art, Board of Trustees Equity and Inclusion Session with Performance Paradigm, October 13, 2021.

[23]"Volunteering in the United States – 2015," Bureau of Labor Statistics U.S. Department of Labor,
accessed October 28, 2022, https://www.bls.gov/news.release/pdf/volun.pdf.

[24]Nicolas J. Duquette, "The Evolving Distribution of Giving in the United States," *Nonprofit and
Voluntary Sector Quarterly* 50, no. 5, (2020), https://doi.org/10.1177/0899764020977691.

CHAPTER TEN: Museums Apologize for Art

[1]Daniel H. Weis and Max Hollein, "Our Commitments to Anti-Racism, Diversity, and a Stronger
Community," The Metropolitan Museum of Art, July 6, 2020, https://www.metmuseum.org
/blogs/now-at-the-met/2020/the-mets-plans-for-anti-racism.

[2]Francis Hals, *Paulus Verschuur (1606–1667)*, 1643, oil on canvas, 46 3/4 x 37 in. (118.7 x 94 cm), The
Metropolitan Museum of Art, New York, https://www.metmuseum.org/art/collection/search/436
620?&exhibitionId=0&oid=436620&pkgids=512.

[3]Johannes Vermeer, *A Maid Asleep*, ca. 1656–57, oil on canvas, 34 1/2 x 30 1/8 in. (87.6 x 76.5 cm),

The Metropolitan Museum of Art, New York, https://www.metmuseum.org/art/collection/search/437878?&exhibitionId=0&oid=437878&pkgids=512.

[4]"In Praise of Painting: Dutch Masterpieces at The Met: Visiting Guide," The Metropolitan Museum of Art, accessed August 14, 2022, https://www.metmuseum.org/exhibitions/listings/2018/in-praise-of-painting-dutch-masterpieces/visiting-guide.

[5]Frans Post, *A Brazilian Landscape*, 1650, oil on wood, 24 x 36 in. (61 x 91.4 cm), The Metropolitan Museum of Art, New York, https://www.metmuseum.org/art/collection/search/437323?&exhibitionId=0&oid=437323&pkgids=512.

[6]"SLAVERY: Ten True Stories," RIJKS Museum, accessed August 14, 2022, https://www.rijksmuseum.nl/en/whats-on/exhibitions/past/slavery.

[7]Margareta Haverman, *A Vase of Flowers*, 1716, oil on wood, 31 1/4 x 23 3/4 in. (79.4 x 60.3 cm), The Metropolitan Museum of Art, New York, https://www.metmuseum.org/art/collection/search/436634?&exhibitionId=0&oid=436634&pkgids=512.

[8]"The African Origin of Civilization: Overview," The Metropolitan Museum of Art, accessed August 16, 2022, https://www.metmuseum.org/exhibitions/listings/2021/african-origin-of-civilization.

[9]Cheikh Anta Diop, *The African Origin of Civilization: Myth or Reality* (1974), xv, xiv.

[10]Diop, *The African Origin of Civilization: Myth or Reality*, 23.

[11]Diop, *The African Origin of Civilization: Myth or Reality* xiv.

[12]Philip Perry, "Black or White? Ancient Egyptian Race Mystery Now Solved," Big Think, January 16, 2022, https://bigthink.com/surprising-science/were-the-ancient-egyptians-black-or-white-scientists-now-know/.

[13]Contemporary Egyptians are no more persuaded by Afrocentric claims. Middle East Eye Staff, "Calls Grow to Cancel Kevin Hart's Comedy Show in Egypt Over 'Afrocentric' Views," *Middle East Eye*, December 16, 2022, https://www.middleeasteye.net/news/calls-grow-cancel-kevin-harts-comedy-show-egypt-over-afrocentric-views.

[14]Diop, *The African Origin of Civilization: Myth or Reality*, xiv.

[15]Frank M. Snowden Jr., "Bernal's 'Blacks,' Herodotus, and Other Classical Evidence," *Johns Hopkins University Press* 22, (1989): 83–95, http://www.jstor.org/stable/26308578.

[16]John Parker and Richard Rathbone, *African History: A Very Short Introduction* (New York: Oxford University Press, 2007), 129.

[17]Kwame Anthony Appiah, *In My Father's House: Africa in the Philosophy of Culture*, (New York: Oxford University Press, 1992), 101.

[18]Old Kingdom, *The King's Acquaintances Memi and Sabu*, ca. 2575–2465 B.C., limestone paint, H. 62 × W. 24.5 × D. 16 cm, 28.8 kg (24 7/16 × 9 5/8 × 6 5/16 in., 63.4 lb.), The Metropolitan Museum of Art, New York, https://www.metmuseum.org/art/collection/search/543899.

[19]Dogon Artist, *Figure: Seated Couple*, 18th–early 19th century, wood-sculpture, H. 28 3/4 × W. 8 5/8 × D. 8 in. (73 × 21.9 × 20.3 cm), The Metropolitan Museum of Art, New York, https://www.metmuseum.org/art/collection/search/310325.

[20]Jan van Eyck, *The Arnolfini Portrait*, 1434, oil on oak panel, 82 cm x 60 cm, The National Gallery, London, https://www.nationalgallery.org.uk/paintings/jan-van-eyck-the-arnolfini-portrait.

[21]Bamana Artisti, *Power Object (Boli)*, First half of 20th century, wood-sculpture, H. 14 1/4 × W. 7 1/4 × D. 20 1/2 in. (36.2 × 18.4 × 52.1 cm), The Metropolitan Museum of Art, New York, https://www.metmuseum.org/art/collection/search/312389.

[22]Middle Knigdom, *Hippopotamus ('William')*, ca. 1961–1878 B.C., faience, L. 20 cm (7 7/8 in.); W. 7.5 cm (2 15/16 in.); H. 11.2 cm (4 7/16 in.), The Metropolitan Museum of Art, New York, https://www.metmuseum.org/art/collection/search/544227.

23Edo Artist, *Plaque: Warrior and Attendants*, 16th–17th century, metal-sculpture, H. 18 3/4 × W. 15 × D. 4 1/4 in. (47.6 × 38.1 × 10.8 cm), The Metropolitan Museum of Art, New York, https://www .metmuseum.org/art/collection/search/316393.

24Doreen Ajiambo, "Witch Doctors Sacrificing Children in This Drought-Stricken African Country," *USA Today*, September 26, 2017, https://www.usatoday.com/story/news/world/2017/09/26 /witch-doctors-sacrificing-children-drought-stricken-african-country-uganda/703756001/.

25Chris Rogers, "Where Child Sacrifice Is a Business," BBC News, October 11, 2011, https://www .bbc.com/news/world-africa-15255357.

26Richard Burton, *The First Footsteps In East Africa* (Whitefish, Montana: Kessinger Publishing, LLC, 2010).

27Holland Cotter, "In 'African Origin' Show at Met, New Points of Light Across Cultures," *New York Times*, January 6, 2022, https://www.nytimes.com/2022/01/06/arts/design/met-museum -african-origin-exhibit.html.

28Kongo Artist and Nganga, Yombe Group, *Mangaaka Power Figure (Nkisi N'Kondi)*, Second half of the 19th century, wood-sculpture, H. 46 7/16 × W. 19 1/2 × D. 15 1/2 in., 53 lb. (118 × 49.5 × 39.4 cm, 24 kg), The Metropolitan Museum of Art, New York, https://www.metmuseum.org/art/collection/ search/320053.

29John Ruskin, *Modern Painters, Vol. 3*, (London: George Routledge & Sons, 1856), 287.

30Margaret Hedeman and Matt Kristoffersen, "Art History Department to Scrap Survey Course," *Yale Daily News*, January 24, 2020, https://yaledailynews.com/blog/2020/01/24/art-history -department-to-scrap-survey-course/.

31Victor Wang, "Student Petition Urges English Department to Diversify Curriculum," *Yale Daily News*, published May 26, 2016, updated May 27, 2016, https://yaledailynews.com/blog/2016 /05/26/student-petition-urges-english-department-to-diversify-curriculum/.

32"Yale Receives $4 Million Mellon Foundation Grant to Support Race Studies Centers across Four Universities," Yale News, January 14, 2020, https://news.yale.edu/2020/01/14/yale-receives-4 -million-mellon-foundation-grant-support-race-studies.

CHAPTER ELEVEN: An Art Museum Cancels Art

1Wendy S. Walters, "Presumptions on the Figure, Given the Absences," in *Fictions of Emancipation: Carpeaux's Why Born Enslaved! Reconsidered*, eds. Elyse Nelson and Wendy S. Walters (New York: The Metropolitan Museum of Art, 2022), 86.

2"Recent Acquisitions, A Selection: 1997–1998," *The Metropolitan Museum of Art Bulletin* 56, no. 2 (1998): 1-81, https://www.metmuseum.org/art/metpublications/Recent_Acquisitions_A_Selection _1997_1998_The_Metropolitan_Museum_of_Art_Bulletin_v_56_no2_Fall_1998.

3Laure de Margerie, "Fountain of the Observatory," in *The Passions of Jean-Baptiste Carpeaux*, eds. James David Draper and Edouard Papet, (New York: The Metropolitan Museum of Art, 2014), 163.

4Sarah Lawrence and Elyse Nelson, "Why Born Enslaved! by Jean-Baptiste Carpeaux, modeled 1868, carved 1873, Purchase, Lila Acheson Wallace, Wrightsman Fellows, and Iris and B. Gerald Cantor Foundation Gifts, 2019 2019.220," The Metropolitan Museum of Art, 2019, https://www .metmuseum.org/art/online-features/metcollects/why-born-enslaved.

5Alex Greenberger, "When Representation Isn't Enough: New Exhibition at the Met Takes Up the Complex Case of a 19th-Century Abolitionist Sculpture," ARTnews, March 10, 2022, https://www .artnews.com/art-news/artists/carpeaux-recast-metropolitan-museum-of-art-1234621559/.

6Rochelle Goldstein, "Professor Wendy Walters Wins 2020 Creative Capital Award," Columbia University School of the Arts, February 20, 2020, https://arts.columbia.edu/news/professor -wendy-walters-wins-2020-creative-capital-award.

7*Fictions of Emancipation: Carpeaux's Why Born Enslaved! Reconsidered*, eds. by Elyse Nelson and

Wendy S. Walters (New York: The Metropolitan Museum of Art, 2022), 16.

[8]Iris Moon, "White Fragility: Abolitionist Porcelain in Revolutionary France," in *Fictions of Emancipation: Carpeaux's Why Born Enslaved! Reconsidered*, eds. by Elyse Nelson and Wendy S. Walters (New York: The Metropolitan Museum of Art, 2022), 46.

[9]Adriano Pedrosa, "History, Histórias" Afro-Atlantic Histories, eds. Adriano Pedrosa and Tomás Toledo DelMonico Books/Museu de Arte de São Paulo D.A.P. New York, (December 7, 2021), 21.

[10]Elyse Nelson "Sculpting about Slavery in the Second Empire," in *Fictions of Emancipation: Carpeaux's Why Born Enslaved! Reconsidered*, eds. by Elyse Nelson and Wendy S. Walters (New York: The Metropolitan Museum of Art, 2022), 52.

[11]Nelson, "Sculpting about Slavery in the Second Empire," 71.

[12]*The Passions of Jean-Baptiste Carpeaux*, eds. James David Draper and Edouard Papet, (New York: The Metropolitan Museum of Art, 2014), 77.

[13]Lisa E. Farrington, "Reinventing Herself: The Black Female Nude," *Woman's Art Journal* 24, no. 2, (2003,2004): 15-23, https://www.jstor.org/stable/1358782.

[14]Manufactured by Minton and Company after Hiram Powers, *The Greek Slave*, 1849, parian porcelain, H. 14 1/2 in. (36.8 cm); Diam. 4 in. (10.2 cm), The Metropolitan Museum of Art, New York, https://www.metmuseum.org/art/collection/search/4140.

[15]Nelson, "Sculpting about Slavery in the Second Empire," 52.

[16]Nelson, "Sculpting about Slavery in the Second Empire," 64.

[17]Greenberger, "When Representation Isn't Enough."

[18]Edouard Papet, "Ugolino," in *The Passions of Jean-Baptiste Carpeaux*, eds. James David Draper and Edouard Papet, (New York: The Metropolitan Museum of Art, 2014), 75.

[19]James Smalls, "Dressing Up/Stripping Down: Ethnographic Sculpture as Colonizing Act," in *Fictions of Emancipation: Carpeaux's Why Born Enslaved! Reconsidered*, eds. Elyse Nelson and Wendy S. Walters (New York: The Metropolitan Museum of Art, 2022), 67.

[20]Smalls, "Dressing Up/Stripping Down: Ethnographic Sculpture as Colonizing Act," 69.

[21]Smalls, "Dressing Up/Stripping Down: Ethnographic Sculpture as Colonizing Act," 68.

[22]Nelson "Sculpting about Slavery in the Second Empire," 52.

[23]Holland Cotter, "'Carpeaux Recast': A Sculptural Gem with a Knotty Back Story," *New York Times*, March 10, 2022, https://www.nytimes.com/2022/03/10/arts/design/carpeaux-recast-met-museum-review.html.

[24]"Two Heroic Sisters Silk Scarf," Kehinde Wiley, accessed September 7, 2022, https://kehinde wileyshop.com/collections/apparel/products/two-heroic-sisters-of-the-grassland-silk-scarf.

[25]Caitlin Meehye Beach, "Reproducing and Refusing Carpeaux," in *Fictions of Emancipation: Carpeaux's Why Born Enslaved! Reconsidered*, eds. Elyse Nelson and Wendy S. Walters (New York: The Metropolitan Museum of Art, 2022), 95.

[26]Beach, "Reproducing and Refusing Carpeaux," 95.

[27]Cotter, "In 'African Origin' Show at Met, New Points of Light across Cultures."

[28]Carol Duncan, "The Art Museum as Ritual," in *The Art of Art History: A Critical Anthology*, eds. Donald Preziosi (New York: Oxford University Press, 2009), 431.

[29]Duncan, "The Art Museum as Ritual," 434.

[30]Sarah E. Lawrence, "Preface," in *Fictions of Emancipation: Carpeaux's Why Born Enslaved! Reconsidered*, eds. by Elyse Nelson and Wendy S. Walters (New York: The Metropolitan Museum of Art, 2022), 11.

[31]"Recent Acquisitions, A Selection: 1997–1998."

[32]Lawrence, "Preface," 9.

[33]Max Hollein, "Director's Forward," in *Fictions of Emancipation: Carpeaux's Why Born Enslaved! Reconsidered*, eds. Elyse Nelson and Wendy S. Walters (New York: The Metropolitan Museum of Art, 2022), 7.

[34]Zeinab Mohammed Salih, "Viewpoint From Sudan - Where Black People Are Called Slaves" BBC, July 26, 2020, https://www.bbc.com/news/world-africa-53147864.

[35]Daniel Gordon, "'Civilization' and the Self-Critical Tradition," *Society* 54, no. 2 (2017), https://doi.org/10.1007/s12115-017-0110-4.

[36]Gordon, "'Civilization' and the Self-Critical Tradition."

[1]Interview with author, January 3, 2021.

CHAPTER TWELVE: Abstainers

[2]John McLaughlin Williams, "Conductor/Violinist John McLaughlin Williams Discusses Bax and His American Premiere Performance of the Violin Concerto," The Sir Arnold Bax Website, January 5, 2013, https://www.arnoldbax.com/conductorviolinist-john-mclaughlin-williams-discusses-bax-and-his-american-premiere-performance-of-the-violin-concerto/.

[3]Interview with author, January 3, 2021.

[4]Email message to author, January 19, 2021.

[5]Williams, "Conductor/Violinist John McLaughlin Williams Discusses Bax."

[6]Email message to author, January 19, 2021.

[7]Quoted in Williams' email message to author, June 4, 2021.

[8]Quoted in Williams' email message to author, June 4, 2021.

[9]Email message to author, July 5, 2021.

[10]"Daniel Bernard Roumain & Mozart: An NJSO Concert Film, Produced by DreamPlay Films," New Jersey Symphony, November 19, 2020, https://www.njsymphony.org/events/detail/daniel-bernard-roumain-mozart.

[11]Daniel Roumain, "I Would LOVE To Compose A Work EXCLUSIVELY For BIPOC Members Of ANY Orchestra. READY!," Facebook, January 31, 2021, https://www.facebook.com/daniel.roumain/posts/2146061338859075.

[12]Daniel Roumain, "Jerry Friedman I'm Writing A Piece Exclusively For BIPOC Orchestral Musicians. If You See That As "Racist" You Clearly Don't Understand What Racism Is Or How It . . ." Facebook, January 31, 2021, https://www.facebook.com/daniel.roumain/posts/2146061338859075.

[13]"Tulsa Race Riot: A Report by the Oklahoma Commission to Study the Tulsa Race Riot of 1921," Oklahoma Historical Society, February 28, 2001, https://www.okhistory.org/research/forms/freport.pdf.

[14]Daniel Bernard Roumain, "Composer Statement," Opera Philadelphia, accessed August 14, 2022, https://www.operaphila.org/whats-on/streaming-2021-2022/they-still-want-to-kill-us/composer-statement/.

[15]Anagha Srikanth, "Tulsa Massacre Memorial Removes Black Composer over 'God Damn America' Lyrics," *The Hill*, March 23, 2021, https://thehill.com/changing-america/enrichment/arts-culture/544479-tulsa-massacre-memorial-removes-black-composer-over/.

[16]"Statement from Tulsa Opera on the 'Greenwood Overcomes' Concert Program," Tulsa Opera, March 21, 2021, https://tulsaopera.com/2021/03/statement-from-tulsa-opera-on-the-greenwood-overcomes-concert-program/#:~:text=General%20Director%20%26%20CEO%20of%20Tulsa,city%2Dwide%20centennial%20commemorative%20events.

[17]Jewel Wicker, "'God Damn America': Tulsa Massacre Opera Drops Black Composer over Lyrics,"

The Guardian, March 22, 2021, https://www.theguardian.com/music/2021/mar/22/black-composer-tulsa-massacre-opera-daniel-bernard-roumain.

[18]"Statement from Tulsa Opera on the 'Greenwood Overcomes' Concert Program."

[19]"About the Project," America/Beautiful, accessed August 14, 2022, https://www.america-beautiful.com/about-the-project.

[20]Daniel Bernard Roumain, "America, NEVER Beautiful," America/Beautiful, accessed August 14, 2022, https://www.america-beautiful.com/composers/daniel-bernard-roumain.

[21]Daniel Bernard Roumain (DBR) (@DBRmusic), "@Tulsaopera Just Decommissoned Me. I Was Asked To Create A New Work For Them. I Composed The Words And Music For A New Aria, And The Last 2 Lines Are, "God Bless America; God Damn America!" They Asked Me To Omit "Damn". I Refused. They Fired Me. Life In Black America.," Twitter, March 19, 2021, https://twitter.com/dbrmusic/status/1373036646803898373.

[22]Justin Curto, "Did the Tulsa Opera Dismiss a Black Composer over One Line?," *New York*, March 29, 2021, https://www.vulture.com/2021/03/tulsa-opera-fires-composer-one-line.html.

[23]Francisco Salazar, "Black Opera Alliance Releases Statement Regarding Tulsa Opera & Daniel Roumain's Removal from 'Greenwood Overcomes,'" Opera Wire, March 25, 2021, https://operawire.com/black-opera-alliance-releases-statement-regarding-tulsa-opera-daniel-roumains-removal-from-greenwood-overcomes/.

[24]Matt Trotter, "Tulsa Opera Cuts Composer from Concert Commemorating Race Massacre over Lyrics Disagreement," Public Radio Tulsa, March 23, 2021, https://www.publicradiotulsa.org/local-regional/2021-03-23/tulsa-opera-cuts-composer-from-concert-commemorating-race-massacre-over-lyrics-disagreement.

[25]David Salazar, "Tulsa Opera Removes Composer Daniel Roumain from Concert Commemorating Race Massacre Over One Word," Opera Wire, March 21, 2021, https://operawire.com/tulsa-opera-removes-black-composer-from-concert-commemorating-race-massacre-over-one-word/.

[26]Curto, "Did the Tulsa Opera Dismiss a Black Composer over One Line?"

[27]Daniel Bernard Roumain, "They Still Want to Kill Us: About the Work," Sozo Artists, March 21, 2021, https://www.sozoartists.com/tswtku-old.

[28]"They Still Want to Kill Us, World Premier," Opera Philadelphia: Operatic Events, 2021, https://www.operaphila.org/whats-on/events/other/2021/they-still-want-to-kill-us/.

[29]Sozo Artists, "THEY STILL WANT TO KILL US feat. J'Nai Bridges & DBR | the uncensored version," Facebook, May 25, 2021, https://www.facebook.com/watch/?v=1079031126252923.

[30]Email message to author, May 27, 2021.

[31]Drew McManus, "Internalizing the Concept of Equity," Adaptistration, October 29, 2020, https://adaptistration.com/2020/10/29/internalizing-the-concept-of-equity/.

[32]"Daniel Bernard Roumain to Become New Jersey Symphony Orchestra Resident Artistic Catalyst," New Jersey Symphony, April 29, 2021, https://www.njsymphony.org/news/detail/daniel-bernard-roumain-to-become-new-jersey-symphony-orchestra-resident-artistic-catalyst.

[33]Tulsa Opera, "Greenwood Overcomes: Celebrating Black Composers & Opera Stars," YouTube video, 2:13:16, May 1, 2021, https://www.youtube.com/watch?v=hRc5EqHuPPo.

[34]"Tulsa Race Riot: A Report by the Oklahoma Commission to Study the Tulsa Race Riot of 1921."

[35]Richard S. Ginell, "Long Beach Opera Reprises *The Central Park Five*, Minimally Staged," Classical Voice, June 21, 2022, https://www.sfcv.org/articles/review/long-beach-opera-reprises-central-park-five-minimally-staged.

[36]Anthony Davis, "The Central Park Five Opera in 3 Acts," PSNY, accessed September 10, 2022, https://www.eamdc.com/psny/composers/anthony-davis/works/the-central-park-five-2/.

37Jessica Gelt, "Arts Groups Raced to Be More Diverse. How One L.A.-Area Company Tripped along the Way," *Los Angeles Times*, July 28, 2022, https://www.latimes.com/entertainment-arts /story/2022-07-28/diversity-inclusion-long-beach-opera-racial-tokenism.

38"About Derell," Derrel Acon, accessed October 29, 2022, http://derrellacon.com/.

39"Dr. Derrell Acon Appointed as Opera Philadelphia's First Vice President of People Operations & Inclusion," Opera Philadelphia, December 16, 2021, https://www.operaphila.org/about/news -press/pressroom/2021/acon/.

CHAPTER THIRTEEN: A New Crime Wave

1Neil MacFarquhar, "Murders Spiked in 2020 in Cities across the United States," *New York Times*, published September 27, 2021, updated November 15, 2021, https://www.nytimes.com /2021/09/27/us/fbi-murders-2020-cities.html.

2Matt Steib, "Homicides Surged in NYC in 2020," *New York*, December 29, 2020, https://nymag .com/intelligencer/2020/12/homicides-surged-in-nyc-in-2020.html.

3Neil MacFarquhar and Serge F. Kovaleski, "A Pandemic Bright Spot: In Many Places, Less Crime," *New York Times*, updated May 28, 2020, https://www.nytimes.com/2020/05/26/us/coronavirus -crime.html.

4Tina Moore and Jorge Fitz-Gibbon, "Big Apple Carjackings Continue to Spike, NYPD Stats Show," *New York Post*, January 13, 2022, https://nypost.com/2022/01/13/nyc-carjackings-continue-to -spike-nypd-stats-show/.

5John Gramlich, "The Gap between the Number of Blacks and Whites in Prison is Shrinking," Pew Research Center, April 30, 2019, https://www.pewresearch.org/fact-tank/2019/04/30/shrinking -gap-between-number-of-blacks-and-whites-in-prison/.

6John Gramlich, "Black Imprisonment Rate in the U.S. Has Fallen by a Third Since 2006," Pew Research Center, May 6, 2020, https://www.pewresearch.org/fact-tank/2020/05/06/share-of-black -white-hispanic-americans-in-prison-2018-vs-2006/.

7E. Ann Carson, "Prisoners in 2019," U.S. Department of Justice Bulletin, October 2020, https:// bjs.ojp.gov/content/pub/pdf/p19.pdf.

8Alejandra O'Connell-Domenech, "Mayor Wants NYPD to Use 'Light Touch' with George Floyd Protesters," *amNY*, May 29, 2020, https://www.amny.com/politics/mayor-wants-to-see-nypd-use -light-touch-with-george-floyd-protesters/.

9Dana Rubinstein and Jeffery C. Mays, "Here's What Led to N.Y.C.'s First Curfew in 75 Years," *New York Times*, June 2, 2020, https://www.nytimes.com/2020/06/02/nyregion/curfew-new-york -city.html.

10"NYPD Eliminating Plainclothes Anti-Crime Units in Move Toward More Community Policing," NBC New York, published June15, 2020, updated June 16, 2020, https://www.nbcnewyork.com /news/local/nypd-eliminating-plainclothes-anti-crime-units-in-move-toward-more-community -policing/2465313/.

11"USE OF FORCE REPORT: 2019," City of New York Police Department, November 3, 2020, https:// www1.nyc.gov/assets/nypd/downloads/pdf/use-of-force/use-of-force-2019-2020-11-03.pdf.

12"USE OF FORCE REPORT."

13"Police Department: Officer Involved Shootings," City of Houston, Texas, accessed October 14, 2022, https://www.houstontx.gov/police/ois/.

14"USE OF FORCE REPORT."

15Interview with author, January 17, 2021.

16Sara Dorn and Dean Blasamini, "Shootings Soar 205 Percent after NYPD Disbands Anti-Crime Unit," *New York Post*, July 4, 2020, https://nypost.com/2020/07/04/shootings-soar-205-percent

-after-nypd-disbands-anti-crime-unit/.

[17] Ashley Southall, "Shootings Have Soared. Is the N.Y.P.D. Pulling Back?," *New York Times*, published July 16, 2020, updated August 26, 2020, https://www.nytimes.com/2020/07/16/nyregion/nyc -shootings-nypd.html.

[18] Rocco Parascandola, Thomas Tracy, and Leonard Greene, "'What the Hell is Going On with the Firearms in NYC?': NYPD Has Made 417 Gun Arrests Already This Year," *New York Daily News*, January 27, 2021, https://www.nydailynews.com/new-york/nyc-crime/ny-cops-make-more- than-400-gun-arrests-this-year-20210127-vy5qsjmsyjeizpxc4ckcs27mna-story.html.

[19] "Overall Crime in New York City Reaches Record Low in 2020," NYPD, January 6, 2021, https:// www.nyc.gov/site/nypd/news/p0106a/overall-crime-new-york-city-reaches-record-low-2020.

[20] Michael Gartland and Rocco Parascandola, "NYPD's Enforcement of Social Distancing Has 'Racist Impact': Councilman Donovan Richards," *New York Daily News*, May 14, 2020, https:// www.nydailynews.com/coronavirus/ny-coronavirus-richards-nypd-racist-public-safety-social -distancing-20200514-otupzlpjyrhb3iabhbk6fok6wu-story.html.

[21] Southall, "Shootings Have Soared. Is the N.Y.P.D. Pulling Back?"

[22] Jeff Asher, "Murder Rose by Almost 30% in 2020. It's Rising at a Slower Rate in 2021.," *New York Times*, updated November 15, 2021, https://www.nytimes.com/2021/09/22/upshot/murder -rise-2020.html.

[23] Bill Hutchinson, "'It's Just Crazy': 12 Major Cities Hit All-Time Homicide Records," ABC News, December 8, 2021, https://abcnews.go.com/US/12-major-us-cities-top-annual-homicide-records /story?id=81466453.

[24] Jessica Anderson, "Baltimore Sees Deadliest January with Latest Homicide; Shootings Continue Monday Night," *The Baltimore Sun*, January 31, 2022, https://www.baltimoresun.com/news /crime/bs-md-ci-cr-weekend-homicides-20220131-hcax43ttxbbibffbaw4v2jimfu-story.html.

[25] Dermot F. Shea, "Crime and Enforcement Activity in New York City," New York City Police Department, July 2021, https://www1.nyc.gov/assets/nypd/downloads/pdf/analysis_and_planning /year-end-2020-enforcement-report-20210721.pdf.

[26] Dermot F. Shea, "Crime and Enforcement Activity in New York City."

CHAPTER FOURTEEN: The Road to Anarchy

[1] Brad Lander (@bradlander), "No One Should Die Over a Traffic Stop. Period.," Twitter, April 12, 2021, https://twitter.com/bradlander/status/1381642219208196099.

[2] TJ Grayson and James Forman Jr., "Get Police Out of the Business of Traffic Stops," *The Washington Post*, April 16, 2021, https://www.washingtonpost.com/opinions/2021/04/16/remove -police-traffic-stops/.

[3] "Officer Who Shot Daunte Wright Arrested, Charged with Second Degree Manslaughter . . . ," Transcripts, The Situation Room, aired April 14, 2021, https://transcripts.cnn.com/show/sitroom /date/2021-04-14/segment/01.

[4] Leily Arzy and Ram Subramanian, "Rethinking How Law Enforcement Is Deployed," November 17, 2022, https://www.brennancenter.org/our-work/research-reports/rethinking-how-law -enforcement-deployed.

[5] "DDACTS: Data-Driven Approaches to Crime and Traffic Safety," National Highway Traffic Safety Administration, March 2014, https://www.nhtsa.gov/sites/nhtsa.gov/files/811185_ ddacts_opguidelines.pdf.

[6] David Giacopassia and David R. Forde, "Broken Windows, Crumpled Fenders, and Crime," *Journal of Criminal Justice* 28, no. 5, (2000): 397-405, https://doi.org/10.1016/S0047-2352(00)00054-4.

[7] Michael Cabanatuan, "Oakland Traffic Deaths Were Up in 2020. Communities of Color Suffered

Most. Here's Why." San Francisco Chronicle, March 23, 2021, https://www.sfchronicle.com/local /article/Oakland-traffic-deaths-jumped-by-22-in-2020-16047513.php#:~:text=Despite%20 reduced%20traffic%20during%20the,to%20recently%20released%20city%20data.

[8]Email message to author, April 17, 2021.

[9]Email message to author, April 16, 2021.

[10]Email message to author, April 16, 2021.

[11]Bob Goldsborough, "After Residents Asked Oak Park to Prevent Crime Village Board Tabled License-Plate-Reading Cameras, Fearing They'd Target People of Color," *Chicago Tribune*, March 25, 2022, https://www.chicagotribune.com/suburbs/oak-park/ct-oak-license-plate-cameras-tl -0331-20220325-hmbsnwkh5fhgbdqvkwuyabskhi-story.html.

[12]Steve Lopez, "Column: Mercedes Crash That Killed 5 Galvanizes an L.A. Movement: No More Fast and Furious," *Los Angeles Times*, August 11, 2022, https://www.latimes.com/california/story /2022-08-11/lopez-column-windsor-hills-crash-speeding-crackdown.

[13]Heather Mac Donald, "Sorry, No Debunking of Racial Profiling Allowed," in *Are Cops Racist?* (Chicago: Ivan R. Dee, 2003), 28–34; David Kocieniewski, "Study Suggests Racial Gap in Speeding in New Jersey," *New York Times*, March 21, 2002, https://www.nytimes.com/2002/03/21 /nyregion/study-suggests-racial-gap-in-speeding-in-new-jersey.html; Matthew T. Zingraff, "Studying Racial Profiling in North Carolina," *NIJ Journal*, no. 250 (2003), https://www.ojp.gov /sites/g/files/xyckuh241/files/archives/ncjrs/jr000250q.pdf.

[14]"2020 Fatality Data Show Increased Traffic Fatalities During Pandemic," NHTSA, June 3, 2021, https://www.nhtsa.gov/press-releases/2020-fatality-data-show-increased-traffic-fatalities -during-pandemic.

[15]"In Response to This Crisis, Earlier This Year USDOT Unveiled the National Roadway Safety Strategy That Is Now Getting Resources from the President's Bipartisan Infrastructure Law," NHTSA, May 17, 2022, https://www.nhtsa.gov/press-releases/early-estimate-2021-traffic-fatalities.

[16]Staff Reports, "Friestleben: Minneapolis Is 'Completely and Entirely Out of Control,'" Minnesota State Wire, September 18, 2020, https://minnesotastatewire.com/stories/555177382-friestleben -minneapolis-is-completely-and-entirely-out-of-control.

CHAPTER FIFTEEN: On Double Standards

[1]Maeve Reston and Stephen Collinson, "President-Elect Joe Biden Seeks to Unite Nation with Victory Speech," CNN Politics, updated November 8, 2020, 2:00 p.m., https://www.cnn .com/2020/11/07/politics/biden-victory-speech-2020-election/index.html.

[2]Matt Stevens, "Read Joe Biden's President-Elect Acceptance Speech: Full Transcript," *New York Times*, November 9, 2020, https://www.nytimes.com/article/biden-speech-transcript.html.

[3]William McGurn, "Joe Biden's Bitter Harvest," *The Wall Street Journal*, November 9, 2020, https:// www.wsj.com/articles/joe-bidens-bitter-harvest-11604963930.

[4]Amber Phillips, "Joe Biden's Victory Speech, Annotated," *The Washington Post*, November 7, 2020, https://www.washingtonpost.com/politics/2020/11/07/annotated-biden-victory-speech/.

[5]Errin Haines and Juana Summers, "Biden: Racism in US Is Institutional, 'White Man's Problem,'" AP News, August 28, 2019, https://apnews.com/article/election-2020-joe-biden-race-and-ethnicity -donald-trump-ap-top-news-88bd58010e75449eb5748499724df2f2.

[6]John Verhovek, "Joe Biden: White America 'Has to Admit There's Still a Systemic Racism,'" ABC News, January 21, 2019, https://abcnews.go.com/Politics/joe-biden-white-america-admit -systemic-racism/story?id=60524966.

[7]Margaret Renkl, "71 Million People Voted for Trump. They're Not Going Anywhere.," *New York Times*, November 9, 2020, https://www.nytimes.com/2020/11/09/opinion/trump-biden-nation -divided.html?smid=tw-share.

[8]"Christine Englehardt Death: Murder Charges Filed in Miami Beach Spring Break Overdoses," FOX 29 Philadelphia, August 5, 2021, https://www.fox29.com/news/christine-englehardt-death -murder-charges-filed-in-miami-beach-spring-break-overdoses.

[9]Michael Majchrowicz and Audra D.S. Burch, "Miami Beach Opened Up and the Revelers Flocked In. Then Came the Crackdown.," *New York Times*, published March 24, 2021, updated June 24, 2021, https://www.nytimes.com/2021/03/24/us/miami-covid-19-spring-break.html.

[10]Brice Helms, "Spring Break Is Business as Usual on South Padre Island," Local 23 Valley Central News, March 13, 2021, https://www.valleycentral.com/news/local-news/spring-break-is-business -as-usual-on-south-padre-island/.

[11]"Protesters Blast McDonald's CEO over Texts Sent to Lightfoot after Adams, Toledo Shooting Deaths," NBC Chicago, November 3, 2021, https://www.nbcchicago.com/news/local/protesters -blast-mcdonalds-ceo-over-texts-sent-to-lightfoot-after-adams-toledo-shooting-deaths/2670681/.

[12]Dahleen Glanton, "You Can't Be a Gang Member and a Good Parent, No Matter How Much You Love Your Kids," *Chicago Tribune*, May 24, 2021, https://www.chicagotribune.com/columns /dahleen-glanton/ct-glanton-jaslyn-adams-black-fathers-gangs-20210524-aidfal3q4jg55ivri27l 5vt7vq-story.html.

[13]"Case Portal: Log # 2021-0001112," Civilian Office of Police Accountability, April 15, 2021, https:// www.chicagocopa.org/case/2021-0001112/.

[14]"Protesters Blast McDonald's CEO over Texts Sent to Lightfoot after Adams, Toledo Shooting Deaths."

[15]Kate Rogers, "Mcdonald's CEO Apologizes after Texts about Chicago Shooting Deaths Surface," CNBC, November 8, 2021, https://www.cnbc.com/2021/11/08/mcdonalds-ceo-apologizes-after -texts-about-chicago-shooting-deaths-surface.html.

[16]The McStrike! (@FastfoodRights), "Mcdonald's Employee Adriana Sanchez Said 'He Doesn't Know The Circumstances Of These Parents' Kempczinski Is 'Putting The Blame On Parents For The Violence In The Streets. He Can't Relate Because He Is Wealthy, And We Are Not, And He Doesn't Understand Our Struggle.,'" Twitter, November 2, 2021, https://twitter.com/Fastfood Rights/status/1455656015802818570.

[17]Maudlyne Ihejirika, "Mom of Jaslyn Adams Demands Mcdonald's CEO Apologize: 'How Dare You Judge Me. You Know Nothing about the 'Hood,'" *Chicago Sun-Times*, November 4, 2021, https:// chicago.suntimes.com/2021/11/4/22763722/mom-jaslyn-adams-mcdonalds-ceo-chris-kempczinski -adam-toledo-apologize-how-dare-you-judge-me.

[18]Lauren Zumbach, "Mcdonald's Protesters Condemn CEO's Comments on Adam Toledo, Jaslyn Adams. 'The CEO Doesn't Understand or Know Our Struggle.,'" *Chicago Tribune*, November 3, 2021, https://www.chicagotribune.com/business/ct-biz-mcdonalds-kempczinski-lightfoot-texts -adam-toledo-20211102-csfswmduvrgnbcwkavko75tufy-story.html.

[19]Rogers, "Mcdonald's CEO Apologizes after Texts about Chicago Shooting Deaths Surface."

[20]Glanton, "You Can't Be a Gang Member and a Good Parent, No Matter How Much You Love Your Kids."

[21]Derick Hutchinson, "'The Thoughts Won't Stop. Help Me.': Police Detail Note, Drawing Teacher Found on Desk of Suspected Oxford High Shooter," Click On Detroit, December 6, 2021, https:// www.clickondetroit.com/news/local/2021/12/06/the-thoughts-wont-stop-help-me-police-detail -note-drawing-teacher-found-on-desk-of-suspected-oxford-high-shooter/.

[22]Corinne Hess, "'The Law Is on Hold in Milwaukee': Youth Are Caught in the Middle of the City's Climbing Homicide Rate," Wisconsin Public Radio, November 5, 2021, https://www.wpr.org /law-hold-milwaukee-youth-are-caught-middle-citys-climbing-homicide-rate.

[23]"School Shootings in 2021: How Many and Where," Education Week, accessed May 28, 2022, https:// www.edweek.org/leadership/school-shootings-this-year-how-many-and-where/2021/03.

24Sneha Dey, et al., "21 Lives Lost: Uvalde Victims Were a Cross-Section of a Small, Mostly Latino Town in South Texas," *The Texas Tribune*, May 27, 2022, https://www.texastribune.org/2022/05/25/uvalde-school-shooting-victims/.

25Sun-Times Wire, "12-Year-Old Girl and 15-Year-Old Boy Shot during Chaotic Weekend Night in Downtown Chicago," *Chicago Sun-Times*, December 7, 2021, https://chicago.suntimes.com/crime/2021/12/6/22821727/12-year-old-girl-wounded-in-downtown-shooting.

26 "Expanded Homicide Data," Federal Bureau of Investigation: Crime Data Explorer, accessed December 27, 2022,https://crime-data-explorer.fr.cloud.gov/pages/explorer/crime/shr.

27James Alan Fox and Mark L. Swatt, "The Recent Surge in Homicides Involving Young Black Males and Guns: Time to Reinvest in Prevention and Crime Control," Issue Lab, December 2008, https://bma.issuelab.org/resources/22889/22889.pdf.

28Troy Clossan and Lola Fadulu, "Columbia University Student Dies in Stabbing Near Campus," *New York Times*, December 3, 2021, https://www.nytimes.com/2021/12/03/nyregion/columbia-student-stabbed.html.

29Nicholas Bogel-Burroughs, "What to Know about Kimberly Potter's Conviction for the Death of Daunte Wright," *New York Times*, published November 30, 2021, updated February 18, 2022, https://www.nytimes.com/2021/11/30/us/daunte-wright-shooting-kimberly-potter.html.

30Sam Raskin, "Two Suspects Charged in Shooting of Baltimore Police Officer," *New York Post*, December 19, 2021, https://nypost.com/2021/12/19/two-suspects-charged-in-shooting-of-baltimore-police-officer/; Lisa Robinson, "Charging Docs Reveal More about Shooting of Officer, Man," WBAL TV Channel 11, December 20, 2021, https://www.wbaltv.com/article/charging-docs-reveal-more-about-shooting-of-keona-holley-justin-johnson/38569185.

31M. Dowling, "Bystander Says Don't Call the Police as Officer Clings to Life after an Ambush," *Independent Sentinel*, December 18, 2021, https://www.independentsentinel.com/bystander-says-dont-call-the-police-as-officer-clings-to-life-after-an-ambush/.

32Andrew McMunn, "FBI: 73 Officers Killed in 2021; 24 Died in Unprovoked Attacks," WCAX Channel 3, May 10, 2022, https://www.wcax.com/2022/05/11/fbi-73-officers-killed-2021-24-died-unprovoked-attacks/.

33Erin Duffin, "Number of Law Enforcement Officers U.S. 2004-2021," Statista, October 11, 2022, https://www.statista.com/statistics/191694/number-of-law-enforcement-officers-in-the-us/.

34"Fatal Force: 1,020 People Have Been Shot and Killed by Police in the Past Year," *The Washington Post*, October 7, 2022, https://www.washingtonpost.com/graphics/investigations/police-shootings-database/?request-id=f4bb182b-6367-4a15-a876-5773188ca9c2&pml=1.

35"Table 47: Law Enforcement Officers Feloniously Killed," Federal Bureau of Investigation, 2014, https://ucr.fbi.gov/leoka/2014/tables/table_47_leos_fk_race_and_sex_of_known_offender_2005-2014.xls.

36"Number of US Police Officers Murdered Up by 59% - FBI," BBC, April 25, 2022, https://www.bbc.com/news/world-us-canada-61218611.

CHAPTER SIXTEEN: A Grim—and Ignored—Body Count

1Joseph Wilkinson, "Philadelphia Pays Walter Wallace Jr.'s Family $2.5 Million in Settlement," *New York Daily News*, October 28, 2021, https://www.nydailynews.com/news/national/ny-walter-wallace-jr-settlement-20211029-qmwucbgpsbdfrox44obk452btq-story.html.

2NBC10 Staff, "Walter Wallace Jr. Struggled with Mental Health Issues, Family Says," NBC Philadelphia, published October 27, 2020, updated October 29, 2020, https://www.nbcphiladelphia.com/news/local/walter-wallace-jr-struggled-with-mental-health-issues-family-says/2575493/.

3Dominique Mosbergen, "Biden, Harris Express Heartbreak after Black Man Is Killed by Philadelphia Police," HuffPost, October 27, 2020, https://www.huffpost.com/archive/au/entry/biden-

harris-express-heartbreak-after-black-man-is-killed-by-philadelphia-police_au_5f98d6adc
5b6c7fe582a1166.

[4]"Crime in the United States Annual Reports," Federal Bureau of Investigation: Crime Data Explorer, https://crime-data-explorer.fr.cloud.gov/pages/downloads; "Fatal Force: 1,039 People
Have Been Shot And Killed By Police In The Past Year."

[5]"Police: 3-Year-Old Boy Hospitalized after Being Shot Twice in Southwest Philadelphia," CBS Philadelphia, October 23, 2020, https://www.cbsnews.com/philadelphia/news/police-3-year-old-boy
-hospitalized-after-being-shot-twice-in-southwest-philadelphia/.

[6]Phillip Jackson, "16-Year-Old Boy Killed, 12-Year-Old Boy Injured in West Baltimore Shooting,
Police Say," *The Baltimore Sun*, October 21, 2020, https://www.baltimoresun.com/news/crime
/bs-md-ci-cr-male-12-year-old-shot-killed-20201021-xvjnlz6qlncvzkxunpqy6wod3u-story.html.

[7]ABC 7 Chicago Digital Team, "Jeffery Manor Shooting: Father of Baby Who Died after Pregnant
Woman Shot, Killed Charged in Their Deaths, Chicago Police Say," ABC 7 Chicago, October 23,
2020, https://abc7chicago.com/chicago-shooting-jeffery-manor-police-stacey-jones/7269258/.

[8]Lexi Sutter, "Lake Shore Drive Became 'Shooting Gallery' When Man Shot Out Woman's Eye, Prosecutors Say," NBC Chicago, October 15, 2020, https://www.nbcchicago.com/news/local/lake-shore
-drive-became-shooting-gallery-when-man-shot-out-womans-eye-prosecutors-say/2354291/.

[9]Snejana Farberov, "Two Suspects Are Arrested in Killing of Baltimore Bus Driver, 51, Who Was
Shot Dead after He Refused to Let Gunman Board and Then Gave Chase When He Stole Victim's
Bag," *The Daily Mail*, October 9, 2020, https://www.dailymail.co.uk/news/article-8823745/Two
-suspects-arrested-killing-Baltimore-bus-driver.html.

[10]Faith E. Pinho, "9-Year-Old Girl among 3 Killed in Spate of Weekend Shootings in Sacramento,"
Los Angeles Times, October 5, 2020, https://news.yahoo.com/9-old-girl-among-3-193740529.html.

[11]"1 Killed, 4 Others Injured in Friday Night Shootings," NBC Chicago, October 2, 2020, https://
www.nbcchicago.com/news/local/1-killed-4-others-injured-in-friday-night-shootings/2348608/.

[12]Paige Fry, "15-Year-Old Boy Killed in Far South Side Shooting, Police Say," *Chicago Tribune*, September 26, 2020, https://www.chicagotribune.com/news/breaking/ct-far-south-side-shooting
-20200927-eqmvgdgvnffnpkqxygp6rvs4uy-story.html.

[13]Jon Jankowski, "'They Killed My Baby!' 3-Year-Old Boy Shot to Death in Orange County Drive-By,"
Click Orlando, September 23, 2020, https://www.clickorlando.com/news/local/2020/09/23
/child-shot-and-killed-in-orange-county/.

[14]Makenzie Koch and Russell Colburn, "Police Identify 1-Year-Old Boy Killed in Triple Shooting in
Kansas City," Fox 4 KC, published Sepbtember 21, 2020, updated September 23, 2020, https://
fox4kc.com/news/police-identify-1-year-old-boy-killed-in-triple-shooting-in-kansas-city/.

[15]"Five People Shot Chicago Near May Street and 122nd Street, Chicago," Cardical News, September 20,
2020, https://www.arlingtoncardinal.com/2020/09/five-people-shot-chicago-near-may-street
-and-122nd-street-chicago/.

[16]Ashley Cole and Dori Olmos, "Grandmother Recalls the Last Time She Saw Her 15-Year-Old
Granddaughter before She Was Shot to Death," KSDK, published September 14, 2020, updated
October 12, 2020, https://www.ksdk.com/article/news/special-reports/cut-short/teenager-shot
-st-louis/63-2af3ae61-f7ed-40ae-8fdc-7db7ac7349a4.

[17]"2 Charged in Michigan Avenue Shooting Attack, Near West Side Pursuit and Crash, Cops Say,"
Chicago Tribune, September 16, 2020, https://www.chicagotribune.com/news/breaking/ct-chicago
-shots-fired-michigan-avenue-charges-20200916-4posirvp5rgqbc2ndnm6vt2kya-story.html.

[18]William Lee and Jeremy Gorner, "Man on House Arrest for Gun Case Accused of Opening Fire at
West Side Birthday Party, Killing 2 And Wounding 3. 'It Makes Your Blood Boil,' Says Chicago's
Top Cop.," *Chicago Tribune*, September 14, 2020, https://www.chicagotribune.com/news/breaking
/ct-south-austin-backyard-birthday-shooting-20200914-zalzrj5vurf5rdvo52tvt6wd7a-story.html.

[19]Tiffany Watson, "Boy, 14, Killed in NE Baltimore," Fox Baltimore, September 11, 2020, https://foxbaltimore.com/news/local/2-separate-baltimore-shootings-within-30-minutes-14-year-old-boy-found-with-gun.

[20]Jorge Fitz-Gibbon, "Chicago Mail Carrier in Critical Condition after Being Shot on the Job," *New York Post*, September 10, 2020, https://nypost.com/2020/09/10/chicago-mail-carrier-in-critical-condition-after-being-shot/.

[21]Bob D'Angelo, "Pennsylvania Girl, 11, Shot in Face While Answering Knock at Family Home," KIRO 7, September 10, 2020, https://www.kiro7.com/news/trending/pennsylvania-girl-11-shot-face-while-answering-knock-family-home/4KNSMFTUDZDUNKFSSYGBBVLYIE/.

[22]Joe Marino, et al., "6-Year-Old Boy among Five People Shot at Brooklyn J'Ouvert Celebration," *New York Post*, September 7, 2020, https://nypost.com/2020/09/07/five-shot-including-child-at-brooklyn-jouvert-celebration/.

[23]Bill Hutchinson, "8-Year-Old Girl Shot to Death in Another Violent Weekend in Chicago," ABC News, September 8, 2020, https://abcnews.go.com/US/year-girl-shot-death-violent-weekend-chicago/story?id=72875434.

[24]Erica Finke, "WATCH: Community Calls for Justice in Shooting That Killed Child Attending Birthday Party," WSBT 22, August 29, 2020, https://wsbt.com/news/local/metro-homicide-called-after-child-shot-in-south-bend#.

[25]"11-Year-Old Girl Shot in Wilmington As City Battles 57% Rise in Gun Violence," 6 ABC, August 31, 2020, https://6abc.com/wilmington-shooting-shot-in-hip-11-year-old-injured-kid/6397258/.

[26]Sara Dorn, "Woman Shot Dead in Bronx among Nearly a Dozen Victims of Overnight Gunplay," *New York Post*, August 22, 2020, https://nypost.com/2020/08/22/woman-shot-dead-in-bronx/.

[27]Rosemary Sobol, et al., "As Detectives Seek Public's Help in Last Week's Shooting of 12-Year-Old Boy, Another Child and His Mother Are Shot on the West Side," *Chicago Tribune*, August 19, 2020, https://www.chicagotribune.com/news/breaking/ct-two-shot-west-side-boy-20200819-suetd6fu3zavhhuho5dcsqgyjy-story.html.

[28]Anthony Johnson, "4-Year-Old Girl Shot While Playing Outside New Jersey Apartment Complex," ABC 7 NY, August 19, 2020, https://abc7ny.com/girl-shot-child-asbury-park-shooting-new-jersey/6377959/.

[29]Chicago Tribune Staff, "9-Year-Old Boy Suffers Graze Wound to the Head While Riding in a Car on South Side," *Chicago Tribune*, August 17, 2020, https://www.chicagotribune.com/news/breaking/ct-boy-shot-chatham-south-side-20200817-2rsrryrorzcdncdiwzvgrx4umy-story.html.

[30]Tina Moore, et al., "Man Fatally Shot at Gun-Violence Memorial As NYC Shootings Rage On," *New York Post*, August 16, 2020, https://nypost.com/2020/08/16/nyc-man-fatally-shot-at-gun-violence-memorial-as-shootings-rage-on/.

[31]Tina Moore and Lee Brown, "76 Injured, 14 Killed by Gunfire This Week As NYC Shootings Skyrocket," *New York Post*, August 16, 2020, https://nypost.com/2020/08/16/nyc-shootings-76-injured-14-killed-by-gunfire-this-week/.

[32]Ashley Cole and Jasmine Payoute, "'That Was My Only Brother' | 14-Year-Old among 15 Children Shot and Killed in 2020," KSDK, August 14, 2020, https://www.ksdk.com/article/news/special-reports/cut-short/14-year-old-boy-shot-killed-st-louis/63-44f2bd4e-3392-406e-b836-95520a20201c.

[33]Stephanie Fryer and Brandon Arbuckle, "11-Year-Old Girl Who Was Shot in Head to Be Removed from Life Support, Family Says," Channel 3000, August 12, 2020, https://www.channel3000.com/family-11-year-old-girl-who-was-shot-in-head-to-be-removed-from-life-support/.

[34]"Police: Man Injured after Gunfire Erupts at Southerwet Philadelphia Apartment Complex," CBS News Philadelphia, Augusgt 11, 2020, https://www.cbsnews.com/philadelphia/news/police-man-injured-after-gunfire-erupts-at-southwest-philadelphia-apartment-complex/.

[35]Peter Hermann, et al., "At Least 20 People Shot, One Fatally, at a Party Attended by Hundreds in Southeast Washington," *The Washington Post*, August 9, 2020, https://www.washingtonpost .com/local/public-safety/at-least-21-people-were-shot-one-fatally-at-a-gathering-in-southeast -washington/2020/08/09/dde4ee6c-da34-11ea-8051-d5f887d73381_story.html.

[36]Robert Moran, "Girl, 6, Stable after Being Shot in West Philly," *The Philadelphia Inquirer*, August 6, 2020, https://www.inquirer.com/news/west-philadelphia-girl-shot-20200805.html.

[37]Chris Palmer, "7-Year-Old Zamar Jones, Shot in the Head in Front of His West Philadelphia Home This Weekend, Has Died, Police Say," *The Philadelphia Inquirer*, August 3, 2020, https://www .inquirer.com/news/7-year-old-zamar-jones-shot-west-philadelphia-charges-20200803.html.

[38]Jonathon Berlin, Jamal R. Brinson, and Kori Rumore, "Devastating Toll of Chicago's Violence: Number of Shooting Victims Younger Than 10 Years Old Three Times Higher Than Last Year," *Chicago Tribune*, August 3, 2020, https://www.chicagotribune.com/news/breaking/ct-viz -young-victims-2020-violence-20200803-xdffjvcr3fhjzesmoavyiinwdq-htmlstory.html.

[39]ABC 7 Digital Staff, "Caleb Reed, VOYCE Activitst, Accidentally Shot and Killed by Friend, Prosecutors Say," ABC 7 Chicago, September 1, 2020, https://abc7chicago.com/caleb-reed-shot-by -friend-charged-in-shooting-accidentally-young-activist-killed/6399602/.

[40]WKYC Staff, "Unsolved Canton Murder: Police Still Hunting for Suspects Who Killed 1-Year-Old Boy," WKYC, September 2, 2020, https://www.wkyc.com/article/news/crime/ace-lucas-murder -canton-surveillance-video/95-0916b21a-6432-419e-8186-30acc84bafc6.

[41]Ramon Antonio Vargas and Paul Murphy, "'They Killed My Baby': 9-Year-Old's Final Moments before New Orleans Triple Shooting Caught on Video," Nola, published July 14, 2020, updated July 22, 2020, https://www.nola.com/news/crime_police/article_6baff696-c613-11ea-a2b2 -8749b7aaf94d.html.

[42]Ashley Southall and Michael Gold, "1-Year-Old Is Shot and Killed at Brooklyn Cookout," *New York Times*, published July 13, 2020, updated July 15, 2020, https://www.nytimes.com/2020/07/13 /nyregion/Davell-Gardner-brooklyn-shooting.html.

[43]WBTV Web Staff, "12-Year-Old Boy Killed in Wadesboro Drive-By Shooting," WBTV, July 8, 2020, https://www.wbtv.com/2020/07/08/year-old-boy-killed-drive-by-shooting-wadesboro/.

[44]Andrew Maykuth, "6-Year-Old Boy among 5 Fatalities in 5 Shootings in Philly in 1 Afternoon; 11-, 15-Year-Old Among Injured," *The Philadelphia Inquirer*, July 5, 2020, https://www.inquirer .com/news/6-year-old-boy-fatally-shot-philadelphia-20200705.html.

[45]Hollie Silverman, "At Least 6 Children Were Killed by Gun Violence across the Nation This Holiday Weekend," CNN, July 6, 2020, https://www.cnn.com/2020/07/06/us/children-killed -holiday-weekend/index.html.

[46]"UPDATED: Coroner Identifies 2 Girls Killed in Delano Shooting; 3 Others Hurt," Bakersfield, July 3, 2020, https://www.bakersfield.com/news/updated-coroner-identifies-2-girls-killed-in-delano -shooting-3-others-hurt/article_cc3e667c-bd40-11ea-9089-4f5524326e13.html.

[47]Morgan Greene, et al., "3-Year-Old Girl Recovering after Shot Outside Her Home on South Side. 'She's Going to Pull Through,'" *Chicago Tribune*, July 1, 2020, https://www.chicagotribune.com/ news/breaking/ct-3-year-old-shot-chicago-violence-20200701-a3b5xr4ov5genfzbcifcz73 pwq-story.html.

[48]Tod Palmer, "Man Charged in 4-Year-Old Legend Taliferro's Murder," KSHB, August 13, 2020, https://www.kshb.com/news/crime/charges-announced-in-legend-taliferros-murder.

[49]Ben Pop and Sam Kelly, "1-Year-Old Dead, Mother Wounded in Englewood Shooting," *Chicago Sun-Times*, June 27, 2020, https://chicago.suntimes.com/crime/2020/6/27/21305650/sincere -gaston-1-year-old-baby-killed-woman-child-shot-englewood-yale.

[50]"3-Year-Old Girl Grazed by Bullet on Chicago's Southwest Side," NBC Chicago, June 22, 2020, https://www.nbcchicago.com/news/local/3-year-old-girl-grazed-by-bullet-on-chicagos

-southwest-side/2293793/.

51 Mike Lowe, et al., "3-Year-Old Boy Shot and Killed in Austin, Reward Offered in Search for Shooter," WGNTV, published June 20, 2020, updated June 22, 2020, https://wgntv.com/news /chicago-news/police-3-year-old-shot-on-west-side-in-serious-condition/.

52 WMAR Staff, "3-Year-Old And Pregnant Mother Killed in Baltimore, Suspect Arrested," WMAR 2 ABC News, published June 19, 2020, updated June 20, 2020, https://www.wmar2news.com/news/region /baltimore-city/woman-toddler-found-shot-to-death-inside-car-in-southwest-baltimore.

53 Kevin Rector, "In South L.A., Police Join Community Leaders to Denounce Gun Violence 'Not Seen in Years'," *Los Angeles Times*, October 2, 2020, https://www.latimes.com/california/story /2020-10-02/in-south-l-a-police-join-community-leaders-to-denounce-gun-violence; "Philly Is Seeing a Spike in Shooting of Children. But Motives and Arrests Are Lagging," *Inquirer*, August 6, 2020, https://www.inquirer.com/news/philadelphia-increase-children-shot-murders-gun -violence-20200806.html.

54 John D. Harden and Justin Jouvenal, "Crime Rose Unevenly When Stay-At-Home Orders Lifted. The Racial Disparity Is the Widest in Years," *The Washington Post*, October 9, 2020, https://www .washingtonpost.com/graphics/2020/local/public-safety/crime-rate-coronavirus/?utm_campaign =wp_main&utm_source=twitter&utm_medium=social.

55 Kim Bell, "Amid 'Indescribable Times,' St. Louis Homicide Rate Reaches Historic Levels," St. Louis Post-Dispatch, September 21, 2020, https://www.stltoday.com/news/local/crime-and-courts /amid-indescribable-times-st-louis-homicide-rate-reaches-historic-levels/article_97b57246 -ae07-5f93-b42a-b5f57fc15c8e.html.

56 "Impact Report: COVID-19 and Crime," CCJ, July 28, 2020, https://counciloncj.org/impact-report -covid-19-and-crime-2/.

57 "Arrest Made in Boy's Death That Sparked Federal Task Force," WMTV, August 14, 2020, https:// www.wmtw.com/article/arrest-made-in-boys-death-that-sparked-federal-task-force/33607204.

58 "Data and Statistics (WISQARS)," Centers for Disease Control and Prevention, last reviewed December 2, 2021, https://www.cdc.gov/injury/wisqars/index.html.

59 Marc Ethier, "USC Marshall Finds Students Were Sincere, But Prof Did No Wrong in Racial Flap," Poets & Quants, September 26, 2020, https://poetsandquants.com/2020/09/26/usc-marshall-finds -students-were-sincere-but-prof-did-no-wrong-in-racial-flap/?pq-category=business-school-news.

60 Peter Baker, "More Than Ever, Trump Casts Himself as the Defender of White America," *New York Times*, published September 6, 2020, updated September 10, 2020, https://www.nytimes .com/2020/09/06/us/politics/trump-race-2020-election.html?searchResultPosition=2.

61 Harden and Jouvenal, "Crime Rose Unevenly When Stay-At-Home Orders Lifted. The Racial Disparity Is the Widest in Years."

62 Brian Klass, "Trump's Racist Strategy Could Backfire — And Biden Can Ensure That It Does," *The Washington Post*, September 2, 2020, https://www.washingtonpost.com/opinions/2020/09/02 /trumps-racist-strategy-could-backfire-biden-can-ensure-that-it-does/.

63 Eugene Robinson, "Trump Is Shouting His Racism. He Must Be Stopped.," *The Washington Post*, Opinion, September 7, 2020, https://www.washingtonpost.com/opinions/trump-is-shouting-his -racism-he-must-be-stopped/2020/09/07/06036768-f13a-11ea-bc45-e5d48ab44b9f_story.html.

64 Jenny Jarvie, "'He's Just Fanning the Flames.' Trump's Vow to Protect Suburbs Rings Hollow in One," *Los Angeles Times*, September 7, 2020, https://www.latimes.com/politics/story/2020 -09-07/hes-fanning-the-flames-trumps-vow-to-protect-suburbs-rings-hollow-in-one.

65 Harden and Jouvenal, "Crime Rose Unevenly When Stay-At-Home Orders Lifted. The Racial Disparity Is the Widest in Years."

66 Kimberlé Williams Crenshaw, "Fear of a Black Uprising," *The New Republic*, August 13, 2020,

https://newrepublic.com/article/158725/fear-black-uprising-confronting-racist-policing.

[67]Baker, "More Than Ever, Trump Casts Himself as the Defender of White America."

[68]Amy Harmon and Audra D. S. Burch, "White Americans Say They Are Waking Up to Racism. What Will It Add Up To?," *New York Times*, published June 22, 2020, updated June 24, 2020, https://www.nytimes.com/2020/06/22/us/racism-white-americans.html.

[69]Kihana Miraya Ross, "Call It What It Is: Anti-Blackness," *New York Times*, June 4, 2020, https://www.nytimes.com/2020/06/04/opinion/george-floyd-anti-blackness.html.

[70]"The Stubborn Racial Gap in Scores on the SAT College Entrance Examination," *The Journal of Blacks in Higher Education*, October 26, 2020, https://www.jbhe.com/2020/10/the-stubborn-racial-gap-in-scores-on-the-sat-college-entrance-examination/.

[71]The Times Editorial Board, "Editorial: An Examination of the Times' Failures on Race, Our Apology and a Path Forward," *Los Angeles Times*, September 27, 2020, https://www.latimes.com/opinion/story/2020-09-27/los-angeles-times-apology-racism.

[72]Elijah Anderson, "The Code of the Streets," *The Atlantic*, May 1994, https://www.theatlantic.com/magazine/archive/1994/05/the-code-of-the-streets/306601/.

[73]"Driver in Custody after Striking Philadelphia Police Sergeant with Pickup Amid Unrest Monday, Sources Say," FOX 29 Philadelphia, published October 27, 2020, updated October 28, 2020, https://www.fox29.com/news/police-sergeant-suffers-broken-leg-after-being-struck-by-pickup-truck-in-west-philadelphia.

[74]Philadelphia law enforcement source, email to author, November 21, 2022.

[75]6abc Digital Staff, "7 More ATM Explosions across Philadelphia Under Investigation," 6 ABC, October 28, 2020, https://6abc.com/atm-explosions-philly-explosion-philadelphia-civil-unrest/7420875/.

[76]Michael Lee, "Philadelphia Man Reportedly Fills Car with Looted Items, Gets Carjacked, and Has Stolen Items Stolen from Him," *Washington Examiner*, October 28, 2020, https://www.washingtonexaminer.com/news/philadelphia-man-reportedly-fills-car-with-looted-items-gets-carjacked-and-has-stolen-items-stolen-from-him.

[77]Philadelphia law enforcement source, email to author, November 21, 2022.

[78]Aubrey Whelan, et al., "Break-Ins at Dozens of Philly Pharmacies Have Owners — And Customers — Shaken," *The Philadelphia Inquirer*, October 29, 2020, https://www.inquirer.com/news/drug-stores-phamacies-looting-community-breakins-theft-walter-wallace-20201029.html.

[79]Crenshaw, "Fear of a Black Uprising."

CHAPTER SEVENTEEN: Mass Shootings, Hate Crimes, and Race

[1]Darlene Superville, "Biden Urges Unity to Stem Racial Hate after Buffalo Shooting," AP News, May 15, 2022, https://apnews.com/article/biden-crime-shootings-new-york-buffalo-065a2ed910a0a09b621ebba57bbba34b.

[2]"Remarks by President Biden and First Lady Biden Honoring the Lives Lost in Buffalo, New York, and Calling on All Americans to Condemn White Supremacy," The White House Briefing Room, May 17, 2022, https://www.whitehouse.gov/briefing-room/speeches-remarks/2022/05/17/remarks-by-president-biden-and-first-lady-biden-honoring-the-lives-lost-in-buffalo-new-york-and-calling-on-all-americans-to-condemn-white-supremacy/.

[3]"Hate Crime in the United States Incident Analysis," Federal Bureau of Investigation: Crime Data Explorer, accessed August 21, 2022, https://crime-data-explorer.fr.cloud.gov/pages/explorer/crime/hate-crime.

[4]Charles Fain Lehman, "Understanding and Reducing Hate Crimes in New York City," Manhattan Institute, March 23, 2022, https://www.manhattan-institute.org/lehman-understanding-reducing-hate-crimes-nyc.

[5]LAPD source, email message to author, May 19, 2022.

[6]"User Clip: Joe Biden Unrelenting Stream of Immigration," C-SPAN, February 17, 2015, https://www.c-span.org/video/?c4926142/user-clip-joe-biden-unrelenting-stream-immigration.

[7]LAPD source, email message to author, May 19, 2022.

[8]Rachel E. Morgan, PhD and Jennifer L. Truman, PhD, "Criminal Victimization, 2019," U.S. Department of Justice, September 2020, https://bjs.ojp.gov/content/pub/pdf/cv19.pdf.

[9]Jamiel Lynch and Christina Mzxouris, "Dallas Police Believe 3 Recent Shootings at Asian-Owned Businesses May Be Connected and Hate-Motivated," CNN, May 14, 2022, https://www.cnn.com/2022/05/14/us/dallas-asian-run-businesses-shootings/index.html.

[10]Chris Boyette, Jamiel Lynch, Michelle Krupa, and Jennifer Henderson, "Man Arrested in Korean-Owned Hair Salon Shooting and Charged with Felony Aggravated Assault," CNN, May 17, 2022, https://www.cnn.com/2022/05/17/us/dallas-hair-salon-shooting-arrest/index.html.

[11]Sarah Trefethen and Amanda Woods, "Three Teens Arrested in Alleged Anti-White Bus Attack," *New York Post*, December 7, 2016, https://nypost.com/2016/12/07/teens-suing-mta-over-alleged-anti-white-attack-on-bus/.

[12]Audrey Conklin, "Woman Assaulted on NYC Subway as Bystanders Do Nothing," FOX News, May 27, 2022, https://www.foxnews.com/us/woman-harassed-nyc-subway-bystanders.

[13]Robby Soave, "CNN Settles Lawsuit with Covington Catholic Student Nick Sandmann," *Reason*, January 7, 2020, https://reason.com/2020/01/07/covington-catholic-cnn-lawsuit-nick-sandmann/.

[14]Aaron Keller, "Covington Catholic's Nick Sandmann Settles $275 Million NBC Lawsuit for 'Confidential' Amount," Law & Crime, December 18, 2021, https://lawandcrime.com/media/covington-catholics-nick-sandmann-settles-275-million-nbc-lawsuit-for-confidential-amount/.; Soave, "CNN Settles Lawsuit With Covington Catholic Student Nick Sandmann."

[15]"Remarks by President Biden and First Lady Biden Honoring the Lives Lost in Buffalo, New York, and Calling on All Americans to Condemn White Supremacy."

[16]Emily Opilo, "Calling Baltimore's Violence 'Beyond Comprehension,' Council Group Orders Police Response Plan by Budget Time," *Baltimore Sun*, May 19, 2022, https://www.baltimoresun.com/politics/bs-md-ci-baltimore-council-crime-budget-20220519-yw5qow3dlzdp3hzskxay4qss6m-story.html.

[17]McKenna Oxenden and Jessica Anderson, "10 People Shot, One Killed, in Three Separate Incidents across Baltimore on a Violent Tuesday," *Baltimore Sun*, May 11, 2022, https://www.baltimoresun.com/news/crime/bs-md-ci-cr-east-baltimore-shooting-20220510-frdq27f7uzgp3j23zwmptjrbkq-story.html.

[18]Jessica Anderson, Lea Skene, and Ngan Ho, "'It's Senseless': Fatal Shooting of Pregnant Woman and Man Angers, Shocks Community," *Baltimore Sun*, May 14, 2022, https://www.baltimoresun.com/news/crime/bs-md-ci-cr-shooting-east-baltimore-pregnant-woman-20220513-ggyz7ydm4nfjhobbh4dgcezng4-story.html.

[19]Jessica Anderson, "After 10 Shot in One Day, Baltimore Residents and Leaders Decry Increasingly Brazen Gun Violence: 'It's Like a Norm Now,'" *Baltimore Sun*, May 11, 2022, https://www.baltimoresun.com/news/crime/bs-md-ci-cr-violence-follow-20220511-xdu75mhhhfbuhmyvwwmnvccvwe-story.html.

[20]Sun-Times Wire, "9-Year-Old Boy Killed, another Young Boy Wounded in Skokie Shooting," *Chicago Sun-Times*, May 14, 2022, https://chicago.suntimes.com/2022/5/14/23072752/9-year-old-boy-killed-skokie-shooting.

[21]Sun-Times Wire, "Two Boys, 6 and 11, among Four Shot While Riding in Car in West Englewood," *Chicago Sun-Times*, May 11, 2022, https://chicago.suntimes.com/2022/5/11/23067830/2-boys-2-adults-injured-in-west-englewood-shooting.

22 "Teen Killed, at Least 4 Others Hurt in Back of the Yards Shooting," NBC Chicago, May 10, 2022, 7:54 a.m., https://www.nbcchicago.com/news/local/1-dead-at-least-3-seriously-hurt-in-back-of -the-yards-shooting/2829216/.

23 Sun-Times Wire, "Chicago's Top Cop Blames Mass Shooting in Back of Yards on Convicted Felon Recently Released on Gun Charge Despite Record," *Chicago Sun-Times*, May 11, 2022, https:// chicago.suntimes.com/crime/2022/5/11/23066714/chicago-shootings-tuesday.

24 Eddie Scarry, "Congrats to the Media for Finally Finding a White Supremacist," *The Federalist*, May 17, 2022, https://thefederalist.com/2022/05/17/congrats-to-the-media-for-finally-finding -a-white-supremacist/.

25 James Varney, "The ADL Murder Report That Cried 'White Supremacist,'" RealClear Investigations, May 26, 2022, https://www.realclearinvestigations.com/articles/2022/05/26/the_anti-defamation_ league_murder_report_that_cried_white_supremacist_834040.html?mc_cid=1ea715361f&mc_ eid=cf98b926c0.

26 Jane Coaston, "New Evidence Shows the Pulse Nightclub Shooting Wasn't about Anti-LGBTQ Hate," *Vox*, April 5, 2018, https://www.vox.com/policy-and-politics/2018/4/5/17202026/pulse -shooting-lgbtq-trump-terror-hate.

27 H.R.350 – Domestic Terrorism Prevention Act of 2022, 117th Congress (2021-2022), https://www .congress.gov/bill/117th-congress/house-bill/350/text.

28 Deirdre Walsh, "Days after Buffalo Mass Shooting, the House Approves a Bill to Fight Domestic Terror," NPR, May 18, 2022, https://www.npr.org/2022/05/18/1099756134/days-after-buffalo -mass-shooting-the-house-approves-a-bill-to-fight-domestic-ter.

29 "The Demented – and Selective – Game of Instantly Blaming Political Opponents for Mass Shootings," Glenn Greenwald, May 15, 2022, https://greenwald.substack.com/p/the-demented-and-selective -game-of?s=r.

30 "Number of US Police Officers Murdered Up by 59% - FBI," BBC, April 25, 2022, https://www.bbc .com/news/world-us-canada-61218611.

31 Marissa Evans, "'When Is the Next One?': After Buffalo Massacre, Black L.A. Residents Consider Their Safety," *Los Angeles Times*, May 21, 2022, https://www.latimes.com/california/story/2022 -05-21/when-is-the-next-one-after-buffalo-shooting-black-la-residents-consider-their-safety.

32 House Committee on the Judiciary Chairman Jerrold Nadler, "House Judiciary Committee Republicans Vote Against Important Domestic Terrorism Legislation," U.S. House Committee On The Judiciary, April 6, 2022, https://nadler.house.gov/news/documentsingle.aspx?DocumentID=394827.

33 Silvia Foster-Frau, Arelis R. Hernández, Scott Clement, and Emily Guskin, "Poll: Black Americans Fear More Racist Attacks after Buffalo Shooting," *The Washington Post*, May 21, 2022, https://www .washingtonpost.com/nation/2022/05/21/post-poll-black-americans/.

34 Heather Mac Donald, *The War on Cops: How the New Attack on Law and Order Makes Everyone Less Safe* (New York: Encounter Books, 2016).

35 Matthew Impelli, "Meena Harris' Tweet Blaming White Men for Boulder Shooting Got 6,500 Retweets, 35K Likes before Deletion," Newsweek, March 23, 2021, https://www.newsweek.com/meena -harris-tweet-blaming-white-men-boulder-shooting-got-6500-retweets-35k-likes-before-1578206.

36 "8 Dead in Atlanta Spa Shootings, with Fears of Anti-Asian Bias," *New York Times*, published March 17, 2021, updated March 26, 2021, https://www.nytimes.com/live/2021/03/17/us/shooting -atlanta-acworth.

37 Kim Christensen, "'I Can't Suffer in Silence Anymore': Demonstrators Remain Vigilant in Protests against Anti-Asian Attacks," *Los Angeles Times*, March 21, 2021, https://www.latimes.com/california /story/2021-03-21/scores-gather-in-garden-grove-to-protest-against-anti-asian-attacks.

38 "Weekends with Alex Witt," MSNBC, March 21, 2021, https://archive.org/details/MSNBCW

_20210321_180000_Weekends_With_Alex_Witt.

39NowThis News, "Pres. Biden and VP Harris Deliver Remarks at Emory University in Atlanta, GA | LIVE," YouTube video, 1:21:15, March 19, 2021, https://www.youtube.com/watch?v=cNj8BSgQ45c.

40Kate Brumback and Jeffrey Collins, "Attacked Spas Had Been Targeted by Prostitution Stings," ABC News, published March 19, 2021, updated March 20, 2021, https://www.wric.com/news/u-s-world/spa-shooting-victims-idd-as-biden-harris-head-to-atlanta/.

41Rebecca Speare-Cole, "Atlanta Suspect Robert Aaron Long Planned Attack on Florida Porn Industry, Police Say," Newsweek, March 17, 2021, https://www.newsweek.com/atlanta-suspect-robert-aaron-long-shooting-florida-porn-industry-1576885.

42Rich McKay, "Motive in Georgia Spa Shootings Uncertain, but Asian Americans Fearful," Reuters, March 17, 2021, https://www.reuters.com/article/crime-georgia-spas/sex-addiction-not-racial-hatred-may-have-driven-suspect-in-georgia-spa-shootings-idINKBN2B925U?edition-redirect=in.

43Emily Baumgaertner, "The Intersection of Sexism, Racism, and Hate," *Los Angeles Times*, accessed November 18, 2022, https://enewspaper.latimes.com/infinity/article_share.aspx?guid=3a73c0ba-db5e-45d0-a092-61668d983305.

44"Remarks by Vice President Harris at Emory University," The White House Briefing Room, March 19, 2021, https://www.whitehouse.gov/briefing-room/speeches-remarks/2021/03/19/remarks-by-vice-president-harris-at-emory-university/.

45Carl Samson, "Man Accused of Fatally Shoving Vicha Ratanapakdee Enters Preliminary Hearing," Yahoo, June 15, 2022, https://www.yahoo.com/video/man-accused-fatally-shoving-vicha-194529813.html?guccounter=1; Associated Press, "San Francisco man to stand trial in death of Vicha Ratanapakdee," ABC 10, June 17, 2022, https://www.abc10.com/article/news/community/race-and-culture/vicha-ratanapakdee/103-cb897c9d-235b-4310-a629-240dccd4944f.

46Marianne Favro, "Elderly Woman Attacked, Robbed by Home Invaders in Daly City," NBC Bay Area, published October 1, 2022, updated October 2, 2022, https://www.nbcbayarea.com/news/local/elderly-woman-attacked-home-invasion-daly-city/3018955/.

47Khanh Tran, "Grandmother, 64, Robbed of $1,000 in Cash for Lunar New Year in San Jose," Yahoo, February 5, 2021, https://www.yahoo.com/entertainment/grandmother-64-robbed-1-000-213216433.html.

48Bill Hutchinson, "Arrest Made in Street Attack of 91-Year-Old California Man," ABC News, February 9, 2021, https://abcnews.go.com/US/arrest-made-street-attack-91-year-california-man/story?id=75777652.

49"75-Year-Old Asian Man Attacked in Oakland Robbery Dies, Suspect Charged with Murder," ABC 7 News, March 11, 2021, https://abc7news.com/oakland-asian-attack-teaunte-bailey-lake-merritt-crime/10408599/.

50"VIDEO: Brazen Attack on Asian Grandma in Broad Daylight Has Family Afraid to Leave Home," CBS Bay Area, February 9, 2021, https://www.cbsnews.com/sanfrancisco/news/video-brazen-attack-on-asian-grandma-in-broad-daylight-makes-family-afraid-to-leave-home/.

51Marlene Lenthang, "3 Arrested in Beating and Robbery of Asian Man in San Francisco Laundromat," ABC News, March 18, 2021, https://abcnews.go.com/US/arrested-beating-robbery-asian-man-san-francisco-laundromat/story?id=76533638.

52Dion Lim, "88-Year-Old Woman Brutally Beaten at San Francisco Park," ABC 7 Chicago, January 11, 2019, https://abc7chicago.com/grandmother-elder-abuse-san-francisco-visitacion-valley-neighborhood/5053585/.

53Anjali Hemphill, "Police File Hate Charges in Subway Attack on Asian Man, DA's Office Still Probing," NBC New York, published March 22, 2021, updated March 23, 2021, https://www.nbcnewyork.com/news/local/man-charged-with-hate-crime-in-subway-attack-that-left-68-year-old-asian-man-bloodied/2957690/.

54Scottie Andrew and Taylor Romine, "Teens Charged with Hate Crimes for Attacking a Woman on a Busand Saying She Caused Coronavirus, NYPD Says," CNN, April 6, 2020, https://www.cnn.com/2020/04/06/us/teens-attack-woman-caused-coronavirus-trnd/index.html.

55Email message to author, March 22, 2021.

56"Arrest Statistics by Bias Motivation Annual 2021," NYC, https://www1.nyc.gov/site/nypd/stats/reports-analysis/hate-crimes.page; Dermot F. Shea, "Crime and Enforcement Activity in New York City," New York City Police Department, July 2021, https://www1.nyc.gov/assets/nypd/downloads/pdf/analysis_and_planning/year-end-2020-enforcement-report-20210721.pdf.

57Nicole Hong and Jonah E. Bromwich, "Asian Americans Are Being Attacked. Why Are Hate Crime Charges So Rare?" *New York Times,* March 18, 2021, https://www.nytimes.com/2021/03/18/nyregion/asian-hate-crimes.html.

58Dion Lim, "Actors Daniel Dae Kim, Daniel Wu Offer $25K Reward after 91-Year-Old Shoved to Ground in Oakland's Chinatown," ABC 7 News, February 5, 2020, https://abc7news.com/man-pushed-to-ground-in-oakland-daniel-dae-kim-wu-violence/10316560/.

59Kim Tran (@but_im_kim_tran), "Listen, If You Don't Understand Why It's Problematic To Offer 25k For Information About A Black Man In Oakland, I Need You To Stay Off All The Goddamned Panels.," Twitter, February 6, 2021, https://twitter.com/but_im_kim_tran/status/1358216610595565568.

60Kim Tran (@but_im_kim_tran), "This Is The Moment We Need To Ask Ourselves, To What End? If It Was For An Accountability Process, Okay, But I Highly Doubt That. Lastly, This Looks A Lot Like A Bounty On A Black Person Funded By Asian American Celebrities. I Have Major, Major Doubts.," February 7, 2021, https://twitter.com/but_im_kim_tran/status/1358313382353399808.

61Cady Lang, "Hate Crimes against Asian Americans Are on the Rise. Many Say More Policing Isn't the Answer," *Time,* February 18, 2021, https://time.com/5938482/asian-american-attacks/.

62Nicole Hong and Jonah E. Bromwich, "Asian-Americans Are Being Attacked. Why Are Hate Crime Charges So Rare?"

63Rebecca Onion, "Coverage of Bay Area Anti-Asian Violence Is Missing a Key Element," *Slate,* March 19, 2021, https://slate.com/news-and-politics/2021/03/anti-asian-violence-bay-area-history-black-communities-race.html.

64Morgan and Truman, "Criminal Victimization, 2019."

65"Afraid: Fear in America's Communities of Color," CNN, March 19, 2021, https://cnnpressroom.blogs.cnn.com/2021/03/19/afraid-fear-in-americas-communities-of-color/.

66Anh Do, Leila Miller, Alejandra Reyes-Velarde, and Joe Mozingo, "A New Generation Hopes to Turn Activism to Fight Asian Hate into a Sustained Movement," *Los Angeles Times,* March 24, 2021, https://www.latimes.com/california/story/2021-03-24/hoping-to-turn-unprecedented-activism-over-asian-hate-into-a-sustained-movement.

CHAPTER EIGHTEEN: The Chauvin Trial and Its Aftermath

1Chandelis Duster, "Waters Calls for Protesters to 'Get More Confrontational' If No Guilty Verdict Is Reached in Derek Chauvin Trial," CNN, April 19, 2021, https://www.cnn.com/2021/04/19/politics/maxine-waters-derek-chauvin-trial/index.html.

2Lou Raguse, "New Court Docs Say George Floyd Had 'Fatal Level' of Fentanyl in His System," Kare 11, August 26, 2020, https://www.kare11.com/article/news/local/george-floyd/new-court-docs-say-george-floyd-had-fatal-level-of-fentanyl-in-his-system/89-ed69d09d-a9ec-481c-90fe-7acd4ead3d04.

3"Remarks by President Biden on the Verdict in the Derek Chauvin Trial for the Death of George Floyd," The White House Briefing Room, April 20, 2021, https://www.whitehouse.gov/briefing-room/speeches-remarks/2021/04/20/remarks-by-president-biden-on-the-verdict-in-the-derek-chauvin-trial-for-the-death-of-george-floyd/.

[4]Lt. Governor Peggy Flanagan (@LtGovFlanagan), Twitter, April 18, 2021, https://twitter.com/LtGov-Flanagan/status/1383868142439440385?ref_src=twsrc%5Etfw%7Ctwcamp%5Etweetembed%7Ctwterm%5E1383868142439440385%7Ctwgr%5E%7Ctwcon%5Es1_&ref_url=https%3A%2F%2Fwww.mediaite.com%2Fnews%2Fmn-lt-gov-peggy-flanagan-minnesota-is-a-place-where-it-is-not-safe-to-be-black%2F.

[5]Cary Aspinwall and Dave Boucher, "'You're Gonna Kill Me!': Dallas Police Body Cam Footage Reveals the Final Minutes of Tony Timpa's Life," *The Dallas Morning News,* July 30, 2019, https://www.dallasnews.com/news/investigations/2019/07/31/you-re-gonna-kill-me-dallas-police-body-cam-footage-reveals-the-final-minutes-of-tony-timpa-s-life/.

[6]Courtney Godfrey, "'Someone Knows Something.' One Year after 11-Year-Old Ladavionne Garrett Shooting," FOX 9 KMSP, May 2, 2022, https://www.fox9.com/news/ladavionne-garrett-j-family-pleads-for-help-someone-knows-something.

[7]Joe Nelson, "Girl, 9, Shot in the Head at Birthday Party in Minneapolis Is 'Fighting for Her Life,'" Bring Me the News, May 17, 2021, https://bringmethenews.com/minnesota-news/girl-9-shot-in-the-head-at-birthday-party-in-minneapolis-is-fighting-for-her-life.

[8]Paul Blume, "'It's Just Not Fair': Families of Children Shot Demand Change in Minneapolis," FOX 9 KMSP, May 17, 2021, https://www.fox9.com/news/its-just-not-fair-families-of-children-shot-demand-change-in-minneapolis.

[9]Kim Hyatt, "'North Side: Speak Up,' Grieving Grandmother Pleads for Answers in Shootings of Children," *Star Tribune*, June 28, 2021, https://www.startribune.com/north-side-speak-up-grieving-grandmother-pleads-for-answers-in-shootings-of-children/600072594/.

[10]Tim Nelson, "6-Year-Old Shot Monday in Minneapolis Gunfire Dies," MPR News, May 18, 2021, updated May 19, 2021, https://www.mprnews.org/story/2021/05/18/third-child-in-critical-condition-after-minneapolis-shooting.

[11]Theo Keith, "Police: Minneapolis Averaging More Than a Carjacking Per Day in 2021," Fox 9, May 20, 2021, https://www.fox9.com/news/police-minneapolis-averaging-more-than-a-carjacking-per-day-in-2021/.

[12]Matt Mckinney and Katie Galioto, "Violent Weekend in Minneapolis: Girl Shot in Head, Police Hurt in Confrontations," *Star Tribune*, May 16, 2021, https://www.startribune.com/violent-weekend-in-minneapolis-girl-shot-in-head-police-hurt-in-confrontations/600057946/.

[13]Bender, Jenkins, Reich, et al., "Transforming Community Safety: Resolution," Minneapolis City of Lakes, accessed August 21, 2022, https://lims.minneapolismn.gov/Download/FileV2/22166/Transforming-Community-Safety-Resolution.pdf.

[14]Karen Scullin, "'We Are Not in Mayberry': Minneapolis Community Leaders Call on City Council to Respond to Recent Violence," FOX 9 KMSP, July 7, 2020, https://www.fox9.com/news/we-are-not-in-mayberry-minneapolis-community-leaders-call-on-city-council-to-respond-to-recent-violence.

[15]Kim Voss, "Why I Am One of Many Former MPD Officers," *Star Tribune*, February 4, 2021, https://www.startribune.com/policing-and-mental-health-why-i-am-one-of-many-former-mpd-officers/600019128/.

[16]Susan Du, "In Minneapolis, Business Owners in George Floyd Square Plead for Safety," *Star Tribune*, March 15, 2021, https://www.startribune.com/in-minneapolis-business-owners-in-george-floyd-square-plead-for-safety/600034338/.

[17]Laura Yuen, Nina Moini, and Riham Feshir, "Here's What We Know about the Fatal Police Shooting Outside a Minneapolis Gas Station," MPR News, January 1, 2021, https://www.mprnews.org/story/2021/01/01/heres-what-we-know-about-the-fatal-police-shooting-outside-a-minneapolis-gas-station.

[18]Anthony Gockowski, "Minneapolis Police Chief Speaks Out against Effort to Abolish MPD,"

Alpha News, October 28, 2021, https://alphanews.org/minneapolis-police-chief-speaks-out
-against-effort-to-abolish-mpd/.

CONCLUSION: Saving Meritocracy, Saving a Civilization

[1]Email message to author, August 16, 2022.

[2]Leanne Son Hing, "The Myth Of Meritocracy in Scientific Institutions: Inaccurate Ideas about
Objectivity And Merit Perpetuate Biases And Inequality In Academia," *Science* 377, no. 6609
(2022): 824, https://doi.org/10.1126/science.add5909.